The 1988 presidential
election in the
South.

$47.95

DATE			

THE 1988 PRESIDENTIAL ELECTION IN THE SOUTH

The 1988 Presidential Election in the South

CONTINUITY AMIDST CHANGE IN SOUTHERN PARTY POLITICS

Edited by Laurence W. Moreland,
Robert P. Steed, and
Tod A. Baker

PRAEGER

New York
Westport, Connecticut
London

Library of Congress Cataloging-in-Publication Data

The 1988 presidential election in the South : continuity amidst change
  in southern party politics / edited by Laurence W. Moreland, Robert
  P. Steed, and Tod A. Baker.
      p. cm.
      Includes bibliographical references and index.
    ISBN 0–275–93145–5 (alk. paper)
      1. Presidents—United States—Election—1988.   2. Southern States—
  Politics and government—1951– .   I. Moreland, Laurence W.
  II. Steed, Robert P.   III. Baker, Tod A.
  JK526   19881
  324.9′730927—dc20   90–23761

British Library Cataloguing in Publication Data is available.

Library of Congress Catalog Card Number: 90–23761
ISBN: 0–275–93145–5

First published in 1991

Praeger Publishers, One Madison Avenue, New York, 10010
An imprint of Greenwood Publishing Group, Inc.

Printed in the United States of America

The paper used in this book complies with the
Permanent Paper Standard issued by the National
Information Standards Organization (Z39.48–1984).

10 9 8 7 6 5 4 3 2 1

Contents

Tables and Figures

TABLES

FIGURES

Preface

ROBERT P. STEED, LAURENCE W. MORELAND,
AND TOD A. BAKER

The post–World War II electoral history of the South prior to 1988 is clear on at least two points. First, there has been a partisan transformation of the region at the presidential election level from one-party Democratic to virtually one-party Republican. Second, the Republican success in presidential elections has not been approximated, much less equaled, in elections for other public offices in the South, especially at the state and local levels. While Republican candidates have certainly enjoyed greater success in gubernatorial and congressional races than formerly, the GOP record is not nearly as strong as for presidential elections; and in other state and local elections (for example, state legislatures), Republican gains have been far less impressive.[1]

An examination of data on the composition of state legislatures in the post–World War II South underscores this observation. Although the GOP showed some strength in states such as Tennessee, Florida, North Carolina, and Virginia, the broader picture prior to the 1980s was consistently one of weakness; and even in Tennessee, where the Republican success was greatest, the proportion of state legislative seats seldom approached a majority in either chamber (rising above 40 percent only rarely).

The 1984 elections in the region confirmed and underscored both these observations.[2] At the presidential level, every southern state gave a substantial majority to the Reagan-Bush ticket. The strength and consistency—approximately 60 percent across the board—of the state-by-state support for the Republican candidates were remarkable. The Walter Mondale–Geraldine Ferraro campaign paid little attention to most of the South and, very soon after the national nominating convention, wrote some states off as impossible to win. In Virginia, for example, it was reported as early as the middle of July that the national Democratic ticket had struck the tents and left the field of battle. With scattered exceptions, state and local Democratic officials in the region maintained a clear distance from Mondale, and what enthusiasm existed waned substantially as Election Day approached. Even in those states where the Democratic standard-bearers campaigned, state and local party leaders were often cool and unenthusiastic.

The Republican presidential landslide in the South had relatively limited impact on down-ticket elections, however. The broader electoral picture was one of Democratic success, particularly at the state and local levels. In Louisiana, for example, the state House of Representatives was still controlled by the Democrats by a margin of 90–17, and the state Senate was controlled by the Democrats by a margin of 37–2. Similarly, in Alabama the respective state legislative chambers were controlled by the Democrats by margins of 93–12 and 31–4, and only fourteen of the state's sixty-seven counties had any Republican local officials.

In states such as Texas and Virginia, the record was better for the Republicans, but the GOP still failed to enjoy the success of its national ticket. In Virginia, for example, incumbent Republican Senator John Warner easily won re-election, and Republicans retained their majority on the state's congressional delegation (6–4); however, Democrats still controlled the bulk of statewide offices on the basis of victories in 1981, and retained their majorities in the state legislative chambers. In Texas, Republican Phil Gramm impressively won a seat in the Senate, and Republicans ran close, albeit losing, races for three major statewide offices (Chief Justice of the Texas Supreme Court, a seat on the Court of Criminal Appeals, and Texas Railroad Commission), and won eighty-four new county offices, thereby doubling the party's previous totals; however, Democrats still controlled the bulk of local offices and, in spite of some losses, maintained their majorities in both houses of the state legislature (97–53 in the House of Representatives and 25–6 in the Senate).

In Congress, southern Republicans fared much better in the 1980s than in previous decades, but they still were a clear minority. The Reagan victory of 1980 was accompanied by Republican victories in both houses which increased the GOP's contingent to ten senators (twice as many as before the election) and thirty-nine House members (up from thirty). These figures remained relatively stable during Reagan's tenure in the White House, standing at ten and forty-three for the Senate and House respectively after his 1984 landslide victory, but dropping slightly after the 1986 midterm elections to six senators and forty House members.[3]

The consistent strength of the Republican presidential vote, even during the Reagan years, then, failed to produce a full-scale realignment of the southern party system. At the same time, Republican breakthroughs occurred in state and local elections. Additionally, there is ample evidence that Republican party organizational strength increased in the region as well.[4]

The 1988 election provided a stern test—full of peril and opportunity—for both parties. For the Democrats, it was clearly important that they be able to take advantage of the absence of a popular incumbent to stem the tide of recent Republican presidential voting. If victory throughout the South was not possible, at least significant gains in Democratic voting, along with victories in some states in the region, were important. For the Republicans, a victory in the South without Ronald Reagan at the head of the ticket would be significant in strengthening and solidifying their presidential coalition and would give them a continuing base for developing party support below the presidential level. Republican failure in the presidential election would, perhaps, signal superficial strength tied disproportionately to the popularity of Reagan, hinder efforts to develop wider and deeper support in the region, and open the door for the Democrats to reverse their recent slide.

The result, of course, was an impressive victory in the South for George Bush and Dan Quayle. This outcome, in the absence of further detailed analyses, does not illuminate the broader dimensions of party development in the region, nor does it clarify the impact of this Republican victory on recent southern electoral trends. This volume examines the 1988 elections in the South with a view toward providing such analyses. Special attention is given to the presidential election contests and results in the region, but there is also some consideration of other elections. The discussions that follow combine South-wide analyses with state-by-state discussions in an attempt to explore both the macro and the micro elements of southern electoral developments. While the editors developed a general outline for the state chapters, each author was given leeway to approach and organize the materials and data as she or he deemed appropriate and relevant to the larger concerns of the volume. Some effort has been made to identify and discuss some common ground both in the state and general chapters, but not at the expense of discussing the diversity of experiences and behaviors that have traditionally characterized the region. The authors of the state chapters were requested to keep discussions of their states' respective political histories and immediate nomination contests to a minimum inasmuch as these topics are the focus of some of the regional chapters, but even there the practice varies in accordance with the authors' judgments about the necessity of including such material for an adequate understanding of the developments in their states. The result, we hope, is a volume that will help clarify the specific events of the 1988 elections in the South and the more general patterns of political development in a rapidly changing region.

We are indebted to a number of people whose assistance at various stages of this project was instrumental to its ultimate completion. First, we gratefully acknowledge the help of our colleagues, who have provided the various chapters of this volume, and to a host of other students of southern politics, whose continuing interest, comments, and suggestions have encouraged this project. Essential financial support was generously provided by The Citadel Development Foundation (CDF); this volume and our related activities concerning the study of southern politics would simply not be possible without the funds made available by the CDF. Finally, we are grateful to our editors at Praeger for their patience and encouragement throughout the project and for their efforts to smooth the publication process.

NOTES

1. For an excellent overview, see Charles S. Bullock III, "Creeping Realignment in the South," in *The South's New Politics: Realignment and Dealignment*, ed. Robert H. Swansbrough and David M. Brodsky (Columbia: University of South Carolina Press, 1988), 220–237. Also see Earl Black and Merle Black, *Politics and Society in the South* (Cambridge, Mass.: Harvard University Press, 1987), chs. 12–13.

For a useful summary of partisan trends in southern congressional delegations, see Charles S. Bullock III, "The South in Congress: Power and Policy," in *Contemporary Southern Politics*, ed. James F. Lea (Baton Rouge: Louisiana State University Press, 1988), 177–193. Research reported by James E. Campbell strongly suggests that the traditional lack of party competition in the South may have contributed to blunting the coattails effect of Republican presidential successes on Republican state legislative efforts; see James E. Campbell, "Presidential Coattails and Midterm Losses in State Legislative Elections," *American Political Science Review* 80 (March 1986): 45–63.

2. Most of the discussion of the 1984 elections in the South is drawn from Robert P. Steed, Laurence W. Moreland, and Tod A. Baker, eds., *The 1984 Presidential Election in the South: Patterns of Southern Party Politics* (New York: Praeger, 1986). The authors of the individual state analyses presented in that volume and utilized in this summary are as follows: Dennis S. Ippolito (Texas); Diane K. Blair (Arkansas); Charles D. Hadley (Louisiana); Alexander P. Lamis (Mississippi); Anne H. Hopkins, William Lyons, and Steve Metcalf (Tennessee); William H. Stewart (Alabama); Mark Stern (Florida); Thomas G. Walker and Eleanor Main (Georgia); Laurence W. Moreland, Robert P. Steed, and Tod A. Baker (South Carolina); Jack Fleer (North Carolina); and Larry Sabato (Virginia). Additional materials may be found in the state analyses presented in Swansbrough and Brodsky, *The South's New Politics*.

3. See the data and discussion in Bullock, "The South in Congress."

4. See, for example, Robert P. Steed, Laurence W. Moreland, and Tod A. Baker, "The Nature of Contemporary Party Organization in South Carolina" (Paper presented at the 1987 annual meeting of the American Political Science Association, Chicago, Ill.); and Lewis Bowman, William E. Hulbary, and Anne E. Kelley, "Party Sorting at the Grassroots: Stable Partisans and Party Changers among Florida's Precinct Officials," in *The Disappearing South? Studies in Regional Change and Continuity*, ed. Robert P. Steed, Laurence W. Moreland, and Tod A. Baker (Tuscaloosa: University of Alabama Press, 1989), ch. 4. In a similar vein, there have been some defections of Democratic public officials to the Republican party in recent years as further possible evidence of growing Republican strength in the region; see, for example, Joe O'Keefe, "The GOP Whistles Dixie," *Campaigns and Elections* 10 (August 1989): 10–11.

PART I

SOUTHERN REGIONAL PERSPECTIVES ON THE 1988 ELECTION

The Nomination Process and Super Tuesday

CHARLES S. BULLOCK III

March 8, 1988, witnessed more people choosing from a larger pool of presidential aspirants across a greater number of states than ever before. Voters in twenty states from Florida to Massachusetts and from Virginia to Hawaii registered their preferences. While the range of participating states was national in scope, media attention focused on the South, where presidential delegates were selected in all eleven states except South Carolina. The Palmetto State, although not voting on March 8, nonetheless contributed to the regional movement with the Republicans staging a primary on Saturday, March 5, while Democrats chose delegates to the national convention on the succeeding Saturday. Thus, in one week the South played its role in the presidential selection process. The region contained 864 of the 2,081 delegates needed to win the Democratic nomination and 564 of 1,139 delegates required for the GOP nomination.

Why did southern leaders decide to mass their primaries together? Were the expectations underlying the united effort met? Did Super Tuesday have unintended consequences? Which candidates won and lost on this historic day and why? These topics will be explored in this chapter.

GROWTH OF THE GIANT

Suggestions that there be a southern regional primary go back at least to 1975.[1] The idea of a united South intrigued local Democratic leaders suffering from the age-old paranoia that the South was ignored by the rest of the country. That the South's preferences deserved greater weight was self-evident to these individuals as they pondered the anemic showing of their party's presidential nominees in 1968 and 1972.[2] If the South spoke with a single voice, national Democratic leaders would have to listen, since no Democrat who failed to carry a majority of the southern states has ever won the presidency. To maximize the region's input, it needed to express its preferences before candidates with a strong southern appeal had been eliminated. Some supporters hoped that Super Tuesday would help a southerner win the Democratic nomination, while those with more modest ambitions agreed with Texas State Senator John Traeger, active in the Southern Legislative Conference (SLC), "We feel that under this new southern primary effort, our region of the country stands a much better chance of keeping its concerns out front."[3]

In anticipation of 1988, the Southern Legislative Conference spearheaded the effort to get additional states to join Alabama, Florida, and Georgia, which had already designated the second Tuesday in March for presidential balloting. In some states this meant changing from a later date that had traditionally been used, while in others it necessitated substituting a primary for an alternative mode of choosing delegates.

Creation of Super Tuesday was premised on several assumptions.[4] First was the belief that one or more conservative, respected southerners would be a candidate. Second, should there be a southern conservative option, he, as the region's favorite son, would exit Super Tuesday with a commanding lead in delegates.[5] Third, the momentum from Super Tuesday would carry over to other regions. A big win in the South would confer credibility and generate campaign funds for the southern winner while simultaneously drying up the resources of some non-southerners, driving them from the field. Fourth, in previous years the inhospitable environments of the early tests of strength (Iowa and New Hampshire) had eliminated southern candidates before they could enjoy a home-field advantage. Fifth, while a southerner would be advantaged by Super Tuesday, the size of the prize would compel all candidates to acquaint themselves with the concerns of southern voters and adopt policy stands acceptable to those voters. Therefore, even if a southerner did not win the nomination, the Democratic standard-bearer in November would be less liberal than George McGovern or Walter Mondale, who had fared poorly nationwide and had endangered southern Democrats running for lower offices. Sixth, southerners would have greater opportunities to meet candidates, which would result in more participation in the selection process.[6] Seventh, the magnitude of a regional primary would be a better test of candidate electability than the New Hampshire primary or the Iowa caucus with their small numbers of participants.[7] Eighth, and finally, a spirited contest with appealing candidates would bring Reagan Democrats back home.

Discussions that predated creation of Super Tuesday were notable for the lack of attention accorded two significant elements of the southern political scene: Republicans and blacks. Since President Reagan was completing his second term, competition for the GOP nomination would divert some conservative voters from the Democratic primary. The remaining Democrats would, therefore, be more liberal than the voters who elected Democrats to the state legislature. The GOP hoped numerous disaffected former Democrats would vote Republican on Super Tuesday, using this event as a way station on the road to realignment.

To the extent that conservatives participated in the Republican primary, the likely beneficiary among Democrats was Jesse Jackson. The black civil rights activist had run well among black voters in 1984. With an additional four years of non-stop campaigning, and in a field that lacked a white candidate having ties to the black community equal to those of Walter Mondale, Jackson might get monolithic black support. In areas having a sizeable black population, Jackson could poll a plurality against a fractured field of white candidates.

THE INITIAL DISAPPOINTMENT

The Democratic Leadership Council (DLC) was formed chiefly by southern officeholders in an attempt to offset the more liberal wing of the party. Many supporters thought that the DLC stars Senator Sam Nunn (D-GA) or Charles Robb, former governor of Virginia, who were both widely respected by party leaders, would seek the presidency. Robb demurred and urged Nunn to run. Nunn was rumored to be on the verge of entering the chase, but in September 1987, he announced that he would not be a candidate.

With Nunn out of the picture, conservative southerners lacked a rallying point. In an attempt to capitalize on Super Tuesday, and with promises of funding, Tennessee's junior senator Albert Gore entered the race. Gore lacked Nunn's conservative record and reputation, so his effort became a test of the ability of regional pride to attract voters.

CANDIDATES' STRATEGIES

Iowa and New Hampshire had their expected winnowing effect. Before Super Tuesday, former Arizona governor Bruce Babbitt (D), former Delaware governor Pete DuPont (R), and General Al Haig (R) withdrew, and Senator Paul Simon (D-IL) chose to husband his resources in the hopes of reviving his campaign by winning his home state, and did not compete in the South.

Democrats

Four Democrats remained active on Super Tuesday. Gore, reacting to unfavorable polls in the North despite a heavy investment of resources, opted to avoid likely defeats and withdrew from the early tests of strength in order to concentrate on the South. To stay in the campaign he had to take several states in addition to his native Tennessee. To win the nomination, Gore needed a smashing success in Dixie. Gore had expected to be the sole moderate-to-conservative Democrat, but instead he had to share that part of the spectrum with Representative Richard Gephardt (MO). While campaigning in the South, Gore attacked Gephardt, hoping that the Missourian would have to foresake the quest after March 8.

Gephardt came South hoping to build on his victory in Iowa. He sought to rejuvenate a campaign that had stumbled in New Hampshire when he ran second, with 20 percent of the vote. A strong showing in the South, coupled with his Iowa victory, would leave Gephardt as the leading moderate Democratic candidate and in good shape to appeal to blue-collar workers and farmers. Some Republican leaders saw Gephardt as the Democrat most able to convert Republicans.[8]

The South had great potential for Jesse Jackson. With his strength being disproportionately among blacks, he was best positioned to win the Deep South states where the percent of blacks is greatest.

Governor Michael Dukakis of Massachusetts targeted Florida and Texas, the region's two least southern states. He campaigned in Spanish among these states' Hispanics and appealed to northerners who had moved to Florida. The publicity given him as the winner in New Hampshire (36 percent of the vote) made Dukakis formidable among the undecided and liberal elements of states beyond the two in which he concentrated his resources. With Jackson to his left and Gore and Gephardt on the right, Dukakis could run as a moderate. He might also pick up support from liberals who thrilled to Jackson's oratory but saw no chance of a black being nominated.

Of the major Democratic contenders, Dukakis risked the least as the campaign, like the baseball teams, went South for a few weeks of spring training. Doing poorly in the South would not wholly offset the boost given by New Hampshire. Any success would contribute to the notion that Dukakis had a growing national appeal, helpful when the campaign reached the industrial heartland. Since Super Tuesday included more than just southern and border states, only if Dukakis won nothing but New England states would he come out the big loser. Conceivably, Dukakis might be hurt if Gephardt or Gore scored such a sweeping victory that Democratic opinion leaders and campaign contributors succumbed to the inevitability of a moderate being nominated.[9] Dukakis saw Gephardt as his chief rival, and continued a barrage of effective television ads, claiming that the Missourian had flip-flopped on Social Security and the Reagan Administration economic reforms.

Republicans

The "bump" that New Hampshire gave Dukakis was matched by the impetus given the candidacy of Vice President George Bush. After an embarrassing third-place finish in the Iowa caucuses, some journalists were willing to count Bush out, and pointed to Senate Minority Leader Robert Dole (KN) as the likely Republican nominee. Bush's 38 to 29 percent victory over Dole in New Hampshire restored the Vice President as his party's leading candidate. A strong showing in the South would propel Bush far ahead of the pack, and might make him unstoppable. The South looked promising for Bush because of the popularity of President Ronald Reagan, with whom Bush was so closely identified, and because of the strength of his organization.

Senator Dole had the best prospects for derailing the Bush express which was now preparing to leave the station. The poorly organized Dole campaign's major asset in the South was Dole's wife, the former Secretary of Transportation. As a native North Carolinian, she was expected to receive a warm reception in her home state and its neighbors. A respectable showing by Dole would signal to party leaders that Bush's nomination was not inevitable. If doubts could be planted, then Dole might capitalize on polls showing him to have broader appeal than the Vice President among Independents and Democrats. The desperation of Dole's plight is visible, however, upon realization that his goal on the eve of Super Tuesday was to keep Bush's share of the delegates allocated nationwide that day below 500.

As important as the South was for Dole, it assumed even greater significance for two more conservative Republicans, Pat Robertson, host of television's "700 Club," and Congressman Jack Kemp (NY). If the evangelist or the congressman from Buffalo had a constituency, it should be in the South or West where voters are more conservative. Since most of the primaries in the West would come relatively late, Robertson and Kemp had to score well on Super Tuesday if they were to survive until attention moved beyond the Mississippi Rover.

Pat Robertson looked expectantly toward the large numbers of born-again Christians in the South. Moreover, Robertson supporters had become active in the GOP, and in some areas had wrested control from Regulars. Finally, the Robertson people were still on a high from their unexpected success in Iowa, where they finished ahead of Vice President Bush. Robertson violated one of the norms of a presidential candidacy and boasted that he would win in South Carolina, the contest that kicked off Super Tuesday week.

Representative Kemp's track record was less promising than Robertson's. Kemp had fewer workers in the South, and faced the traditional regional suspicion of northerners, which was especially great in the case of New York Yankees. His best hope was that business leaders who had hailed the Kemp-Roth tax cuts of the early 1980s would rally to his banner. In a desperate effort to create a viable candidacy, Kemp spent heavily on television advertising in South Carolina.[10]

SUPER CAMPAIGN FOR SUPER TUESDAY?

Super Tuesday's creators expected that the concentration of convention delegates would force candidates to devote more time and attention to the South.

Super Tuesday certainly got the attention of the candidates, but it did not result in the kind of retail politics lavished on Iowa and New Hampshire. The campaign styles pursued in the South were dictated by the very magnitude of the stakes. With only three weeks between New Hampshire and Super Tuesday, candidates had to mount media campaigns. Candidates who had money invested heavily in television ads.

All candidates tried to augment their advertising dollars by staging media events near major airports. Prominent in the campaign were fly-ins, where the candidate would touch down at an airport and be greeted by a clutch of local party officials, campaign workers, and reporters. The candidate would make "the speech" to the cheering enthusiasts, mingle briefly with the crowd, and with a hearty wave at the top of the steps, disappear back into the campaign airplane to fly to the next event. Charles Hadley and Harold Stanley have quoted a reporter's observation: "These guys saw more runways than a Delta Air Lines commuter pilot."[11]

While precise enumerations are not available, it seems likely that states with major airports received more attention. Atlanta, Charlotte, and Dallas–Fort Worth, with their airports and media outlets, were particularly attractive. Smaller cities had to content themselves with visits by relatives of the candidates.[12] To the extent that campaign spending indicates the seriousness of competition, Michael Binford has noted that "at least seven of the southern states did not receive much emphasis."[13] Alabama's Democratic chair complained: "We've got virtually no campaign going on. We had the candidates here all the time [in 1984. In 1988] we're way up in the bleachers."[14]

To the extent that Super Tuesday became a television campaign, candidate efforts were no different than they would have been if the region had received less attention. There was simply not time for candidates to walk down many main streets or discuss issues over dessert and coffee in many living rooms. Washington political observer Norman Ornstein saw the southern advertising as less effective than elsewhere, in part because of the magnitude of Super Tuesday. The television ads were

not meshing nearly as much as the ads that work in single states when the contest was more focused and when you had more debates going on and more of an opportunity for voters to see all of the elements working together. Super Tuesday is such a crazy quilt there of different states, with different messages . . . that these ads haven't done very much.[15]

Concentrating the selection of so many delegates on a single day may have actually reduced the likelihood that voters would have personal contact with candidates. Had the southern primaries been scattered over a longer period, states that were largely ignored prior to Super Tuesday might have attracted visits from candidates who chose to pass up non-southern states where they expected to do poorly and instead concentrated on a particular southern state in hopes that they would emerge at the end of a primary day with at least one victory. For example, had Arkansas and Alabama had primaries on the same date as Illinois, they might have received more attention from Gore if he figured he could win those two while there was little chance for success against two home-staters (Jesse Jackson and Paul Simon) in the Land of Lincoln.

The magnitude of Super Tuesday prompted the candidates to try various approaches. Jesse Jackson relied on black voters throughout the region. Unlike in 1984, when some black leaders, particularly in Atlanta and Birmingham, endorsed Walter Mondale, Jackson had near-universal support in black communities in 1988. Gore sought to win credibility through association. He lined up the endorsements of 800 leading Democrats, including noncandidates Sam Nunn and Chuck Robb.[16] Like a high-jumper who passed on the initial tests in Iowa and New Hampshire, Gore needed to excel in the South to create an attitude of inevitability for his nomination.

Like Gore, Bush and Dole mounted efforts throughout the region. Bush's advisors saw in the South the potential to nail down the nomination, while Dole may have feared that failure to contest the entire region successfully would make his continuation in the chase untenable. Dole, however, was at a serious disadvantage in facing the Vice President. Of all the candidates in both parties, only Bush had the name recognition, funding, and following to mount a serious campaign in all states.

Despite Gephardt's Iowa success, his resources were so scarce that he was unable to use television effectively to publicize the protectionist stand that had served him well in Iowa. Southerners concerned about mill closings caused by cheap textile imports might have rallied to his charges that Korean protectionism pushed the price of a K-car to almost $50,000. Gephardt's problem was that relatively few southerners heard that message.[17] He led the Democratic aspirants in campaign spending only in Louisiana, and relied on the endorsements of southerners with whom he had served in Congress.[18]

Some candidates targeted certain states. Dukakis focused on Florida and Texas. Robertson, and to a lesser degree Kemp, lavished attention on South Carolina. They calculated that success in South Carolina on Saturday would give their candidacies an essential boost going into the remaining states.

RESULTS

Democrats

Jesse Jackson emerged as the leader in the southern portion of Super Tuesday, taking half the states and 286 delegates. Jackson carried every state that had been wholly covered by the Voting Rights Act in 1965. His share of the vote in these states, as reported in Table 1.1, ranged from 35 percent in Louisiana to 45 percent in Virginia. He also received the bulk of the delegates chosen in the South Carolina caucuses.

Table 1.1
Democratic Candidates' Share of the Vote in the South on Super Tuesday
(in percent)

State	Dukakis	Gephardt	Gore	Jackson
Alabama	8	7	37	44
Arkansas	19	12	37	17
Florida	41	14	13	20
Georgia	16	7	32	40
Louisiana	15	11	28	35
Mississippi	9	6	34	44
North Carolina	20	6	35	33
Tennessee	3	2	72	21
Texas	33	14	21	24
Virginia	22	4	22	45

Source: Compiled by the author from figures reported in the New York
Times (10 March 1988), 11.

Albert Gore was second to Jackson in delegates (259) and states carried, taking
Arkansas and North Carolina in addition to winning a landslide in his native
Tennessee. Gore trailed Jackson in Georgia, Virginia, Alabama, and Mississippi,
despite spending more money in these states than any other Democrat and despite
endorsements from leaders like Georgia House Speaker Tom Murphy.[19]

Dukakis's narrow strategy paid off as he took the two states that he had
targeted, the only southern states in which he was the top spender among Democrats. He won Florida easily, doubling the vote of his nearest rival, and enjoyed
a 9-point lead in Texas, where he polled a third of the vote. However, outside
those states, Dukakis led in only three congressional districts in the remainder
of the South.[20] Almost 70 percent of Dukakis's 193 delegates came from the
two states he won.

The Democrats' big loser was Dick Gephardt, who was sharply attacked by
Dukakis and Gore, and won no southern state.[21] Gephardt's lone Super Tuesday
victory came in his home state of Missouri. In the South, Gephardt's greatest
strength was in Florida and Texas, where he got one vote in seven. In six of
the states, he failed to attract even 10 percent of the electorate.

Exit polling provides insights into the types of voters attracted to the various
candidates. The most pronounced relationship is between race and support for
Jackson. In the CBS News/New York Times surveys Jackson is estimated to have
gotten 91 percent of the black vote, while ABC News showed Jackson with 96
percent of the black vote.[22] Near-unanimous black support enabled Jackson to
win all but one congressional district in which blacks cast at least 30 percent of
the Democratic ballots.[23] Jackson ran substantially worse among other groups.
Among Hispanics he was estimated to have gotten between 21 (CBS) and 37
(ABC) percent of the vote. His share of the white vote was estimated at between
7 (CBS) and 10 (ABC) percent. Jackson was the first choice among women,

with between 31 (CBS) and 37 (ABC) percent of their votes. Among males, his estimated share of the vote was between 25 (CBS) and 29 (ABC) percent.

The ABC poll showed Jackson leading in every age group up to age forty to forty-nine. His strongest support came among those in the thirty- to thirty-nine-year age bracket, where he got 40 percent of the votes contrasted with 23 percent for Gore and 21 percent for Dukakis. Jackson did very well among the economically disadvantaged voters to whom he pitched his message.

Albert Gore was the leader among whites with slightly more than a third of the vote. He ran particularly well among those in the fifty- to fifty-nine-year age bracket (ABC), and finished about evenly with Dukakis among the over-sixty group. Gore was also the top vote-getter among white Protestants, with 40 percent of their votes (CBS). The Tennessean showed strength among non-Democrats including voters who had supported Reagan in 1984 (ABC). "By and large, the [congressional] districts Gore won were politically marginal—ones where the Democrats have long held the House seat but rarely have won in recent presidential elections."[24]

Gore was helped by late converts, taking 35 percent of the voters who decided between Saturday and Monday and 27 percent of those who made up their mind on primary day (CBS). Many of these may have come at Gephardt's expense. Late converts were insufficient, however, to offset the loss of expected support from millions of conservatives who voted in the Republican primary. Had whites voted in the Democratic presidential primary at rates similar to their participation in past Democratic primaries to select local, state, and congressional nominees, Gore would have carried some of the Deep South states.

Strength among whites, particularly those who voted for Reagan in 1984, lent credence to Gore's claims that he could lure back to the Democratic party voters who had been sorely missed in the recent debacles. The senator's showing, however, was too weak to convince contributors and northern voters that a moderate-to-conservative approach held the greatest promise for November. Super Tuesday, then, rather than launching a successful effort, was the beginning of the end for Tennessee's junior senator.

Dukakis was the clear choice among white liberals, with 39 percent of the vote. He finished second among whites, and was the top choice among Hispanics in the CBS poll, with 49 percent of their votes. The ABC poll showed him running second to Jackson among Hispanics, with 33 percent of the vote. As the heir apparent to the Democratic liberal wing, Dukakis did better among voters who had supported Mondale in 1984 than did any other white candidate.

When asked to explain their preferences, Jackson's supporters stressed that their candidate would help poor people, curb unemployment, and care for the elderly (ABC and CBS). Of those who stressed the need for strong leadership in foreign affairs, 53 percent believed that Jackson would be effective on that dimension, which suggests that his meetings with world leaders had paid off. Perceptions of Jackson's honesty and empathy for people like the respondent were additional strong points.

Table 1.2
Republican Candidates' Share of the Vote in the South on Super Tuesday
(in percent)

State	Bush	Dole	Kemp	Robertson
Alabama	64	16	5	14
Arkansas	47	26	5	18
Florida	62	21	5	11
Georgia	54	24	6	16
Louisiana	58	18	5	18
Mississippi	66	17	4	13
North Carolina	45	40	4	10
South Carolina*	48	21	12	19
Tennessee	60	22	5	12
Texas	64	14	5	15
Virginia	53	25	4	15

*South Carolina Republicans held their primary on Saturday before the rest of the region voted on Tuesday.

Source: Compiled by the author from figures reported in the New York Times (10 March 1988), 11, for all states except South Carolina. South Carolina figures were reported in R. W. Apple, Jr., "In Victory Bush Seems Beneficiary of a Legacy," New York Times (7 March 1988), 11.

Dukakis voters pointed to his experience and management abilities—themes Dukakis would continue to stress. Dukakis voters believed their man would reduce the deficit and, relatedly, would promote economic growth.[25]

Gore did particularly well among voters concerned about national defense and, not surprisingly, those who wanted a candidate from the South. Unfortunately for Gore, national defense was the primary factor in the vote of only 10 percent of the Democrats. Those who thought it important to have a southern candidate were even fewer, only 3 percent of those sampled (CBS).

To the extent that Democratic voters were concerned about trade and oil import fees, they were attracted to Richard Gephardt, who emphasized his efforts to curb the U.S. trade imbalance. Unfortunately for the Missouri congressman, these items were of great concern to only 12 and 6 percent of the electorate, respectively (CBS). The trade aspect did not carry over to a perception that Gephardt would be particularly effective in handling foreign affairs, where only 5 percent mentioned him.

Republicans

As Table 1.2 shows, George Bush swept the South with a majority of the vote in all but three states, a feat achieved only in one state by a Democrat (Gore in Tennessee). Dole was a distant second in most states, seriously challenging Bush only in North Carolina, where the Senate Minority Leader came within 14,000 votes of the Vice President. In all but one of the other states, Bush got at least twice the vote that Dole received.

Dole's performance was so poor that in several states, he ran neck-and-neck with Robertson, and actually was bested by Robertson in Texas. Robertson, while always getting at least 10 percent of the vote, performed best in South Carolina (19 percent), the state he had boasted he would win. As poorly as Robertson did, Kemp's performance was worse. Kemp got a tenth of the Republican vote only in South Carolina, and was eliminated from consideration.

Bush got a majority of the Republican votes among most southern groups. Fundamentalist Protestants may have been an exception, with CBS reporting a 47–30 split between Robertson and Bush.[26] There is a curvilinear relationship between age of voter and share of vote for Bush. The Vice President ran well among younger and older voters, and did best with the over-sixty group, getting two-thirds of their vote. Moreover, while Bush was supported by 62 percent of those who approved of Ronald Reagan's performance as president, he lost to Dole by a 43–37 margin among Republican voters who saw flies in the Reagan ointment. However, since 83 percent of the Republican participants approved of the President, the loss to Dole among the dissidents was relatively insignificant, and pointed up the wisdom of a Bush campaign that portrayed him as Reagan's chief lieutenant and heir.

The breadth of support registered by Bush across states is also manifest in the range of explanations offered by his supporters. ABC respondents supported Bush because of his strong leadership, expected stability in a crisis, experience in government (79 percent), and an ability to "understand people like me."[27] As Reagan's heir, Bush was expected to be able to handle foreign affairs (76 percent), hold down unemployment (75 percent), and keep taxes low (69 percent). A majority of the voters also were attracted to Bush in anticipation that under his administration the economy would remain strong and that government spending would be held in check. No new taxes and a strong United States abroad and economically at home continued to be Bush themes throughout the campaign.

Dole ran better among voters who decided late, doing best among those who decided on Super Tuesday, but even there he was bested by a 49 to 28 margin (CBS). Among those who had made their choices prior to 1988, he lost to Bush by a six to one margin. In retrospect, to win, Dole had to unsettle enough Republicans to break their commitment to Bush. Victory in New Hampshire might have done that.

Support for Robertson was most likely to be attributed to his honesty and an expectation that he would produce change. Robertson also attracted voters concerned about care for the poor and elderly. Robertson's greatest strength, not surprisingly, was among those concerned about moral decline.

SUPER TUESDAY: AN EVALUATION

Super Tuesday helped clarify the electoral scene, although not in the way anticipated by its creators. The results did not predict the Democratic nominee, since Dukakis led among neither black nor white voters in the South. However, on the Republican side, Super Tuesday all but sealed the fate of those challenging George Bush.[28]

Bush's southern triumph, augmented by his success in the non-southern Super Tuesday states, eliminated Kemp and Robertson, and left Dole's candidacy hanging by the slenderest of threads.[29] The magnitude of the Bush sweep was accentuated, since Republican rules did not require proportional distribution of delegates. Thus, while Bush received 54 percent of the popular vote in Georgia, he took all forty-eight delegates. Throughout the region, Bush's share of the delegates (85.7 percent) far exceeded his share of the vote.[30]

Several other Democratic expectations were unfulfilled by Super Tuesday. As the Gore candidacy evaporated like dew on a summer's morn, it became obvious that carrying the Democratic portion of the southern white vote was insufficient to win the Democratic nomination. Endorsements from many of the region's Democratic leaders failed to hold enough of the traditional, conservative voters within the party for Gore to overcome Jackson's black support.

The second-place finish proved to be Gore's one moment of triumph. However, southern and border states all voting on a single day deprived the native son of potential follow-up victories on succeeding weeks. After faring poorly in Illinois and then being unable to rebound, even with the help (or kiss of death?) of New York City Mayor Ed Koch, Gore's quest ended.

If Super Tuesday failed to nominate a southerner, did it succeed in prompting a more conservative choice among Democrats than in 1984? Although the eventual nominee, Michael Dukakis, was more conservative than Jesse Jackson and probably to the right of Illinois Senator Paul Simon, his choice was not attributable to Super Tuesday. After all, Dukakis finished third in the region, well behind the leading vote-getter, Jesse Jackson, who was the most liberal candidate. Of the three Democrats who carried southern states on Super Tuesday, Dukakis would fall in the middle ideologically. Nonetheless, he was perceived by southern voters as being to the left of Al Gore, who cast his campaign in conservative hues.

Another objective was to encourage presidential candidates to articulate views more in line with southern policy preferences. A difficulty not foreseen by Super Tuesday's creators was the range of those preferences. As illustrated by the result in which three Democrats carried states, black southerners supported Jackson's calls for redistribution, many whites backed Gore with his more conservative message, and a not insignificant number responded positively to a message of competence. Gephardt's trade message was favorably received by those southerners who heard it. Candidates' messages in the South were essentially the same that they articulated in other regions. Super Tuesday did not—and with our national media, could not—result in the adoption of uniquely southern themes. There were complaints that in the three-week southern campaign, little was said about specific concerns of the South.[31]

The goal of providing southerners with a wider range of options was partially achieved. It is true that some lesser candidates had already fallen by the wayside, and the Simon candidacy was on hold awaiting a post-Illinois coup de gras. Despite the available alternatives, southern voters were no more favorable to Kemp and Robertson, the most conservative candidates in the field, than were primary voters in other states.

The expectation that candidates would spend more time in the South seems to have been met. According to the Southern Legislative Conference,[32] in the eight months leading up to Super Tuesday, the four active Democrats averaged 75 days each in the South, while Bush, Dole, and Robertson averaged 51 days in the region.[33] Gore's emphasis on the South led him to spend 121 days campaigning there, which far exceeded anyone else in either party. Jackson was the only other candidate to spend more time in the South than in Iowa and New Hampshire.[34] It is not clear, however, whether candidates were in the South more than they would have been had southern primaries been scattered over a longer period. That serious candidates often passed up debates in the South sheds additional light on the relative significance of the region.

Super Tuesday was expected to increase turnout, and approximately 3.9 million Republicans and 7.1 million Democrats participated.[35] As the first time in twelve years that both parties had active challengers, turnout would have risen even without Super Tuesday. Assessing the increase in turnout, then, is tricky, because there are alternative baselines one might use. To compare GOP turnout in 1988 with the turnout in the uneventful 1984 primary would be meaningless. Another consideration is that in previous years fewer states had used primaries. It makes little sense to compare participation in caucuses with numbers of voters in a primary. Comparing Democratic activity in 1988 with that in states that held primaries in 1984 reveals declines in Alabama (20 to 17 percent), Georgia (30 to 24 percent), and North Carolina (45 to 32 percent).[36] Democratic turnout rose by 4 points in Florida, 10 points in Tennessee, and doubled to 37 percent in Louisiana, where Governor Edwin Edwards had actively discouraged participation in the 1984 primary.

Among Republicans, turnout gains were particularly impressive when 1988 is compared with 1980.[37] Republican voters more than doubled in Georgia, Louisiana, and Mississippi, and almost doubled in Texas. Sizeable increases were registered in all other southern states except Alabama.

GOP turnout rose because Super Tuesday enticed many whites to vote in a Republican primary for the first time in their life. Exit polls found that less than 10 percent of the participants in GOP primaries in states without party registration identified themselves as Democrats, but this may miss a bigger point.[38] Haley Barbour, Mississippi Republican National Committeeman, explained:

Republican strategy as specifically agreed to by the 13 GOP State Chairmen in October 1987 was to attract into the GOP Super Tuesday contests the voters who typically vote Republican every General Election but who had always voted in state Democratic primaries. Cross-over Democrats, in the literal sense, were never the target.[39]

The Republican strategy seemingly worked, as ABC found only 8 percent of the voters in the Democratic primary to have been Republicans. Thus, Super Tuesday may have furthered the realignment process by getting additional voters to extend their period of Republican behavior from November back to March. The GOP could look with expectancy toward many of the participants in the Democratic primary. A survey on the eve of Super Tuesday found white Democrats evenly split when asked which party's nominee they would likely support in November.[40]

Some Democrats had hoped that the excitement of Super Tuesday, especially if it produced a southern Democratic standard-bearer, would bring voters who had supported Reagan back to the Democratic party. When Bush went through the South in the general election like General Sherman through Georgia, the pattern of a generation during which Democrats have carried the South only once was maintained. That Dukakis was shunned less than Mondale should provide little comfort to Democrats, especially since Mondale faced the "Great Communicator," Ronald Reagan. To the extent that a more moderate Democrat was nominated without scoring well on Super Tuesday, it did not affect the outcome of the general election in the South. Indeed, as a *New York Times* writer warned on Super Tuesday, Florida and Texas are so non-southern that even Dukakis victories there would "prove little or nothing about the ability to carry a region the Democrats have grown accustomed to losing in national elections."[41]

In the wake of the general election, some comments made before Super Tuesday have a serendipitous quality. South Carolina Democratic spokesman Donald Fowler asserted that a Democrat who could win in the South could carry the industrial heartland.[42] Dukakis did not carry the South in the primaries or in November—nor did he beat Bush in the industrial states. SLC Director Charley Williams was prophetic when he said, "Super Tuesday is the big barometer. It is the meteorological forecast of what is likely to happen in the November general election."[43] The Vice President polled more votes in the South than did Dukakis on Super Tuesday. Bush outpolled the Massachusetts governor even in the two states in which the latter was the Democratic plurality winner in March.

The ultimate test of the success of Super Tuesday will be if it is repeated. A second coming seems improbable, with Arkansas and Virginia particularly likely to change.[44] Even before the votes were counted, some smaller states felt they had been overshadowed by neighbors who could offer more delegates.[45] Perhaps if the "ideal southern candidate" chooses to run in some subsequent election, it may be possible to pull off another extravaganza like that of 1988. Even then, however, a wiser strategy might be to have clusters of southern states scattered throughout the primary season so that the southern candidate, like Antaeus who renewed his strength each time he touched the ground, could return to the homeland for bursts of electoral success to help carry him or her through the long primary season.

ACKNOWLEDGMENTS

I appreciate the helpful comments on an earlier draft by Haley Barbour, Brad Lockerbie, and Bob Swansbrough.

NOTES

1. "Early Southern Regional Primary Moves Closer to Reality for 1988," Southern Legislative Conference press release, February 7, 1986, 1.

2. Hubert Humphrey carried Texas; George McGovern carried no states, and carried only one state nationally.

3. "Texas Joins Southern Primary—Largest Single Bloc of Southern Delegate Votes," Southern Legislative Conference press release, September 30, 1986, 1.

4. For an extended discussion of the background of Super Tuesday, see Harold W. Stanley and Charles D. Hadley, "The Southern Presidential Primary: Regional Intentions with National Implications," *Publius* 17 (Summer 1987): 83–100.

5. Charley Williams, Executive Director of the Southern Legislative Conference, contends that Super Tuesday was not intended to help any candidate but to be fair to all (Charley Williams, comments made at the Super Tuesday Roundtable at The Citadel Symposium on Southern Politics, Charleston, S.C., March 3–4, 1988). After the fact, Charles Robb also denied that he and the other progenitors had any intent to help promote the candidacy of a southern conservative (quoted in Charles D. Hadley and Harold W. Stanley, "An Analysis of Super Tuesday: Intentions, Results, and Implications" [Revision of paper presented at the annual meeting of the Midwest Political Science Association, Chicago, Ill., April 14–16, 1988], 3).

6. Bob Graham, "Super Tuesday Good for Nation, Better for Voter," *Atlanta Constitution*, February 22, 1987, E-1.

7. Charlie Capps, "Why Super Tuesday?" in *Challenge to the Candidates: The Southern Vein*, Special Report of the Sunbelt Institute in Cooperation with the Congressional Sunbelt Caucus (n.d.), 4.

8. Michael Oreskes, "G.O.P. Seeking to Lure Democrats to Tuesday Primaries and Beyond," *New York Times*, March 7, 1988, 10.

9. E. J. Dionne, "South Carolina Result Sets Stage for a Bush Showdown with Dole," *New York Times*, March 7, 1988, 1, 10.

10. Norman Ornstein, transcript of the "MacNeil/Lehrer Newshour," March 7, 1988, 5.

11. Hadley and Stanley, "Analysis of Super Tuesday," 13.

12. Compare David Castle, comments made on the Super Tuesday Roundtable at The Citadel Symposium on Southern Politics, Charleston, S.C., March 3–4, 1988.

13. Michael B. Binford, "An Analysis of Super Tuesday in the South: Patterns of Campaign Spending" (Paper presented at the annual meeting of the Southern Political Science Association, Atlanta, Ga., November 3–5, 1988), 6.

14. Quoted in Mark Mayfield, "The Democratic Primary in Alabama Gets Lost in 'Super' Shuffle," *USA Today*, February 29, 1988, 7A.

15. Ornstein, "MacNeil/Lehrer Newshour," 5.

16. Hadley and Stanley, "Analysis of Super Tuesday," 18.

17. Kevin Phillips, transcript of the "MacNeil/Lehrer Newshour," March 7, 1988, 9.

18. Binford, "Analysis of Super Tuesday in the South," 8.

19. Ibid., Table 4.

20. Rhodes Cook, "A Now-Mighty Bush Has Flaws Democratic Ticket May Exploit," *Congressional Quarterly Weekly Report* 46 (March 26, 1988): 791.

21. Kevin Sack, "Dukakis Turns Aggressor at Debate," *Atlanta Journal and Constitution*, February 28, 1988, 1-A; E. J. Dionne, "Gore and Gephardt Struggling for Survival in Contests Today," *New York Times*, March 8, 1988, 1.

22. Survey results reported in the next several paragraphs come from the CBS News/ *New York Times* "Super Tuesday" poll and from results provided by the ABC News Polling Unit. ABC provides results for each individual state. The CBS News/*New York Times* figures include, in addition to the states that are the subject of this chapter, Kentucky and Oklahoma.

23. CBS News/*New York Times*, "Super Tuesday" poll.

24. Cook, "Now-Mighty Bush," 791.

25. While ABC voters gave Dukakis a 42 to 27 lead over Gore in ability to reduce the federal deficit, CBS respondents rated the two candidates equally at 32 percent.

26. The ABC poll showed Robertson getting 35 percent among white, born-again Christians compared to Bush's 40 percent, and 25 percent among white evangelicals compared with 47 percent for Bush.

27. This perception of empathy by Bush as early as March foreshadowed polls in October that saw Bush as less elitist than Dukakis.

28. A few days before Super Tuesday, Jay Hakes, who had promoted the concept of a southern regional primary while on the staff of Florida's Senator Bob Graham, observed:

Yeah, we talk a lot about unintended consequences, but I have a vision of twenty years from now an historian sitting down to write the story of Super Tuesday and saying those Democrats were a lot cagier than people thought they were because they constructed a system that made it easier for George Bush to get the Republican nomination.

To which Donald Fowler, a South Carolina Democratic leader and a critic of Super Tuesday, rejoined, "Well, Jay, if that was your purpose, you are a hell of a lot smarter than I thought you were, and I congratulate you" (Comments made at the Super Tuesday Roundtable at The Citadel Symposium on Southern Politics, Charleston, S.C., March 3–4, 1988). Bush's success in the general election was perhaps the ultimate unintended consequence for Democrats! Some prescient observers foresaw early the strength of Bush's appeal in the South (Merle Black and Earl Black, "Don't Underestimate Bush," *New York Times*, March 13, 1988, 27).

29. While Dole pressed Bush more closely in some non-southern states, losing by 1 percentage point in Missouri and 2 points in Oklahoma, the reports, focusing on winner– loser, stressed the universality of the Bush triumph.

30. Bush took 409 of 477 delegates won on Super Tuesday in the South. These figures exclude Virginia, where the outcome was not binding, and South Carolina, which voted two days earlier. Bush and Dole entered Super Tuesday even in the delegate count; Bush emerged with 74 percent of all pledged delegates (Hadley and Stanley, "Analysis of Super Tuesday," 5).

31. R. W. Apple, Jr., "Super Tuesday: An Experiment Whose Time May Be Past," *New York Times*, March 8, 1988, 11; Steve Harvey, "Jackson, Dukakis Score Big with

Sample of Georgia Viewers,'' *Atlanta Journal and Constitution*, February 28, 1988, 14-A.

32. ''Southern Regional Primary Update,'' Southern Legislative Conference press release, March 10, 1988, 1.

33. Time in the South was not reported for Kemp. If the SLC counted the time spent in its member states, the figures reported here exceed the time spent in the eleven-state South, since the SLC includes Kentucky, Maryland, Oklahoma, and West Virginia.

34. Hadley and Stanley, ''Analysis of Super Tuesday,'' 11–12.

35. ''The Numbers Are In: Super Tuesday Turnout a Huge Success,'' Southern Legislative Conference press release, March 10, 1988, 2; plus figures on South Carolina GOP voting reported in R. W. Apple, Jr., ''In Victory Bush Seems Beneficiary of a Legacy,'' *New York Times*, March 7, 1988, 11.

36. Southern Leadership Conference, ''Backgrounder,'' April 1988, 2.

37. Ibid., 1, 7; Southern Leadership Conference, ''Backgrounder,'' February 1988, 2.

38. According to Oreskes, ''G.O.P. Seeking,'' 3 percent of the voters in South Carolina's GOP primary were Democrats. ABC and CBS found 5 and 7 percent, respectively, of Super Tuesday's GOP participants to be Democrats.

39. Letter from Haley Barbour to Chris Henick, February 6, 1989.

40. Steven V. Roberts, ''Southern Democrats Go Home Again,'' *New York Times*, March 2, 1988, 12.

41. Dionne, ''Gore and Gephardt,'' 10.

42. Donald Fowler, comments made at the Super Tuesday Roundtable at The Citadel Symposium on Southern Politics, Charleston, S.C., March 3–4, 1988.

43. Charley Williams, Super Tuesday Roundtable.

44. Southern Leadership Conference, ''Backgrounder,'' May 1988, 3.

45. Castle, Citadel Symposium; but for an opposing view, see Jay Hakes, comments made at the Super Tuesday Roundtable at The Citadel Symposium on Southern Politics, Charleston, S.C., March 3–4, 1988.

2

The Reagan Legacy and Party Politics in the South

HAROLD W. STANLEY

In assessing the legacy of the Reagan presidency for political parties, the mixed record contrasts clearly with the high hopes at the start. In 1980, the signs depicted by Reagan's decisive presidential victory, an unexpected Republican U.S. Senate majority for the first time in thirty years, and the surge in the proportion of people thinking of themselves as Republicans, led some political commentators to conclude that partisan realignment, and perhaps even an era of Republican dominance, were imminent.

The South figured prominently in such assessments. In 1980, Republicans picked up twelve Senate seats, including four in the South, which were critical to majority control. In the House of Representatives, the size of the Democratic majority in 1981 enabled Republicans and southern Democratic conservatives ("Boll Weevils") to form a working majority. If the "Reagan Revolution" realigned the parties, such conservatives would be a principal building block for an expanded Republican party.

The rosier Republican scenarios went mostly unrealized over the course of the Reagan presidency. As Reagan's presidency drew to a close in 1988, both parties emphasized the South as a newly competitive region: Republicans to consolidate previous gains, and Democrats to recover what had been lost. Both national nominating conventions were held in the South, and Super Tuesday helped focus southern voters on the presidential field.

The years of the Reagan presidency gave Republicans strong encouragement in the South and in the nation, but Democrats had some reasons to cheer. Partisan realignment did not occur, and Republican electoral gains were often matched by Democratic recoveries. The landslide Reagan win over Mondale in 1984 was a personal victory, and Reagan's coattails, like Bush's in 1988, did not prove capable of pulling Republicans into office. The midterm elections provided grounds for Democratic optimism: In 1982, House Democrats picked up twenty-six seats (gaining twelve in the South) to enfeeble the Boll Weevils, and in 1986, Democrats netted eight Senate seats (four in the South) and reclaimed majority control. In 1988, Bush's presidential victory was accompanied by net Republican losses for most levels of office.

This chapter assesses the legacy of the Reagan years for partisan politics in the South, with special emphasis on electoral changes. Partisan changes in the electorate, and not the institutionalization of such changes through government policy, will be the focus.

Presidents are often credited or blamed with whatever happens during their presidency. Certain partisan changes that registered during the Reagan years continued trends begun before Reagan took office. Moreover, certain changes set in motion during the Reagan years depend for their continuation and culmination on those who follow Reagan.

The strengthening of the Republican party during Ronald Reagan's presidency fell short of a partisan realignment. Definitions of realignment vary.[1] Here it means an enduring alteration in the partisan balance of supporters. An enduring alteration need not produce a new majority party, but it should be sizeable. Even if partisan changes during the Reagan years had been larger, two qualifications caution against the realignment conclusion. First, realignments require durability, and too little time has passed to test the durability of partisan changes. Second, dealigning forces continued to characterize partisan politics, and their significance cannot be easily dismissed.

President Reagan worked to bring about partisan change. A former Democrat, Reagan frequently made pointed appeals to Democratic voters, not merely for voting support but also for partisan conversion. In working to promote the Republican party, Reagan met with prominent Democrats who might be induced to switch over and run as Republicans, helped recruit Republican candidates for major offices, spoke often at Republican fund-raisers, lent his name to direct mail appeals, and appeared often on behalf of Republican candidates.[2] Previous presidents made similar efforts, but Reagan entered the presidency with clear prospects for a partisan realignment.

Expectations ran high early in the beginning. In 1980, Republicans won the presidency, majority control of the Senate, and thirty-three House seats. Commentary repeatedly raised the possibility of partisan realignment.[3] Republican leaders had high hopes to solidify the gains of 1980 and build a new governing coalition, even hoping to take majority control of the House of Representatives in 1982. Voters dashed these hopes in the 1982 midterm elections. Although initially overly optimistic about the prospects for taking control, particularly in light of the 1981–1982 recession, Republicans arguably had the advantage in campaign finance, candidate quality, redistricting, and public opinion.[4]

Reagan's decisive re-election win in 1984 renewed talk of realignment. Reagan himself claimed realignment, remarking in 1985 that "the other side would like to believe that our victory last November was due to something other than our philosophy. I just hope they keep believing that. There's a change happening in America. Realignment is real."[5]

REPUBLICAN FORTUNES: ELECTED OFFICIALS

The Republican record in winning elective office is one salient benchmark for gauging partisan changes. Watergate had laid the Republicans low in the mid-1970s. Conditions under Jimmy Carter—hostages, high inflation, and soaring interest rates—revived Republican hopes. Reagan helped Republicans to capitalize on those conditions, and won the 1980 popular vote by 10 percentage points.[6] Reagan's forty-nine-state re-election over Mondale in 1984, like his forty-four state win over Carter in 1980, was an impressively large victory margin. Bush followed with a forty-state sweep, yielding the fifth Republican presidential win in six tries.

In the three presidential elections of the 1980s, only one southern state cast its electoral votes for a Democrat—Georgia, in 1980, for favorite son and incumbent president Jimmy Carter. Of course, Democratic candidates did not fare well elsewhere either. Only eleven other states and the District of Columbia backed a Democratic candidate in the 1980s.

Below the presidential level, Republicans have had less to cheer about in recent years. The most notable accomplishment was capturing a U.S. Senate majority in 1980. However, congressional Republicans have slipped from those heights, and Reagan left office with fewer Republicans elected to federal office than when he entered. In the Senate, 53 Republicans served after the 1980 elections; this dropped to 45 after 1988. In the House, 192 Republicans were elected in 1980, only 173 in 1988.

Similar slippage marked the South. Republicans held 10 of the 22 Senate seats after 1980, but only 7 after 1988. Republicans held 39 southern House seats in 1980 and 1988, but redistricting had upped southern representation from 108 to 116, so holding steady marked a relative decline.[7] Moreover, Republicans in 1988 did not even contest one out of every four southern House seats.[8]

Republican presidential victories were followed by midterm losses—common occurrences, but particularly disappointing in 1982 and 1986, suggesting realignment had not taken hold at the congressional level. In 1982, Republicans lost twenty-six seats in the House, the worst loss by a president's party in the first midterm election since Republicans lost seventy-five seats under Warren Harding in 1922.[9] In 1986, Republicans lost eight U.S. Senate seats and majority control of the chamber.

At the state level throughout the nation and in the South, Republicans have not registered notable gains: twenty-three Republican governors were in office after the 1980 elections, and twenty-two after those of 1988. Republicans comprised about 40 percent of state legislators after both the 1980 and 1988 elections. The number of state legislatures in which the Republicans controlled both chambers did slip from fifteen after the 1980 elections to eight after the 1988 elections. Democratic control has edged up from twenty-eight to twenty-nine legislatures, and the number in which different parties control different chambers has increased from six to twelve.[10]

In the South, Republicans were governors in five states after both the 1980 and 1988 elections. However, this similarity masks considerable turnover. During the 1980s, of the eleven southern states, only Georgia and Mississippi failed to elect a Republican as governor. The patronage, appointment, and bargaining powers of southern governors make such Republican victories potentially critical for party building.[11] In the face of seemingly entrenched Democratic state legislatures and local county elites, Republican governors can seek to safeguard partisan interests that would otherwise get short shrift in redistricting and kindred matters.

Republicans remain outnumbered among southern state legislators. Republicans held one out of every six seats at the start of the decade. In 1989 they held one out of every four. These regional figures suggest that Republicans are far from majority control of southern legislative chambers. However, in several southern states Republicans have made strong strides toward competitiveness. As of 1981, Republicans held one-third of the legislative seats or more only in Tennessee and Florida. In 1989, North Carolina, Texas, and Virginia joined this group, with South Carolina just outside the circle with 28 percent. Recent developments in Florida and North Carolina in which Republicans have allied with conservative Democrats to exert control of legislative chambers indicate a far more potent position for Republicans than even these numbers suggest.

These electoral results at levels below the presidency in the nation and in the South scarcely mark the emergence of a new Republican majority.[12] Despite winning the presidency by convincing margins three times in a row, and in five out of the last six tries, such Republican success has yet to spill over to produce similar Republican successes at lower levels. The Reagan years raised Republican hopes, but they did not appreciably raise the number of Republican officeholders below the presidential level.

The less than compelling Republican record in nonpresidential elections can be considered to reveal the institutional barriers to partisan change. Incumbency voting, most evident in House elections, benefits Democrats who disproportionately enjoy the benefits of incumbency. Rather than revealing Republican failure, the restricted lower level Republican success can be viewed as ''more a sign of the extent to which the House and state governments have insulated themselves from emerging political forces.''[13]

How high are such barriers to partisan change? Strong partisan gains have marked even recent years. As Raymond Wolfinger noted, in 1980 when Reagan secured 51 percent of the presidential vote, House Republicans gained ten open seats and defeated twenty-eight Democratic incumbents, losing only three incumbents and one open seat: "Incumbency alone does not provide much protection to a party on the short end of a strong partisan tide."[14]

Moreover, partisan realignment entails a restructuring of partisanship. Restructuring resulting in split-ticket voting suggests dealignment, not realignment—dealignment in which party ties mean less. "What kind of realignment leaves so little imprint beyond the presidential level?"[15] Kevin Phillips calls such a result a "split-level realignment."[16] One can question the wisdom of terming such changes realignments, even partial ones. Beck has expressed the relevant concerns well:

Surely no realignment has occurred if it is based on new "reconstructed partisans" who do not follow up their Republican presidential preferences by supporting candidates of the same party for other offices. Partisanship is a loyalty to a party, not to a candidate, and as such should serve as an enduring guide to voting behavior. If the politics of the 1980s greatly diminishes its role, then it is a politics of dealignment rather than realignment.[17]

Former White House Political Director Mitchell E. Daniels, Jr., underscored the problems of party realignment in a period when parties mean less: "Had Ronald Reagan come along 20 or 30 years earlier, he would have left a much deeper political imprint. But party affiliation doesn't mean as much to people now as it did before. We are in an era of departisanization."[18]

PRESIDENTIAL APPROVAL

President Reagan's popularity and personal appeal, Republicans hoped, would attract new supporters to the Republican party, offering candidates across the ticket a broader base on which to build. As Reagan's term ended, critics and supporters commented that Reagan's strong appeal had not been institutionalized within the party.

Reagan enjoyed the reputation of having high public approval ratings—as the "Teflon president," to whom problems supposedly did not stick. The reality is otherwise. After his honeymoon ended, Reagan's ratings plummeted steadily throughout 1981 and 1982, rebounded in early 1983, and continued climbing until late 1986, with a slight downturn in early 1985. The performance of the economy—recession in the early years, and recovery in the later years—is a critical component of these fluctuations.[19]

The striking aspects of Reagan's approval ratings are the peaks he attained and sustained throughout the fifth and sixth years of his administration, which were higher even than the approval rating chalked up during his first year in office.[20] However, the unraveling of the Iran-Contra affair took its toll on

Reagan's approval rating in late 1986 and 1987, a loss that was only partially recouped.[21]

Reagan's initial election in 1980, when Republicans gained thirty-three House seats and twelve Senate seats, suggested that he had coattails. In subsequent elections, however, Reagan's appeal did not translate readily into support for his fellow Republicans. Indeed, in 1982 Reagan was not even welcome in some Republican campaigns.[22] In 1986, Reagan put in campaign appearances in sixteen states after Labor Day, but Republican Senate candidates won in only four of these states; indeed, in only one state did Reagan's active support affect the outcome.[23]

Even when Reagan was on the ticket, questions about his coattails lingered. His lopsided re-election in 1984 was accompanied by the loss of two Republican seats in the Senate and a gain of only fourteen seats in the House. The Republican share of House seats (41.8 percent) was the lowest ever for the party of a winning presidential candidate—lowest, that is, until Bush won with a 40.2 percent House share.[24] Reagan's personal popularity, such as it was, did not signify an ability to carry large numbers of Republicans into office.

PARTY IDENTIFICATION

Republican wins in five of the last six presidential elections have occurred despite a Democratic edge in partisan identifiers. Republican gains in party identification during the Reagan years eroded but did not reverse this traditional Democratic advantage in the nation and in the South. Although polls sometimes showed roughly equal percentages of Republican and Democratic identifiers, such readings did not persist. The authors of an extensive study of political attitudes in early 1987 bluntly concluded: "We see no evidence of a Republican realignment or an emerging Republican majority."[25] More competitive parties, not a newly dominant Republican party, have resulted from the changes in partisan identification.[26]

Table 2.1 presents partisan identification in the South from 1952 to 1988. It charts the decline of the Democrats and the rise of the Republicans, revealing that much of the change occurred prior to Reagan's election in 1980. Since 1980, these trends have continued, among both whites and blacks (although the fluctuations, perhaps due to the small sample of blacks, are grounds for caution). After 1982 a majority of southern whites no longer identified with the Democratic party.[27]

Patterns of partisanship offer some comfort to Democrats. According to Table 2.1, the Democratic edge in southern partisans was only reduced from 30 to 22 percent. However, the political reality behind the numbers diminishes that edge further. Republicans turn out at higher levels, and greater Democratic partisan defections, certainly at the presidential level, mean that even with a 20-point Democratic lead in identifiers, the Republican party can be considered the majority party in the South for presidential voting.[28]

Table 2.1
Partisan Identification in the South, 1952–1988*

Year	All Southerners Dem	Ind	Rep	Whites Dem	Ind	Rep	Blacks Dem	Ind	Rep	Sample Size All	Wh	Bl
1952	68	2	13	80	2	14	56	1	14	450	316	96
1956	65	5	21	69	6	22	48	3	19	434	354	80
1958	66	7	19	71	7	18	44	3	22	361	297	64
1960	58	11	23	62	12	22	37	7	25	295	229	44
1962	58	8	24	58	9	26	55	0	14	360	309	51
1964	71	8	17	70	8	21	77	8	5	487	288	199
1966	61	12	23	61	12	24	62	10	18	293	243	50
1968	67	11	21	61	13	25	94	2	2	446	316	130
1970	58	15	26	51	17	30	92	5	3	480	365	115
1972	58	14	25	54	15	29	73	13	12	705	563	142
1974	57	16	22	53	16	25	78	14	6	443	360	80
1976	58	15	25	53	16	30	79	11	7	575	455	115
1978	57	14	26	53	14	30	71	14	10	647	526	118
1980	57	13	27	53	14	31	80	6	10	471	392	79
1982	61	9	28	55	11	32	93	2	5	423	354	67
1984	52	14	31	46	15	37	73	13	10	651	509	139
1986	57	12	29	49	13	36	83	8	8	702	530	170
1988	55	10	33	48	11	38	76	4	16	645	492	149

*Partisans include strong and weak identifiers as well as those who lean toward one party. Apolitical and "other" are counted in the base on which percentages are figured but are not shown in the table. All figures, except for sample size, are reported in percent. The following abbreviations are used in the table: Dem = Democratic, Ind = independent, Rep = Republican, Wh = white, and BL = black.

Source: Calculated by author using National Election Studies data (Center for Political Studies, University of Michigan, Ann Arbor, Michigan) for the years indicated.

In addition to shifts in the overall level of partisan identification, the party coalitions have undergone alterations during the Reagan years. One prominent group indicative of Reagan's appeal beyond the traditional Republican base—"Reagan Democrats"—is emblematic of the failure to convert Reagan's personal strength to long-lasting Republican advantage. Bill Brock, former Republican National Committee (RNC) chairman, put it well in 1988: "The phrase 'Reagan Democrat' ought to be a contradiction in terms. They ought to be Republicans by now."[29] In 1988, the Democrats who had voted for Reagan in 1984 split evenly between Bush and Dukakis.[30]

Under Reagan, Republicans have registered marked gains among white fundamentalists, white southerners, and youth. Judging by the 1988 results, Bush retained those gains. Reagan received two out of three votes cast by white fundamentalists in 1980. In 1984 and 1988, the Republican nominee received four out of five. Bush in 1988, like Reagan in 1984, received two out of three votes cast by white southerners, but here Reagan had built on what went before: Republican advances in the white South have been underway for decades.[31]

Youth have identified more strongly with the Republicans than the Democrats, a differential given impetus by the contrast between Carter and Reagan.[32] However, youth gave the same vote share to Reagan in 1984 as did older voters, and the actual implications of youth partisanship are a matter of dispute. Thomas Cavanagh and James Sundquist see Republican tendencies among the young as ominous for the Democrats since that party can no longer count on having its ranks rejuvenated at the previous rates.[33] Raymond Wolfinger has cautioned that youth have typically voted similarly to other age groups, and that the youth vote in one election predicts little about the next election.[34]

PARTY ORGANIZATION

Organizationally, the Republican party has continued to improve during the Reagan presidency.[35] In terms of recruitment, fund-raising, and services provided to state and local parties and candidates, Republican developments have outstripped those of the opposition and left the Democrats seeking to catch up. Despite Democratic improvements, the Republican National Committee and the Republican Senate and House campaign committees still outraised and outspent their Democratic counterparts by more than two to one.

These organizational developments, begun when Bill Brock took over the RNC in 1977, expanded during the Reagan presidency. In 1984 the RNC played a major role in coordinating campaign workers throughout the nation for Reagan's re-election—quite a contrast with Nixon's re-election drive, which was run through the Committee for Reelection of the President (CREEP), independent of the RNC.

Reagan committed himself to building the Republican party and broadening the Republican base. Appearances at fund-raisers and appeals in speeches for support of and identification with the Republican party were frequent. Less visible but politically telling were Reagan's personal, persuasive efforts to recruit compelling candidates for selected contests. Although some Republicans (most notably, House Minority Leader Robert Michels) criticized Reagan in 1984 for playing it safe and doing less than he might have done to seek to elect Republicans, in 1986 Reagan's active support for Republican candidates raised questions among his supporters about whether he was endangering his own political standing with his partisan zeal.[36]

Reagan, a converted Democrat himself, sought to convert other Democrats to the Republican cause. He made public appeals and he also took part in some targeted attempts to switch key Democratic officeholders to the Republicans. As the RNC chairman said of the more general pattern in early 1986: ''The legacy of the Reagan Revolution may be nothing less than partisan realignment. The momentum of his elections has resulted in more than 200 Democratic office-holders changing their affiliation to the Republican Party.''[37]

The benefits of better organization can be telling. When Democrats and Republicans claim roughly similar numbers of identifiers, organization can provide the winning edge. Voter registration drives in 1984 suggest the possibility of organizational one-upmanship.

For the 1984 elections, both national parties and over fifty national organizations mounted major voter registration campaigns.[38] Low registration rates were evident among traditionally Democratic groups. Pro-Democratic organizations hoped to mobilize the unregistered in order to produce Democratic victories. The Democratic efforts for 1984 succeeded in raising registration totals, but they failed to deliver a Democratic advantage. Republicans had countered with registration drives that carefully targeted Republican supporters.[39] The more diffuse pro-Democratic drives pushed up registration totals with many who ultimately turned out to vote for Reagan.[40] The well-publicized 1985 attempt to switch registered Democratic voters to Republican registration—''Operation Open Door,'' targeting Florida, Louisiana, North Carolina, and Pennsylvania— met with less success.[41]

The 1984 registration drives advantaged the Republicans. A longer look at registration also shows Republican advantage, but not one attributable to Reagan. In the nation, party registration figures point to an improved competitive position for the Republican party, not because of a rising share of Republican voters, but because of the declining Democratic share of registered voters. Between 1976 and 1986, the Democratic percentage of registered voters in the twenty-eight states reporting registration by party declined from 56.1 to 49.5. Most of that Democratic decline predated the Reagan years (56.1 to 50.4 in 1980). The Republican percentage stood at 31.3 percent in 1976 and 31.8 percent in 1986, having dipped to 30.0 percent in 1980.[42]

In the South, only three states have party registration, but in these three, Republican registration shares have risen and Democratic shares have declined. Louisiana Republicans lag, with 16 percent of the registrants, up from 7 percent in 1980. The percentage of North Carolina Republicans rose from 24 to 30 percent over the same period, and Florida Republicans rose from 30 to 39 percent. Democratic registration shares have declined by similar percentages, leaving Florida Democrats in 1988 with 54 percent of the registered voters, North Carolina Democrats with 65 percent, and Louisiana Democrats with 75 percent.[43]

Reagan actively worked to build the Republican party, but some think Reagan's political success in some senses worked against organizational development. Brock, former RNC chairman, suggested that in recent years there has been a tendency to neglect party building because "Reagan was running so strong and popular."[44]

CONCLUSION

The Reagan years have witnessed a strengthening of the Republican party in the South and in the nation. Several Republican gains merit mention. Democratic partisan identifiers still outnumber the Republicans, but by a much narrower margin than they did prior to 1980. Roughly equal shares of partisan identifiers make the party struggle much more competitive and leave Republicans better positioned for possible emergence into majority party status. Republican party organization improved further in the Reagan years, and can provide the winning edge as partisan competition tightens.

Republican strengthening stopped short of a realignment, and Republicans may not secure a realignment soon. Republicans remain presidentially oriented, having been frustrated in efforts to build on Reagan's base to win office below the presidency. The Republican leaders who follow Reagan and their skill in defending and building on the gains of the Reagan years will determine whether the Republican party becomes the new majority party, extending its success across the different levels of government and solidifying its supporters into partisan loyalists. If they fail, the Republican gains during the Reagan years will have made Republicans more competitive, but dominance will elude them.

NOTES

1. Discussions of the realignment concept, the literature, and recent southern experience can be found in Harold W. Stanley, "Southern Partisan Changes: Dealignment, Realignment or Both?" *Journal of Politics* 50 (1988): 64–88; and John R. Petrocik, "Realignment: New Party Coalitions and the Nationalization of the South," *Journal of Politics* 49 (1987): 348–375.

2. Rhodes Cook, "Reagan Nurtures His Adopted Party to Strength," *Congressional Quarterly Weekly Report* (1985): 1927–1930; Maxwell Glen, "Marketing Reagan," *National Journal* (1987): 2156–2159.

3. Austin Ranney, "Reagan's First Term," in *The American Elections of 1984*, ed. Austin Ranney (Washington, D.C.: Duke University Press and the American Enterprise Institute for Public Policy Research, 1985), 2.

4. Albert R. Hunt, "National Politics and the 1982 Campaign," in *The American Elections of 1982*, ed. Thomas E. Mann and Norman J. Ornstein (Washington, D.C.: American Enterprise Institute for Public Policy Research, 1983), 5–7, 40.

5. Quoted in Phil Gailey, "Republicans Start to Worry about Signs of Slippage," *New York Times*, August 25, 1985, E5.

6. Reagan gained only 0.6 percent more of the popular vote in 1980 than Carter had in 1976. The landslide look resulted from gaining Senate control, polls suggesting the race was too close to call, and Reagan racking up 91 percent of the electoral vote. In 1984, Reagan earned 98 percent of the electoral vote and 59 percent of the popular vote

(Harold W. Stanley and Richard G. Niemi, *Vital Statistics on American Politics*, 2d ed. [Washington, D.C.: CQ Press, 1989], 106).

7. Republican congressional growth in the South, although constant in the 1980s, has not constituted a steadily expanding base on which Republicans have built. In the last quarter century, at least twenty-three districts that elected a Republican have later reverted to a Democrat (Hastings Wyman, Jr., "The Gingrich Victory: A New GOP Strategy," *Southern Political Report*, April 4, 1989, 2).

8. Democrats did not contest 8 percent of the southern House seats—calculated from *Congressional Quarterly Weekly Report* (October 8, 1988): 2819; (May 6, 1989): 1074–1080.

9. Stanley and Niemi, *Vital Statistics on American Politics*, 185.

10. *National Journal* (November 12, 1988): 2885–2886; U.S. Bureau of the Census, *Statistical Abstract of the United States 1987*, 107th ed. (Washington, D.C.: Government Printing Office, 1986), 238–239.

11. The potential can outrun the actual: "As for the GOP's four new[ly elected] governors strengthening the state parties, they'll have to do better than their recent Republican predecessors—Edwards (S.C.), Holshouser (N.C.), Treen (La.), White (Ark.), etc.—whose regimes left little imprint on their states' political landscape" (Hastings Wyman, Jr., "Democrats Sweep Southern Senate Races: GOP Gains Governorships," *Southern Political Report*, November 11, 1986, 2).

12. Another indicator of local Republican presence: Only 132 of 1,103 southern counties (12 percent) have Republican sheriffs. Although precise county designations are unavailable, 47 (36 percent) of these Republican sheriffs are from North Carolina, Tennessee, or Virginia—states with strong pockets of traditional Republicanism in the mountain regions (Hastings Wyman, Jr., "Don't Run against the Sheriff," *Southern Political Report*, May 30, 1989, 2–3).

13. John E. Chubb and Paul E. Peterson, "Realignment and Institutionalization," in *The New Direction in American Politics*, ed. John E. Chubb and Paul E. Peterson (Washington, D.C.: Brookings Institution, 1985), 17.

14. Raymond E. Wolfinger, "Dealignment, Realignment, and Mandates in the 1984 Election," in *The American Elections of 1984*, ed. Austin Ranney (Washington, D.C.: Duke University Press and American Enterprise Institute for Public Policy Research, 1985), 285.

15. Paul Allen Beck, "Incomplete Realignment: The Reagan Legacy for Parties and Elections," in *The Reagan Legacy: Promise and Performance*, ed. Charles O. Jones (Chatham, N.J.: Chatham House, 1988), 167.

16. Paul R. Abramson, John H. Aldrich, and David W. Rohde, *Change and Continuity in the 1984 Elections* (Washington, D.C.: CQ Press, 1986), 287.

17. Paul Allen Beck, "Incomplete Realignment," 168.

18. Quoted in Paul Taylor, "For GOP and Nominee, a Fight to Hold Ground; Reagan Era Marked by Missed Opportunities," *Washington Post*, August 14, 1988.

19. James W. Ceaser, "The Reagan Presidency and American Public Opinion," in *The Reagan Legacy: Promise and Performance*, ed. Charles O. Jones (Chatham, N.J.: Chatham House, 1988), 172–210; D. Roderick Kiewiet and Douglas Rivers, "The Economic Basis of Reagan's Appeal," in *The New Direction in American Politics*, ed. John E. Chubb and Paul E. Peterson (Washington, D.C.: The Brookings Institution, 1985), 69–90.

20. Previous presidents have failed to find such favor. Indeed, the longer they were

president, the less they were liked (Thomas E. Cronin, *The State of the Presidency*, 2d. ed. [Boston: Little Brown, 1978]).

21. James W. Ceaser, "The Reagan Presidency and American Public Opinion," in *The Reagan Legacy: Promise and Performance*, ed. Charles O. Jones (Chatham, N.J.: Chatham House, 1988), 201–205.

22. Hunt, "National Politics and the 1982 Campaign," 39.

23. *Congressional Quarterly Weekly Report* (November 8, 1986): 2813.

24. Bush carried 98 of the South's 116 congressional districts (84 percent), but 60 of these districts returned Democratic members of Congress. (Only one southern district went for Dukakis and a Republican congressman—Louisiana's 8th.) The South's 53 percent rate of split district outcomes compares with 27 percent for the rest of the nation (calculations based on unpublished *Congressional Quarterly* data).

25. The authors note that once higher Republican voter turnout and partisan loyalty are taken into account, the Democratic lead in identification "virtually disappears," leaving the parties "almost dead even" (Norman Ornstein, Andrew Kohut, and Larry McCarthy, *The People, the Press, and Politics: The "Times Mirror" Study of the American Electorate* [Reading, Mass.: Addison-Wesley, 1988], 2, 21, 75).

26. Thomas E. Cavanagh and James L. Sundquist, "The New Two-Party System," in *The New Direction in American Politics*, ed. John E. Chubb and Paul E. Peterson (Washington, D.C.: The Brookings Institution, 1985), 33–68.

27. For a consideration of whether the National Election Studies understate Republican identification in the South, and for results from other polls, see Earl Black and Merle Black, *Politics and Society in the South* (Cambridge, Mass.: Harvard University Press, 1987), 236–240.

28. Stanley, "Southern Partisan Changes," 79.

29. Quoted in Taylor, "For GOP and Nominee."

30. Exit poll results in this and the following paragraph are from the *New York Times/ CBS News Poll* as reported in Stanley and Niemi, *Vital Statistics on American Politics*, 100–101.

31. Harold W. Stanley, William T. Bianco, and Richard G. Niemi, "Partisanship and Group Support over Time: A Multivariate Analysis," *The American Political Science Review* 80 (1986): 969–976; Wolfinger, "Dealignment, Realignment, and Mandates," 287–290; and Black and Black, *Politics and Society in the South*, 232–316.

32. Helmut Norpoth, "Under Way and Here to Stay: Party Realignment in the 1980s?" *Public Opinion Quarterly* 51 (1987): 376–391.

33. Cavanagh and Sundquist, "The New Two-Party System," 48–49.

34. Wolfinger, "Dealignment, Realignment, and Mandates," 291–292.

35. A. James Reichley, "The Rise of National Parties," in *The New Direction in American Politics*, ed. John E. Chubb and Paul E. Peterson (Washington, D.C.: Brookings Institution, 1985), 186–195.

36. Cook, "Reagan Nurtures His Adopted Party to Strength."

37. Frank J. Fahrenkopf, Jr., "Preface," *1984–1985 Election Summary* (Washington, D.C.: Republican National Committee, 1986).

38. *New Republic*, May 7, 1984, 40. For a discussion of the 1984 voter registration drives focusing on the South, see Harold W. Stanley, "The 1984 Presidential Election in the South: Race and Realignment," in Robert P. Steed, Laurence W. Moreland, and Tod A. Baker, eds., *The 1984 Presidential Election in the South: Patterns of Southern Party Politics* (New York: Praeger, 1986), 303–335.

39. Reichley, "The Rise of National Parties," 193–194.

40. One nonpartisan study reported that new registrants backed Reagan over Mondale by a margin of two to one. New registrants also favored Republican House candidates with 54 percent of their vote (Curtis B. Gans, *Non-Voter Study '84–'85* [Washington, D.C.: Committee for the Study of the American Electorate, 1985]; *New Republic*, February 25, 1985, 15; and Susan L. Farmer, "The Republican Registration Drive 1984," [Paper delivered at the 1985 Annual Meeting of the American Political Science Association, New Orleans, 1985]). Given Reagan's comfortable margin of victory, net registration gains did not prove essential to his re-election, but they helped.

41. Cook, "Reagan Nurtures His Adopted Party to Strength," 1928.

42. The percentage of others or Independents rose from 12.5 to 18.6 percent from 1976 to 1986 (*Republican Almanac: 1987 State Political Profiles* [Washington, D.C.: Republican National Committee, 1987], ix, 9).

43. Percentages calculated from official registration statistics obtained from the Secretary of State or State Election Board in each state.

44. An unnamed, former high-ranking Reagan administration official termed this the "Hollywood syndrome," and elaborated:

In politics, the enterprise is larger than the star, and we failed to institutionalize the popularity of the star, to stretch it beyond him to the party and beyond his tenure in office. His core managers, the California group and the First Lady, always concentrated on making the star popular. (Taylor, "For GOP and Nominee")

PART II

THE CAMPAIGN AND ITS CONSEQUENCES: THE DEEP SOUTH

3

Alabama: Further Steps toward a Competitive Party System

PATRICK R. COTTER

The 1988 general election in Alabama was a very low-key, but still potentially critical, affair. The Democratic and Republican presidential and vice presidential candidates largely ignored the state. Neither of the state's U.S. Senate seats was up for election. Only one of the state's incumbent congressmen was seriously challenged, and that challenge turned out to be not too serious. The campaigns for positions on the Alabama Supreme Court and the Public Service Commission attracted little media or public attention. None of the constitutional amendments on the ballot were controversial.

Alabama had not enjoyed (or suffered—depending upon your perspective concerning campaigns) such a low-key election in a number of years. The 1980 presidential election in the state was very close, with Ronald Reagan ultimately winning by only about 1 percent of the vote. That year also saw the election of the state's first Republican U.S. senator since Reconstruction. In 1982, George Wallace overcame tough primary and general election opponents to win his fourth term as governor. Both Ronald Reagan and incumbent Democratic Senator Howell Heflin easily won their campaigns in 1984. However, there were several close congressional races that year. The loud, rough-and-tumble, and anything but dull, character of the state's electoral politics perhaps reached its peak in 1986. In that election the outcome of the nomination process produced a deep split within the Democratic Party, which in turn led to the election of the state's first Republican governor in more than one hundred years. At the same time, Congressman Richard Shelby narrowly defeated (with 50.3 percent of the vote) incumbent Republican U.S. Senator Jeremiah Denton.

While certainly important events, these earlier elections did not produce or accompany any immediate and major change in the balance of Democratic and Republican party identifiers within the Alabama electorate. Throughout the 1980–1986 period, Democrats consistently outnumbered Republicans in the state, though the size of the Democratic advantage fluctuated over time.[1] Even the upheavals associated with the 1986 election did not alter this fact. Indeed, the number of Democratic and Republican identifiers in the state at the end of the 1986 campaign was almost exactly the same as had existed at the beginning of the contest.[2]

Ironically, given the bland nature of the campaign, important changes did occur in the state's electorate during the 1988 campaign. Specifically, at the conclusion of the contest there were more Republican than Democratic party identifiers in Alabama.

It is far too early to tell whether the partisan change that occurred in 1988 is permanent or only temporary. Even if it is only temporary, however, the shift in the distribution of party identification that occurred during 1988 signals that important political changes are taking place within Alabama. A review of the 1988 campaign within the state will provide information concerning why the distribution of party identification changed. This review will also provide insight into the present and future politics of Alabama.

THE CAMPAIGN

The Presidential Campaign

As it approached the Atlanta convention, the Alabama Democratic party faced two problems. The first was a possible split between the supporters of Jesse Jackson (who had narrowly won the state's Super Tuesday primary) and those now supporting Michael Dukakis (many of whom originally backed the second-place finisher on Super Tuesday, Albert Gore). As was the case nationally, this possible split involved differences over issues, the priority given to different policy areas, and the role that Jackson and his supporters were to play within the party.[3]

The second problem involved whether Michael Dukakis, the party's soon to be confirmed nominee, had a chance to win in Alabama. For months some of the state's Democratic leaders had said that in order to win in Alabama the national party had to move back into the "political mainstream." In October 1987, for example, Speaker of the Alabama House Jimmy Clark argued:

the people of this state are tired of that so-called intelligentsia element in Washington, New York, New England running the nation, when that is no longer the center of the

mainstream thought of this nation. The Democratic Party either is going to reach back
. . . or they're going to get throttled here, and it's going to go right down to the grassroots
of this state.[4]

Dukakis's nomination campaign gave many Alabama Democratic leaders a
greater sense of optimism about the upcoming presidential campaign than they
had felt in a number of years. This optimism existed despite the fact that the
Massachusetts governor had largely ignored the state during his pre-convention
campaign. Even with this heightened optimism, however, many Alabama party
leaders and officeholders were still concerned about Dukakis's chances in the
state. Thus, in the days leading up to the convention, Alabama officials urged
Dukakis to position himself within what they considered to be the political
mainstream.[5] For example, U.S. Senator Richard Shelby said that Dukakis had
to "reach out and show us that he's a mainstream American and sensitive to the
issues we care about, and that he's not another eastern liberal in the Kennedy
mold coming out of Massachusetts."[6] The best way to demonstrate his position
in the mainstream, many of the state's leaders argued, was for Dukakis to select
a southerner for his vice presidential running mate.[7]

The tone and events of the Atlanta convention, particularly the reconciliation
between Dukakis and Jackson and the selection of Texan Lloyd Bentsen to be
the party's vice presidential candidate, addressed the problems the Alabama
Democratic party faced going into the convention. As a result, the state's Democrats left the convention more unified and enthusiastic for its national ticket
than they had been in years. At a post-convention meeting, Paul Hubbert, leader
of the influential Alabama Education Association, said, "We've come together
for the first time in eight years. The local and state candidates won't have to
run from the ticket this year. They won't have to say, 'I'm an Alabama Democrat.' Instead they can say, 'I'm a Democrat.' "[8] Reflecting this sense of
enthusiasm and scent of victory (aided by the findings of post-convention national
surveys), many of the state's Democratic officeholders publicly expressed support
for Dukakis and took leadership positions in his campaign.[9]

Official support for Dukakis perhaps reached its peak during Dukakis's first
(and, as it turned out, only) post-convention visit to Alabama. After meeting
with Dukakis, House Speaker Jimmy Clark, the former critic of the Washington–
New York–New England axis, said, "The issues he [Dukakis] is bringing up
are issues that the majority of Alabamians are concerned about."[10] Similarly,
U.S. Senator Howell Heflin said, "There are more Democratic officeholders
than I have seen in many years involved in this presidential campaign. I have
never seen so many Democrats energized."[11]

Meanwhile, Republican leaders were expressing guarded confidence about the
presidential campaign.[12] Alabama's delegation to the New Orleans convention
was firmly behind George Bush (who had swept the state's Super Tuesday
presidential primary). Not even the controversy surrounding Dan Quayle's nomination as the party's vice presidential candidate diminished this support.[13]

At the convention, Alabama Republicans quickly picked up the Bush strategy of attacking Dukakis as being out of touch with most citizens.[14] The outlines of this strategy, however, were evident well before the convention. Specifically, in June, Dukakis made a brief campaign visit to Montgomery. Shortly before this event (which occurred about one month before the Democratic convention and about two months before the Republican gathering), a Birmingham-based Republican organization released information criticizing Dukakis' position on the Pledge of Allegiance, the death penalty, and the use of national guard troops in Central America.[15] At about the same time as Dukakis's visit, state GOP Chairman and Montgomery Mayor, Emory Folmar, attacked the Massachusetts Governor "as a member of the American Civil Liberties Union [ACLU], an opponent of the death penalty, an advocate of gun control and as 'weak' on defense."[16] Similarly, Folmar called the Democratic nominee a "typical tax–spend Northeastern liberal" and "a soul mate of George McGovern and Walter Mondale and a prophet of the Teddy Kennedy school of politics."[17] Subjects such as the death penalty, the ACLU, the Pledge of Allegiance, and national defense were, of course, topics that George Bush would later bring up throughout the general election campaign. Folmar even called Dukakis, as Bush would do later, a "card carrying member of the American Civil Liberties Union."[18]

After the Republican convention, little happened within Alabama in terms of specific campaign events. Neither George Bush nor Michael Dukakis campaigned in the state. Dan Quayle made two brief stops in Alabama, once in early September and then again just days before the November election. Most surprisingly, neither fellow southerner Lloyd Bentsen nor Jesse Jackson made any campaign visits to the state.

Undoubtedly, a major reason the candidates ignored the state was the results of public opinion polls that showed Bush with a strong lead in Alabama. For example, a survey conducted in late August by Southern Opinion Research for the *Birmingham News* found Bush with a 52 to 32 percent lead (Table 3.1).[19] Other polls conducted within the state revealed similar results.[20] Republican officials expressed pleasure over the survey results and said that they accurately reflected the opinions of Alabamians. They vowed, however, not to let their guard down until the November election.[21]

While the state's Democrats remained publicly optimistic,[22] the lopsided survey results were soon followed by rumors and speculation that the Dukakis campaign had written off Alabama and the entire South.[23] These rumors were quickly denied, but no effective actions were taken to improve Dukakis's position within the state. As a result, a late September *Birmingham News* survey found that Bush now led by a 54 to 33 percent margin, an increase from the 17 percent advantage he had held a month earlier.[24]

Dukakis's poor showing in the polls led some Alabama Democratic leaders to criticize the candidate and his campaign organization. For example, John Baker, Chairman of the Alabama Democratic Party, said, "I don't believe that the Dukakis campaign could have run a worse campaign than they've run."[25]

Table 3.1
Pre-Election Presidential Preferences (in percent)*

Candidate	August 27-31	September 27-29	November 2-5
Bush	52	54	57
Dukakis	32	33	36
Don't know/no answer	15	13	8
Totals	99	100	101
(N)	(502)	(504)	(692)

*In the November survey, Dukakis' name was listed before Bush. Unde-
cided but "leaning" respondents were included in candidates' percentages in the November survey. Percentages in this table and the following tables may not sum to 100 percent because of rounding error.

Source: Birmingham News/Southern Opinion Research surveys for the
dates indicated.

Some prominent Democrats, including Baker (who later tempered his criticism of the Dukakis campaign), continued to hold out some hope for victory. Birmingham Mayor and national campaign co-chair Richard Arrington, however, reported that Dukakis has given up on Alabama.[26]

The final pre-election surveys found Bush well in front of Dukakis. According to the *Birmingham News* study, Bush led by a 57 to 36 percent margin among likely voters.[27]

These and previous survey results had, by this point in the campaign, changed many of the state's Democrats' enthusiasm for the national ticket to frustration over lost opportunities. Now some of the party's office seekers sought to disassociate themselves from the Dukakis-Bentsen ticket. Anger and disgust with the strategy and tactics of the Bush campaign were one of the few elements that unified Democratic leaders.[28]

State Campaigns

The presidency was not the only office being contested in the November election. In addition to choosing candidates for the House of Representatives, Alabama voters selected five members of the state Supreme Court, one judge on the Court of Civil Appeals, and the president of the Alabama Public Service Commission. A number of local government positions were also up for election. None of the congressional races generated much news or attention. Indeed, three of the incumbents faced no major party opponent, and in only one of the races was a challenger given any chance for victory.

In the Supreme Court races, supporters and opponents of "tort reform" had conducted relatively visible and hard-fought campaigns in the Democratic primary (with the "anti" position coming out slightly ahead). In the general election, however, the judicial and Public Service Commission races attracted little attention. Indeed, about the only news generated by the contests occurred when it was revealed that (a) the Democratic candidate for Chief Justice had once been a leader of the pro-segregationist Citizens' Council, while (b) his Republican opponent was the object of three different law suits including one brought by his own campaign advertising agency.[29]

RESULTS AND ANALYSIS

The Presidential Election

George Bush easily won the presidential election in Alabama, receiving 59.2 percent of the vote compared to Dukakis's 39.9 percent. If attention is limited to the two-party vote, Bush won by a 59.7 to 40.3 percent margin.[30]

As Table 3.2 shows, younger and more educated voters were more likely than others to support Bush. About 69 percent of white voters and a surprisingly high 26 percent of black voters supported Bush. Bush was supported by about two-thirds of the respondents from nonunion households compared to about 45 percent of those residing in a union household. Little difference in presidential voting was found between males and females. Not surprisingly, Republican party identifiers were more likely to support Bush than were Democratic identifiers.

Bush's victory in Alabama was not a case of the state's voters selecting the lesser of two evils. Rather, most Alabama voters genuinely liked the Republican candidate. As Table 3.3 shows, throughout the general election campaign, more voters evaluated Bush positively than negatively. In the final pre-election survey, about half (51 percent) of the state's voters gave the GOP candidate a "positive" rating, while only about 26 percent evaluated him negatively. Michael Dukakis, however, was consistently rated more unfavorably than favorably. In the November *Birmingham News* survey, negative evaluations of the Democratic candidate outnumbered positive ratings by a 43 to 28 percent margin.[31]

Voters' beliefs concerning Bush's personal and professional qualities, and their expectations concerning what he would accomplish as president, were also quite positive. Specifically, in the late September and the November *Birmingham News* surveys, respondents were asked whether a series of statements involving traits such as honesty and reliability best described George Bush or Michael Dukakis. Respondents were also asked which of the two candidates would do the better job as president in several different policy areas, such as holding down taxes and protecting the environment.

An easy way in which to summarize the information gathered in these survey questions is to calculate the ratio between the number of respondents who said that Bush had a particular trait, or would do a better job in a particular policy area, and the number of respondents believing that Dukakis had more of that trait or would do the better job. In this ratio, scores greater than 1.0 indicate

Table 3.2

Presidential Preferences by Socio-Demographic Characteristics of Registered Voters (in percent)*

Characteristic	Bush	Dukakis	Total	(N)
Age				
18-40 years	65	35	100	(298)
41-60 years	61	39	100	(202)
61+ years	50	50	100	(125)
Education				
Less than high school	48	52	100	(106)
High school	58	42	100	(228)
More than high school	68	32	100	(297)
Race				
White	69	31	100	(499)
Black	26	74	100	(122)
Union Household				
Yes	45	55	100	(130)
No	65	35	100	(492)
Gender				
Male	66	34	100	(276)
Female	58	42	100	(363)
Party Identification				
Republican	86	16	100	(245)
Independent-Republican	93	7	100	(82)
Independent-Independent	72	28	100	(39)
Independent-Democrat	29	71	100	(35)
Democrat	15	85	100	(189)

*Voters expressing no preference are excluded from the calculations.

Source: Birmingham News/Southern Opinion Research survey for 2-5 November 1988.

that Bush received more ''support'' regarding a characteristic or policy area than did Dukakis. Scores less than 1.0 indicate the reverse.

The results of the analysis show that for each of the personal and professional traits examined, Bush received more support than did Dukakis (Table 3.4). Bush had an especially strong advantage over his Democratic opponents in the area of professional competence (namely, having ''the experience necessary to be president,'' the ''skills and personality needed to be a good leader,'' and the ability to ''make good decisions in times of crisis''). Respondents also generally believed that Bush was more likely than Dukakis to ''stand up for what he believes is right.'' The two presidential candidates were evaluated more equally in the areas of being honest in ''dealing with people'' and in their ability to understand ''the needs of the average citizens.''

Respondents also believed that Bush would do a better job than Dukakis in

Table 3.3
Feelings toward Candidates (in percent)

Candidate	August 27-31	September 27-29	November 2-5
George Bush			
Positive	45	49	51
Neutral/Don't know	32	25	23
Negative	23	26	26
Totals	100	100	100
(N)	(502)	(501)	(692)
Michael Dukakis			
Positive	23	28	28
Neutral/Don't know	40	36	30
Negative	37	37	43
Totals	100	101	101
(N)	(502)	(501)	(692)

Source: Birmingham News/Southern Opinion Research surveys for the dates indicated.

most of the policy areas examined. Bush enjoyed a particularly large advantage over Dukakis in the area of foreign and defense policy. Additionally, voters were about twice as likely to say that Bush rather than Dukakis would do a better job in the areas of "holding down taxes" and "fighting crime." Bush had a smaller advantage over Dukakis in the areas of "protecting the environment," "promoting jobs and economic development," "reducing the federal deficit," and "improving education."

Only in social-welfare policy–related areas (such as "treating rich and poor citizens equally" or "improving education") was Dukakis evaluated more favorably than Bush. Even in these traditionally Democratic areas, however, Dukakis had only a small advantage.

Bush's victory in Alabama was also aided by Alabamians' attitudes concerning the present and future condition of the country as a whole. In November, almost half the state's voters said that the country was "better off" than it was four years ago (Table 3.5). Only about 18 percent said the country was "worse off." Of those believing that the country was better off, an overwhelming number (about 87 percent) supported George Bush.

Similarly, about 60 percent of the state's voters believed that the country would be better off during the next four years if the Republican party won the presidential election (Table 3.6). Only about one in three voters said that the country would be better off if the Democrats won. Of those saying that the country would be better off with a Republican victory, more than 90 percent supported Bush. Similarly, about 90 percent of those saying the country would improve if the Democrats won voted for Dukakis.

Table 3.4
Ratio of Bush/Dukakis Responses on Personal Characteristics and Policy Items

Item	September 27-29	November 2-5
Personal Traits*		
Has the experience necessary to be president	2.53	2.29
Has the skills and personality needed to be a good leader	1.63	1.91
Will make good decisions in times of crisis	1.76	1.85
Will stand up for what he believes is right	1.51	1.50
Is honest in his dealings with people	1.41	1.31
Understands the needs of the average citizen	1.01	1.23
Policy Items**		
Negotiating with the Soviet Union	2.44	2.73
Maintaining the national defense	2.43	2.52
Holding down taxes	1.85	2.06
Fighting crime	1.65	2.01
Protecting the environment	1.31	1.51
Promoting jobs and economic development	1.20	1.34
Reducing the federal deficit	1.29	1.33
Reducing the use of illegal drugs	1.45	***
Improving education	1.29	***
Treating rich and poor citizens equally	0.93	0.98
Helping the elderly, poor, and homeless	0.86	***
Improving health care	0.84	***

*"Do each of the following statements best describe George Bush or Michael Dukakis?"
**Which of the presidential candidates, George Bush or Michael Dukakis, do you believe would do the best job in the following areas?"
***Item not included in the November survey.

Source: Birmingham News/Southern Opinion Research surveys for the dates indicated.

State Elections

In the nonpresidential races, Alabama voters re-elected each of the state's five Democratic and two Republican congressional representatives. The closest of these races was Republican Sonny Callahan's victory over State Board of Education member John Tyson by a 59 to 41 percent margin.

Democrats won each of the statewide judicial positions on the November ballot, receiving between 55 and 61 percent of the vote. Among these winning candidates was Oscar Adams, the only black statewide official in Alabama. Adams was re-elected to a second term on the Supreme Court. The incumbent president of the Public Service Commission, Jim Sullivan, was re-elected with

Table 3.5

Voter Perception of the State of the Country as Compared with Four Years Earlier (in percent)*

Intended Vote	Better	Same	Worse
Bush	87	54	12
Dukakis	13	46	88
Totals	100	100	100
(N)	(242)	(181)	(93)

*Voters expressing no preference are excluded from the calculations.

Source: Birmingham News/Southern Opinion Research survey for 2-5 November.

Table 3.6

Voter Perception of Which Party Will Be Better for the Country, by Intended Vote (in percent)*

Intended Vote	Democrat	No Difference	Republican
Bush	10	45	94
Dukakis	90	55	6
Totals	100	100	100
(N)	(163)	(20)	(291)

*Voters expressing no preference are excluded from the calculations.

Source: Birmingham News/Southern Opinion Research survey for 2-5 November.

58 percent of the vote.

In local races, the Republican party picked up about sixty positions, essentially doubling the number of offices held by the GOP. Republican officials claimed that these gains signaled that Alabama had become a true two-party state. Democratic party officials disputed such statements, pointing out that its candidates had won all the statewide races in 1988 and continued to hold the vast majority of the approximately 3,000 elected local government offices within Alabama.[32]

CONCLUSION

Clearly, the 1988 presidential election in Alabama represents an impressive personal victory for George Bush. The state's voters generally liked and admired him, and believed he would accomplish good things as president. Similarly, the positive feelings that Alabamians generally had for the Vice President, and their beliefs concerning the present and future conditions in the nation, means that the 1988 election was also a victory for Ronald Reagan. Conversely, given the amount of support he had among Democratic party leaders, the 1988 election was a very serious defeat for Michael Dukakis. It was also a serious defeat for the national Democratic party, since it is uncertain whether the state's leaders and officeholders will commit themselves so strongly to future presidential candidates.

Was the 1988 election in Alabama anything beside a personal triumph for the Republican ticket? Specifically, was this contest, as GOP leaders claimed, the event that broke the Democratic stranglehold on Alabama politics and moved the state into a new, two-party competitive era? On the other hand, was the 1988 election, as Democratic leaders claimed, an event that, like previous Republican presidential victories, did not alter the basic political balance within the state?

Determining the significance of the 1988 election will become easier in the future when additional information has been collected and more elections completed. Still, even at this point in time there is evidence that suggests that the 1988 election represents an important point in Alabama's political development.

It is true that Democratic candidates won each of the state offices filled in the 1988 election, yet the margin of victory in these contests was not overwhelming, particularly compared to the results of previous statewide contests. For example, the GOP did not even contest the Supreme Court positions selected in the 1984 election (1986). When Republican Guy Hunt convincingly won the governorship in 1986, the GOP's candidates for Lieutenant Governor and Secretary of State received slightly less than 40 percent of the vote.

It is also true that the Democratic party continues to hold the overwhelming majority of local government positions within the state (as well as more than 90 percent of state legislative seats and, with the exception of the governorship, all the state's constitutional offices). Still, the limited gains that the GOP has made at the local and state legislative levels represent important progress for the party. One of the problems the Republican party has traditionally faced in Alabama is the recruitment of good candidates. The election of Republicans to local and state legislative offices represents the development of a pool of candidates on which the GOP can draw in future elections.

Perhaps the most important piece of evidence indicating that the 1988 election was an important event in Alabama's political development concerns changes that occurred in the number of Democrats and Republicans within the state. In the first of the *Birmingham News* election surveys, Democratic party identifiers among registered voters in Alabama outnumbered Republican identifiers by a 37 to 26 percent margin (Table 3.7). This result is roughly similar to those that were found in Alabama earlier in the 1980s.[33] If the preferences of "Independent-leaners" are considered, the survey showed an equal number of Democratic and Republican identifiers in the state. Similar results were obtained in the second of the election surveys.

The final pre-election survey, however, found more Republican than Democratic identifiers. Specifically, about 39 percent of the state's registered voters

Table 3.7
Party Identification among Registered Alabama Voters (in percent)*

Identification	August 27-31	September 27-29	November 2-5
Republican	25	29	39
Independent-Republican	18	18	16
Independent-Independent	10	7	8
Independent-Democrat	7	10	6
Democrat	36	36	31
Totals	96	100	100
(N)	(462)	(479)	(644)

*Voters expressing no preference are excluded from the calculations.

Source: Birmingham News/Southern Opinion Research surveys for the dates indicated.

identified themselves as Republicans, compared to 31 percent who said that they were Democrats. When Independent-leaners are included, Republicans outnumber Democrats in Alabama by a 55 to 37 percent margin.

At least some of the change in party identification that occurred in Alabama is probably the result of the specific, low-key way in which the 1988 campaign was conducted in the state. In particular, Bush's strong lead, Dukakis's general absence throughout the campaign, and the lack of any strong and visible Democratic candidate contesting a statewide election meant that the information to which Alabama voters were exposed in 1988 flowed largely in the Republican direction. Several recent studies have shown that party identification is sensitive to individuals' evaluations of current political events.[34] Thus, because of the information available to them, many Alabama citizens shifted their party identification in the Republican direction during the 1988 general election campaign.

What is not clear at this time is the permanence of these changes in party identification. Thus, it is premature, and perhaps inaccurate, to declare Alabama a Republican state.[35] A post-election return to a more normal balance of partisan information may result in a reversion to a Democratic advantage in party identification. Conversely, a return to normalcy may not produce any change in individuals' "standing decisions." Instead, change will only occur when an event, such as a recession or a government scandal, produces a heavily pro-Democratic or anti-Republican political context.

Regardless of the speed of future shifts in party identification, the changes that did occur in 1988 suggest that currently, many Alabama voters, including those who say that they are Democrats or Republicans, are not strongly attached to either political party. For political scientists, the shifting balance of Democrats and Republicans, and the apparent weakness of individual party attachments, raises questions concerning the concept of party identification and, specifically, suggests a need to gain better understanding of what is really being measured by the party identification questions in polls.

For future Alabama politics, the shifting distribution of party identification suggests that the state has moved into a more competitive period. Even with the 1988 Republican gains, neither party appears to have a large, guaranteed, and firm basis of support within the electorate. Thus, the outcome of future Alabama elections may depend even more than normal on campaign-related factors such as candidate recruitment, fund-raising, and advertising.

NOTES

1. Patrick R. Cotter and James Glen Stovall, "Party Identification and Political Change in Alabama," in *The South's New Politics*, ed. Robert H. Swansbrough and David M. Brodsky (Columbia: University of South Carolina Press, 1988), 142–157.

2. Patrick R. Cotter and James Glen Stovall, "The 1986 Election in Alabama: The Beginning of the Post-Wallace Era," *PS* 20 (Summer 1987): 655–663.

3. *Montgomery Advertiser* and *Alabama Journal*, July 16, 1988; *Montgomery Advertiser*, July 18, 1988.

4. *Tuscaloosa News*, October 31, 1987.

5. *Birmingham Post-Herald*, June 20, 1988.

6. *Birmingham News*, May 29, 1988.

7. Ibid.

8. *Birmingham News*, July 23, 1988.

9. *Birmingham News*, July 24, 1988; September 11, 1988; *Tuscaloosa News*, September 5, 1988. No statewide polls were published during this period.

10. *Tuscaloosa News*, August 19, 1988.

11. *Montgomery Advertiser*, August 19, 1988.

12. *Birmingham News*, July 24, 1988; *Birmingham Post-Herald*, August 17, 1988.

13. *Montgomery Advertiser*, August 17, 1988.

14. *Birmingham Post-Herald*, August 17, 1988.

15. *Birmingham News*, June 18, 1988.

16. *Birmingham Post-Herald*, June 20, 1988.

17. *Montgomery Advertiser* and *Alabama Journal*, June 19, 1988.

18. *Montgomery Advertiser* and *Alabama Journal*, June 19, 1988.

19. *Birmingham News*, September 4, 1988. The election surveys conducted by Southern Opinion Research for the *Birmingham News* are based on telephone interviews with random samples of registered Alabama voters. A random-digit dialing method of sampling was used in the study.

20. A *Birmingham Post-Herald* survey (October 3, 1988) found Bush ahead of Dukakis by a 55 to 38 percent margin. A Capstone Poll survey (*Tuscaloosa News*, September 18, 1988) found that Bush led Dukakis by 54 to 38 percent.

21. *Birmingham News*, September 4, 1988; *Birmingham Post-Herald*, October 3, 1988.

22. *Birmingham News*, September 4, 1988.

23. *Birmingham Post-Herald*, September 12, 1988; September 30, 1988.

24. *Birmingham News*, October 2, 1988.

25. *Birmingham News*, October 8, 1988.

26. *Birmingham News*, October 16, 1988; *Tuscaloosa News*, October 8, 1988.

27. *Birmingham News*, November 6, 1988. Among all respondents, Bush led by a 56 to 36 percent margin. The final *Birmingham Post-Herald* survey (November 5, 1988) found Bush ahead by 59 to 38 percent.

28. *Tuscaloosa News*, October 20, 1988; *Birmingham News*, October 30, 1988; November 6, 1988.

29. *Birmingham Post-Herald*, November 5, 1988.

30. Voter turnout in the 1988 Alabama election was down by about sixty thousand votes compared to 1984. About 46 percent of the state's eligible voters participated in the 1988 presidential election compared to an estimated 49 percent nationally (*Birmingham Post-Herald*, November 24, 1988).

31. Both Lloyd Bentsen and Dan Quayle ended the campaign with about an equal number of positive and negative ratings. Specifically, Bentsen was rated positively by about 29 percent of the respondents in the November survey, while an equal number gave him a negative evaluation. In the late-August survey, Bentsen was rated favorably by about 21 percent of the respondents and negatively by about 24 percent. Quayle received a positive rating in the November survey from about 29 percent of the respondents and a negative evaluation from 28 percent. Over the course of the campaign, the number of respondents rating Quayle negatively increased from 18 percent to 28 percent, while his positive ratings remained relatively unchanged (31 percent to 29 percent).

32. *Tuscaloosa News*, November 10, 1988; November 11, 1988; November 13, 1988.

33. Cotter and Stovall, "Party Identification."

34. Charles H. Franklin and John E. Jackson, "The Dynamics of Party Identification," *American Political Science Review* 77 (December 1983): 957–973; Charles H. Franklin, "Issue Preferences, Socialization and the Evolution of Party Identification," *American Journal of Political Science* 28 (August 1984): 459–478; Richard A. Brody and Lawrence S. Rothenberg, "The Instability of Partisanship: An Analysis of the 1980 Presidential Election," *British Journal of Political Science* 18 (October 1988): 445–466.

35. A December 1988 Southern Opinion Research survey showed that among registered voters, the number of self-identified Democrats was again greater than the number of self-identified Republicans. If Independent-leaners are included among party identifiers, however, Republicans still outnumber Democrats in Alabama.

4

Georgia: Ripe for the Picking—Presidential Politics in the Peach State

ALAN I. ABRAMOWITZ AND WENDY DAVIS

For Georgia Democrats, the 1988 presidential campaign began with high hopes. Following the Democratic convention, which was held in Atlanta from July 18 to July 21, national polls showed Democratic nominee Michael Dukakis leading his probable opponent, Vice President George Bush, by margins ranging from 15 to 20 percentage points. Even in the South, Dukakis held a comfortable lead. George Bush was widely viewed as a "country club" Republican with much less appeal to the average Georgia voter than Ronald Reagan. Despite the nomination of Dukakis, a northern governor with a relatively liberal image, the leadership of the state Democratic party was much more unified than it had been four years earlier. In 1984, Governor Joe Frank Harris and most of the other top Democratic elected officials in Georgia had shunned the party's national ticket of Walter Mondale and Geraldine Ferraro. In 1988, Harris, along with Lieutenant Governor Zell Miller, State House Speaker Tom Murphy, and both of Georgia's U.S. senators, Sam Nunn and Wyche Fowler, endorsed and promised to work for the Dukakis-Bentsen ticket. Dukakis's choice of Lloyd Bentsen, a conservative Texan, as his running mate, had helped to overcome the reluctance of many conservative Democratic leaders to associate themselves with the national ticket. Many Georgia Democrats even saw Jesse Jackson as a potential asset to the presidential campaign if Jackson could stimulate black voter turnout without alienating moderate-to-conservative white voters.

In the end, of course, the hopes that many Georgia Democrats had held of carrying the state for the Dukakis-Bentsen ticket were crushed under an avalanche of votes for George Bush and Dan Quayle. Nationally, the Democratic ticket won 46 percent of the popular vote, an improvement of 5 percentage points over 1984. In Georgia, however, the Dukakis-Bentsen ticket received the same share of the popular vote that the Mondale-Ferraro ticket had received four years earlier—40 percent.

George Bush's landslide victory raises several questions about the nature of presidential politics in Georgia. The most frequently asked question is, what went wrong for the Democratic campaign in Georgia, and what went right for the Republican campaign there, between the time of the Democratic convention in July and November 9? This question may be misleading, however, because it rests on the assumption that the Dukakis-Bentsen ticket had a realistic chance of carrying Georgia and simply blew that chance. A more fundamental question about the 1988 presidential election is whether the Democrats ever had a realistic chance of carrying Georgia. In order to answer this question, it is necessary to place the 1988 presidential campaign in historical perspective by examining the development of presidential politics in Georgia since the end of World War II, and particularly since 1964, when the Republican party's "Southern Strategy" was first implemented.

THE DEVELOPMENT OF TWO-PARTY COMPETITION

From the end of Reconstruction in 1876 until 1964, the Democratic party carried the state of Georgia in every presidential election. In 1928, when the Democrats nominated a Roman Catholic presidential candidate, Governor Alfred E. Smith of New York, five southern states rebelled and cast their electoral votes for Republican Herbert Hoover.[1] However, even the nomination of a Catholic was not enough to break the attachment of a majority of Georgians to the Democratic party—Smith carried the Peach State by a margin of 57 to 43 percent.

The onset of the Great Depression and the New Deal policies of Franklin Delano Roosevelt (FDR) reinforced Georgia's loyalty to the Democratic party. In his first election in 1932, Roosevelt received an overwhelming 91.6 percent of the vote in Georgia. Even in his final bid for the White House in 1944, FDR received 81.7 percent of the vote in Georgia. Only Mississippi and South Carolina cast a higher percentage of their votes for Roosevelt.

Figure 4.1 compares the Democratic share of the presidential vote in Georgia with the Democratic share of the national popular vote between 1932 and 1988. A positive score for a given election indicates that the Democratic candidate received a larger share of the vote in Georgia than in the entire nation; a negative score indicates that the Democratic candidate received a smaller share of the vote in Georgia than in the nation as a whole.

In the four presidential elections in which Franklin Roosevelt was the Democratic candidate, the Georgia electorate was about 30 percentage points more

Figure 4.1
Deviation of Georgia Democratic Vote from National Presidential Vote,
1932–1988

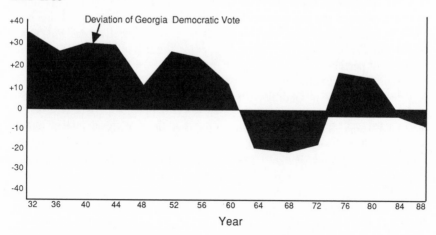

Source: Compiled by authors.

Democratic than the nation as a whole. The first significant break between Georgia voters and the national Democratic party occurred in 1948. Not surprisingly, the issue that precipitated that break was civil rights. In 1948, the Democratic National Convention, at the urging of a young mayor of Minneapolis named Hubert Humphrey, adopted a civil rights plank calling for congressional action to guarantee equal rights for blacks in voting, employment, personal security, and military service.[2] Following the adoption of this plank, a group of conservative southern Democrats walked out of the convention.

Three days after the close of the Democratic convention in Philadelphia, disgruntled southern Democrats gathered in Birmingham, Alabama for a States' Rights Party convention. Although thirteen southern states were supposedly represented, there were no delegates present from several states, including Georgia. The delegates to the States' Rights Party convention chose Governor Strom Thurmond of South Carolina as their presidential candidate and Governor Fielding Wright of Mississippi as their vice presidential candidate. In November, the Dixiecrats, as they were called, carried Alabama, Louisiana, Mississippi, and South Carolina—the only states in which the Thurmond-Fielding ticket was able to obtain the Democratic label on the ballot. President Harry Truman, the Democratic nominee, carried every other southern state, including Georgia, in which he received 61 percent of the popular vote compared with 20 percent for Thurmond and 18 percent for the Republican nominee, Governor Thomas E. Dewey of New York.[3]

A substantial majority of Georgia voters remained loyal to the Democratic party in 1948. Nevertheless, the Dixiecrat revolt served to demonstrate the

potency of the civil rights issue in the South and the potential division between
the liberal and conservative wings of the Democratic party. For the next sixteen
years, however, the issue of civil rights remained largely dormant in presidential
politics. Civil rights was not a major issue in the three presidential elections
between 1952 and 1960. In 1952, however, for the first time since 1928, a
Republican presidential candidate, Dwight D. Eisenhower, carried several southern states: Florida, Tennessee, Texas, and Virginia. Four years later, Eisenhower
added a fifth southern state—Louisiana—to his victory column. In 1960, the
Republican nominee, Vice President Richard Nixon, carried Florida, Tennessee,
and Virginia in his unsuccessful bid to succeed Eisenhower. It was probably
only the presence of native son Lyndon Johnson as the vice presidential candidate
on the Democratic ticket that allowed John F. Kennedy to carry the state with
the largest number of electoral votes in the South—Texas. In national politics,
the loyalty of the South to the Democratic party had already eroded considerably
by 1960.

In both 1952 and 1956, the Democratic presidential candidate, Senator Adlai
Stevenson of Illinois, ran about 25 points ahead of his percentage of the national
popular vote in Georgia. Thus, compared with the nation as a whole, Georgia
remained almost as Democratic in 1956 as it had been during the Roosevelt
years. In 1960, however, John F. Kennedy's share of the popular vote in Georgia
was only 12 percentage points greater than his share of the national popular vote.
Even in Georgia, Democratic dominance in presidential politics was eroding.
Until 1964, however, the process of erosion appeared to be a gradual one.

Richard Nixon in 1960, like Dwight Eisenhower in both 1952 and 1956, made
his strongest showings in the South in the traditionally Republican mountainous
areas, where opposition to secession and support for the Union had been strongest
during the Civil War, and in the metropolitan areas where an influx of affluent,
new residents was providing the GOP with a base of support. Most of these
areas of Republican strength were found in the rim South rather than the Deep
South. In Georgia, the traditional Republican base was confined to a few sparsely
populated counties in mountainous north Georgia. In 1960, four of these counties
gave Richard Nixon his largest share of the vote in the state—Fannin County
(66 percent), Pickens County (57 percent), Union County (56 percent), and
Gilmer County (56 percent). Outside these isolated pockets of traditional Republican strength, the strongest support for the GOP was found in the growing
metropolitan areas of the state. In 1960, Richard Nixon carried Richmond County
(Augusta) with 55 percent of the vote, Muscogee County (Columbus) with 53
percent, and Chatham County (Savannah) with 52 percent, and fell just short of
a majority in the Atlanta metropolitan area, with 50 percent of the vote in Dekalb
County and 49 percent in Fulton County.

In 1964, civil rights re-emerged as a major issue in presidential politics for
the first time since 1948 and with much more dramatic results. Led by President
Lyndon Johnson, the Democratic party adopted a civil rights plank in its national
platform that called for full voting rights for blacks and an end to legal segregation

of schools, housing, and public accommodations. The Republican standard-bearer in 1964, Senator Barry Goldwater of Arizona, offered the South and the nation "a choice, not an echo" on civil rights—Goldwater strongly opposed all the civil rights legislation favored by President Johnson. By raising the issue of civil rights, the Republican presidential candidate very deliberately sought to splinter the Democrats' traditional southern base. It was the first Republican attempt to implement a distinctive Southern Strategy.

Although Lyndon Johnson won the 1964 presidential election in a landslide, the GOP's newfound Southern Strategy met with considerable success. Along with his home state of Arizona, Goldwater carried five southern states—Alabama, Georgia, Louisiana, Mississippi, and South Carolina. Four of these states—Alabama, Georgia, Mississippi, and South Carolina—had not given their electoral votes to a Republican presidential candidate since the end of Reconstruction.[4]

Barry Goldwater received 87 percent of the popular vote in Mississippi, 69 percent in Alabama, 59 percent in South Carolina, 57 percent in Louisiana, and 54 percent in Georgia. However, Goldwater failed to carry several southern states that had previously supported Dwight Eisenhower—Florida, North Carolina, Tennessee, Texas, and Virginia. Together, these five states had far more electoral votes (75) than the five southern states that Goldwater carried (47).

Barry Goldwater's overt appeal to white racial fears, although playing well in most of the Deep South, evidently alienated some moderate Republican voters in the growing metropolitan areas of the region as well as some traditional Republican voters in the mountainous areas of the rim South. In Georgia, the Republican presidential vote increased by almost 17 percentage points between 1960 and 1964. However, in six traditionally Republican counties located in the north Georgia mountains, the Republican presidential vote actually decreased by an average of 10 percentage points. The Republican presidential vote also declined slightly in the Atlanta metropolitan area (Fulton and Dekalb counties), although Goldwater did improve on Richard Nixon's showing in most of the smaller metropolitan areas of Georgia. To be successful in the South, a Republican presidential candidate would have to combine the support of conservative white Democrats alienated by the pro–civil rights stance of the national Democratic party with the support of affluent suburban voters in the growing metropolitan areas and traditional Republicans in the mountainous areas of the rim South.

The 1968 presidential election provided graphic evidence of the salience of racial concerns among the white electorate in various southern states. Running as the candidate of the American Independent Party, Governor George Wallace of Alabama based his campaign heavily on an appeal to white racial fears, emphasizing opposition to busing and federal interference in southern racial customs. Wallace received only 13.5 percent of the national popular vote, but he carried five southern states—Alabama (with 66 percent of the vote), Arkansas (with 39 percent), Georgia (with 43 percent), Louisiana (with 48 percent), and Mississippi (with 64 percent). The Republican presidential candidate, former

Vice President Richard Nixon, won the election with 43.4 percent of the national popular vote and a clear majority of the electoral votes. Nixon carried five southern states—Florida (with 40 percent of the vote), North Carolina (with 40 percent), South Carolina (with 38 percent), Tennessee (with 38 percent), and Virginia (with 43 percent). The Democrats' presidential candidate in 1968, Vice President Hubert Humphrey, carried only one southern state, Texas, the home state of outgoing Presidential Lyndon Johnson, with 41 percent of the vote.

Hubert Humphrey's showing in the 1968 presidential election demonstrated the severity of the southern revolt against the national Democratic Party. Despite the rapid growth in the size of the black vote in the South after the passage of the federal Voting Rights Act in 1965, Humphrey received only 19 percent of the vote in Alabama and only 23 percent of the vote in Mississippi. In Georgia, Humphrey finished a poor third to Wallace (43 percent) and Nixon (30 percent), with only 27 percent of the vote, his third worst showing in the nation.

In 1968, the candidacy of George Wallace prevented Richard Nixon from successfully carrying out the GOP's Southern Strategy. Wallace's appeal to white racial fears kept Nixon from uniting white racial conservatives with the new metropolitan Republicans and the traditional mountain Republicans. It is not surprising, then, that Nixon and his political operatives were obsessed about preventing another third-party bid by Wallace in 1972.

Once George Wallace announced that he would not run for the presidency as a third-party candidate in 1972, the way was cleared for Richard Nixon to unite these three disparate elements behind his candidacy and thereby complete the GOP's Southern Strategy. That task was made even easier when the Democrats nominated Senator George McGovern of South Dakota as their presidential candidate. McGovern's ultra-liberal positions on issues ranging from welfare to national defense were anathema to the overwhelming majority of voters in the South. The result was a landslide comparable in magnitude to those enjoyed by Democratic presidential candidates during the era of one-party dominance. Richard Nixon carried every southern state by at least a two to one margin. He carried Georgia with 75 percent of the vote, his second best showing in the entire nation. Only Mississippi gave Nixon a larger share of the vote (78 percent) than Georgia.

The three presidential elections between 1964 and 1972 marked the low ebb in the fortunes of the national Democratic party in Georgia. In these three contests, the Democratic presidential candidates fell an average of 14 percentage points below their national vote share in Georgia. After 1972, the only consolation for Georgia Democrats was that things had to get better because they could not get any worse. As it turned out, things got a lot better a lot faster than even the most optimistic Democrat could have expected. The reason for the rapid turnaround in the fortunes of the Democratic party in Georgia was, of course, Jimmy Carter.

The Watergate scandal and the nomination of Jimmy Carter, an ex-governor of Georgia and an ex-peanut farmer, as the Democratic presidential candidate in 1976 temporarily short-circuited the GOP's Southern Strategy. Carter carried every southern state except Virginia, and he carried his home state of Georgia by better than a two to one margin, the best showing by a Democratic presidential candidate since 1952.

As the first major party presidential candidate from the Deep South since Zachary Taylor in 1848, and as an ideological moderate, Jimmy Carter was able to split the coalition of racial conservatives, affluent suburbanites, and traditional Republicans that Richard Nixon had assembled four years earlier. What also made this feat possible, however, was the lessening of racial tension in the South.[5] By 1976, most southern whites had come to accept the end of legal segregation, and race baiting as a political strategy had gone out of style.

The lessening of racial tension in the region helped to ease the feelings of hostility of many southern white voters toward the national Democratic party, and made it possible for a Democratic candidate like Jimmy Carter to forge a biracial coalition of black and moderate white voters. However, even though Jimmy Carter ran about 15 percentage points ahead of his national vote share in Georgia in both 1976 and 1980, the biracial coalition that supported him was quite fragile. It was probably only loyalty to a native son that kept Georgia from joining the rest of the states in the South in the Republican column in 1980.

In the 1984 presidential election, the Democrats virtually wrote off the South by picking two northern liberals, former Vice President Walter Mondale of Minnesota and Congresswoman Geraldine Ferraro of New York, as their standard-bearers against President Ronald Reagan. Mondale's campaign staff was frequently criticized for its lack of understanding of southern politics and its reluctance to accept the advice of southern leaders. According to Atlanta Mayor Andrew Young, Mondale's staff consisted of a bunch of "smart-ass white boys who think they know it all."[6]

The one major effort made by the Mondale campaign to appeal to southerners was the appointment of Bert Lance as chairman of the Democratic National Committee. However, this effort backfired when Mondale withdrew Lance's appointment after allegations of unethical financial activities by this former head of the Office of Management and Budget (OMB) resurfaced. After the Lance fiasco, the Mondale campaign was not able to gain the enthusiastic support of most Georgia Democratic leaders. Mayor Young's early support waned, and Governor Joe Frank Harris was conspicuously absent on most occasions. Former President Carter appeared at only one Mondale-Ferraro rally, and Senator Sam Nunn made only a minimal effort on behalf of the ticket.

The results of the 1984 election in the South were predictable: Ronald Reagan easily carried every southern state, including Georgia. However, the Mondale-Ferraro ticket did not do much worse in the South than it did in the rest of the nation. The 40 percent vote that the Democratic ticket received in Georgia was only 1 percentage point below its national total.[7]

What did the results of the 1984 election imply about the status of the Republican party's Southern Strategy? Perhaps Ronald Reagan's landslide victory and the lessening of regional differences that went with it meant that the Southern

Strategy was no longer unique to the South: Voters in all regions of the country were now responding positively to the GOP's conservative philosophy and to a more subtle appeal to white racial fears—an appeal that took the form of opposition to the "coddling" of criminals, affirmative action, welfare programs, and other policies that appeared to benefit blacks at the expense of whites. In short, the Southern Strategy was now a national strategy. The 1988 presidential election provided the first test of whether the new, nationalized version of the GOP's old Southern Strategy could survive the departure of Ronald Reagan from the national political scene.

THE 1988 PRESIDENTIAL CAMPAIGN IN GEORGIA

Georgia Democrats began the 1988 presidential campaign with high hopes because of the results of the 1986 midterm elections. In his first term in the Senate, Mack Mattingly, the first Republican elected to a statewide office in Georgia since the end of Reconstruction, had succeeded in establishing a good record for constituent service, and he did not make any big mistakes in Washington. The Republicans were fairly confident that he could retain his seat, especially since his challenger was Congressman Wyche Fowler. Fowler represented the majority-black Fifth District, which includes most of the city of Atlanta. With a reputation and voting record that were very liberal by Georgia standards, Fowler looked like an easy target for the GOP. However, Fowler used a folksy, down-home campaign style to convince rural and small-town voters that he was no big-spending city slicker but "good old Wyche," who understood their needs and would work hard to represent them. On the stump, Mattingly was no match for Fowler. Fowler received endorsements and campaign support from most leading Georgia Democrats, including Sam Nunn. Although Mattingly led in the polls for most of the race, in the end Fowler squeaked through to victory with 50.4 percent of the vote.

Fowler's election put both Senate seats safely back in Democratic hands: Nunn, who has gained national prominence for his work in the Senate as chairman of the Armed Services Committee, is expected to face only nominal Republican opposition in 1990 when he seeks his fourth term. The election of 1986 also revealed Republican weakness in the Fourth Congressional District. First-term GOP incumbent Pat Swindall narrowly fought off the challenge of Ben Jones, a political newcomer and former actor who had played "Cooter" on The "Dukes of Hazard" television show. Jones's campaign was aided by allegations that Swindall had taken a huge loan from a private businessman suspected of past involvement in drug trafficking in order to build a million-dollar mansion in Stone Mountain. The allegation that Swindall knowingly took drug money was very damaging to his reputation, and the subsequent investigation resulted in Swindall's indictment on several counts of perjury. Jones's strong campaign and the scandal surrounding Swindall contributed to the former's victory in 1988 by a 20 percentage point margin.

Swindall's political problems gave Georgia Democrats new optimism as election year 1988 unfolded. In addition, the national spotlight was on Atlanta as the host city for the Democratic National Convention. Although the goal of the Super Tuesday primary had not been achieved, and a not-so-moderate non-southerner, Michael Dukakis, was the obvious party nominee, Georgia Democrats put forward a united effort to bring off a successful convention that would boost Atlanta and the Democratic party. If all the happy, welcoming faces were only an act, the actors got lost in their roles as party boosters. Every major Georgia Democratic leader publicly endorsed Michael Dukakis, and spirits soared when Texas Senator Lloyd Bentsen was selected by Dukakis as his running mate. The "Boston-Austin" connection, which had helped carry John F. Kennedy to victory in 1960, gave many Georgia Democrats renewed hope of a Democratic victory in 1988. Bentsen's selection carried even more symbolic value because Bentsen had defeated George Bush in a 1970 Texas Senate race. "Beat Bush Again!" was the resounding cry at Democratic pre-convention rallies.

Jesse Jackson's role at the Democratic convention was a source of some concern in the days leading up to the nomination, but Jackson got enough of the concessions he was seeking to permit a warm embrace on the podium following Dukakis's stirring acceptance speech. Dukakis, who had often appeared to be a bloodless technocrat, was transformed for the evening into a leader of passion and conviction. The telegenic spectacle of an enthusiastic and unified Democratic party sent Dukakis's standing in the polls soaring to the highest level of the campaign at nearly 55 percent.[8]

Many Georgia Democrats had shunned the party's 1984 ticket as too liberal and too beholden to labor unions and left-wing interest groups. In 1988, however, the nomination of the liberal Governor of Massachusetts was balanced by the selection of a southern city for the convention and a moderate southern Senator as the vice presidential candidate. With a jump start from the successful convention, Georgia Democrats were off and running, ready to take advantage of George Bush's perceived weaknesses.

Another factor contributing to the optimism of Georgia Democratic leaders was a split within the Georgia Republican party. A dispute raged over the selection of delegates to the Republican National Convention. On opposing sides were supporters of Christian broadcaster Pat Robertson and party regulars, who supported George Bush. (In the Republican presidential primary on Super Tuesday, Bush had received 54 percent of the vote to 16 percent for Robertson.) This battle resulted in a divided state convention in May. At the convention, which was dominated by Bush supporters, Robertson's supporters staged a walkout and selected their own slate of national convention delegates. Thus, the Georgia Republican party sent two delegations to the party's national convention in New Orleans.[9]

With George Bush unopposed for the presidential nomination, the goal of Republican party leaders was to have a mishap-free convention in New Orleans that would allow Bush to quickly regain the ground he had lost since the Democratic convention. National party leaders also wanted to keep the newly active religious right firm in support of Bush, so the Georgia delegation dispute was resolved by being very generous to the Robertson supporters. All the uncontested delegates were seated, and the remaining slots were evenly split between the two factions. Georgia GOP Chairman John M. Stuckey, Jr., a Bush supporter, then threatened to resign because the convention seats had not been allocated in proportion to the primary vote. The Bush camp in Georgia was on the verge of mutiny; although Stuckey decided to keep his position, many leaders were worried that this schism would result in a loss of enthusiasm and fund-raising difficulties.

The dilemma of seating the delegation was the beginning of several problems within the Georgia Republican delegation; conflicts also developed over the selections of the delegation chairman and the representative to the national committee. The early favorite for the delegation chairmanship was Brant Frost IV, Pat Robertson's state campaign chairman. Frost, however, was deemed unacceptable by leaders of the Bush forces at the convention. At this point in the controversy, Georgia's two Republican U.S. representatives—Pat Swindall and Newt Gingrich—joined the fray. Much to the delight of Georgia Democrats, the scandal-plagued Swindall was chosen to chair the delegation. To further complicate the situation, three men were in the running for national committeeman— Representative Gingrich; incumbent Carl Gillis, who was supported by the Robertson faction; and businessman Joe Rogers, who was the choice of the party regulars. The selection of Gingrich might have helped to unify the party, but Gillis was chosen for the position. This outcome left George Bush's Georgia campaign in shambles: The Bush campaign was saddled with Swindall's ethical problems, had slighted an important supporter in Gingrich, and faced uncertain financial waters in the state.[10]

For Georgia Republicans, August had been a difficult month. By the end of the month, however, things had cooled down a bit as state party leaders tried to put their differences behind them and display some unity. State Senator Paul Coverdell, Chairman of the Republican Southern Steering Committee, held a press conference to announce a united effort on behalf of the Bush-Quayle ticket. His statement had only a limited impact, since he brought no other party members with him, but later in the week Stuckey released $300,000 in state Republican funds to the Bush campaign. This was a positive development, but the Republicans had to admit that their campaign was a month or more behind schedule. A twenty-one-member steering committee for the Georgia campaign was chosen; the committee included many former supporters of Senator Robert Dole but only two Robertson followers. Significantly, Brant Frost was left off the committee.[11]

Although the Republican National Convention ended on a high note with George Bush's stirring acceptance speech, the Georgia Republican party was still reeling from its internal divisions. Georgia Democrats were hoping to capitalize on this Republican division. Many Georgia Democrats also felt, along with other southern Democrats, that 1988 would be different from 1984; as

Virginia State Senator Stanley C. Walker so eloquently put it, "Congressmen are not hiding behind barns and stuff when the candidates come around."[12]

Even conservative state legislators got into the act. When Lloyd Bentsen's wife Beryl Ann made a late-August swing through Georgia accompanied by Colleen Nunn, she was met at each stop by prominent local politicians. Lloyd Bentsen was scheduled to meet his wife and many Georgia Democratic leaders at an Atlanta press conference to announce the Dukakis campaign's Georgia steering committee. However, mechanical difficulties with his campaign plane prevented the vice-presidential candidate from appearing; nevertheless, the Democratic show of unity, although delayed and somewhat dampened in enthusiasm, took place. Governor Harris, Senator Nunn, and some seventy-five state Democratic leaders expressed their support for the Dukakis-Bentsen ticket and announced the selection of eight co-chairpersons for the state campaign committee. The eight Democrats chosen were Governor Harris, senators Nunn and Fowler, Fifth District Congressman John Lewis, President Carter, Mayor Young, State Party Chairman John Henry Anderson, and Elaine B. Alexander, a personal friend of Michael Dukakis. Praising the selection of Lloyd Bentsen as Michael Dukakis's running mate, Senator Nunn noted that Bentsen was multilingual in that he spoke English, Spanish, and "Southern."[13]

Nationally, the New Orleans convention had given the Bush campaign an enormous boost. The only fly in the ointment for the GOP was the nomination of Indiana Senator Dan Quayle for vice president. Although the nomination was a shock to many Republican leaders, they quickly united behind Bush's choice. The press, however, had a field day with the relatively young and nationally inexperienced senator. Somehow, the questions raised by the press about Quayle's background and qualifications only seemed to strengthen the Republican ticket. Quayle even bragged about being a punching bag for the press because it allowed George Bush to avoid critical questions.

Bush himself took the high road in the fall campaign, speaking frequently about the need for "a kinder, gentler nation." However, immediately following the Republican convention, the GOP launched a massive negative advertising campaign, attacking Dukakis on such issues as the Pledge of Allegiance, gun control, Boston Harbor, the American Civil Liberties Union, and prison furloughs. The Republican advertising campaign was cleverly designed to arouse white racial fears without antagonizing moderate voters. The most frequently aired GOP spot emphasized Michael Dukakis's opposition to the death penalty and his support for a prison furlough program in Massachusetts—a program that had resulted in the murder of a Maryland family by a furloughed convicted murderer named Willie Horton. By election day, Willie Horton's name had become a household word. Although the Bush-Quayle campaign's ads did not specifically mention that Horton was black, that fact, along with Horton's picture, was widely disseminated in newspaper and television news stories. The racial overtones of the Bush-Quayle campaign ads were surely not lost on white voters in Georgia or elsewhere.

For weeks, while the Bush campaign blasted away at Michael Dukakis's record and reputation, Dukakis refrained from striking back. When Dukakis finally did respond, he gave complicated explanations for his past actions and positions instead of simple, straightforward answers to the GOP's charges. Bush was clearly setting the tone of the campaign, and his images were hitting home hard, especially in the South.

In Georgia, the state Republican party focused on sticking the "liberal" label on Dukakis and any Georgia Democrat who supported him. Republican Chairman Stuckey claimed that this support proved that Georgia's Democratic leaders had abandoned their conservative heritage and embraced the liberalism of the national Democratic party. In response to Stuckey's charges, Senator Nunn affirmed his support for the Democratic ticket while admitting that he did have differences of opinion with Michael Dukakis on certain issues. However, Nunn stressed his belief that Dukakis would maintain a strong national defense. Governor Harris, also criticized by Stuckey, explained that his support for Dukakis was based not on agreement on every issue but on respect for a hardworking fellow governor. House Speaker Tom Murphy's response to Stuckey's attack was more succinct: "Mr. Stuckey is not only an unmitigated liar but nearly a total idiot. He's the fellow that turned his party over to Pat Swindall down in New Orleans, and that ought to tell you something about that."[14]

At the start of the campaign, many political observers thought that the presidential contest in Georgia would be highly competitive. In early September, the *Atlanta Constitution* claimed that Georgia's twelve electoral votes were up for grabs, and predicted that both Bush and Dukakis would frequently campaign in the state. During the first six weeks of the campaign, however, neither presidential candidate visited Georgia. The Bush campaign did, however, send many surrogates into the state on behalf of the ticket. During September, the Vice President's son, George W. Bush, campaigned in Atlanta, and Dan Quayle and former Labor Secretary William Brock also visited the metropolitan area. During this same period, several cities in south Georgia were visited by Florida Governor Bob Martinez and by Marvin Bush, another son of the Vice President. On the Democratic side, Lloyd Bentsen made a brief stop in the state as did his wife, Beryl Ann. Michael Dukakis's daughter-in-law, Lisa Dukakis, also made an early September campaign stop in Atlanta.

The Democratic campaign had gotten a huge head start in Georgia because of the publicity generated by the Democratic convention, and the enthusiasm arising out of the July spectacle kept the Democrats going for a while. A sophisticated computer program developed by Jim Flowers, an Emory University political science graduate student, aided the Democrats in their goal of voter targeting within the state. A large phone bank was set up in their Atlanta headquarters with a plan for a huge election day push to get voters to the polls, particularly in predominantly black areas of Atlanta.[15] Organizationally, they were well ahead of the feuding Republicans.

Contrary to State Senator Coverdell's claim of unity, the Republicans remained badly split. Carl Gillis, the national committeeman, organized his own campaign for Bush in south Georgia. His effort focused on registering and cultivating support among evangelical Christians, and was not coordinated with the Atlanta-based Bush campaign.[16]

In spite of their organizational superiority, however, the Democrats could not control the campaign's issues. The Iran-Contra scandal, the budget and trade deficits, and other problems of the Reagan-Bush administration were overshadowed by the success of the national GOP campaign in painting Dukakis as a "liberal" who opposed the Pledge of Allegiance and favored gun control and furloughs for convicted killers. The GOP strategy was simple. As Republican State Representative Fred Cooper said, "We have to attract the Reagan Democrats. If he's a good old boy, we've got to make sure he knows that Dukakis is going to take his gun away."[17]

The end of September brought some renewed hope for the Democrats with the first presidential debate. The Democrats hoped that the debate would provide Dukakis with a good opportunity to effectively answer the GOP's negative advertising campaign. However, in debates, as in presidential primaries, expectations influence the results. The Republicans made sure that the public expected Bush to get clobbered by the Harvard professor, so when Bush did not commit any huge errors, the public reaction was that he had done rather well. Dukakis's campaign staff had a poor start in preparing for the debate and, as usual, did not accept any outside suggestions on how to improve Dukakis's performance. Although most debate coaches scored Dukakis as the "winner," he did not effectively rebut the GOP's charges. By failing to define his own positions clearly, Dukakis allowed the Republicans to define them for him.

After the first debate, the Democrats still felt that they had a flickering hope in Arkansas, Texas, Georgia, North Carolina, Tennessee, Kentucky, and Louisiana. However, the Bush campaign kept hammering away at Dukakis in the South, using their gut-level issues. "We're getting killed on the pledge thing, on the national defense thing, on furloughs," said one southern state Democratic chairman, who requested anonymity. "They're tying the ACLU around [Dukakis's] neck. Those things are killing us in the South."[18]

In addition to these problems, the Dukakis campaign was being accused of abandoning the South. In the week following the debate, George Bush made a sweep of the South that included his first trip to Georgia. At a rural cattle ranch just south of Atlanta in Clayton County, Bush donned khaki trousers and a blue western shirt and attacked Michael Dukakis on the issue of "values." He told an estimated one thousand supporters gathered for the rally that "my values are your values, and they are not the values of the ACLU."[19]

During the same September weekend as the first debate, the Southern Governors Association convened at Sea Island, the most exclusive of Georgia's Golden Isles. Although this meeting was a bipartisan event, the group was heavily slanted toward the Democratic party. Governor Harris was the chairman, and Mayor Young was the keynote speaker. Young was "carefully non-partisan" in his address, but speaking afterward to reporters, he strongly attacked George Bush for his participation in Reagan administration policy mistakes, and referred to Dan Quayle as "a flake." Representatives of both presidential candidates were at the conference, as well as the national party chairmen, Paul Kirk of the Democratic National Committee (DNC) and Frank Fahrenkopf of the Republican National Committee (RNC). However, neither presidential candidate attended the conference, and Governor Harris was publicly upset that Dukakis could not fit it into his schedule because of the debate.[20]

Tensions were running high in the Georgia Democratic camp as the final month of the campaign approached. The Dukakis campaign finally managed to get Jesse Jackson involved in a major effort to get out the black vote. Jackson made a late-September stop in Atlanta on behalf of the Dukakis-Bentsen ticket. However, many southern Democratic party leaders who were willing to work for the ticket were not getting any clear direction from Boston. Mayor Young announced that he had cleared time on his October calendar and was tired of waiting for Dukakis's people to arrange his schedule. Without his trusted long-time advisor John Sasso, who had been sent into political exile for spreading "vicious truths" about an opponent during the Democratic primary campaign, Dukakis had been trying to run the campaign himself. In October, Sasso was finally brought back in an attempt to rescue the floundering Dukakis campaign, and began developing a plan for using surrogates.[21] Sasso also began to seek advice from party professionals outside Dukakis's own narrow circle of advisors.

While the Democrats were organizing their surrogates, Georgia Republicans were spending a hundred thousand dollars on a week-long negative advertising blitz and attempting to raid the Democrats' home base. In support of five black GOP candidates in the state, the Republicans held a twenty-five-dollar per plate dinner at Paschal's Motor Hotel. This effort to court the black vote received mixed reviews. During the dinner the GOP speakers did not mention the Reagan administration, but referred instead to past Republican leaders such as Frederick Douglass, Abraham Lincoln, and Earl Warren. Democratic Party State Executive Director Robert Kahn responded predictably to the event: "I don't think it has much credibility given what Bush and his pals have done for civil rights in the last eight years."[22] Another unusual GOP function was a rally in Atlanta's Piedmont Park for the local Hispanic community. These Republican efforts to court minority voters, though yielding few tangible results, demonstrated a great deal of confidence in the security of the GOP's own electoral base.

Frustration was growing in the Democratic camp. A strategy session in Atlanta for the entire southern campaign provided an opportunity for many southern Democratic leaders to voice complaints about the conduct of the campaign. The strategy session pointed to five target states still considered winnable: Georgia, Arkansas, Tennessee, Kentucky, and North Carolina. However, the Dukakis campaign was unwilling to allocate much in the way of additional resources to these states.[23]

The message from southern Democrats to the national campaign was that it was time to get down in the trenches and fight back. The Dukakis campaign had finally launched some negative ads: The commercials criticized the Quayle nomination, and portrayed Bush as merely a product of skilled handlers. However, these ads did not pack the same emotional wallop as the GOP spots, and they came too late to undo the damage done to Dukakis's reputation.

Early October brought Tom Murphy's withdrawal of support for the Dukakis-Bentsen ticket. The continued Republican attacks on Michael Dukakis's liberalism had become too much for the conservative House Speaker, who was facing a significant Republican challenge for the first time in his career. Murphy officially withdrew his endorsement of Dukakis, citing differences of opinion on the death penalty and gun control. Generous Republican financial contributions to his opponent probably also influenced his decision. The only consolation for the Dukakis campaign was that Murphy did not endorse the GOP ticket but chose to remain neutral in the presidential race. As he eloquently explained it, "I don't like Bush either."[24] All Georgia's other Democratic leaders remained at least nominally in the Dukakis camp through the end of the campaign. Nevertheless, Murphy's defection was a clear signal that support for Dukakis among conservative Democrats had eroded badly.

Shortly after Murphy's announcement, another noted conservative Democrat made his views known. Although no longer active in Georgia politics, former Governor and restaurateur Lester Maddox held a press conference in early October to denounce Michael Dukakis as a "socialist and revolutionary leftist." He pledged to conduct an anti-Dukakis campaign in six southern states. In addition, Maddox echoed the Republican condemnation of Democratic party leaders in the state for supporting Dukakis.[25]

The Dukakis campaign finally got around to planning a trip to Georgia by the candidate for mid-October. However, almost all the state's Democratic leaders announced that they would be unavailable to campaign with Dukakis because of scheduling conflicts, and the trip was canceled. Georgia Republicans gleefully took note of the Democrats' scheduling problems. State Representative Stanley Baum observed that, "Dukakis doesn't come. [Lieutenant Governor] Zell Miller goes to Greece [on vacation]. The Governor is in Australia [on a trade mission]. Sam Nunn is staying in Washington, and the Speaker has taken a walk. There's definitely a change in attitude. It's beginning to break our way."[26]

As the Democratic campaign sagged, the Republicans hit the state again. Dan Quayle returned to the Atlanta suburbs just prior to his vice presidential debate. George Bush's son Jeb stumped in suburban Gwinnett County, opened a new headquarters in Decatur, and hosted a celebration in the Atlanta headquarters during the vice presidential debate. Henry Kissinger came to opulent Buckhead for a thousand-dollar per person dinner in a private home. The Republicans topped off this flurry of activity with their second hundred-thousand-dollar week-long television advertising blitz.[27]

The vice presidential debate improved Lloyd Bentsen's popularity but did little for the Democratic ticket. Bentsen's strong showing did not even help in the

South, and time was running out. An early October poll conducted by the *Atlanta Journal Constitution* showed Bush leading Dukakis by 12 percentage points in the South. Many southern Democrats found themselves wishing that the positions of the two candidates on their ticket could be reversed. Republican leaders were starting to think about mandates and coattails, while Democratic leaders were increasingly concerned about cutting their losses.[28]

The Georgia Democratic campaign continued to flounder. A rally in Douglasville featured Senator Nunn; however, he was scheduled only at the last minute, so the rally was not well publicized or well attended. After this fiasco, the last Democratic hope was the traditional Democratic barbecue to be held in the south Georgia town of Hawkinsville on October 22.[29] Governor Dukakis and every prominent Democratic leader in the state were scheduled to attend. The Democratic plan for Senator Nunn to introduce Dukakis before a huge, enthusiastic crowd worried Georgia Republicans; Dan Quayle was sent to the state for the third time. While Quayle proudly called himself the "lightning rod" for the Bush campaign, the Democrats broke out their "Honk if you're smarter than Dan Quayle" bumper stickers.[30]

Some five thousand Democratic party activists and leaders journeyed to Hawkinsville, including Jimmy Carter, Sam Nunn, Wyche Fowler, Joe Frank Harris, and Andrew Young. Nunn's introduction was very partisan, and very well received. He again stressed Michael Dukakis's belief in a strong national defense. Following Nunn's speech, Wyche Fowler inspired the crowd with the story of his own come-from-behind victory over Mack Mattingly: "Take off your coat, Mike Dukakis. Tear up the polls. The people of Georgia are about to speak." Dukakis himself was warmly applauded when he said that he was planning "to fight like a Georgia Bulldog." However, the rest of the speech failed to make any clear regional appeal.[31] Nevertheless, the Hawkinsville rally did appear to briefly renew the hopes of Georgia Democrats. If they could not carry Georgia for the Dukakis-Bentsen ticket, at least most Democrats felt confident that they could keep George Bush's coattails very short.

The following week, Dan Quayle was once again sent to Atlanta to counter any post-Hawkinsville Democratic surge. The Republicans appeared to be worried that the Democratic ticket might gain back some ground during the last week of the campaign as Michael Dukakis barnstormed the nation in a final nonstop campaign blitz. However, by this time the Dukakis campaign was concentrating on those states that were still viewed as winnable. Significantly, the only southern state visited by Dukakis during the final week of the campaign was Texas, the home state of Lloyd Bentsen. At this point, most Georgia Democrats were more concerned about state and local Democratic candidates than about the fate of their party's presidential candidate. In a last-ditch effort to save his seat in Congress, Pat Swindall got into trouble with the Bush campaign by distributing thousands of "Bush/Swindall" lawn signs. The national Republican campaign did not want George Bush to be dragged down by Pat Swindall's coattails.

During the final week of the campaign, the Georgia Democratic party made its first effort to counter the state Republican party's supplemental media buys. Radio spots focused on Pat Swindall's attempt to ride George Bush's coattails, and criticized Bush over issues like drugs and the budget deficit. The Democrats wanted to unleash even more negative advertisements, but the Georgia campaign was looking to Boston for approval and funds. What the state party received instead were five additional field-workers.[32] It was a classic case of too little, too late.

EXPLAINING THE RESULTS: THE BUSH COALITION IN GEORGIA

On November 9, the Bush-Quayle landslide extended to every section of Georgia: The GOP ticket carried 134 of Georgia's 159 counties. Of the twenty-five counties carried by Michael Dukakis and Lloyd Bentsen, fifteen had black populations of greater than 50 percent according to the 1980 census, while six had black populations of between 40 and 50 percent. The Democratic ticket carried only four counties in the state with black populations of less than 40 percent.

The Republican ticket carried every metropolitan area in Georgia including Macon (Bibb County) with just over 50 percent of the vote, Savannah (Chatham County) with 58 percent of the vote, Columbus (Muscogee County) with 55 percent of the vote, and Augusta (Richmond County) with 57 percent of the vote. In the five-county Atlanta metropolitan area (Fulton, Dekalb, Cobb, Gwinnett, and Clayton counties), the Bush-Quayle ticket received 57 percent of the vote. The GOP ticket did especially well in the booming suburbs north and east of Atlanta, winning 73 percent of the vote in Cobb County and 76 percent of the vote in Gwinnett County.

In order to explain the Republican presidential victory and the nature of the Bush-Quayle coalition in Georgia, we conducted a regression analysis of the results of the 1988 presidential election in Georgia's 159 counties. Our dependent variable was the Republican percentage of the major party vote.

To control for the racial composition of the electorate, we included the black percentage of each county's population in 1980 as an independent variable. Despite widespread discontent among blacks about Michael Dukakis's treatment of Jesse Jackson, black voters generally remained loyal to the Democratic party in 1988. According to network exit polls, almost 90 percent of black voters nationwide and in the South cast their ballots for the Dukakis-Bentsen ticket.

Since 1964, the GOP's Southern Strategy in presidential elections has been to combine the support of conservative Democrats alienated by the racial liberalism of the national Democratic party with that of affluent suburbanites in the growing metropolitan areas and traditional Republican voters in the mountainous areas of the South. We used the results of the 1968 presidential election in Georgia to distinguish between two bases of support for the Republican ticket

Table 4.1

Regression Analysis of 1988 Republican Presidential Vote in Georgia Counties*

Independent Variable	B	S.E.	Beta
Black population	-.243	.043	-.438
Population growth	.234	.043	.288
Traditional Republicanism	.382	.103	.369
White racial conservatism	.316	.072	.403

Constant = 38.907

Adjusted R^2 = .70

(N = 159)

*Dependent variable is percentage vote for George Bush in 1988 presidential election. All of the estimated coefficients are statistically significant at the .001 level. Black population was measured by black percentage of population in 1980; population growth was measured by percentage increase in population between 1980 and 1986; traditional Republicanism was measured by percentage vote for Richard Nixon in 1968; and white racial conservatism was measured by percentage vote for George Wallace in 1968.

Source: Data compiled by authors. County election results for 1988 are from the Atlanta Journal (9 November 1988); black percentage of population is from the 1980 Census; population growth from 1980 to 1986 is taken from an estimate by the Census Bureau in Current Population Reports; results of the 1968 election are from Richard Scammon and Alice V. McGillivray (eds.), America Votes.

in 1988—traditional Republicanism and racial conservatism. Traditional Republicanism was measured by the vote for Richard Nixon in 1968, while racial conservatism was measured by the vote for George Wallace. Our measure of traditional Republicanism includes both the mountain Republicanism of north Georgia and the metropolitan Republicanism that had developed by 1968. However, in order to capture the impact of the continuing influx of new Republican voters into the metropolitan areas, we included an additional independent variable in our analysis: the percentage change in population in each county between 1980 and 1986.[33]

The results of the regression analysis are presented in Table 4.1. All four of our independent variables had substantial and statistically significant effects on the outcome of the 1988 presidential election. Together these four variables explain 70 percent of the variance in the Republican presidential vote across counties. A comparison of the standardized regression coefficients indicates that traditional Republicanism and white racial conservatism were about equally important in explaining support for the Bush-Quayle ticket. In addition, population growth in recent years has added significantly to the GOP base, especially in the burgeoning suburbs north and east of Atlanta.

These results appear to offer little encouragement to Democratic leaders as they contemplate their party's future prospects in presidential elections in Georgia. Against almost any candidate representing the northern liberal wing of the Democratic party, the GOP should be able to hold together its coalition of affluent suburbanites, traditional Republicans, and racial conservatives. Moreover, the Republican base in Georgia should continue to grow as more and more young, upwardly mobile executives and professionals move into the Atlanta suburbs. Between 1980 and 1986, Gwinnett County, which supported George Bush by a three to one margin over Michael Dukakis, grew by 66 percent, adding almost 110,000 new residents. During this same period, Cobb County, which gave 73 percent of its vote to Bush, grew by 32 percent, adding almost 95,000 new residents. A number of counties on the outskirts of the Atlanta metropolitan area also experienced rapid growth during the 1980s. Between 1980 and 1986, Rockdale County, which gave 74 percent of its vote to George Bush, grew by 29 percent; Forsyth County, which gave 77 percent of its vote to Bush, grew by 34 percent; and Cherokee County, which gave Bush 77 percent of its vote, grew by 45 percent. These Republican strongholds should experience rapid growth during the 1990s as the Atlanta metropolitan area continues to expand outward.

Even if he had run a brilliant campaign, Michael Dukakis's chances of carrying Georgia in 1988 would probably have fallen somewhere between slim and none. Moreover, as long as the Democratic party nominates a certifiable liberal as its presidential candidate, Georgia will probably remain in the GOP column in presidential elections. The results of the 1988 presidential election showed that simply putting a moderate southerner on the ticket for the vice presidency is not enough to lure a substantial number of moderate-to-conservative white voters back into the Democratic camp. Barring a major economic downturn, the only hope the Democratic party has of carrying Georgia in 1992 is if the party nominates a moderate-to-conservative candidate for the presidency: a Bentsen-Dukakis instead of a Dukakis-Bentsen ticket. Unfortunately for the Democrats, the current presidential nominating system makes such an outcome highly unlikely.

Perhaps the most interesting question raised by the outcomes of the 1988 and other recent presidential elections is how long the Georgia Democratic party can maintain its dominant position below the presidential level. Following the 1988 elections, Democrats controlled 189 of 236 seats in the state legislature and 9 of Georgia's 10 seats in the U.S. House of Representatives; the only Republican to win a U.S. Senate seat from Georgia since the end of Reconstruction was defeated in his first bid for re-election in 1986, and no Republican has been elected governor in the past 112 years, although a Republican candidate did receive a plurality of the popular vote in a three-way race in 1966.[34]

The Republican party has made some inroads in state and local elections in recent years. Between 1980 and 1989, the GOP increased its representation in the state legislature from 28 to 47 seats, and Republicans now control most of the local governing bodies in the suburban counties surrounding Atlanta. These gains have provided the GOP with something it has long lacked in Georgia—a cadre of experienced officeholders who can make credible candidates for statewide office. Several of these Republican officeholders, including State Representative Johnny Isaakson and former Mayor George Israel of Macon, are now contemplating a bid for the statehouse in 1990. Depending on the outcome of the Democratic gubernatorial primary, in 1990 Georgians could witness something they have not experienced for almost a quarter of a century—a truly competitive two-party contest for the governorship. Both Lieutenant Governor Zell Miller and Atlanta Mayor Andrew Young, two of the leading candidates for the Democratic gubernatorial nomination, are regarded as moderate-to-liberal national Democrats. Young, of course, also happens to be black. If either Miller, who is currently considered the front-runner, or Young, who is considered a long shot, should win the Democratic nomination, Republican strategists believe that their candidate would have a realistic chance of winning the governorship.

In the long run, the demographic trends described above should continue to add to the size of the Republican base in state and local as well as presidential elections. In addition, the continued domination of the presidential nominating process by the northern liberal wing of the Democratic party may place pressure on conservative officeholders at the state and local level, many of whom are Democrats in name only, to bring their party affiliation in line with their political philosophy. If Jesse Jackson or a candidate with similar views were to win the Democratic presidential nomination in 1992 or some future presidential election year, wholesale defections to the GOP by conservative Democratic officeholders would not be out of the question. Even without such an apocalyptic event, however, the most likely prospect for the future is a continued increase in two-party competition in state and local elections. As the 1990s approach, Republican strategists clearly have Georgia on their minds.

NOTES

1. The five southern states carried by Hoover were Florida, North Carolina, Tennessee, Texas, and Virginia. In addition to Georgia, Smith carried Alabama, Arkansas, Mississippi, and South Carolina.

2. Congressional Quarterly, *Guide to U.S. Elections* (Washington, D.C.: Congressional Quarterly Press, 1985), 100–101.

3. For an excellent discussion of the causes and consequences of the Dixiecrat revolt, see V. O. Key, Jr., *Southern Politics in State and Nation* (Knoxville: University of Tennessee Press, 1984), 329–344.

4. See Bernard Cosman, *Five States for Goldwater: Continuity and Change in Southern Presidential Voting Patterns* (University, Ala.: University of Alabama Press, 1966). See also Earl Black and Merle Black, *Politics and Society in the South* (Cambridge, Mass.: Harvard University Press, 1988), and Alexander P. Lamis, *The Two-Party South* (New York: Oxford University Press, 1988).

5. See ibid., 31–37.

6. Thomas Walker and Eleanor Main, "Georgia," in *The 1984 Presidential Election in the South*, ed. Robert P. Steed, Laurence W. Moreland, and Tod A. Baker (New York: Praeger, 1985), 107.

7. For a thorough discussion of the 1984 presidential election in Georgia, see Walker and Main, ''Georgia,'' 96–122.

8. ''Anatomy of a Victory,'' *Newsweek*, November 21, 1988, 14.

9. A. L. May and Tom Baxter, ''Georgia GOP Chief May Quit as Dissents Rule Delegation,'' *Atlanta Constitution*, August 11, 1988, A-1.

10. Tom Teepen, ''Georgia GOP Split Leaves Bush Campaign in the State Hamstrung,'' *Atlanta Constitution*, August 19, 1988, A-23.

11. A. L. May, ''State GOP Vows Unity at Launch of Bush Campaign,'' *Atlanta Constitution*, August 26, 1988, A-7.

12. Tom Baxter, ''Southern Legislators Say Democratic Ticket Looks Like a Winner,'' *Atlanta Constitution*, August 23, 1988, A-6.

13. Raad Cawthon, ''Bentsen's a No-Show, but Political Show Goes on at Georgia Capitol,'' *Atlanta Constitution*, August 27, 1988, A-8.

14. A. L. May, ''Georgia Democrats Have Sold Out, GOP Charges,'' *Atlanta Constitution*, September 9, 1988, A-5.

15. A. L. May, ''Both Parties Setting Sights on Georgia,'' *Atlanta Constitution*, September 18, 1988, A-1.

16. Ibid., A-14.

17. Ibid.

18. Tom Baxter and Kevin Sack, ''Dukakis's Debate Aim: Turn the Tide in South,'' *Atlanta Constitution*, September 25, 1988, A-1, A–9.

19. John W. Mashek, Kevin Sack, and Mike Christensen, ''Bush Camp Backs Off on Abortion,'' *Atlanta Constitution*, September 27, 1988, A-4.

20. A. L. May and Tom Baxter, ''Young: Politics of Race Dead,'' *Atlanta Constitution*, September 27, 1988, B-1, B-7.

21. Priscilla Painton, ''Team of Democratic Surrogates Posed for Late Surge for Dukakis,'' *Atlanta Constitution*, September 30, 1988, A-4.

22. A. L. May, ''Georgia GOP Pitches for Votes in Democrats' Black Stronghold,'' *Atlanta Constitution*, September 30, 1988, A-15, A-22.

23. ''Dukakis Strategists Meet in Effort to Salvage South,'' *Atlanta Constitution*, October 2, 1988, A-11.

24. A. L. May, ''House Speaker Murphy No Longer Backs Dukakis,'' *Atlanta Constitution*, October 1, 1988, D-1, D-7.

25. A. L. May, ''Maddox Visits State Capitol to Denounce Dukakis,'' *Atlanta Constitution*, October 5, 1988, A-13.

26. A. L. May, ''GOP Almost Tasting Victory in Georgia as Dukakis Stumbles,'' *Atlanta Constitution*, October 8, 1988, A-8.

27. Ibid.

28. Tom Baxter, ''Southern Poll Shows Bush Pulling Away from Dukakis,'' *Atlanta Constitution*, October 9, 1988, A-1, A-18.

29. A. L. May, ''Douglasville Rally Draws Party Heavyweights, Few Voters,'' *Atlanta Constitution*, October 16, 1988, B-2.

30. A. L. May, ''Quayle Visit to Savannah Signals Georgia Still Viewed as Wavering,'' *Atlanta Constitution*, October 22, 1988, A-12.

31. A. L. May and Kevin Sack, ''Top Democrats in Georgia Greet, Embrace Dukakis,'' *Atlanta Constitution*, October 23, 1988, A-1, A-18.

32. A. L. May, ''Georgia Democrats' Ads Point to Swindall Riding Bush Coattails,'' *Atlanta Constitution*, November 1, 1988, A-7.

33. Two additional independent variables, 1985 per capita income and the change in per capita income between 1980 and 1985, were dropped from the analysis because they had negligible effects on the Republican presidential vote.

34. Republican Howard "Bo" Calloway received 46.5 percent of the vote to 46.2 percent for Democrat Lester Maddox and 7.3 percent for Independent write-in candidate Ellis Arnall. Under the provisions of the Georgia constitution, since no candidate had received a majority of the vote, the state legislature chose between the top two finishers. The overwhelmingly Democratic legislature chose Maddox.

5

Louisiana: Race, Republicans, and Religion

CHARLES D. HADLEY

Continuity continues amidst change in Louisiana politics. The state political trends examined in my essay on the 1984 presidential election—the growing electoral presence of blacks and Republicans and the higher voter turnout in presidential over gubernatorial elections—continue amidst revelations of and convictions for political corruption.[1] Most noteworthy, Republican U.S. Attorney John Volz prosecuted Governor Edwin W. Edwards for selling hospital certificates of need in very long (twenty-one weeks altogether), intensely publicized trials that ended first in a hung jury, and then in acquittal.[2] While the flamboyant governor survived the trials with juries of his working-class peers, he did not survive the ultimate political trial with the Louisiana electorate as his jury, a story to which we will turn shortly.

Federal prosecutors continue to investigate and uncover extortion by state and local officials who ultimately are convicted and sent to federal prison.[3] The helpfulness of raw political influence appears to touch all aspects of public affairs from massive state bond issues,[4] to the persistent award and re-award of lucrative contracts to companies with records of substandard work,[5] to lucrative state jobs demanding little work, if any.[6] By creating and staffing the Office of the Inspector General in 1988 and appointing an aggressive Inspector General, the current state administration is dealing directly with reported improprieties.

Although the percentage increase in voter registration by blacks reached its

Table 5.1
Louisiana Voter Registration by Race, 1980–1988

Race and Year	Number Registered	Percent Increase	Percent of Voting Age Population	Percent of Total
Blacks				
1980	465,000	14.4	60.7	23.1
1984	561,000	20.6	65.7	24.8
1988	583,000	3.9	66.8	26.1
Whites				
1980	1,550,000	13.5	74.8	76.9
1984	1,701,000	9.7	76.3	75.2
1988	1,637,000	-3.9	72.5	73.9*

*Includes those responding "other."
Sources: State of Louisiana, Commissioner of Elections, "Report of Registered Voters [October close of voter registration]" (Baton Rouge, 1980-1988); U. S. Bureau of the Census, Statistical Abstract of the United States (Washington, D.C.: Government Printing Office, 1986), 257; U. S. Bureau of the Census, "Projections of the Population of Voting Age, for States: November 1988," Current Population Reports, Series P-25, No. 1019 (January 1988), 9.

lowest level (3.9) in the contemporary period during the 1984–1988 election cycle, black voter registrants continued to increase vis-à-vis their age-eligible numbers (Table 5.1). Of the black voting age population (VAP), the proportion registered increased from 60.7 percent in 1980 to 65.7 in 1984 and 66.8 in 1988, and the registration gap between blacks and whites decreased from 14.1 percentage points to less than 6 over the eight-year interval.[7] The black share of the total number of registered voters incrementally increased from 23.2 percent in 1980 to 24.8 in 1984 and 26.1 in 1988 as the white share drifted downward. Moreover, the number of black elected officials increased from 438 to 505 (15.3 percent) between 1984 and 1987.[8]

While proportionately small next to Democratic party adherents, the Louisiana Republican party made great strides in voter registration over the Reagan years. Those choosing to affiliate with the GOP increased from 7.4 percent in 1980 to 11.3 percent in 1984 and 16.4 percent in 1988 (Table 5.2). Importantly for Republicans, the percentage of those unaffiliated or associated with another political party appears to have stabilized at just over 8 percent of those registered.

Moreover, though the elections are separated by about one year, with that for governor earlier, the phenomenon of a higher voter turnout in presidential than gubernatorial elections first appeared in 1968 (up 7.4 percent). The current set of elections is no exception. Voter turnout in the 1988 presidential election was 2.03 percentage points higher than that in the 1987 gubernatorial election.

MAJOR REPUBLICAN SETBACKS

With U.S. Senator Russell B. Long's announced retirement well in advance of the 1986 election, both the Republican and Democratic parties tried to make

Table 5.2
Louisiana Voter Registration by Political Party, 1980–1988

Year	Total Number	Percent Democratic	Percent Republican	Percent Other
1980	2,015,402	86.6	7.4	6.0
1984	2,262,101	80.6	11.3	8.1
1988	2,231,857	75.2	16.4	8.4*

*Over 99 percent are independent or unaffiliated with a party.

Source: See Table 5.1 for sources.

it a two-candidate race between their respective U.S. representatives, W. Henson Moore and John B. Breaux, and invested heavily in them. Among prominent campaigners on Moore's behalf, President Reagan visited Louisiana twice, and Vice President Bush four times. In what became a crowded field, Moore outspent Breaux by two to one, and was expected to win the contest outright with 50 percent of the vote in the open primary. He came up short, 44.2 percent to Breaux's 37.4. Twelve other contenders together received the remaining 18.4 percent, including three well-known Democrats, who together took 15 percent of the vote, indirectly helping Moore, either by accident or design. They later endorsed Breaux in the runoff.[9]

Whether due to overconfidence, poor timing, or clumsy handling, Republicans created an issue in the primary that put their candidate on the defensive in the runoff and gave Democrat Breaux momentum. They initiated a voter registration purge that affected 34,000 blacks, many of whom did not learn of their removal until they went to vote in the primary. Just two weeks prior to the runoff, a New Jersey U.S. District Court Judge released the smoking gun that Republican attorneys had attempted to suppress. The national Republican party had hired Ballot Integrity Group, Inc., to target voting precincts in which President Reagan received less than 20 percent of the vote, precincts that happened to be predominantly black. The RNC staff memo read in part:

I don't want anything to fall between the cracks on our end. I know this race is really important to you. I would guess the program will eliminate at least 60–80,000 folks from the rolls. . . . If it's a close race . . . which I am assuming it is, this could keep the black vote down considerably.

While Moore denounced the memo and denied involvement, a campaign headquarters paid staffer was mentioned in it by name. A fire storm of protest was thus unleashed.[10]

A Watergate-style cover-up was alleged by Breaux and other prominent Democrats. Likely due to the voter purge controversy, voter registration increased by 38,054 between the traditional Saturday state election and the rare November Tuesday balloting reserved strictly for federal general elections. Voter turnout increased 14.4 percent from one election to the next. Black ministers all over the state urged their congregations to vote, and rang their church bells on Election Day as a constant reminder. Black voter turnout surged. Breaux reversed the primary outcome by garnering 52.8 percent of the vote to Moore's 47.2.[11]

After Moore's unanticipated defeat, state and national Republicans regrouped behind and invested heavily in U.S. Representative Robert L. "Bob" Livingston to wrest control of the state from incumbent Governor Edwin W. Edwards. In part because of damage from adverse publicity generated by his protracted trials, and because of the economic downturn causing serious budget problems, Edwards was perceived as vulnerable and was challenged from within his own party by U.S. representatives W. J. "Billy" Tauzin from Edwards's own Cajun southwest and "Buddy" Roemer from northeast Louisiana, and by Secretary of State James H. "Jim" Brown, as well as three minor candidates. Edwards, who gathered in the solid support of blacks and their political organizations, organized labor, and endorsements from elected Democratic officials, consistently ran neck and neck with Livingston in the polls.[12]

Then, four weeks before the primary, the New Orleans *Times-Picayune* endorsed Roemer in a front-page editorial; all the other major newspapers soon followed suit. North Louisiana money that was being held back from Livingston for fear he could not beat Edwards began to flow to Roemer, a telegenic candidate who carried his low-budget campaign message directly to the voters via television. Roemer moved from fifth place in the polls to a stunning first-place finish, garnering 33.1 percent of the primary vote to Edwards's 28.1. Livingston placed a distant third with 18.5 percent, winning majorities in only three of the state's 64 parishes: Jefferson, St. Bernard, and St. Tammaney, all of which are in his congressional district. Other Republican strongholds such as Caddo Parish (Shreveport) went overwhelmingly for Roemer. Livingston attributed his lackluster performance to Moore's post-election claim that a good Republican could never beat an acceptable Democrat in a statewide race. Edwards stunned his supporters and the electorate with his early-morning withdrawal from the runoff, an act appearing gracious in making Roemer his successor, which let him walk away without suffering the ignominy of a landslide defeat and with over a million dollars in campaign funds in his pocket.[13]

CONTINUED REPUBLICAN SUCCESS, DEMOCRATIC MISFORTUNE

Despite the 1983 electoral rout of incumbent Republican Governor David C. Treen at the hands of Edwin W. Edwards and the two statewide losses noted above, a Republican was elected Lieutenant Governor to serve with Roemer, and Republicans gained two congressional seats to control half the state delegation (four of eight seats). Incumbent Lieutenant Governor Robert L. "Bobby"

Freeman, closely tied to Edwards, blacks, and organized labor, was challenged by three Democrats, including former Commissioner of Education Bill Dodd. Republicans rallied around former Secretary of State Paul Hardy, who endorsed Treen, was given a high-level position in the Treen administration, and left the Democratic party for his new Republican political home. Freeman placed first with 40 percent of the vote, followed by Hardy with 29 percent. Given the lackluster showing of Livingston, the Republican party, with its campaign organization in place, redoubled its efforts for Hardy, who went on to win the low-turnout runoff with 53 percent of the vote.[14]

In 1986 Republicans retained W. Henson Moore's congressional seat. State Representative Richard H. Baker, who was an elected Democrat until he became a Republican a year earlier, won it outright with a 51.0 percent margin in the open primary. The eventual Republican win in the Eighth District was a pleasant surprise. In that district, U.S. Representative Gillis W. Long, a powerful national Democrat with a compatible constituency, was succeeded by his wife Cathy in a special election after his death in early 1985. She chose not to seek re-election. Republicans came together around Clyde Holloway, whom both Gillis and Cathy Long had handily defeated in the open primaries, when he garnered but 25 (1980) and 16 percent of the vote. Blacks rallied around Faye Williams, a bright, articulate lawyer who was the only black candidate, though she had not lived in the district or state since 1962. Both made the runoff, with Williams leading Holloway 26 to 23 percent.

During the runoff, the Alexandria *Daily Town Talk* editorialized about a tragic 1971 California incident in which Williams's estranged husband, who was a popular television sports broadcaster, claimed to have seen her through her window in bed with a white political activist, went home for his rifle, killed him, beat her, and fled; later to be arrested, tried, and convicted of murder. According to Williams:

It is unfortunate that the Alexandria *Town Talk* has been on a witch hunt since the day I announced I was going to run. . . . When they couldn't find anything wrong with my qualifications, they moved to my personal life. . . . Since that time I have built a life of my own. . . . Those rumors were going on all during the primary. The people who voted for me were never interested in my personal life. They were more interested in how I could help them.

Were this not enough, close to the runoff election day, Williams was accused of being "a PLO sympathizer" in a letter to the news media from Shelly Beychok, a former aide to Edwards and a Jewish member of the Louisiana State University (LSU) Board of Supervisors. Beychok urged Democrats to reject her candidacy. Because of all this, Holloway only won by 5,412 votes, or 51 percent, to become the district's first Republican congressman since Reconstruction.[15]

With the election of Buddy Roemer as governor, candidates lined up to compete in the special election for his congressional seat in the northwestern area of the state. Though fifteen Republican candidates expressed an interest, only seven showed up for interviews by district Republican delegates in a closed meeting. At its conclusion, Jim McCrery, a business lobbyist and Roemer's former congressional aide, who had just changed his partisan affiliation from Democrat to Republican a month earlier, emerged with the party's official endorsement. While Republicans united behind McCrery, nine Democrats, including former U.S. Representative Claude Leach and State Senator Foster Campbell, both Roemer rivals dating back to 1978–1980, jumped into the open primary.

Outdistancing his nearest rival by a comfortable 31 to 19 percent vote margin on Super Tuesday 1988, Republican McCrery faced Democrat Campbell in the runoff. A fire storm of protest broke out when, just five days prior to the runoff, a longtime Roemer friend told a group of some 150 Roemer campaign volunteers at a McCrery reception that Roemer planned to vote for McCrery. Danny Walker related: "He [Roemer] said Jim McCrery worked hard and long and knows the job well; he represents the winds of change. He represents a new breed, if you will, in politics, and he plans this Saturday to vote for Jim McCrery." McCrery went on to edge out Campbell by less than 1 percent of the vote, 50.5 to 49.5. Another Reconstruction barrier fell. All three newly elected Republican congressmen won re-election in 1988.[16]

Another Republican success was the conversion of elected conservative Democrats to their party. As noted, two of the three new Republican congressmen were Democrats who switched to the Republican party just prior to running for Congress. While such switching began in the late 1970s, it was very evident in the course of the 1984 presidential campaign or just shortly thereafter, with one Democratic state senator and six Democratic state representatives having made the move. By the 1987 state elections, elected Democratic state legislators making the move to the Republican party included four state senators and fourteen state representatives.

This class of Republican converts is a good test of the incumbent protection provided by the open elections system. Of the sixteen seeking election, only three were forced into runoff elections, in which two were defeated (by a Republican and by a former Republican running without a party designation on the ballot). One was defeated in an attempt to move up to the Senate, although two successfully made the transition. One, Baker, moved on to Congress. Today, largely through the success of their conversion program, Republicans hold 5 of 39 Senate seats and 18 of 105 House seats.[17]

DEMOCRATIC PARTY REACTION

From the mid-1970s, Louisiana Republicans built a substantial party organization, well funded and well staffed; systematically expanded their voter registration base; methodically converted elected conservative Democrats to their party; and made substantial inroads in the election of national and state legislators, among other elected officials. Though Republicans suffered some major setbacks along the way, their accomplishments provoked state Democratic reaction.

Democratic National Committeeman Tucker Melancon credits the 1985 election of Jim Brady as party chair and the 1986 election of John Breaux as U.S. senator with the establishment of the ''modern-day'' Louisiana Democratic party. Brady, according to Melancon, built a stable financial base that enabled the party to install a state-of-the-art computer, build a statewide voter data base, and hire a professional staff. With the help of U.S. senators J. Bennett Johnston and Breaux, Brady brought elected officials onto the Democratic State Central Committee, in 41 of 210 seats, to make the party more representative of average Louisiana Democrats. The ''modern-day'' party even targeted twenty-seven Republican state legislators and parish-wide elected officials in 1987, and provided Democratic opponents with direct mail, telephone banks, polling, and campaign field coordinators; five Republicans were defeated.[18]

THE CAMPAIGN

Early Stages

Six presidential candidates built extensive Louisiana campaign organizations well in advance of and in preparation for Super Tuesday: Republicans George Bush, Bob Dole, Jack Kemp, and Pat Robertson, and Democrats Jesse Jackson and Al Gore. Vice President Bush, who began well over a year in advance, had the most elaborate organization, with over a thousand committed volunteers by mid-January 1988. Dole hired Representative Bob Livingston's gubernatorial campaign manager, and built on that following. Robertson, on the other hand, headquartered his campaign in Protestant north Louisiana and built his campaign organization outside the state Republican hierarchy, and especially among churchgoers.

Among the early Democrats, Reverend Jesse Jackson, like Vice President Bush, began building his campaign organization in the state well over a year in advance. Instrumental on behalf of Jackson were black clergy and black state legislators, especially State Representative Sherman Copelin (D-New Orleans), who co-directed the 1984 Jackson effort. By early January 1988, they claimed to have organized ''virtually all members of the Black Legislative Caucus, New Orleans Mayor Sidney Barthelemy and most of the politically active black clergy and business people.''[19]

While Jackson's presidential campaign did not begin in Louisiana it received an important boost in New Orleans at the Conference of Southern Black Democrats, where black political leaders from around the South came together for organizational purposes and to settle on a campaign endorsement strategy. The conference had the misfortune of meeting in New Orleans where Jackson was well organized. State Representative Copelin, a delegate, quickly positioned himself as the conference point man for Reverend Jackson. He forcefully sounded an early warning to the 157 registered participants in advance of the scheduled business meeting: "We have an opportunity with Super Tuesday. . . . I am going to try to kill this presidential endorsement [the resolution he held in his hand]. This resolution to run a favorite son in each state is an attempt to try to stop Jesse." When the business meeting, which was closed to the press, did convene, the eighteen noncontroversial resolutions enclosed in delegate packets were read by title, given a brief explanation, and passed unanimously.[20]

The "Presidential Endorsement" resolution, a modified version of the favorite son resolution alluded to by Copelin, was believed to be controversial and, therefore, was considered last. It was an attempt by prominent southern black political leaders, pragmatists all, to let their delegates at the Democratic National Convention support a consensual, electable Democratic presidential candidate sensitive to black concerns. The resolution, in reality, encouraged conference state affiliates to endorse both Reverend Jesse Jackson and a second-choice nominee. According to Joe L. Reed, leader of the Alabama Democratic Conference and a New Orleans conference organizer:

There are two things one can say for certain about the outcome of the Democratic convention. One is that the nominee will not be black. And two is that the nominee will be white. We need a spare tire strategy which indicates our second choice and to have a spare tire in the trunk is not insult to the good tire that is rolling down the road.

The fight over the proposed resolution became one between Jesse Jackson supporters and pragmatists who favored the endorsement of both Jackson and another candidate, a two-candidate strategy.[21]

The heated and sometimes acrimonious discussion focused both on Jesse Jackson's presidential candidacy and on the importance of leaving the conference united. As one resolution opponent observed:

I am a supporter of Jesse Jackson. My reservation runs deeper. A lot of people are not here. We cannot leave here divided. We would send a message to the grassroots people who worship the ground Jesse walks on. Other problems in the black community need addressing much more than this [resolution].

State Representative Reverend Avery C. Alexander (D-New Orleans) cautioned those assembled, "It suggests that Jesse Jackson cannot win. With that attitude, I would not be here [as an elected official]." During the business meeting, moreover, consummate politician and tactician Copelin skillfully scuttled the resolution in a close 50 to 45 vote by making sure his Louisiana people were in attendance, forging a coalition with the Texas delegation, and sending delegates from the meeting to round up and bring back resolution opponents from the hotel and street. Having won the battle of the Presidential Endorsement resolution, Copelin attempted to punish conference organizers and resolution supporters by running candidates, including himself, against the recommended slate of conference officers. After losing to Birmingham Mayor Richard Arrington for Chair by 16 to 49, and after State Representative Diana E. Bajoie (D-New Orleans) and Jesse Jones lost to Joe L. Reed for Secretary-Treasurer by 21 and 20 to 56, Copelin "withdrew in the interest of unity." Having won the battle, he proceeded to tell reporters, "this group doesn't have the right to come up with some back-door scheme that sends a message to the rest of America that Jackson doesn't have support from Southern blacks."[22]

Super Tuesday Strategies

While Democratic state legislators, principally through the organizational ef-forts of the Southern Legislative Conference, created Super Tuesday with the intention of helping the presidential nominees of their party, Republicans seized the opportunity it presented and attempted to use Super Tuesday to their own advantage.[23] The Southern Republican State Chairmen's Association, Southern Republican Exchange, and the Southern Republican Leadership Conference, which met in New Orleans, all presented two basic themes: (1) All Democratic presidential candidates are liberal and out of step with southern voters, while all of our Republican candidates are compatibly conservative with southern voters; and (2) conservative and moderate southern voters are welcome in the Republican Super Tuesday primaries.[24]

According to President Ronald Reagan:

"Super Tuesday" presents our party with a tremendous opportunity—to convince those who share our values to vote for the Republican candidate of their choice in the Republican primary. Now, in my humble opinion, it shouldn't be too hard to get a majority of Southern voters interested in our primary. . . . Republican candidates all agree with the people of the South. . . . Yes, the values of Southern voters are best represented by our Republican candidates. . . . So, please, go out and encourage participation in the Republican primary in your States on March 8.

The President's remarks were echoed by Republican National Committee Chair Frank J. Fahrenkopf Jr.: "Southern Democrats intended Super Tuesday to be a way to moderate their party. . . . In so doing, the Democrats have handed us a tremendous opportunity to win over the disaffected majority of their party." He then went on to castigate every "liberal" Democratic presidential candidate individually, especially U.S. Senator Albert Gore.[25]

Louisiana Republicans began a concerted effort in January 1988 to bring registered Democrats, Independent and No Party designees, and newly eligibles into their party before the close of registration for Super Tuesday. Registered Independents in Jefferson Parish, for example, received a personal letter from State Representative Charles D. Lancaster, Jr. (R-Metairie), U.S. Representative Bob Livingston, and former Governor David C. Treen. The letters, which in-cluded cards to change voter registration, explained that the open election system did not apply to presidential primaries, and that only registered Republicans could participate in and choose among Republican candidates on Super Tuesday, as was the case for registered Democrats.

It was a statewide voter registration effort by elected Republican officials, many of whom paid for it at their own expense. The state Pat Robertson organization, moreover, worked with the state party and was an integral part of the voter registration campaign in north Louisiana. Voter registrars in Caddo (Shreveport), where Robertson had his state headquarters, and Rapides (Alexandria) parishes credited Robertson with much of the registration activity:

We haven't seen anything like it [in Caddo Parish] since the heyday of George Wallace back in the 1960s. When we got here on Friday, there was already a long line forming. In this part of the state, the Robertson folks have had an impact.

A lot of people coming in to change their registration have mentioned Pat Robertson. I'd say he's a big factor up here [in Rapides Parish].

When the final registration change for Super Tuesday was tallied, the Louisiana Republican party had gained 25,063 new adherents within the five months since the close of registration for the gubernatorial primary, a gain largely at the expense of the Democratic party.[26]

The Louisiana Republican party itself mounted a second voter registration campaign for the presidential election. It mailed a hundred thousand packets with voter registration verification cards to insure that all eligible Republicans in a household with a Republican registrant were on the voter roles. Through this and continued efforts by Republican elected officials, an additional 36,100 Republicans were registered by the general election, bringing the party share to 16.4 percent of the state total (Table 5.2).[27]

In contrast to the concerted Republican efforts focused on Louisiana, the South, and Super Tuesday, the Louisiana Democratic party organized a Super Tuesday Summit which was held in early January to showcase the Democratic presidential candidates, explain the delegate selection process, and stress the importance of a high Super Tuesday voter turnout. Iowa and nature, however, worked against it. While four of the seven presidential candidates committed to appear, only Al Gore was there; the others felt it imperative to remain campaigning in Iowa. Even the scheduled appearance of Democratic National Committee Chair Paul Kirk was canceled when Washington National Airport was snowed in. Were those unexpected turn of events not enough, Governor-elect Buddy Roemer showed little interest in his party's presidential candidates when he addressed the assembled delegates.[28]

Super Tuesday Results, Political Maneuvering

Of the major presidential contenders, Republicans, and especially Robertson, Dole, and Bush, spent two to three times more on their Louisiana campaigns than did Democrats: 14 to 20 percent of the Federal Election Commission state limit versus 2 to 7 percent for Dukakis, Gore, and Gephardt. Though the Jackson campaign spent 2 percent, or $28,000, in Louisiana, it was the campaign average for the Super Tuesday states. The small campaign investment was reflected in their collective invisibility, especially for Democratic candidates.[29]

For example, a field operations staff member from Reverend Jesse Jackson's national headquarters in Chicago came to New Orleans two and a half weeks before Super Tuesday because of complaints that Jackson campaign co-chair Copelin and the legislative Black Caucus members were letting the campaign slide. She and a coalition of groups created an alternative campaign with operations in Baton Rouge, New Orleans, and Shreveport. Ultimately, the field organizer's Rainbow Coalition held an alternative victory party in a New Orleans community center, while Copelin, Mayor Sidney Barthelemy, and the official Louisiana campaign organization did the same at New Orleans' Lakefront Airport. Open animosity existed between the rival groups of Jackson supporters.[30]

Louisiana experienced a comparatively high Super Tuesday voter turnout, 24 percent of its voting age population in contrast to 1980 and 1984 turnouts of 14 and 11 percent. Too, Republicans increased their share of the turnout to 19 percent from respective proportions of 10 and 5 percent in 1980 and 1984.[31] Louisiana Republican activists and their presidential candidates appear to have reaped the benefits of the party strategy of concentrating on voter registration and participation. Vice President George Bush garnered all available Republican delegates by placing first in each of the congressional districts (twenty-four delegates) with victory margins from 46 to 67 percent, and first statewide (ten delegates) with a comfortable 58 percent to 24, 21, and 5 percent for Robertson, Dole, and Kemp. Robertson bested Dole in four congressional districts stretching from Monroe (Fifth) and Alexandria (Eighth) through the Cajun territory (Third and Seventh), and split District Four (Shreveport) with Dole (Table 5.3).[32]

Seven additional delegates, officially uncommitted, were selected by the Republican State Central Committee (RSCC) at its March 19, 1988, meeting held to swear in the new committee; to select officers, including national committee members; and also, to select national convention alternate delegates. With 1992 in mind, the Robertson organization had the election of RSCC members as an important secondary goal, and "instructed [its] voters by direct mail and telephone campaigns to mark their ballot slots for state central committee as well."[33] In coalition with arch-conservative RSCC members favoring Kemp, some 58 of the 140 total, the Robertson coalition attempted to seize the Louisiana Republican party by electing its members to all available positions, including the uncommitted delegates and alternate delegates.[34]

Overnight hardball political maneuvers eliminated the Robertson campaign's candidate for party Chair although it went on to capture the positions of RSCC Secretary and National Committeeman in the secret balloting. Among the well-established Louisiana Republicans who were elected for the seven delegate positions was the Robertson coalition candidate for party Chair. In large part due

Table 5.3

Super Tuesday Republican Vote and Allocation of National Convention Delegates, by Congressional District

CD*	Dukakis			Gephardt			Gore			Jackson			Other**	
	Vote	%	Del.	Vote	%	Del.	Vote	%	Del.	Vote	%	Del.	Vote	%
1	16,891	31	1	6,423	12	0	12,623	23	1	9,298	17	1	8,841	16
2	10,326	14	0	2,544	3	0	5,466	7	0	51,488	69	6	5,133	7
3	18,361	23	1	9,148	11	0	19,251	24	2	20,924	26	2	12,852	16
4	12,608	13	0	9,517	10	0	34,525	35	2	27,864	29	2	13,225	14
5	5,876	7	0	9,336	12	0	28,314	36	2	29,871	38	3	6,135	8
6	10,265	14	0	6,026	8	0	27,426	37	3	23,241	31	2	7,534	10
7	11,211	14	0	15,135	20	2	23,644	30	2	20,164	26	2	7,434	10
8	9,806	11	0	8,757	10	0	22,802	26	3	37,149	42	4	9,689	11
Totals:														
	95,347	15	2	66,886	11	2	172,683	27	15	224,899	36	21	70,843	11

*CD = congressional district.
**Includes Frank Ahern, Bruce Babbitt, Norbert G. Dennerll, Jr., David E. Duke, Gary Hart, Richard B. Kay, Lyndon LaRouche, and Paul Simon.

Source: Calculated by the author from congressional district figures made available by Philip J. Jones, Executive Director, Louisiana Democratic Party, 13 January 1989.

to dwindling meeting attendance, the Robertson coalition went on to prevail in three of the seven-at-large Alternate Delegate positions.[35] Former RSCC Chair George J. Despot sent a letter of warning to RSCC members:

The Robertson project apparently covers a four year period with a target date of 1992. . . . Procedurally, the coalition will cast its 58 votes as a unit on those issues which affect those long-range objectives. . . . [T]hey will attempt . . . to motivate and acquire 12 independent votes, and then they will prevail on that issue. Such an issue would be the filling of vacancies on the committee [RSCC].[36]

The Democratic result mirrored that of 1984. Campaign conflict aside, Reverend Jesse Jackson had a clear first-place statewide finish with 36 percent of the vote, and was followed closely by Al Gore with 27 percent. Massachusetts Governor Michael Dukakis trailed with 15 percent, just edging out U.S. Representative Richard Gephardt who received 11 percent. Jackson came out far ahead in the two nationally oriented congressional districts (Second—New Orleans and Eighth—from Alexandria stretching down river to just outside New Orleans), which were those with the largest black populations, split the Third and Fifth districts with Gore, and placed behind Gore in the Fourth, Sixth, and Seventh districts. Dukakis placed first in the First District, suburban metropolitan New Orleans (Table 5.4).

Due in part to the 15 percent delegate allocation floor, Jackson translated his 36 percent statewide win into 53 percent (twenty-one) of the allocated delegates, given very high voter turnouts coupled with disproportionate wins in his two strongest congressional districts. Gore earned fifteen delegates (38 percent), while

Table 5.4

Super Tuesday Democratic Vote and Allocation of National Convention Delegates, by Congressional District

CD*	Bush			Dole			Kemp			Robertson			Other**	
	Vote	%	Del.	Vote	%	Del.	Vote	%	Del.	Vote	%	Del.	Vote	%
1	19,584	66	3	5,198	18	0	1,625	5	0	2,905	10	0	267	1
2	8,088	67	3	2,271	19	0	648	5	0	917	8	0	196	2
3	7,442	52	3	2,509	18	0	645	4	0	3,608	25	0	150	1
4	14,714	61	3	4,206	17	0	1,009	4	0	3,882	16	0	240	1
5	9,837	56	3	2,429	14	0	798	5	0	4,438	25	0	166	1
6	11,055	56	3	4,071	21	0	1,579	8	0	2,919	15	0	174	1
7	7,698	46	3	2,870	17	0	923	6	0	4,918	30	0	173	1
8	4,863	49	3	2,055	21	0	519	5	0	2,427	24	0	104	1
Totals:														
	83,281	58	24	25,609	18	0	7,746	5	0	26,014	18	0	1,470	1

*CD = congressional district.
*Includes Pierre "Pete" DuPont and Alexander M. Haig, Jr.

Source: Calculated by the author from congressional district figures made available by the Louisiana Republican Party.

Dukakis and Gephardt each earned two (5 percent). The selection of party leaders and at-large delegates by the Democratic State Central Committee on June 4, 1988, gave Jackson an additional ten delegates for a total of thirty-one, Gore eight (for twenty-three), and Dukakis four (for six). Gephardt received none. The complete delegation included fourteen officially uncommitted super delegates, delegates by virtue of their elected office or party position.[37]

Though a super delegate and traditionally the head of the state delegation by virtue of office, Governor Buddy Roemer opted not to attend due to pressing state business. On the other hand, the governor was no friend of the state Democratic establishment, which was criticized openly by one of his key aides in a workshop at the party's Super Tuesday Summit. Roemer, too, had back-handedly endorsed Republican Jim McCrery, who went on to win the seat Roemer held in Congress, and displayed an initial open coolness for the vice presidential candidacy of U.S. Senator Lloyd Bentsen. The Democratic establishment, then, was not displeased when Roemer was reduced to a minor role at the national convention nor when he announced his intention to stay home. With Roemer out, the delegation was headed by U.S. Senator John Breaux.[38]

Though the Jackson delegates expressed irritation when Dukakis picked up the twenty-five delegates pledged to Gore and Gephardt to come within one vote of Jackson, thirty-two to thirty-one, the visible emphasis among Louisiana delegates was unity and mended fences. By the convention roll call, ten additional delegates had moved to Dukakis, one had gone to Jackson, and one had moved to Gephardt, bringing their respective totals to forty-one, thirty-three, and one. When the convention and maneuvering among the Louisiana delegates in anticipation of campaign roles had both ended, Breaux, the clear choice from the

Table 5.5

Summary Statistics for Super Tuesday Democratic and Republican Primaries, by Candidate—Delegates Allocated by Congressional District and At-Large

Party and Candidate	% of Primary Vote	CD* Delegates	% of CD Delegates	At-Large Delegates	% of At-Large Delegates	Total Delegates
Democrats						
Dukakis	15	2	5	4	18	6
Gephardt	11	2	5	0	0	2
Gore	27	15	38	8	36	23
Jackson	36	21	53	10	45	31
Republicans						
Bush	58	24	100	17**	100	41
Dole	18	0	0	0	0	0
Kemp	5	0	0	0	0	0
Robertson	18	0	0	0	0	0

*CD = congressional district.
**Ten at-large delegates went to Bush because he won statewide; the remaining seven were elected by the Republican State Central Committee at its 19 March 1988 meeting in Baton Rouge.

Source: Calculated by the author from congressional district figures made available, for the Democrats, by Philip J. Jones, Executive Director, Louisiana Democratic Party, 13 January 1989, and, for the Republicans, by the Louisiana Republican Party.

beginning, was named Chair, and his aide, Norma Jane Sabiston, was named state coordinator of the Louisiana Dukakis-Bentsen campaign. Copelin, with his controversial background, was pushed to the sidelines, while State Senator William Jefferson emerged as the consensus co-chair. In a compromise to Jackson, Mayor Sidney Barthelemy received a position on an expanded Democratic National Committee.[39]

With a united Bush delegation of party activists in a united party, Louisiana Republican National Convention delegates had no need to position in contrast to their Democratic counterparts (Table 5.5). Delegation chair U.S. Representative Richard Baker, a delegate handpicked by George Bush, became chair of the Louisiana Bush for President organization. Just as it had been in the Super Tuesday voter registration effort, and with an eye toward the future, the Robertson organization was welcomed as an integral part of the Bush campaign in the state. According to RSCC Treasurer and Bush organizer Scott Sewell, "Pat Robertson . . . offered to come to Louisiana as often as possible to organize a lot of Louisiana churches and get issues to fundamentalist groups." With an organization in place, a hired field staff, a Baton Rouge state campaign headquarters, and campaign offices in every major city, the Bush delegates enthusiastically left the convention to plunge into the presidential campaign, to work in a coordinated, united effort.[40]

From Convention to General Election

After the Republican National Convention, held in New Orleans, nominees wasted no time campaigning throughout Louisiana. Vice presidential candidate Dan Quayle kicked off a southern campaign swing September 1 in Baton Rouge on the LSU campus, and then toured the huge Exxon refinery before moving on to Shreveport. He returned September 26 to tour the National Aeronautics and Space Administration (NASA) Michoud Assembly Facility, and to speak to National Alliance of Business members gathered in New Orleans for their twentieth annual meeting. Several weeks later, Quayle returned to the state again, speaking at an Oil Industry For Bush rally in Lafayette and then to students on the University of Southwestern Louisiana campus.[41]

Louisiana was not being taken for granted. Just days before the presidential election, George Bush's son Jeb made a November 2 swing through Baton Rouge, Lafayette, Houma, and Franklin. Barbara Bush campaigned in Baton Rouge and worked with campaign workers there on November 3. Dan Quayle returned one more time on November 4, and campaigned in Monroe.[42]

The Dukakis-Bentsen campaign, in contrast, got off to a late, unenthusiastic start. Substituting for vice presidential candidate Lloyd Bentsen, Governor Buddy Roemer told the assembled Louisiana Women For Dukakis that he would vote for but not support Dukakis. Also, he noted "I've never seen a more unfocused, unorganized, non-issue campaign in my life."[43] The campaign finally got off the ground officially the following Saturday, September 24. A week earlier, however, Bentsen spoke at a Shreveport rally, and he returned there on Election Day itself, this time speaking to a rally of union members.[44]

Reverend Jesse Jackson made three widely publicized Louisiana campaign appearances on behalf of the Democratic ticket. September 22 he spoke at a rally on the Southern University campus, a rally at which he announced support for District Eight congressional candidate Faye Williams in her rematch against incumbent Republican Clyde Holloway. Williams accepted his endorsement, calling him "the real President of the United States." Furthermore, his National Rainbow coalition was to conduct "a nine-day, 42-community blitz of the district stumping for Williams and encouraging voter participation and registration." A week later, September 26, Jesse Jackson, Jr., rallied Southern University students to register, and led nearly 200 to do so. Reverend Jackson himself campaigned in New Orleans on October 19 on the campuses of Dillard and Tulane universities, and spoke at a United Auto Workers Union convention. The following week, he returned to New Orleans and spoke to large crowds on the campuses of Southern University and Delgado Community College in New Orleans.[45]

Governor Michael Dukakis himself received an enthusiastic, responsive reception from an overflow crowd of several thousand at the University of New Orleans on Friday night, October 21, an event that left several hundred to 1,000 disappointed supporters outside the facility. With many important Democratic leaders and elected officials from around the state present, as well as important business and education leaders, Dukakis easily dismissed the Willie Horton attack as packaged by the Republicans with a gripping personal story about the beating death of his father. More important for this audience, he defined his offshore drilling policy as consistent with current Louisiana practice. Unfortunately, it was too little, too late. Privately, Louisiana Democrats, especially black political leaders, were furious with the ineptness of his campaign, especially since all their advice on campaign strategy had been ignored. Rather than actively build a biracial coalition as did John Breaux in his successful comeback to defeat Henson Moore "using economic appeals and the argument that Ronald Reagan and the congressional Republicans have ignored the Southern economy," Dukakis stayed out of the South.[46]

RESULTS AND ANALYSIS

Not unexpectedly, and consistent with the presidential elections since President Jimmy Carter's 1976 Louisiana win, the Bush-Quayle ticket defeated that of Dukakis-Bentsen by a 54.3 to 44.1 percent margin, the remainder going to four minor candidates. Voter turnout in the lackluster or even invisible contest, while better than the national average, was a very low 51.3 percent of the state's voting age population. Consistent with 1984, the strongest Republican areas of the state in the presidential vote were the north Louisiana parishes, including those in the central area and the cities of Alexandria, Monroe, and Shreveport, as shown in Figure 5.1. Another area of strong Republican voting in the 1988 presidential election was that surrounding Orleans Parish (New Orleans) and including the parishes of Jefferson, St. Bernard, and St. Tammany. Lafayette and East Baton Rouge parishes, with the cities of Lafayette and Baton Rouge, moreover, turned in votes close to the 60-plus percent range for the Bush-Quayle ticket, with 59.4 and 58.8 percent, respectively.

Conversely, the strongest Democratic areas were those with the largest black populations, Orleans Parish (New Orleans) and the parishes in the Eighth Congressional District, which are outlined in Figure 5.1; and to the far southwestern area of the state, the home territory of Breaux. Interestingly, Reverend Jesse Jackson's endorsement and campaigning in the Eighth District on behalf of Faye Williams aside, Williams lost the rematch by about the same margin (43.2 to 56.8 percent for Republican incumbent Holloway) that the Dukakis-Bentsen ticket won it (56.1 percent).

CONCLUSION: CONTINUITY AMIDST CHANGE

Louisiana, especially New Orleans, was at the center of several presidential campaign strategies. A potentially divisive two-candidate strategy among black political leaders—Reverend Jesse Jackson plus an electable white Democrat— was derailed there at the Conference of Southern Black Democrats. The Southern

Figure 5.1
Distribution of the 1988 Republican Vote by Parish

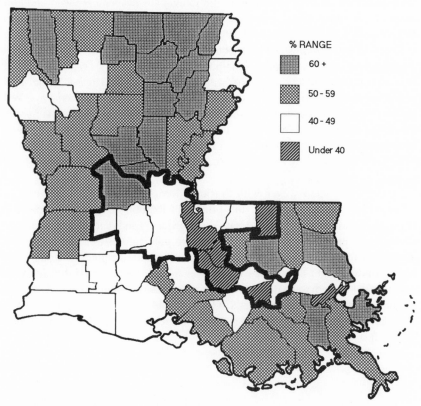

Note: Eighth Congressional District is outlined.
Source: Prepared by author.

Republican Leadership Conference rallied party activists from around the region and showcased the Super Tuesday voter registration/participation strategy, inviting conservative and moderate southern Democrats to choose among compatibly conservative Republican presidential candidates. The Republican National Convention launched an uncharacteristically aggressive, unrelenting George Bush on the road to the White House, even with his unexpected and controversial running mate U.S. Senator J. Danforth "Dan" Quayle (R-IN).

The Louisiana Republican party was organized and unified to do the work it does best, and this time had the cooperation of Pat Robertson and his state organization at all stages of the presidential selection process. It successfully expanded its voter registration and participation for both Super Tuesday and the general election. United, it added one more presidential victory to its string of wins. While the party had recently lost the important statewide U.S. Senate seat and gubernatorial battles, at the same time it continued to expand its base of congressional seats, arguably with the indirect help of Democratic Governor Buddy Roemer. The party, aided by the open elections system, maintained its foothold in the state legislature with the re-election of members who had converted after having been elected as Democrats, a feat usually accomplished in the primary.

An important driving force in Louisiana electoral politics, if not the most important, is race. Its impact on the political process, besides maneuvering for positions in the Dukakis campaign, was highlighted in the Breaux-Moore U.S. Senate contest. More telling was the 1988 electoral re-run between Faye Williams, a bright, articulate, and well-qualified black woman actively supported by Reverend Jesse Jackson, and incumbent Republican Clyde Holloway, which took place in the Eighth District with its nationally oriented constituency. Williams lost the contest by about the same margin that the Dukakis-Bentsen ticket won it.

Presidential contests, even with President Ronald Reagan out of the picture, provide continued leverage for the Louisiana Republican party to expand its base. That achievement, coupled with serious viable candidates, should continue to move the party toward a more competitive political position. The continued activity of the Robertson organization/coalition, while helping move the party forward now, might be a mixed blessing as it could surface as a divisive force when strong enough to challenge the Republican establishment itself. Its success within the party could be to Louisiana Republicans what blacks are to Louisiana Democrats, a necessary coalition partner for electoral success but an electoral barrier in broader constituencies.

NOTES

1. Charles D. Hadley, "Louisiana," in *The 1984 Presidential Election in the South*, ed. Robert P. Steed, Laurence W. Moreland, and Tod A. Baker (New York: Praeger, 1986), 21–29.

2. See, for example, Johnny Greene, "John Volz v. Edwin Edwards," *Southern Magazine* 1 (October 1986): 49–51, 74–80; Nancy Lemann, "The Trials and Jubilations of Governor Edwin Edwards: An Education in Louisiana Politics," *Esquire*, May 1987, 79–89; Allan Katz, "The Last Hurrah," New Orleans *Times-Picayune*, November 1, 1987, A-29; and Mark Muro, "The State of Scandal: Louisiana's Bad Old Boys," *Boston Globe*, March 8, 1988, 61.

3. For example, Charles M. Hargroder, "Sudden Twist in Marsellus Case," New Orleans *Times-Picayune*, October 6, 1987, A-11; Steve Cannizaro, "Ex-Causeway Chief Given 2-Year Term," New Orleans *Times-Picayune*, January 12, 1989, B-1; Steve Cannizaro, "Former City Tax Official Admits Accepting Liquor-Permit Bribes," New Orleans *Times-Picayune*, January 19, 1989, B-1, B-2.

4. Anne Veigle, "DLJ Battles for Louisiana Business," New Orleans *Times-Picayune*, December 6, 1987: G-1; Anne Veigle, "How a Giant Public Bond Deal Happened," New Orleans *Times-Picayune*, December 6, 1987, G-1; Bill Lynch, "Bond Counsel Firm's Big Role in La. Bonds," New Orleans *Times-Picayune*, December 6, 1987, G-

1. Compare W. John Moore, "New Rules of the Game in Louisiana," *National Journal*, April 30, 1988, 1118.

5. Rebecca Theim and Robert Rhoden, "Airport Land Deals Help Consultant," New Orleans *Times Picayune*, January 12, 1989, 1.

6. John LaPlante, "Guste Says Kiefer Owes La. $423,291," Baton Rouge *Morning Advocate*, October 6, 1988, 1; James Gill, "Mr. Blake and Old-Style Politics," New Orleans *Times-Picayune*, April 22, 1988, A-19.

7. Louisiana completed computerized and centralized voter registration in the Department of Elections and Registration in early 1987. The purge of duplicate entries among parishes likely led to the small 1988 registration increase among blacks and the decline among whites.

8. U.S. Bureau of the Census, *Statistical Abstract of the United States* (Washington, D.C.: Government Printing Office, 1988), 247.

9. Ellen Hume, "GOP, Aided by Democratic Scandals, Sees Chance To Elect Its First Louisiana Senator in 100 Years," *Wall Street Journal*, September 18, 1986, 54; David Maraniss, "In Louisiana, Race Is in the Race," *Washington Post National Weekly Edition*, August 25, 1986, 14; "Campaign Price Tag is $9 Million," New Orleans *Times-Picayune*, December 16, 1986, B-6; Richard M. Scammon and Alice V. McGillivray, comps. and eds., *America Votes 17* (Washington, D.C.: Congressional Quarterly, Elections Research Center, 1987), 204.

10. Alan Katz, "Black Voters Purge Target, Memo Shows," New Orleans *Times-Picayune*, October 25, 1986, 1, A-4; Jack Wardlaw, "Purge Campaign May Cost Moore Dearly," New Orleans *Times-Picayune*, October 25, 1986, 1, A-4; "Cover-up Is Charged in Vote Purge," New Orleans *Times-Picayune*, October 28, 1986, B-1, B-2; Bill Lynch, "GOP Voter Purge Issue Narrows Moore-Breaux Race," New Orleans *Times-Picayune*, October 28, 1986, A-15.

11. "Cover-up Is charged," B–2; Scammon and McGillivray, *America Votes 17*, 199; Iris Kelso, "The Blacks Journey to the Polls," New Orleans *Times-Picayune*, November 9, 1986, B-3; Jack Wardlaw, "Voter Sidelights," New Orleans *Times-Picayune*, November 9, 1986, B-3.

12. Drew Broach, "Livingston Reaps Rewards of Party Loyalty," New Orleans *Times-Picayune*, August 16, 1987, 1, A-4; Bill Lynch, "Black Voting Bloc May Break up in Governor's Race," New Orleans *Times-Picayune*, September 15, 1987, A-13; Iris Kelso, "Gov. Edwards and the Battle for Endorsements," New Orleans *Times-Picayune*, September 17, 1987, A-29; "Edwards' Report Shows $100,000 Campaign Donation," New Orleans *Times-Picayune*, October 17, 1987, B-5.

13. John McQuaid and Allan Katz, "Strategy, Endorsements Put Roemer on Fast Track," New Orleans *Times-Picayune*, October 25, 1987, 1, A-10; Jack Wardlaw and Allan Katz, "Edwards Quits the Runoff; Roemer Is Elected Governor," New Orleans *Times-Picayune*, October 25, 1987, 1, A-10; Alex Martin, "Opponents' Strongholds Fell Prey to Roemer," New Orleans *Times-Picayune*, October 26, 1987, 1, A-5, A-6; Bridget O'Brian, "Edwards Decided Quickly, Alone," New Orleans *Times-Picayune*, October 26, 1987, 1, A-5, A-6; Bridget O'Brian, "Finale: Good Times Roll to a Halt for Edwards," New Orleans *Times-Picayune*, October 26, 1987, 1, A-5, A-6; Secretary of State, "Proclamation of Election Returns," Baton Rouge *State-Times*, November 5, 1987, 6-C.

14. Voter turnout was off by one-third from the primary to just over 30 percent of the voting age population. (U.S. Census Bureau; Secretary of State; *Statistical Abstract*;

"Proclamation," November 5, 1987; "Proclamation of Election Returns," Baton Rouge *State-Times*, December 3, 1987, 17-D).

15. "Candidate's Tragic Past Resurrected," New Orleans *Times-Picayune*, October 18, 1986, A-17; "Congressional Candidate Blasted as Soft on PLO," New Orleans *Times-Picayune*, October 30, 1986, B–12; Barri Marsh, "8th District Candidates Study in Contrasts," New Orleans *Times-Picayune*, November 2, 1986, C-1, C-2; Michael Barone and Grant Ujifusa, *The Almanac of American Politics 1988* (Washington, D.C.: National Journal, 1987), 501–503.

16. "GOP Endorses Former Aide to Run for Roemer's Seat," New Orleans *Times-Picayune*, November 26, 1987, B-6; John LaPlante, "McCrery, Campbell Win Spots in 4th District Runoff," Baton Rouge *Morning Advocate*, March 9, 1988, 11A; Thomas Fitzgerald, "McCrery, Campbell in Runoff to Fill Roemer's Seat in House," New Orleans *Times-Picayune*, March 9, 1988, A-8; "Roemer, Hardy Back McCrery in 4th District Race," Baton Rouge *Morning Advocate*, April 14, 1988, 10B; Thomas Fitzgerald, "Roemer's Nod for GOP Angers State Democrats," New Orleans *Time-Picayune*, April 22, 1988, 1; "Jim McCrery Official 4th District Winner," Baton Rouge *Morning Advocate*, April 20, 1988, 11A; Scammon and McGillivray, *America Votes 17*; Richard M. Scammon and Alice V. McGillivray, comps. and eds., *America Votes 14* (Washington, D.C.: Congressional Quarterly, Congressional Research Center, 1981), 180–181.

17. Hadley, "Louisiana," 36–37; Charles D. Hadley and Elizabeth A. Rickey, "Louisiana Republicans after the 1987 Democratic Revolution: Continuing on the Road toward Realignment?" (Paper presented at The Citadel Symposium on Southern Politics, Charleston, S.C., March 3–4, 1988). Compare Joan McKinney, "McCrery Win Renews Debate over Open Primary System," Baton Rouge *Sunday Advocate*, May 1, 1988, 15B.

18. Tucker Melancon, "Democrats Rebuilding in La.," Baton Rouge *Sunday Advocate*, March 13, 1988, 7B. Compare Hadley, "Louisiana," 25; Hadley and Rickey, "Louisiana Republicans," 14–17.

19. Allan Katz, "6 Candidates Hold an Edge in Organizing," New Orleans *Times-Picayune*, January 24, 1988, B-1, B-4.

20. Charles D. Hadley, Delegate, Conference of Southern Black Democrats, New Orleans, "Personal Notes," November 14, 1987.

21. A relevant section of the resolution read: "The delegates pledged to that candidate endorsed by the State Affiliate are encouraged to confer with the delegates from other states, and support the candidate, who in their opinion, is best for blacks, who can unify the Party and be elected in November, 1988" (Reed quoted in Ron Smothers, "Jackson Supporters Block Efforts by Black Democrats on Strategy," *New York Times*, November 16, 1987, 8). See also Luix Overbea, "Black Southern Politicians Seek United Front for Super Tuesday," *The Christian Science Monitor*, December 10, 1987, 5.

22. Hadley, "Personal Notes"; Copelin quoted in Smothers, "Jackson Supporters." On the endorsement strategy, see also Adam Pertman, "Some Black Leaders Back Jackson . . . and Look for Second Choice," *Boston Globe*, December 23, 1987, 14.

23. On its creation and expectations, see Harold W. Stanley and Charles D. Hadley, "The Southern Presidential Primary: Regional Intentions with National Implications," *Publius: The Journal of Federalism* 17 (Summer 1987): 83–100; and, for their assessment of the event, Charles D. Hadley and Harold W. Stanley, "Super Tuesday 1988: Regional Results, National Implications," *Publius: The Journal of Federalism* 19 (Summer 1989), 19–37.

24. The Southern Primary Project, Southern Republican State Chairmen's Association,

Super Tuesday: A Super Republican Day (n.d.); Haley Barbour, "Memorandum to the Southern Republican Exchange on the Southern Republican Primary Project," January 9, 1988 (Southern Republican Leadership Conference, New Orleans, 11–13 February 1988).

25. President Ronald Reagan, Videotaped Remarks to the Southern Republican Leadership Conference, New Orleans, February 11, 1988; Frank J. Fahrenkopf, Jr., Remarks to the Southern Republican Leadership Conference, New Orleans, February 12, 1988.

26. Allan Katz, "GOP Gains La. Voters; Robertson Credited," New Orleans *Times-Picayune*, February 13, 1988, B-1, B-2; Allan Katz, "La. Voters Flocking to Republican Party," New Orleans *Times-Picayune*, February 16, 1988, B-1, B-2; copies of personal mailings from State Representative Charles D. Lancaster, Jr., U.S. Representative Bob Livingston, and former Governor David C. Treen; Louisiana Department of Elections and Registration, "State Wide Report of Registered Voters," September 25, 1987; Louisiana Department of Elections and Registration, "State Wide Report of Registered Voters," February 18, 1988.

27. "Election 88: Packets Mailed," Baton Rouge *Morning Advocate*, October 7, 1988, 2B; Department of Elections and Registration, "Special Report of Registered Voters," October 14, 1988.

28. "Dear Democrat" letter to party activists from James J. Brady, Chairman, Democratic State Central Committee of Louisiana, December 1, 1987; Charles D. Hadley, Delegate, Super Tuesday Summit, January 8–9, 1989; Iris Kelso, "Gore Talks to the Louisiana Pros," New Orleans *Times-Picayune*, January 10, 1988," A-27.

29. See Hadley and Stanley, "Super Tuesday 1988," Table 3.

30. Allan Katz, "Worker for Jackson Campaign Raps Efforts of Copelin, Caucus," New Orleans *Times-Picayune*, March 10, 1988, A-13.

31. Hadley and Stanley, "Super Tuesday 1988," Table 5. Compare "The Numbers Are In: Super Tuesday Turnout a Huge Success," Southern Legislative Conference, Press Release, March 10, 1988.

32. For nearly complete returns by congressional district which are unavailable from the Secretary of State, see "Updated Louisiana Totals," New Orleans *Times-Picayune*, March 10, 1988, A-13.

33. Bill Lynch, "Former Treen Aide to Head La. GOP," New Orleans *Times-Picayune*, March 20, 1988, B-1, B-2.

34. Allan Katz, "Robertson Forces Pull Off Coup on State GOP Panel," New Orleans *Times-Picayune*, March 18, 1988, 1, A–4. This article was used by Republican party regulars to beat back the Robertson coalition's attempted takeover.

35. Lynch, "Former Treen Aide"; Bill McMahon, "La. GOP Puts Nungesser in Top Post," Baton Rouge *Sunday Advocate*, March 20, 1988, 1B. Also from "Republican State Central Committee Minutes," March 19, 1988, and my personal observations.

36. George J. Despot, "Selective Mailing to the Republican State Central Committee [RSCC] Membership," March 29, 1988. Subsequently, the Robertson coalition, on two occasions, prevailed in filling four RSCC vacancies by this writing.

37. See Democratic State Central Committee, "Louisiana's Delegate Selection Process for the 1988 Democratic National Convention" (n.d.); Allan Katz, "Dukakis Picks Up 25 More Delegates from La.," New Orleans *Times-Picayune*, July 18, 1988, A-7, gives the complete list of delegates, including super delegates.

38. Zack Nauth, "Roemer on the Sidelines," New Orleans *Times-Picayune* (July 20,

1988), A-14; Joan McKinney, "Buddy Roemer No Favorite of Democrats at Convention," Baton Rouge *Sunday Advocate*, July 24, 1988, 13B.

39. Katz, "Dukakis Picks Up"; Allan Katz, "Jackson Backers from N.O. Hope Rift is Mended," New Orleans *Times-Picayune*, July 15, 1988, A-2; Allan Katz, "La. Delegation Mended Fences before Atlanta," New Orleans *Times-Picayune*, July 18, 1988, A-7; Allan Katz and Zack Nauth, "Breaux, Jefferson Will Lead," New Orleans *Times-Picayune*, July 22, 1988, A-12; Joan McKinney, "La. Demo Establishment Embraces Dukakis," Baton Rouge *Morning Advocate*, July 22, 1988, 10A; Alex Martin and Allan Katz, "Barthelemy Wins Spot on Panel," New Orleans *Times-Picayune*, July 23, 1988, A-2; Clancy DuBos, "In-Fighting in Atlanta," *Gambit*, July 26, 1988, 11.

40. Marsha Shuler, "La. Delegation Made Up of Party Activists," Baton Rouge *Sunday Advocate*, August 14, 1988, 12A; Marsha Shuler, "Robertson Forces to Aid Bush in La.," Baton Rouge *Morning Advocate*, August 18, 1988, 10A: Marsha Shuler, "La. Delegates Shift into Campaign Gear," Baton Rouge *Morning Advocate*, August 19, 1988, 1, 12A.

41. John LaPlante, "Quayle Hits Oil Issues in BR Talk," Baton Rouge *Morning Advocate*, September 1, 1988, 1, 6A; Joe Guan, Jr., "Quayle Pledges GOP's Support of Space Program," Baton Rouge *Morning Advocate*, September 27, 1988, 1B, 2B; Allan Katz and John McQuaid, "Quayle: Record Speaks to Ability," New Orleans *Times-Picayune*, September 27, 1988, 1, A-4; "Quayle Says Bush Will Help Oil Industry," October 15, 1988, 1B, 2B. On Quayle's New Orleans visit and campaign strategy, see B. Drummond Ayres, Jr., "Script for Quayle: Local and Low Key," *New York Times*, September 28, 1988, 11.

42. "Bush's Son campaigns in 4 La. Cities," Baton Rouge *Morning Advocate*, November 2, 1988, 10A; Marsha Shuler, "Barbara Bush Campaigns in BR," Baton Rouge *Morning Advocate*, November 4, 1988, 1, 6A; Merrill Hartson, "Quayle Cites Overdraft," Baton Rouge *Morning Advocate*, November 5, 1988, 6A; Allan Katz, "Monroe Easy Town for Quayle to Take," New Orleans *Times-Picayune*, November 5, 1988, B-7.

43. Quoted in Iris Kelso, "Cranking Up the Dukakis Campaign in Louisiana," New Orleans *Times-Picayune*, September 22, 1988, A-29.

44. Steven Komarow, "Bentsen Says Demos on the Upswing," Baton Rouge *Morning Advocate*, September 16, 1988, 4B; "Bentsen Tells La. Rally 'We're on your side,' " Baton Rouge *Morning Advocate*, November 8, 1988, 6A.

45. Ed Anderson, "Jackson Backs La. Candidate," New Orleans *Times-Picayune*, September 22, 1988, B–8; Bill McMahon, "Jackson Sees Dukakis Win in Debates," Baton Rouge *Morning Advocate*, September 22, 1988, 1B, 2B; John McQuaid, "Jackson Arrives on Revival Mission," New Orleans *Times-Picayune*, October 19, 1988, A-2; Iris Kelson, "Jackson Lights Fire at Delgado," New Orleans *Times-Picayune*, November 2, 1988, B-1, B-2; Janet McConnaughey, "Jackson Tells Tulane Crowd that 'passion' Isn't the Issue," Baton Rouge *Morning Advocate*, October 19, 1988, 5B; Karen Didier, "Jesse Jackson Jr. Visits Southern," Baton Rouge *Morning Advocate*, September 27, 1988, 2B.

46. James O'Byrne, "Dukakis: Get Rigs Going Again," New Orleans *Times-Picayune*, October 22, 1988, 1, A-4; and especially, Allan Katz, "Duke in Dixie," New Orleans *Times-Picayune*, October 30, 1988, B-3.

6

Mississippi: Electoral Conflict in a Nationalized State

STEPHEN D. SHAFFER

The 1988 elections in Mississippi promised to be a fascinating contest between a traditionally dominant Democratic party and an increasingly powerful Republican party. Enormous changes had swept across the state in recent decades, as the Democratic party was transformed from the party of white supremacy to an accommodating coalition including blacks as well as disadvantaged whites. The Republican label was no longer a curse word, as many moderate and conservative whites supported attractive federal candidates offered by that party. In effect, Mississippi voters were undergoing the twin processes of dealignment and realignment, as the numbers of Independents and Republicans had risen at the expense of Democrats, who nevertheless continued to comprise a plurality of the electorate. However, factions threatened the unity of both parties, as Democratic candidates were occasionally defeated by racial splits within their party when normally Democratic voters refused to support candidates not sharing their race, and the Republican party was sometimes split into moderate and conservative wings.[1]

Republican party gains in Mississippi were especially evident in federal elections in the 1970s and 1980s. As occurred in most areas of the country, the state generally voted Republican for President, supporting Richard Nixon in 1972 and Ronald Reagan in 1984 with landslide margins, and narrowly supporting Reagan in 1980 (though narrowly supporting Democrat Jimmy Carter in 1976). In 1978 the presence of a black independent Senate candidate split the normally Democratic vote and helped elect the first Republican to the U.S. Senate from Mississippi since Reconstruction—moderate conservative Thad Cochran. The Nixon landslide of 1972 also marked the beginning of Republican control of two of the state's five U.S. House seats.

However, by the mid-1980s the state's Democratic party had also demonstrated considerable strength as a reinvigorated ''populist'' coalition of blacks and lower and middle socioeconomic-status whites. Democrats were especially successful at the state level, as they divorced themselves from the unpopular ''liberal'' image of the national Democratic party. The 1987 state elections continued the trend established during Reconstruction of every state official elected statewide being a Democrat. Despite a strong challenge by progressive Republican Jack Reed, Mississippians elected Democratic reformer Ray Mabus to the Governor's Mansion—a 39-year-old Harvard graduate. In 1986 Democrats also showed surprising strength at the federal level, as young, aggressive Mike Espy unseated conservative Republican Congressman Webb Franklin of the Second District (which incorporated the Mississippi River Delta region) to become the first black elected to Congress from the state since Reconstruction. Espy had successfully attacked Franklin for supporting Reagan's domestic budget cuts which had hurt his district, plagued as it was by high unemployment and the greatest poverty in the nation.

These last two elections, therefore, gave Democrats reasons for hope in 1988 despite long-term Republican electoral gains. The Democrats were fielding a strong slate of congressional candidates, including three House incumbents and two attractive candidates for the open seats. The Democratic Senate nominee for the open seat created by Democratic Senator John Stennis's retirement was Congressman Wayne Dowdy, who had been successful in the Fourth District in constructing the type of biracial coalition that Democratic candidates required for victory. Even the national Democratic party gave reason for hope, selecting Michael Dukakis, who was initially portrayed in nonideological terms as a competent leader who could promote economic development, as its presidential nominee. While the Republican party also offered attractive candidates, some like Senate candidate Trent Lott who had represented the conservative Fifth District were viewed as possibly too conservative to adequately represent such a poor state that was so heavily dependent on federal assistance.

What went wrong for the Democrats? On Election Night, Mississippi voted for Republican presidential candidate George Bush by a landslide, and found itself with two Republican senators for the first time since Reconstruction. However, voters also returned Democratic House incumbents to Congress by overwhelming margins, including liberal Mike Espy. In this chapter we shall examine the nature of the campaigns for the presidential, senatorial, and congressional offices, and how they shaped the decisions of voters in the state.

THE CAMPAIGN

The Presidential Campaign

Dukakis's problems in Mississippi were foreshadowed by the primary campaign, as he lacked a significant core of active supporters. Jesse Jackson had strong support in the large black community and was endorsed by the legislative Black Caucus. In visits to the state, he stressed popular issues to attract more white support, like the need for more and better paying jobs, improved education, and an effective drug fight.[2] In his campaign stops to the state, Gore reminded Mississippians that he was the region's favorite son, and announced the names of 150 Mississippi Democratic party and public officials supporting his candidacy.[3] Jackson and Gore were both endorsed by the powerful Mississippi Association of Educators.[4] As such, it was not surprising that despite a first-place victory in New Hampshire and the attendant publicity, Dukakis won only 9 percent of the Democratic primary vote in Mississippi, as Jackson came in first with 44 percent and Gore second with 34 percent. On the Republican side, Bush's victory in New Hampshire and President Reagan's great popularity in Mississippi helped Bush sweep the state with 66 percent of the Republican vote compared to only 17 percent for Dole.[5]

Eager for victory after eight years of a Republican presidency, many southern Democratic public officials endorsed Dukakis after he had sewn up the nomination, evoking memories of the Democratic party unity that had helped elect Carter in 1976. Flanked by Democratic congressional candidates from the Fourth and Fifth districts, Governor Ray Mabus endorsed Dukakis at a June campaign stop in Biloxi, where Dukakis "talked tough" on drugs and promised to appoint a federal "drug czar." Rejecting the "liberal" label, Mabus touted Dukakis as a competent, pragmatic progressive, who supported job creation and improved education. Setting the theme for the fall campaign, state Republicans counterattacked with their own news conference in which Republican State Party Chairperson Evelyn McPhail assailed Dukakis as "an ultra-liberal" who was "soft on crime." McPhail attacked the Democratic standard-bearer's support for abortion and gun control, and his opposition to the death penalty, school prayer, and mandatory prison sentences for drug dealers.[6]

Public opinion polls up until August gave the Democrats some hope for victory. One Mason-Dixon poll revealed that Mississippians had relatively centrist views on many specific issues, especially involving economics. Mississippians supported more federal spending to help the poor, improve education, support social security, fight acquired immune deficiency syndrome (AIDS), and help the farmer. Residents were divided on the issues of abortion and whether to cut defense spending.[7] Meanwhile, support for Dukakis grew as the Democratic party unified behind him. While Bush's support remained steady at 50 percent, Dukakis's support in Mississippi grew from 39 percent in a June 9–12 Mason-

Dixon poll to 43 percent by August 1–3.[8] However, presaging the fall campaign, in which symbols would become so important to many voters, 71 percent of Mississippians opposed removing the replica of the Confederate battle flag from the state flag, an action sought by some black leaders.[9]

The state Dukakis campaign continued to mount a serious campaign to carry the state. In early August, Michael Dukakis himself became the first presidential candidate since Reagan in 1980 to visit the Neshoba County Fair, the most prominent forum for political speech making in the state. Dukakis reminded the crowd of the Democratic party's domination of state offices, and praised Governor Mabus and retiring Senator Stennis. He attacked the Reagan administration's management of government in the areas of fiscal policy, Attorney General Edwin Meese's legal problems, and White House dealings with Panamanian strongman Manuel Noriega and the Iranians, and promised a real war against drugs. However, the modest crowd of 3 to 5,000 alternated between jeers and cheers, and some held signs ranging from "Stop Abortion, Stop Dukakis" to "No More Comedians in the White House." One small group of protesters organized by white supremacist Richard Barrett carried a sign reading, "Real Democrats have red necks, white skin, and blue collars."[10]

Perhaps the most telling speech at the Neshoba County Fair had come the day before from George Bush's son, Neil. Referring to his father as a man who believed in "basic values, in family, in patriotism," he attacked Dukakis as being a tax-and-spend liberal who opposed prayer and the Pledge of Allegiance but favored abortion and gun control. Trumpeted Neil Bush, Dukakis "is a card-carrying member of the American Civil Liberties Union . . . We can't afford to return to the day when liberals controlled the presidency and when the liberals controlled both houses of the Congress."[11] State Democratic officials valiantly sought to defend Dukakis, as Secretary of State Dick Molpus accused Neil Bush of "the same old liberal-conservative, mean-spirited rhetoric of 20 years ago" that had divided the state. State Treasurer Marshall Bennett labeled Dukakis's speech as a "solid pride in America speech" to which the crowd was receptive. Democratic State Party Chairman Ed Cole, the only black state party chairman in the country, concluded that Dukakis was "a lot like the average Mississippian. He's for decent housing and good jobs."[12]

Meanwhile, state Republicans geared up for the tough campaign. Former state legislator Charles Pickering of Laurel sounded the Republican theme, claiming that Dukakis's only experience in government was in "raising taxes," and touted the Reagan years. "We've had it so good the past eight years. There is peace and prosperity."[13] Quickly unifying the Republican party, former Dole supporter Thad Cochran was selected as chief advisor on agriculture issues to the Bush campaign, and was included in the teams of "truth squads," teams of Republican speakers touring the country on Bush's behalf.[14] Also selected by the state Republican party to lead the effort for the national and congressional tickets, Cochran enumerated the Bush assets of "competence, strength, a sense of direction, and proven leadership ability."[15] Former Reagan White House aide

Haley Barbour of Yazoo City and longtime party activist Clarke Reed were also picked by the Bush camp to aid the presidential effort.[16]

State Democrats continued to plan a serious effort to carry the state for Dukakis. The Dukakis state campaign effort was led by a veteran of the Espy and Mabus campaigns, Michael Matthews, and Democratic activist Shirley Terry from Natchez. Assisted by two staff members from the Democratic National Committee, the Dukakis campaign pooled its resources with other Democratic campaigns in the state in voter registration, phone banks, and voter turnout efforts.[17] In a speech to the state American Federation of Labor and Congress of Industrial Organizations (AFL-CIO) convention in Biloxi on August 23, Dukakis's son promised "a good job at a decent wage" if his father were elected, and also talked about his support for plant-closing legislation, social security cost of living adjustments, and agriculture. Lashing out at the Republicans, he termed the Republican convention a "festival for the far right, a Mardi Gras for the Moral Majority."[18]

The selection of Quayle as Bush's vice presidential running mate momentarily gave the Democrats an important issue. Democratic activist and Dean of Jackson State University Graduate School Leslie McLemore said that the choice indicated that "Bush and his people didn't exercise the best of judgment."[19] At a visit to the largely black universities Mississippi Valley State and Jackson State to encourage voter registration, Jesse Jackson attacked Quayle for a lack of appreciation for the plight of the poor, dispossessed, and those who are discriminated against. He also accused Bush of being born wealthy and therefore lacking an understanding of the disadvantaged. Borrowing a line from Jim Hightower's speech at the Democratic convention, Jackson added, "George Bush was born on third base and thought he hit a triple." Ridiculing the Republicans, Jackson said, "George Bush wants to hide Quayle and hide from Noriega, but there is no hiding place. Can you imagine President Quayle? The last time there was a great flood, the Lord sent a dove from out of the sky. He did not pull a Quayle from under a Bush."[20] Some Democratic state officials also expressed disappointment at Quayle's speech before the Southern Legislative Conference. House Speaker Tim Ford pointed out that "his speech didn't have much substance," and state Representative Charlie Capps of Cleveland felt that "he didn't get into the issues that separate the Democrats from the Republicans."[21]

Meanwhile, political observers were giving high marks to Dukakis's running mate, Lloyd Bentsen. At the same conference, many legislators praised Bentsen's knowledgeable criticisms of the Republican ticket. "Bentsen's experience and knowledge was [sic] certainly evident," commented Speaker Tim Ford.[22] While touring the University of Mississippi Medical Center's children's hospital in Jackson, Bentsen promised more spending for rural health care and infant care programs. The state's First Lady, Julie Mabus, praised Bentsen for authoring legislation that led to more Medicaid funding, especially for mothers and babies.[23] Senator Stennis praised Bentsen: "This man . . . no one excels him. . . . This man is qualified, this man is dedicated, this man is devoted." However, syndicated columnist Carl Rowan claimed that Dukakis had decided to "lay low and let running mate Bentsen sell him in the South." Rowan concluded that "Dukakis had better get off his butt, and out of Massachusetts, and go sell himself in the South and the border states."[24]

By mid-September it was becoming evident that the Dukakis campaign had not caught on in Mississippi. A Mississippi State University poll showed Bush with 55 percent and Dukakis dropping to 33 percent. The state's veteran political columnist Bill Minor captured the mood of the state in his quote of a veteran Democratic political observer:

Dukakis is just not perceived as being "one of us." He's from Massachusetts and he has a funny-sounding name and he is perceived as not sound on national defense and the flag-waving issues that are big with Mississippians. . . . Bush's campaign pitch on patriotism, abortion, and anti-liberalism is tailor-made to appeal to the Mississippi electorate.[25]

By late September there were reports that the Dukakis campaign would soon begin pulling back budget and staff from southern states like Mississippi that were likely to go for Bush, prompting top Dukakis aides to deny these reports and even add a press secretary to its Mississippi staff.[26]

The hemorrhage continued. In the face of Bush's greater sympathy for civil rights compared to Reagan's, state Republicans hoped to attract more black support with efforts like their mentor program, in which Republican leaders volunteer to be a political godparent to younger blacks.[27] At a three-day meeting of the directors of the National Association for the Advancement of Colored People (NAACP) in Jackson, black leaders contended that both presidential candidates had ignored issues of major concern to blacks or dealt with them only in platitudes and generalities. NAACP Executive Director Benjamin Hooks complained that the campaign was focusing on "whether somebody can drive a tank or pledge allegiance to the flag" instead of major concerns. He maintained that there was "an absence of enthusiasm over the election, which could affect the turnout."[28] In late October, Fayette Mayor Charles Evers, brother of slain civil rights leader Medgar Evers, endorsed Bush because of "his experience and his relationship with Ronald Reagan. They're working to try to bring America around. People have to have jobs, and I'm for people working for a living." According to Evers, Dukakis "thinks you should have welfare and food stamps and all that bull."[29]

Things continued to go well for the Bush campaign. By mid-October, about thirty Bush-Quayle campaign offices were spread across the state, and yard signs and bumper stickers covered the landscape.[30] State political observers felt that Bush had performed very well in the second televised debate, being "warm and relaxed," while Dukakis was the "cold, rational technocrat . . . whining and disjointed."[31] In a last-ditch effort, on October 31, Halloween, Democratic party leaders held seven press conferences across the state to denounce the Bush attacks on Dukakis. "For the past three months, George Bush and Dan Quayle have been celebrating Halloween at the expense of Mississippians and the American people,'' said Bill Collins, head of the Oktibbeha County Democratic Executive Committee, at one conference. "They have served up a campaign cauldron full of trickery and deceptions. They have lied about Mike Dukakis and Lloyd Bentsen and have distorted their own records.'' Collins argued that Dukakis supported the right to bear arms, would not raise taxes, and was not soft on defense, and he pointed out that the Massachusetts furlough program had been started by a previous Republican governor.[32]

In the final days of the campaign, most newspapers endorsed the Bush candidacy. Endorsing Bush, the Jackson *Clarion Ledger,* the major statewide newspaper, cited the "growth, peace, and prosperity for the past eight years,'' and lauded his support for the free marketplace, a strong military, and a "gentler America.'' Dukakis was accused of being,

clearly out of step with the views of Mississippians. He has barely asked voters of this state to support him, and has offered few reasons why they should. . . . He was one of the weaker candidates of the weak Democratic field as far as the South and Mississippi is [sic] concerned. The governor of Massachusetts simply does not translate in Mississippi.[33]

Meanwhile, Republican state leaders were touring the state, warning voters to guard against overconfidence and to head to the polls on November 8. They said that the party had had 5,000 volunteers working statewide, and that GOP workers would be in 1,500 precincts on election day.[34] On the Sunday before Election Day, these front page headlines in the *Clarion Ledger/Jackson Daily News* greeted Mississippians: "Bush, Lott way out front in statewide polls; Republican hopeful leads Dukakis by 2–1 margin,'' and "Bush jabs at 'liberal' opponent; Dukakis targets middle class.''[35] Election Day had become anticlimactic.

The Senate Campaign

The Senate campaign promised to be a very tough contest between a middle-of-the road Democrat, Wayne Dowdy, and a conservative Republican, Trent Lott. Throughout the campaign at rallies with the party faithful, Lott trumpeted his conservative philosophy. In rural Pike County, he said:

I'm a conservative and that means get the government off their backs, out of their pockets and out of their lives. . . . Hey, federal government, don't try to control our guns; leave us alone; we will defend ourselves and we will live our lives in Mississippi without you telling us how to do it.[36]

At a Clarksdale appearance he declared, "The best thing the federal government can do for you, other than to provide basic things like roads, is to get off the back of businessmen and women and industry, and let the American free enterprise system work."[37] At Mississippi College he asserted, "Dowdy looks for all solutions from Washington. I look for solutions from the people, from the individual, from the family, from the community, from the church or synagogue, from the people and it rises up to Washington."[38]

Dowdy, on the other hand, projected a more moderate image of liberalism on public works and entitlement programs that benefited a poor state like Mississippi, and conservatism on defense, foreign, and social issues.[39] In a meeting with the Jackson *Clarion Ledger* editorial board, Dowdy described himself as a "progressive," and outlined his support for extending the Voting Rights Act and protecting the environment.[40] Many political observers felt that Lott was vulnerable on the issues, as he had voted against civil rights issues like the Voting Rights Act, the Civil Rights Restoration Act, the Martin Luther King holiday, and sanctions against South Africa, while voting to cut funding from many domestic programs like social security, child nutrition, homeless assistance, college student aid, catastrophic health insurance, hazardous waste cleanup, and the Clean Water Act. Dowdy had voted to support these domestic and civil rights programs.[41]

Lott anticipated the Dowdy camp's attacks on his record by saturating the airwaves with a series of attractive television advertisements produced by the Robert Goodman agency in Washington, D.C. Columnist Bill Minor pointed out that in national political circles, Goodman's nickname was "Dr. Feelgood," because of his ability to portray his candidates in a very positive light. One ad pictured Lott as a defender of social security cuts proposed by Washington bureaucrats, and cited David Stockman's quotation of Lott's reaction to one set of proposed cuts, "No Way. Period. End of discussion."[42] Nonetheless, reports circulated in newspapers that Lott had only a 60 percent rating from the National Committee to Preserve Social Security and Medicare, while Dowdy boasted a 100 percent rating.[43] When questioned by an elderly citizen at a fish fry, Lott responded, "My mother is 75 and lives on Social Security and [Dowdy's] family is worth $60 million. Which one of us is going to be more likely to support Social Security?"[44] Dowdy forces countered with a ten-second television ad stating: "Trent Lott has voted to cut Social Security and Medicare. For his true record write: 'CUTS' in care of the Dowdy campaign headquarters."[45]

Another classic ad had Lott talking with college students, explaining that a college grant had helped him attend school. The ad claimed that when the Washington budget cutters tried to cut student loans, Lott said no and saved the program. The powerful Mississippi Association of Educators (MAE) endorsed and actively supported Dowdy, praising his 100 percent rating from that organization on votes concerning education, and condemning Lott's "dismal zero" rating in the last Congress.[46] Lott responded by pointing out the Democratic party orientation of the MAE: "They almost universally endorse liberals and Democrats."[47]

Yet another attractive television ad featured Lott dressed in khaki pants and a plaid flannel shirt with the sleeves rolled up, inviting viewers to "take a ride with me" in a pickup truck as he outlined his commitment to four-laning rural highways like "bloody 98."[48] Dowdy campaign manager Dean Pittman accused Lott of voting to cut highway money at least thirteen times since 1981, and of misleading voters with this ad as well as the social security and education ads.[49] Dowdy also held a news conference at the intersection of two of the highways for which Lott had allegedly voted to cut federal funding, and pointed out that forty-three deaths had occurred on one stretch in recent years.[50]

Meanwhile, Lott's voting record had also gotten him in trouble with various environmental groups. Environmental Action placed Lott on the group's "Dirty Dozen" list of "bench-sitters in the war against pollution." Lott's press secretary Tom Bagwill called it "a partisan election-year attack . . . by a left-wing liberal organization with its head in the sand."[51] The National Toxics Campaign claimed that Lott had "one of the worst environmental records in the House of Representatives," and the Mississippi chapter of the Sierra Club endorsed Dowdy as a "friend of the environment."[52]

Negative campaign ads were also evident in the campaign. Lott attacked Dowdy's attendance record on roll call votes, which had dipped to 68 percent by the end of 1987, picking up an issue used by Dowdy's opponent for the Democratic senate nomination, Secretary of State Dick Molpus.[53] Dowdy attacked Lott's use of a chauffeur-guard provided to House leaders. Showing a gray limousine driving across the countryside, the announcer said, "That chauffeur must be more important to Trent Lott than the people of Mississippi." The ad showed the limousine driving past poor people in dilapidated housing while discussing Lott's votes to cut domestic programs. The ad concluded by saying that voters had the chance to "vote for a party politician who looks at life through tinted windows or . . . vote for a senator who sees Mississippi through the eyes of its people."[54]

The Lott campaign promptly countered with a thirty-second television ad featuring George Awkward, the chauffeur-guard, wearing a large handgun in his leather shoulder holster. The black guard explained that he had been a Washington, D.C., law enforcement veteran for twenty-seven years: "Mr. Dowdy, I'm nobody's chauffeur. Got it?"[55] At a televised debate in Jackson, Dowdy pursued his attack by exhorting the voters to "cut George." Lott responded that Dowdy had voted for the appropriation bill providing the chauffeur-guard, and then deadpanned: "I've got a better idea. Let's cut Wayne. At least George shows up for work and he makes less than you do."[56] At a forum in late September, the moderator expressed the concerns of many political observers about the course of the campaign: "We have two good candidates for the U.S. Senate, and I'm just sorry they're dissipating so much energy on negativism."[57]

Another important campaign issue of Dowdy's was the cry that "Mississippi can't afford two Republican Senators." Columnists like Sid Salter and Bill Minor also expressed concerns that the state might lose influence and federal funds by failing to have at least one Senator from the party that controlled the Senate.[58]

Lott pointed out that he had been able to effectively serve his district for sixteen years as a member of the minority party, and that two Republican Senators would work well with a Republican-controlled White House if Bush were elected.[59]

Lott continued to stress themes often relied on by incumbents, such as influence in Washington and constituency service. Newspaper pictures showed House Minority Whip Trent Lott meeting with other prominent political leaders like Senate Minority Leader Dole.[60] In campaign stops, Lott promised to immediately be a force for Mississippi in the upper chamber:

I just won't be hanging around. The first day on the floor they won't be asking, "Who's the new guy from Mississippi?" . . . I know Bob Dole, Bob Byrd, Howard Metzenbaum, Ted Kennedy—some of them I'd just as soon not know. But I know them, and I've already done battle with them and against them.[61]

Lott also defended his political philosophy: "I may vote against some of these national programs, but if it passes, I will work to make sure Mississippi gets more than its share." On the Gulf Coast, Lott claimed credit for the $8 million Fort Bayou Bridge in Ocean Springs, and in Hattiesburg his spokesperson claimed that Lott had secured federal funding for flood control projects in Hattiesburg and Laurel.[62] In a stop in northeast Mississippi, Lott pledged more jobs and improved roads.[63] The Republican also received strong support from business, receiving an in-person endorsement in Jackson from the head of the U.S. Chamber of Commerce and the Guardian of Small Business award from the National Federation of Independent Business.[64]

Initially, most political observers expected Lott to do poorly among black voters because of Republican traditional weaknesses among this liberal group and because of Dowdy's stronger record on civil rights.[65] Consistent with Lott's pledge to serve all Mississippians, a group called Blacks for Trent Lott was formed, headed by Isadora Hyde of Moss Point. Hyde argued that Lott would be more effective than Dowdy, and would bring more jobs and promote economic development for the state.[66] Lott even courted the black vote at the annual Delta Blues Festival in Greenville, where some festivalgoers who derided welfare were impressed with his pledge to bring more jobs to the state.[67] In mid-September, Drew lawyer Cleve McDowell, a former state NAACP field director for the Delta counties, announced that he was working for Lott because of his jobs pledge and because he looked like he would win the election.[68] Fayette Mayor Charles Evers also endorsed Lott, and expressed a hope that his conservative philosophy would gradually be modified.[69] Columnist Bill Minor saw support for Lott emerging among younger blacks, black businessmen, and professionals.[70]

In late September, the Dowdy forces unleashed the stunning news that Lott had hired only 2 blacks among the 163 people he had hired since 1972.[71] Lott claimed that he had hired "many" blacks, but declined to provide specific numbers because "I don't keep count."[72] Later, he said that he had hired 5 or

6 blacks, and that "with one or two exceptions, I've hired every black that's come to me for a job." Since Lott's Fifth District is only 17 percent black and Lott is a conservative Republican, it is quite plausible that very few blacks did ask him for a job, though that itself demonstrated a political problem in attracting black support for this campaign. Lott pledged that blacks would comprise a larger percentage of his Senate staff if he were elected.[73]

Meanwhile, Dowdy used his good ole country boy, homespun, aw-shucks approach to communicate earnestness and humility.[74] Country music stars like Mel Tillis made radio ads for him, aimed primarily at rural north Mississippi.[75] Consistently down in the polls by about 8 points, Dowdy mounted the "Victory Express" for a 1940s style whistle-stop train tour, evoking memories of Truman's come-from-behind victory. However, symbolic of the campaign's overall difficulties, the train was hindered by two derailments.[76]

In addition to the heavy focus on the candidates' personal qualities and issue positions, party politics also played an important role in the campaigns. Lott's campaign was assisted by a $5,000 picture-taking, fund-raising dinner in Washington, D.C., with President Reagan, prompting Dowdy's campaign manager to joke, "We give away our pictures for free."[77] At the Neshoba County Fair, Lott asked the audience: "Do you want one that is going to follow in the line of McGovern, Mondale, O'Neill, Wright, Jackson, and Dukakis? Or do you want one that's going to continue the Reagan revolution and elect George Bush President?" He also linked himself with popular Republican Senator Thad Cochran by quipping, "Thad and Trent. TNT is dynamite."[78] Cochran campaigned for Lott, calling him a man of influence, character, and power, who would be a very valuable asset and resource for the state.[79] The Lott campaign also received boosts from visits by Representative Jack Kemp, former Tennessee Governor Lamar Alexander, and Republican senators John McCain of Arizona, John Warner of Virginia, Nancy Kassebaum of Kansas, Robert Kasten of Wisconsin, Orrin Hatch of Utah, and Don Nickles of Oklahoma.[80]

Dowdy forces initially were eager to tag Lott as a Republican party loyalist. "It is obvious that Trent Lott has voted straight party loyalty throughout his career and against some things that could have helped rural Mississippians," said one Dowdy supporter.[81] "He has gone along with every cut in education," said national Democratic party campaign officials.[82] Popular southern Democratic Senators such as Albert Gore of Tennessee, Lloyd Bentsen of Texas, Sam Nunn of Georgia, and J. Bennett Johnston of Louisiana, stumped the state on behalf of Dowdy.[83] Dowdy especially linked himself with popular Senator John Stennis, who boosted Dowdy at a Washington fund-raiser in May, provided a written endorsement in August, and then made a television commercial for him in the closing days of the campaign. Stennis stressed Dowdy's sincerity, his sense of purpose, and his commitment to the people, saying, "[he] understands the real needs of Mississippi, and I have full confidence that he will be a valued and effective member of the Senate."[84] In late October, Dowdy, "whose silence about Democratic presidential candidate Michael Dukakis [was] deafening," expressed concern that Dukakis's lagging presidential campaign in Mississippi was hurting his own prospects for election.[85]

An important advantage of the Lott effort throughout was superior campaign resources. In an early October newspaper headline, "Lott Campaign Resources Dishearten Dowdy Camp," it was estimated that Lott would outspend Dowdy by $3.5 million to $1.5 million. (A post-campaign report indicated that Lott's advantage was not as great as anticipated, however, as Lott reported spending $3.2 million to Dowdy's $2.1 million.) "People are running scared, but it's not at a panic level yet," observed Democratic Party Chairman Ed Cole about the Republican advantage in the polls, money, yard signs and bumper stickers, and campaign county and precinct organization.[86] After saving his money for the last few weeks of the campaign, Dowdy forces launched a series of "talking-head," thirty-second television commercials with the candidate discussing various economic issues.[87] In the final days of the campaign, despite Dowdy's reputation in his previous elections for coming from behind at the last minute, it looked as if Lott's lead would hold. Lott toured the state counseling against complacency and urging his supporters to turn out on election day. He also pictured himself as a defender of the working class against a tax-hungry federal government.[88] After the Jackson *Clarion Ledger* endorsed Wayne Dowdy, the Lott forces purchased an ad in that newspaper that reprinted the Memphis *Commercial Appeal*'s endorsement of Lott.[89] The final pre-election poll commissioned by the *Clarion Ledger/Jackson Daily News* found Lott leading Dowdy by a 48 percent to 34 percent margin with 18 percent uncommitted.[90] On the day before the election, Dowdy greeted workers at a shift change at a Natchez tire and rubber plant, while Lott campaigned in his hometown of Pascagoula after voting on Election Day.[91]

The House Campaigns

A major theme of the congressional incumbents was constituency service—keeping in touch with their constituents and bringing jobs and federal projects to their districts. During his first term, Second District Congressman Mike Espy spoke to numerous chambers of commerce, Rotary Clubs, and black churches. He boasted of helping his district by creating the Lower Mississippi River Delta Development Commission, attracting federal funds for an extension of the Greenwood-Leflore County airport runway and a federal loan for an electronics company that brought eighty-five new jobs to Yazoo City, and establishing National Catfish Day and increasing the Defense Department's purchase of the district's pond-raised catfish.[92] In August he had toured the Delta Pride catfish processing plant in Indianola with potential client U.S. Army Secretary John Marsh, had had a catfish lunch with several dozen Delta mayors and supervisors, and had discussed steering other military purchases to the impoverished district.[93]

Another important theme of incumbents was their seniority and power in Washington. The power of veteran congressmen Jamie Whitten of the First

District, Chair of the powerful Appropriations Committee, and Sonny Montgomery of the Third District, Chair of the Veterans Affairs Committee and a leading "Boll Weevil" conservative, was quite evident to political observers. Regarding freshman Espy, in July, House Majority Leader Thomas Foley of Washington attended a fund-raiser for him in Greenville.[94] In late October, senators Nunn and Johnston praised Espy at a news conference, touting his influence and his success at helping the state's image and uniting the white and black communities.[95]

By early 1988 it was evident that Congressman Espy was expanding upon the 10 percent of whites who had supported him in 1986. In February it was reported that at least 30 percent of his campaign contributions had come from white delta farmers.[96] In April he announced a campaign committee with biracial coordination in each county that included many prominent white public officials, farmers, businessmen, and teachers.[97] On Labor Day, Hiram Eastland, second cousin to one-time segregationist former Senator James Eastland, hosted a biracial gathering in honor of Espy at the Eastland family's Adair Plantation Home in Doddsville.[98]

Meanwhile, Espy's conservative Republican challenger, Jack Coleman, a former Reagan appointee to the Commerce Department and head of a defense contractors trade association, aggressively publicized the Congressman's liberal voting record.[99] Espy's liberal record included support for more federal domestic spending for child care, housing, catastrophic health care, and adult illiteracy and reduced defense spending for the Strategic Defense Initiative, the MX missile, the B-1 bomber, and aid to the Nicaraguan Contras. Espy also supported federal funding for abortions for poor women, a sixty-day notice plant-closing provision, and a strengthened Fair Housing Act and Civil Rights Restoration Act.[100] However, Espy also touted some of his conservative postures, such as supporting the death penalty for drug kingpins, a balanced budget amendment, and opposing gun control, for which he received the endorsement of the National Rifle Association.[101] When Coleman charged that Espy's support for defense cuts could hurt defense industries in the district, Espy's spokesperson responded that the Congressman was currently traveling with several Greenville businessmen to meet with Boeing Company executives about steering more contract work to the district.[102]

At a speech before the state's AFL-CIO convention, Espy expressed concern that possible Bush and Lott coattails could defeat him, and in October one poll showed Coleman only 10 points behind the Congressman.[103] However, prominent Republicans like Senator Cochran declined to campaign with Coleman, and columnist Bill Minor accused the Republican challenger of skirting "close to injecting racism into the campaign."[104] In the face of numerous prominent political leaders campaigning for Espy, Coleman was reduced to publicizing a campaign visit by Assistant Secretary of the Agriculture Department, George Dunlop.[105]

Coleman was not the only challenger who faced the frustrating experience of trying to gain enough name recognition to defeat an incumbent. Black Independent Second Congressional District candidate Dorothy Benford, who had earlier been fined $1,000 for malicious mischief in smashing the car window of Jesse Jackson's state campaign coordinator after being told that her support was not welcomed, was fined $67 for reckless driving after allegedly almost hitting three children as her car ran down Espy campaign signs.[106] Congressman Sonny Montgomery's Republican challenger Jimmie Bourland, an excavating contractor making his first bid for public office, became so frustrated over his inability to receive media coverage that he climbed up a 500-foot television tower.[107]

Closer races were expected for the open seats being vacated by Fourth District Congressman Dowdy and Fifth District Congressman Lott. In the Fourth District, Moderate conservative Brookhaven funeral home owner Mike Parker faced conservative Republican Tom Collins. The son of a Baptist preacher, Parker had upset more politically prominent Democrats in the primary by touting grassroots support, a no-strings-attached campaign theme, and a television campaign helped by a personal loan.[108] Collins, a prisoner of war (POW) during the Vietnam War and former director of the Mississippi Veterans Home Purchase Board, credited his nomination to a grass-roots campaign, support by veterans groups and the elderly, and a last-minute surge of support.[109]

Throughout the campaign Collins sought to place the unpopular "liberal" label on Parker. He charged that Parker had "bought" the Democratic party nomination, and that he had accepted campaign contributions from "out-of-state liberal organizations" like House Speaker Jim Wright, the Democratic Campaign Committee, and pro-labor political action committees.[110] "My opponent's party can't wait to get to Washington so they can raise taxes. . . . My opponent is obligated to the liberal agenda," said Collins. Parker shrugged off identification with ideological terms by saying, "I'm a Mike Parker Mississippi Democrat."[111] One unidentified campaign brochure even contained the following excerpt from the conservative magazine *Human Events*: "Like the Viet Cong that Thomas Collins once faced in the elephant grass of Southeast Asia, Democratic nominee Mike Parker is an enemy that is difficult to find but very deadly."[112]

Meanwhile, Parker, touting the endorsement of the Mississippi Association of Educators, continued to use his spending advantage for effective television commercials that projected his homespun values of earnestness and dedication.[113] In a meeting with Jackson police officers on the Sunday before the election, Parker stressed his homespun, I'm-just-like-you appeal. He told officers that his brother was a police officer, and that he understood the psychological pressures that officers faced. Admitting that he was not a brilliant man, but was "just like you are, just an everyday person," he pledged to bring common sense to Congress.[114]

Two conservatives associated with local and state reform efforts faced off in the Fifth Congressional District. Popular Harrison County Sheriff Republican Larkin Smith of Pass Christian was benefited by a sizeable funding advantage over Democratic State Legislator Gene Taylor of Bay St. Louis. Among the issues, Smith argued the need for a Republican in Washington if Bush were elected President, while Taylor cited his legislative accomplishments and familiarity with state issues.[115] Forgoing liberal political action committee (PAC) money because of his conservative positions, Taylor's funding woes were helped a little by Governor Mabus, who endorsed him, hosted a $100-per-ticket lunch, and made a ten-second commercial.[116] The state Democratic party dispatched its executive director, Brian Martin, to help run the Taylor campaign while remaining on the state party's payroll.[117]

RESULTS AND ANALYSIS

Election Day in Mississippi provided few surprises, as all the pre-election favorites won. Heavily entrenched Democratic incumbents Jamie Whitten and Sonny Montgomery won re-election with 78 and 89 percent respectively of the vote. The power of incumbency had become so potent that even a black freshman Congressman like Mike Espy was re-elected by a landslide 66 percent of the vote in a state that had historically been preoccupied with the race question. In the open districts, popular pre-election favorites were elected with 55 percent of the vote each—Democrat Mike Parker in the Fourth District and Republican Larkin Smith of the Fifth District. Popular, well-funded Republican Trent Lott was elected to the U.S. Senate with a more narrow 53 percent of the vote in a tough campaign. Mississippians also voted for Republican George Bush for President by a landslide 61 percent of the vote.

In each case it appears that the candidate's overall image, especially as shaped by the mass media, was the key in winning the election.[118] Bush, for example, was advantaged by the issues and by his personal attributes. Twenty-four percent of voters mentioned issues as a reason for voting for Bush, while only 15 percent mentioned issues as a reason for their vote for Dukakis (Table 6.1). Bush was especially advantaged by general issue comments of a nonideological nature, such as "I like his issue positions" and "I like his stand on economics." While 14 percent favored Bush's conservative views on issues generally, or on taxes, defense, and moral issues specifically, a sizeable 11 percent of voters favored Dukakis's liberal positions on issues generally or on domestic economic, moral, or civil rights policies.

In addition to general issue concerns, candidate attributes also helped Bush. Thirteen percent of voters said they preferred Bush's ability, experience, qualifications, or empathy, or said they just "liked him," while only 4 percent of voters made similar comments about Dukakis. While 31 percent of voters mentioned partisan considerations for their vote, these factors benefited both candidates equally. While Dukakis was benefited more by being a Democrat and by arguing that it was "time for a change," Bush was helped more by voter approval of Reagan and Reagan's performance in office over the past eight years.

In the Senate race, Trent Lott was benefited by an image of superior personal qualities and performance in office. Seventeen percent of voters preferred Lott's

Table 6.1
Reasons Voters Offered for Their Candidate Preferences, by Candidate
(in percent)*

Reason	Dukakis	Bush	Dowdy	Lott
Party identification	13	9	12	9
Party performance	1	3	0	1
Liked Reagan	0	3	0	0
Change is needed	2	0	1	0
Party-related factors, total	16	15	13	10
Ideology	1	7	1	4
Economics	1	3	0	1
Taxes	0	1	0	0
Liberal on domestic economic programs	8	0	4	0
For minorities	1	0	1	0
Social-moral issues	1	4	0	0
Defense	0	2	0	0
Quayle factor	0	2	0	0
Issues in general	3	5	4	6
Issues, total	15	24	10	11
General candidate factor--liked candidate	2	8	4	8
Ability, experience, qualified	1	4	2	5
Influential in Washington	0	0	0	2
Empathy, trust him	1	1	1	2
Candidate factors, total	4	13	7	17
Performance--general approval	2	2	2	8
Helped Mississippi	0	0	1	3
Absent voting record	0	0	0	1
Know more about him; had contact with him	0	0	2	3
Performance factors, total	2	2	5	15
Other responses	0	1	0	1
Don't know	3	5	4	7
Total responses for each candidate	40	60	39	61

*Cell entries indicate the percentage of votes for each office who indicated the listed reasons for voting for a preferred candidate. Underlined numbers are totals for groups of factors. Responses for the first two columns total 100 percent, as do the responses for the third and fourth columns.

Source: Mississippi State University poll, September 1988; the poll is a statewide, random-digit telephone survey of likely voters.

experience, ability, and qualifications to his opponent's; cited his influence and empathy with the voters; or just said they "liked him" (Table 6.1). A smaller number (7 percent) of voters cited similar reasons for a vote for Dowdy. Regarding job performance, 15 percent of voters preferred Lott because they knew more about him, felt he had helped Mississippi, or just felt he had "done a good job." Fewer voters (5 percent) gave similar reasons for voting for Dowdy. Since the election outcome was significantly closer than this particular poll found in early September, these numbers for Lott are inflated, but they still illustrate the basic themes that helped elect him to the Senate.

Policy issues and partisanship did not appear to be significant factors in the outcome of the Senate election. While 10 percent of voters preferred Lott for partisan reasons, such as his Republican affiliation or his party's performance in the White House in recent years, 13 percent of voters liked Dowdy for similar partisan reasons, such as his Democratic affiliation or their feeling that a change in party control of government was needed. Only 21 percent of voters mentioned issues as the reason for their Senate vote, compared to 39 percent who had mentioned issue reasons for their presidential vote. On balance, neither senate candidate was benefited significantly by issues, since 11 percent of these issue comments favored Lott while 10 percent favored Dowdy. While some conservative Lott backers later claimed that his ideology had helped elect him, only 4 percent of voters said that they had supported Lott because of his "conservatism." On the other hand, 6 percent of voters preferred Dowdy because of his general liberalism, liberalism on domestic economic programs, or support for civil rights.

This analysis does not completely rule out the impact of ideological concerns on presidential and senate voting, since some of the general comments about liking the candidate or his job performance may have been affected by ideological issues that were not specifically mentioned. It is, therefore, interesting to compare voters' own ideological preferences with those of the candidates, and examine the ideological images that voters had of the candidates.

The ideological center of Mississippi voters is basically the moderate conservative philosophy. Twenty-three percent of voters call themselves moderate conservative; in the immediately adjacent categories, 29 percent are conservatives and 29 percent are moderates or have no preference; only 19 percent of voters are liberal or moderate liberal (Table 6.2). Because of the moderate conservative orientation of many voters, many political observers expected a close senate race between moderate Wayne Dowdy and conservative Trent Lott. In September, many voters misperceived Dowdy as being more liberal than he really was, as 24 percent labeled him a liberal. Compared to voters themselves, Dowdy was perceived as more liberal by 14 percent and as less conservative by 19 percent. By Election Day this misperception gap may have narrowed as the race narrowed, and, if Dowdy had had more money for television advertising, the gap might have been erased.

Lott, on the other hand, was successful at portraying himself as a moderate conservative with his television commercials. Indeed, 14 percent of voters labeled Lott a liberal or moderate liberal and 34 percent as a moderate, while only 35 percent accurately perceived him as a conservative. Lott's moderate conservative image was more in line with the voters' own political philosophy than was their perception of Dowdy's position.

In the presidential race, Bush's moderate conservative philosophy was very much in line with Mississippi voters' views, while Dukakis's moderate liberal

Table 6.2
Voter Perceptions of Candidate Ideology (in percent)*

Item	Liberal	Moderate Liberal	Moderate/ Don't Know	Moderate Conserv- ative	Conserv- ative
Voter Perceptions					
All voters	10	9	29	23	29
Perception of Dowdy	24	14	44	8	10
Perception of Lott	9	5	34	17	35
Perception of Bush	8	4	29	20	39
Perception of Dukakis	41	15	34	3	7
Deviation					
Dowdy - Voters	+14	+ 5	+15	-15	-19
Lott - Voters	- 1	- 4	+ 5	- 6	+ 6
Bush - Voters	- 2	- 5	0	- 3	+10
Dukakis - Voters	+31	+ 6	+ 5	-20	-22

*Cell entries listed under "voter perceptions" reflect voters' own ideo-
logical positions and their perceptions of the candidates' positions.
Each row totals 100 percent.

Source: Mississippi State University poll, September 1988.

philosophy was regarded as too liberal. Indeed, 41 percent of voters felt that
Dukakis was a liberal, which posed a problem for him since only 10 percent of
voters called themselves liberals (table 6.2). While 52 percent of voters regarded
themselves as conservatives or moderate conservatives, only ten percent of voters
attached the same labels to Dukakis. In short, voters perceived Dukakis's philosophy as being too liberal compared to their own political values.

As Mississippi politics nationalizes and voters respond to the same kinds of
candidate appeals as do voters in other states, electoral differences between social
groups have also come to mirror those that exist nationally.[119] In the 1988
electoral decisions, ideological and partisan divisions were quite evident, as self-
identified liberals and Democrats were much more likely to vote for Dukakis
and Dowdy compared to conservatives and Republicans, who favored Republicans Bush and Lott more (Table 6.3). Socioeconomic status (SES) differences
were also large, as lower income and less-educated groups were substantially
more likely to support Democratic candidates than were higher SES groups, who
preferred Republicans. Racial differences were also as great as those that existed
nationally, as whites were much more likely to vote Republican compared to
blacks, who were heavily Democratic. Gender, age, and residency length were

Table 6.3
Voter Preferences by Selected Demographic Groups (in percent)*

Demographic Group	Dukakis	Bush	Dowdy	Lott
Ideology				
Liberal	64	36	75	25
Moderate	58	42	44	56
Conservative	20	80	31	69
Party				
Democratic	78	22	74	26
Independent	17	83	26	74
Republican	4	96	16	84
Income				
Under $10,000	72	28	61	39
$10,000-20,000	50	50	59	41
Over $20,000	27	73	31	69
Education				
Less than high school	63	37	55	45
High school graduate	32	68	52	48
Some college/college graduate	30	70	29	71
Race				
White	21	79	28	72
Black	83	17	85	15
Gender				
Male	35	65	45	55
Female	43	57	42	58
Age				
18-30	42	58	55	45
31-60	36	64	39	61
60+	50	50	44	56
Years lived in Mississippi				
15 years or less	33	67	38	62
More than 15 years	39	61	45	55

*Each cell entry represents the percentage of the identifed group voting
for the Democratic and Republican candidates for President and U. S.
Senate. Numbers in each row total 100 percent for each race.

Source: Data from the Mississippi State University poll for September
1988 (for the presidential race) and for April 1988 (for the U. S.
Senate race).

much less important factors in separating Mississippi voters into different candidate preference groups in 1988.

A closer examination of the partisan and racial groups sheds additional insight into the election outcomes. Republican identifiers were more supportive of their candidates than were Democrats, who constitute a more diverse and divided party. In pre-election polls, Bush and Lott were supported by 96 and 84 percent respectively of Republicans, while Dukakis and Dowdy were favored by more modest margins of 78 and 74 percent of Democrats. Independents went 83 percent for Bush and 74 percent for Lott, suggesting the popularity of the candidate-centered, nonpartisan themes of the two Republican nominees. Republican candidates also appeared poised to do somewhat better among blacks than previous party nominees, as Bush and Lott were drawing 17 and 15 percent of black support. Democratic candidates in the polls appeared relatively weak among whites, with only 21 and 28 percent support.

CONCLUSION

It is important to observe that Mississippi politics has been significantly nationalized as state voters are affected by the same forces that affect voters in other states. In the era of partisan dealignment and modern television advertising, Mississippians respond primarily to the overall images that the candidates provide. As in the rest of the nation, it is extremely difficult to defeat an incumbent because of his or her ability to concentrate on nondivisive issues like constituency service, casework, and attracting federal projects. Even Senate candidates for open races who have served in the U.S. House can deemphasize ideologically consistent voting records by stressing constituency service themes.

The increased nationalization of Mississippi politics and dealignment of voters away from both parties has also led to very intense and competitive electoral contests in open races. The 1988 election outcomes continue the trend of recent decades toward a true two-party system, especially in federal elections. The Republicans carried the state in their third consecutive presidential election, and captured the second U.S. Senate seat, though Democrats won four of the five U.S. House races. However, while Republicans came close in the 1987 gubernatorial election by winning 47 percent of the popular vote, Democrats have won all gubernatorial elections since Reconstruction, and heavily dominate state and local politics. The future promises increasingly fierce battles between the two state parties to win the hearts and minds of the increasingly independent Mississippi voter.

ACKNOWLEDGMENTS

The author gratefully acknowledges funding assistance from Mississippi State University and its Social Science Research Center, and the valuable graduate assistance provided by Yanru Chang.

NOTES

1. The turbulent changes the swept the state in the 1960s and 1970s are outlined in Jack Bass and Walter DeVries, *The Transformation of Southern Politics* (New York: Basic Books, 1976), 186–217. The salience of race in contemporary state electoral politics is discussed in Alexander P. Lamis, *The Two-Party South* (New York: Oxford University Press, 1984), 44–62. An excellent analysis of the extent to which realignment and dealignment are simultaneously sweeping the South is provided by Harold W. Stanley,

"Southern Partisan Changes: Dealignment, Realignment, or Both?" *Journal of Politics* 50 (February 1988): 64–88. How these twin processes have shaped Mississippi politics in the 1980s is detailed in Stephen D. Shaffer, "Changing Party Politics in Mississippi," in *The South's New Politics: Realignment and Dealignment*, ed. Robert H. Swansbrough and David M. Brodsky (Columbia: University of South Carolina Press, 1988), 189–203.

   2. *The Jackson Clarion-Ledger*, January 3, 1988, 1-B; January 15, 1988, 1-A; February 6, 1988, 4-B.
   3. *Clarion-Ledger*, February 12, 1988, 1-B.
   4. *Clarion-Ledger*, February 9, 1988, 2-B.
   5. *Clarion-Ledger*, March 9, 1988, 5-A.
   6. *Clarion-Ledger*, June 18, 1988, 1-A.
   7. *Clarion-Ledger*, February 11, 1988, 1-A.
   8. *Clarion-Ledger*, August 6, 1988, 3-B; *Starkville Daily News,* June 22, 1988, 4-A.
   9. *Clarion-Ledger*, January 31, 1988, 1-A.
   10. *Clarion-Ledger*, August 5, 1988, 1-A.
   11. *Clarion-Ledger*, August 5, 1988, 1-B.
   12. *Clarion-Ledger*, August 4, 1988, 1-B; August 5, 1988, 12-A.
   13. *Starkville Daily News*, August 31, 1988, 3-A.
   14. *Clarion-Ledger*, August 16, 1988, 1-A.
   15. *Clarion-Ledger*, August 31, 1988, 3-B.
   16. *Starkville Daily News*, June 23, 1988, 12.
   17. *Clarion-Ledger*, August 14, 1988, 2-H; July 4, 1988, 1-B.
   18. *Clarion-Ledger*, August 24, 1988, 3-B.
   19. *Clarion-Ledger*, August 27, 1988, 1-B.
   20. *Clarion-Ledger*, October 7, 1988, 1-A.
   21. *Clarion-Ledger*, August 25, 1988, 14-A.
   22. *Clarion-Ledger*, August 25, 1988, 14-A.
   23. *Starkville Daily News*, August 27, 1988, 2-B.
   24. *Clarion-Ledger*, September 4, 1988, 5-G.
   25. *Clarion-Ledger*, September 18, 1988, 3-H.
   26. *Memphis Commercial Appeal*, September 28, 1988, 1-A; September 30, 1988, 12-A.
   27. *Clarion-Ledger*, August 17, 1988, 6-A.
   28. *Clarion-Ledger*, October 14, 1988, 20-A.
   29. *Clarion-Ledger*, October 21, 1988, 3-B.
   30. *Columbus Commercial Dispatch*, October 11, 1988, 7-A.
   31. *Clarion-Ledger*, October 14, 1988, 1-A.
   32. *Commercial Dispatch*, November 1, 1988, 1-A.
   33. *Clarion-Ledger*, October 23, 1988, 4-H.
   34. *Clarion-Ledger*, November 4, 1988, 3-B.
   35. *Clarion-Ledger*, November 6, 1988, 1-A.
   36. *Clarion-Ledger*, October 29, 1988, 3-B.
   37. *Clarion-Ledger*, October 28, 1988, 1-B.
   38. *Clarion-Ledger*, October 28, 1988, 3-B.
   39. *Clarion-Ledger*, October 30, 1988, 18-A.
   40. *Clarion-Ledger*, October 4, 1988, 1-B.
   41. *Clarion-Ledger*, October 30, 1988, 18-A.
   42. *Clarion-Ledger*, October 9, 1988, 3-I.

43. *Clarion-Ledger,* May 1, 1988, 1-B.
44. *Clarion-Ledger,* September 18, 1988, 13-A.
45. *Clarion-Ledger,* August 23, 1988, 3-B.
46. *Clarion-Ledger,* May 10, 1988, 4-B.
47. *Clarion-Ledger,* September 27, 1988, 3-B.
48. *Starkville Daily News,* May 25, 1988, 4-A.
49. *Clarion-Ledger,* June 7, 1988, 1-B.
50. *Clarion-Ledger,* July 16, 1988, 3-B.
51. *Clarion-Ledger,* September 9, 1988, 3-B.
52. *Clarion-Ledger,* November 2, 1988, 3-B.
53. *Clarion-Ledger,* February 25, 1988, 1-A.
54. *Clarion-Ledger,* September 13, 1988, 1-A, 10-A.
55. *Clarion-Ledger,* September 13, 1988, 1-A.
56. *Starkville Daily News,* September 8, 1988, 4.
57. *Clarion-Ledger,* September 20, 1988, 1-B.
58. *Clarion-Ledger,* September 25, 1988, 3-H; October 9, 1988, 3-I.
59. *Clarion-Ledger,* September 27, 1988, 1-B.
60. *Starkville Daily News,* August 3, 1988, 5.
61. *Clarion-Ledger,* October 22, 1988, 1-A.
62. *Clarion-Ledger,* September 25, 1988, 3-B; July 24, 1988, 3-B.
63. *Clarion-Ledger,* October 12, 1988, 3-B.
64. *Clarion-Ledger,* October 14, 1988, 6-B.
65. *Clarion-Ledger,* February 28, 1988, 1-B.
66. *Clarion-Ledger,* August 28, 1988, 1-B.
67. *Starkville Daily News,* September 19, 1988, 5.
68. *Clarion-Ledger,* September 20, 1988, 1-A.
69. *Clarion-Ledger,* October 21, 1988, 3-B.
70. *Clarion-Ledger,* November 6, 1988, 3-H.
71. *Clarion-Ledger,* September 28, 1988, 1-A.
72. *Clarion-Ledger,* September 29, 1988, 1-B.
73. *Clarion-Ledger,* October 2, 1988, 1-B.
74. *Clarion-Ledger,* September 18, 1988, 3-H; *Clarion-Ledger,* October 30, 1988, 3-H.
75. *Starkville Daily News,* August 2, 1988, 3.
76. *Clarion-Ledger,* September 8, 1988, 1-B.
77. *Clarion-Ledger,* May 18, 1988, 1-A.
78. *Clarion-Ledger,* August 5, 1988, 1-B.
79. *Clarion-Ledger,* September 11, 1988, 1-B, 6-B.
80. *Commercial Dispatch,* November 1, 1988, 1-A; *Starkville Daily News,* August 31, 1988, 6-A.
81. *Starkville Daily News,* March 10, 1988, 3-B.
82. *Clarion-Ledger,* March 10, 1988, 3-B.
83. *Clarion-Ledger,* November 5, 1988, 1-B; October 27, 1988, 1A; see also issue of May 15, 1988, 3B.
84. *Starkville Daily News,* May 27, 1988, 4; *Clarion-Ledger,* August 25, 1988, 1-B.
85. *Clarion-Ledger,* October 20, 1988, 1-A; November 6, 1988, 2-B.
86. *Clarion-Ledger,* October 3, 1988, 1-A; December 15, 1988, 1-B.
87. *Clarion-Ledger,* October 6, 1988, 1-B.

88. *Clarion-Ledger*, November 2, 1988, 1-B.

89. *Clarion-Ledger*, November 7, 1988, 4-A.

90. *Clarion-Ledger*, November 6, 1988, 1-A.

91. *Clarion-Ledger*, November 8, 1988, 1-B.

92. *Clarion-Ledger*, November 3, 1988, 3-B; February 21, 1988, 5-B; October 24, 1988, 1-A.

93. *Clarion-Ledger*, August 13, 1988, 8-B.

94. *Clarion-Ledger*, July 11, 1988, 1-B.

95. *Clarion-Ledger*, October 27, 1988, 3-B.

96. *Clarion-Ledger*, February 14, 1988, 1-B.

97. *Clarion-Ledger*, April 26, 1988, 1-B.

98. *Clarion-Ledger*, September 6, 1988, 1-A.

99. *Starkville Daily News*, October 24, 1988, 2.

100. *Clarion-Ledger*, November 3, 1988, 9-A.

101. *Clarion-Ledger*, October 26, 1988, 3-B.

102. *Clarion-Ledger*, September 8, 1988, 3-B.

103. *Clarion-Ledger*, August 25, 1988, 3-B.

104. *Clarion-Ledger*, October 2, 1988, 3-H.

105. *Clarion-Ledger*, November 2, 1988, 3-B.

106. *Clarion-Ledger*, September 7, 1988, 1-B.

107. *Clarion-Ledger*, October 7, 1988, 2-B.

108. *Clarion-Ledger*, February 14, 1988, 19-A; March 30, 1988, 1-A.

109. *Clarion-Ledger*, March 10, 1988, 1-B.

110. *Clarion-Ledger*, October 13, 1988, 3-B; October 25, 1988, 1-B.

111. *Clarion-Ledger*, July 29, 1988, 3-B.

112. *Clarion-Ledger*, October 21, 1988, 1-B.

113. *Clarion-Ledger*, September 18, 1988, 6-B; October 6, 1988, 4-B.

114. *Clarion-Ledger*, November 7, 1988, 1-B.

115. *Clarion-Ledger*, October 28, 1988, 3-B; October 23, 1988, 1-B.

116. *Starkville Daily News*, October 21, 1988, 5.

117. *Clarion-Ledger*, September 4, 1988, 3-G.

118. The data from this section are derived from two statewide telephone surveys of likely voters using two-stage, random-digit dialing procedures, conducted by the Mississippi State University Survey Research Unit of the Social Science Research Center. The April 11–24 poll surveyed 433 likely voters, and the August 29–September 17 poll surveyed 692 likely voters. The data were weighted by demographic characteristics to adjust for households that lacked telephones.

119. Shaffer, "Changing Party Politics," 194–199.

7

South Carolina: Different Cast, Same Drama in the Palmetto State

LAURENCE W. MORELAND, ROBERT P. STEED, AND
TOD A. BAKER

Both Michael Dukakis and southern Democrats had great expectations that 1988 would be a year in which Democrats would once again become competitive with Republicans in presidential contests across the South. For South Carolina Democrats, their state was no exception to this general hope. Although there were some who warned early on that the Republicans could and would successfully depict Michael Dukakis as "Teddy Dukakis,"[1] and therefore anathema to much of the white South, the state's top Democrats entertained the idea that the Dukakis-Bentsen ticket would not be the albatross that quadrenially seemed to compel many South Carolina Democrats to flee from any association with their presidential candidate. Certainly the state's Democrats were hungry for a presidential victory for, other than in 1976 when the party had nominated a former Deep South governor (Jimmy Carter of Georgia), the state had not voted for a Democrat presidential candidate since 1960.

Early surveys were suggestive that Dukakis would run considerably better than the 1984 ticket had run. For example, a poll reported by South Carolina's only statewide newspaper, the *State* (published in Columbia, the state capital), in late May had George Bush leading Dukakis by a substantial margin (53 to 41 percent),[2] but even so, Dukakis was running stronger than Walter Mondale had run four years earlier when he had attracted only a little more than a third of the state's popular vote.[3] Moreover, the subsequent choice of U.S. Senator

Lloyd Bentsen of Texas as the Democratic vice presidential nominee (a choice that the state's most prominent Democrat, U.S. Senator Ernest "Fritz" Hollings, had recommended as one of the keys to carrying the South) further fueled the early optimism. As a consequence, Democratic leaders generally expressed the view that 1988 was not going to be a repeat of 1984. Indeed, the prospects seemed good enough that the state's Democratic establishment—including such leaders as Lieutenant Governor Nick Theodore, popular former Governor Richard Riley, and Charleston Mayor Joseph P. Riley, Jr.—was optimistic that the Dukakis-Bentsen ticket was one that Democratic state and local candidates could happily embrace.[4]

If South Carolina Democrats were cautiously optimistic in 1988, the state's Republicans were abundantly so. A booming Sunbelt economy with low unemployment, together with a popular presidential candidate, convinced most Republicans that the presidential election was theirs to lose. With an impressive 1984 presidential win in the state and a Republican gubernatorial victory in 1986, Republicans felt poised to carry the state decisively once again.

POLITICAL CONTEXT

Changes in the State's Party System

The early optimism of many Democrats in 1988 ran counter to the state's recent political history.[5] To be sure, Democrats had been the beneficiaries of a one-party system during the first half of the century, when the state remained largely rural and underdeveloped.

From the Civil War through the general economic depression of the 1930s, South Carolina was a static society. The earlier political dominance of South Carolina's plantation owners had generally faded with the political rise of white supremacists in the late 1800s. But, when unified under the Democratic banner, rich and poor white Democrats did not need black voters to win statewide elections. . . . A die-hard States' Rights view, one-crop cotton agriculture, racial segregation, and a general intellectual malaise kept the state isolated from the nation well into the twentieth century.[6]

The state's political environment during those years also remained static, with the Democratic party constituting virtually a one-party system. However, events after World War II transpired to fundamentally alter the economic and social environments. A new political leadership in the legislature and the governor's office, which was oriented toward business and economic development, the out-migration of substantial numbers of blacks, the in-migration of middle-class whites to the state, the industrialization and urbanization that generally characterized the Sunbelt states after World War II— all contributed to creating an environment in which a one-party system largely based on race could no longer survive. The additional pressure of external forces—the enactment of the Civil

Rights Act of 1964 and the Voting Rights Act of 1965—sounded the death knell of the old politics.

Because of a national Democratic party that, since the late 1940s, had increasingly moved toward embracing the political goals of blacks and of a national Republican party in the 1960s that largely had stayed aloof from the political agenda of black Americans, South Carolina Democrats in the 1960s inherited a new black constituency, whether they wanted it or not, as blacks were effectively enfranchised across the state. On the other hand, an emergent Republican party in South Carolina began to develop rapidly in the 1960s and 1970s, based largely on middle-class white suburbanites (a traditional Republican support group outside the South), business-oriented in-migrants to the state, middle-class retirees (many from outside the South), and finally, native South Carolinians who were refugees from the newly black Democratic party. A few Democratic office holders switched parties in the 1960s, most notably the legendary U.S. Senator Strom Thurmond, who switched to the Republicans in September of 1964 and supported the presidential candidacy of Barry Goldwater.

Emergent Republicanism in South Carolina developed as a top-down political phenomenon, with the Republican party able to attract the most votes at the presidential level, fewer votes at the statewide level, and fewer still at the local level. This Republican success at the presidential level reflected the willingness of many whites in the state to split their ballots between parties, but it was also due in part to the success of Democrats, particularly local Democrats, in disassociating themselves from their own national party.

Electorally, these developments resulted in the increasing deterioration of Democratic strength, particularly at the presidential level. Although not one county had voted for a Republican presidential nominee from 1900 to 1944, with the Democratic vote almost always above 90 percent, in 1948 the state's nearly all-white voting population began to move away from its long-time Democratic one-partyism by voting for the third-party candidacy of Strom Thurmond, who—then still a Democrat—left the party briefly to protest the strong civil rights stance that the party had adopted at its 1948 national convention. In the years after 1948, the Democrats were never again able to muster the huge majorities that had once been commonplace.

In 1964 the Republicans began what was to become an almost unbroken string of presidential victories in South Carolina. Led by their new leader, Senator Thurmond, the Republicans carried the state for Barry Goldwater with 59 percent of the vote. In 1968 and 1972, the state voted for Republican Richard Nixon. Indeed, Thurmond's pre-nomination support in 1968 had been instrumental for Nixon in earning his party's nomination. In 1972, Nixon won every county in the state, some by margins close to 90 percent, as white South Carolinians deserted the Democratic party by large margins. In 1976 the Democrats succeeded in carrying the state for the first time in sixteen years, but only because of a unique short-term factor—the Democratic nominee (former Georgia Governor Jimmy Carter) was a southern Democrat from a neighboring state, running with the image of being outside the national Democratic party establishment. The Democrats could not repeat this in 1980, and the state narrowly gave its electoral votes to Republican Ronald Reagan (who won 51 percent of the popular vote). In 1984, Republican presidential ascendancy continued the trend begun in the 1950s, and the Reagan-Bush team carried the state with two-thirds (nearly 64 percent) of the popular vote.

At other levels, too, the Republican party began to make inroads in what had been a Democratic lock on virtually all state and local offices. Even so, Republican success at the sub-presidential level has been much less consistent. Thurmond, of course, was re-elected to his sixth term in 1984 (with over two-thirds of the vote). Otherwise, however, the Democrats continued to show considerable strength in the mid-1980s. After the 1984 elections they held more than three-fourths of the membership in each house of the state legislature, and they continued to dominate local offices, winning nearly 80 percent of them.

The 1986 Elections

The last statewide elections before the 1988 presidential contest were held in 1986. That year, the Republicans failed to unseat the state's most senior Democrat, Senator Hollings. In his bid for a fourth full term, Hollings decisively defeated former U.S. Attorney Henry McMaster with over 63 percent of the vote, carrying forty-five of the state's forty-six counties (losing narrowly only in the suburban-rural county of Lexington, just outside the capital city of Columbia).

The Republicans did succeed in 1986 in electing only the second Republican governor in this century—then U.S. Representative Carroll Campbell, who had served as 1980 Reagan campaign chairman in South Carolina. Campbell, aided considerably by strongly carrying his Greenville-Spartanburg congressional district (the Fourth), narrowly defeated Democratic Lieutenant Governor Mike Daniel with 51.0 percent of the vote.[7] Campbell's running mate in 1986 was another U.S. Representative, First District Congressman Tommy Hartnett of Charleston, and together the two comprised the Republican "dream team" of 1986—two U.S. Representatives from two of the state's three principal metropolitan areas. However, as a congressman, Hartnett had been less visible statewide, as well as less articulate than the smooth and photogenic Campbell. Hartnett's vote in 1986 generally ran slightly behind his running mate's, and he failed to run as well in his Charleston congressional district as Campbell ran in his Greenville-Spartanburg district. As a consequence, Hartnett lost the lieutenant governorship to State Senator Nick Theodore of Greenville, who won with 50.5 percent of the vote. (Theodore carried his home county, Greenville, which was otherwise a strongly Republican area.)

The Greenville-Spartanburg area surprised the Republicans in another way as well as they failed to hold the congressional seat Campbell was vacating to run for governor. Liz Patterson, daughter of former U.S. Senator Olin Johnston, won the district with 51.4 percent of the vote. On the other hand, Republicans held on to Hartnett's Charleston congressional seat as colorful Arthur Ravenel, with 52.0 percent of the vote, defeated the Democratic nominee, former state legislator Jimmy Stuckey. The third Republican incumbent, Second District Congressman Floyd Spence of Columbia, ran for re-election, and he defeated the state Democratic party's executive director, Fred Zeigler, with 53.6 percent of the vote. The state's other three congressional seats— all more rural than the three districts held by Republicans prior to the 1986 elections and all held by Democrats—easily returned incumbents. Third District Congressman Butler Derrick was re-elected with 68.4 percent of the vote, and Sixth District Congressman Robin Tallon won with 75.5 percent. Fifth District Congressman John Spratt was unopposed.

Summary: The South Carolina Party System

The status of South Carolina politics on the eve of the 1988 presidential election can be summarized by noting that the last forty years of economic, social, and political change in the state have resulted in five discernible political trends. First, the Republican party has built its strength primarily in the suburban areas of the state's metropolitan districts (twelve of the state's counties fall into Standard Metropolitan Statistical Areas, roughly centered in three regions: Charleston–North Charleston, Columbia, and Greenville-Spartanburg). The white middle class in South Carolina has responded to the appeal that the Republican party has succeeded in making to the middle class nationally, particularly during the Reagan era. Second, the Republicans have had trouble penetrating the rural areas of the state, many of which retain their traditional Democratic loyalties, even in presidential contests. In 1980, for example, Jimmy Carter lost the state even though he carried thirty-five of the forty-six counties; the counties he carried, however, tended to be rural, less populated, and often highly black counties (on the other hand, Carter lost eight of the ten most populous counties).[8]

A third trend has been the overwhelming support that blacks have given the Democratic party. In 1984, for example, blacks voted for Walter Mondale at over 90 percent. On the positive side, this has given the party a large base on which to build, as 26.7 percent of registered voters were black in 1988.[9] On the other hand, some white voters have perceived the Democratic party as a party of minorities, particularly the black minority; in a Deep South state like South Carolina, this has not necessarily been advantageous.

A fourth trend has been the emergence of a party system that ideologically has begun to delineate rather clearly between the two parties. Many of those who have strong party identifications have tended to cluster rather distinctively, particularly the Republicans in the state. A survey of delegates to the 1988 state party conventions indicated that 68 percent of the Democrats described themselves as "liberal" (with 16 percent responding "middle-of-the-road" and 17 percent as "conservative"); for the Republicans, in a remarkable display of ideological homogeneity, 98 percent described themselves as "conservative."[10] This movement toward "party sorting" has given the two parties increasingly clear centers of gravity.

Finally, many white South Carolina voters have developed an impressive willingness to split their ballots between parties. In 1986, for example, Republican Carroll Campbell decisively won the most Republican county in the state (Lexington) with over 70 percent of the vote in his race for governor at the same time that Democrat Fritz Hollings was winning nearly half the vote in that same county in his race for re-election to the U.S. Senate. Much of the explanation for ticket splitting lies in the fact that South Carolinians have increasingly moved away from identification with the Democratic party. This dealignment has resulted in the formation of a large group of Independents (and it has provided fertile ground for conversion of some into Republican identifiers as well). A poll by the *State* newspaper in 1986 found that 38 percent of those sampled considered themselves to be Independent, with 36 percent identifying with the Democratic party and 26 percent identifying with the Republican party.[11] Ticket splitting has also attested to the success of state and local Democrats in orienting at least some voters in the direction of perceiving substantive differences between national Democrats and and those on the state and local level.

On the eve of the 1988 elections, despite the summer hopes of many Democrats regarding their presidential ticket, the recent political omens were not encouraging. South Carolina had in the 1970s and 1980s developed a vigorous and healthy Republican party (led in 1988 by an incumbent governor), the state had a nearly thirty-year trend of presidential Republicanism, and the Democrats had nominated a candidate (a northeastern liberal) against whom South Carolina Republicans virtually itched to run. Indeed, Republican optimism more than matched Democratic hopes; Tony Denny, the South Carolina Republican party's executive director, took the view in August that, if George Bush could not carry South Carolina, he would not win any states at all.[12]

THE CAMPAIGN

The Democrats

South Carolina Democrats came out of their national convention uncharacteristically unified. While perceptions of the way in which Jesse Jackson had been treated at the convention by Michael Dukakis had a divisive potential for the party, that division was downplayed even before the delegates left Atlanta. Native-son Jackson had had great support among black Democrats in the state (and, in the March party caucuses, had garnered over half the state's delegates to the national convention), and at the convention, two of the state's leading Democrats—Senator Hollings and Sixth District Congressman Robin Tallon— had made the symbolic unifying gesture of casting their votes as super delegates for Jackson.[13] A leading black Democrat, S.C. Human Affairs Commissioner

James E. Clyburn, told the South Carolina delegates at the convention that he had been to five national conventions, that he had never seen the party more cohesive, and that "you all ought to be proud."[14] Longtime State Senator Isadore Lourie contended that Jackson's Atlanta speech was the best convention address since 1948, and said he would be delighted to campaign with Jackson for the national ticket in Columbia, Charleston, or even New York. Barbara Williams, one of the state's leading political commentators (writing for the Charleston *Post-Courier* papers), noted that Lourie is Jewish and that "Lourie's remarks were considered particularly significant in view of Jackson's past problems with the Jewish community."[15]

After the convention, Dukakis surged in several national public opinion polls, giving him a substantial early lead over Bush. In late July, Dukakis appointed South Carolina native Marcia Hale (who had held administrative posts with a number of South Carolina Democrats and who had served as convention manager for Dukakis in Atlanta) to head his transition team to the White House, a team that was to begin its work immediately.[16]

Despite the early optimism of many of the state's top Democrats, conservative Democratic elected officials who had not been part of the convention enthusiasm were more cautious in their acceptance of the national nominees. Still, unlike 1984, when most Democratic public officials below the level of governor abandoned the national ticket, they were at least open to persuasion. State Representative Joe Wilder of Barnwell expressed well the views of many of the state's Democrats whose party loyalty often weakened or disappeared at the presidential level:

I supported Jimmy Carter, but I did not support Mondale personally, and I'm not going to be out working for Michael Dukakis. I'm not very happy with George Bush, but as far as his positions are concerned, I'm more inclined to support the positions that I know about that have been espoused by Bush than those that have been espoused by Dukakis. I think we need to see what happens on the campaign trail between now and November, and how their positions play and who makes the most mistakes.[17]

Democratic State Representative T. W. Edwards, another Reagan voter in 1984, was reassured by the addition of Bentsen to the ticket: "I think with the appointment of Bentsen, that is showing to the South and to South Carolina that there is room for conservative Democrats within the party, and that's what I consider myself."[18] Anderson County Sheriff E. E. Cooley summed up the situation for many white South Carolina Democrats when he observed that "they've lost a lot of Democrats, people I know have voted Democrat all their lives, the last two times they voted Republican. I think they'll bring some of them back. The next few months, [Dukakis is] going to have to prove to people he's going to do what's right."[19]

Bentsen's presence on the ticket provided an opportunity for the Dukakis campaign to staunch the bloodletting suffered in 1980 and 1984 among white conservative South Carolina Democrats. He provided someone on the ticket with whom Democratic officials and white traditional Democratic voters could identify; Bentsen thus became a symbol, leaving open the possibility in voters' minds that they had not been forgotten by the national party. Of course, in late July, the question remained unanswered whether that presence would be enough to reverse the Republican presidential tide that had regularly swept over the state since 1960.

The Republicans

Just as the Jackson candidacy provided a potentially divisive influence among South Carolina Democrats, the Pat Robertson candidacy had provided a similar danger for South Carolina Republicans. Before 1987, the state's growing number of Republican partisans had little to divide them. However, in 1987 newcomers to the party—organized as the Carolina Conservative Coalition (CCC) and consisting mostly of fundamentalist Christians supporting Robertson for president— turned out in large numbers at the Republican precinct reorganizations. They gained control of the Charleston County Republican party, and seemingly did so as well in Richland County (Columbia). Considerable bitterness surrounded the Robertson effort. In Charleston County, party regulars, led by North Charleston Mayor John E. Bourne, Jr., sought to overturn their ouster from party positions by (unsuccessful) appeals to the party apparatus. In Richland County, party regulars had maintained control by declaring ineligible most of the CCC delegates on the ground that they had not been registered to vote in their precincts at least thirty days prior to reorganization; these denied delegates filed suit (which was later dropped) in state court.[20] Inasmuch as South Carolina Republicans were utilizing a presidential primary in 1988 (with delegates being bound to the primary winner for two ballots), these maneuverings made sense only if the balloting at the convention went to three or more ballots, an eventuality expected by the Robertson camp; then, the actual people casting the ballots would become important, and the Robertson forces hoped to have their own people in place.

For the Robertson nomination campaign, the South Carolina Republican presidential primary was a do-or-die effort. If Robertson could not win in South Carolina despite his considerable success in the 1987 precinct caucuses, it was doubtful that he could win elsewhere. The Robertson campaign took out full-page advertisements in South Carolina newspapers attacking Bush. Titled "Who Hijacked the Reagan Revolution?" the advertisements singled out "Eastern Republicans," headed by Bush, who would not "let Reagan be Reagan." The solution, asserted the ads, was to elect "solid conservatives from the beginning," not "wimps."[21]

Despite the Robertson effort and Senator Thurmond's endorsement of yet another Republican contender (Bob Dole), George Bush easily won the primary. With the help of Governor Campbell and campaign manager Lee Atwater (another South Carolina native), Bush carried all six congressional districts, winning with

48.6 percent of the primary vote (Dole followed with 20.7 percent, and Robertson came in third with 19.2 percent).[22] Together with New Hampshire Republicans, South Carolina Republicans provided the momentum that Bush needed to sweep through Super Tuesday three days later and on to the nomination.

Despite the bitterness that surrounded some of the Bush-Robertson maneuvering in the spring of 1988, South Carolina Republicans had healed their differences by the time of their New Orleans national convention. In late July, Robertson joined a Republican rally in Charleston, where he urged his supporters to support Bush.[23] Robertson also excoriated Dukakis at length, attacking him as "the most liberal candidate any party has nominated for the presidency," a theme that the Bush campaign was soon to make its own.

By the beginning of the campaign season in September, Bush seemed in good shape in South Carolina: He had carried the state in a much-publicized primary just a few months earlier, he had the backing of a relatively unified state party, he had the enthusiastic support of a popular Republican governor, and as heir to the Reagan legacy, he had the good will, not only of Republicans, but also of (white) Democrats and Independents across the state who had overwhelmingly supported the Reagan-Bush ticket just four years earlier.

The Campaign

Both campaigns had high-visibility figures to chair their respective efforts in the state. While Governor Campbell served as the Bush overall southern chair, Tommy Hartnett (having returned to business in Charleston after his defeat for Lieutenant Governor) served as the Bush-Quayle state campaign chair.[24] Campbell's predecessor as Governor, Democrat Richard Riley, chaired the state Dukakis-Bentsen campaign.[25]

South Carolina was a much-visited state during the primary caucus season, when a number of candidates (Bush, Robertson, Dole, Jack Kemp, Jackson, and Richard Gephardt) saw the state as an important key to winning the nomination and therefore campaigned in the state. However, in the general election the state became of little strategic value, and neither Dukakis nor Bush appeared during the traditional campaign period (Labor Day to Election Day), although both had been in the state just before their respective national conventions. In June, Dukakis visited Florence, S.C., where he attacked the evils of drug use. Even then, however, in Dukakis's swing across the South, he was denounced by various Republicans as an "ultra-liberal," out of step with the mainstream of southern voters.[26] In late July, on the day Dukakis accepted the Democratic nomination in Atlanta, Bush visited Greenville for the purposes of raising campaign funds for other Republicans and supporting the Republican challenger for Governor Campbell's old Fourth District House seat.[27] In Greenville, Governor Campbell took the occasion to recommend to Bush that he select either Jack Kemp or Bob Dole as his running mate as well as to sound the theme that Bush would later use so effectively against Dukakis in the fall campaign: Dukakis, said the Governor, was "masquerading as a moderate. He's well on the left. He's a card-carrying member of the ACLU. He's a liberal. And if he came out and campaigned like an honest liberal like Walter Mondale, we probably wouldn't be using that word very much."[28]

The only national candidate to visit South Carolina during the campaign was Dan Quayle, who visited Darlington on Sunday, September 4, the day before the traditional Labor Day campaign kickoff. There he officially commenced the Darlington 500, the famous stock car race, by intoning, "Gentlemen, start your engines."[29]

The presidential campaign in South Carolina was a fairly desultory affair. The state has only eight electoral votes, and a stiff campaign was to be expected only if Bush faltered and Dukakis soared. By early September, a poll sponsored by the *State* newspaper indicated that the 12-point Bush lead in May had doubled to 24 points (58.6 percent to 35.8 percent)—a margin equaled at that point in the campaign in only two other states (Utah and New Hampshire).[30] In September, the director of the Dukakis campaign (young attorney Det Bowers, Jr., an activist in a number of Democratic gubernatorial campaigns) had to begin denying reports that the state was being written off by the Democrats. This was a denial that, at least for the record, he continued to make through late October, although appearances inescapably suggested otherwise. Lloyd Bentsen, for example, canceled altogether an appearance in the state that had been scheduled for late September. The Dukakis campaign was run by just three full-time workers (compared with ninety paid staffers in neighboring—and more competitive—North Carolina).[31] In early October, the Dukakis campaign chair (former governor Riley) conceded a Bush lead but continued to hold out hope, contingent on all the breaks going for Dukakis: "The dynamics are out there. If the vote were held today, Bush would win. But I think with a couple of breaks and some further strengthening of the Dukakis-Bentsen ticket, we could certainly win here."[32] Riley hoped that the Quayle candidacy would be the break that would cause what he saw as a large contingent of only superficially committed voters to shift to Dukakis.

While the Quayle candidacy caused a ripple in South Carolina (what Charleston's *Evening Post* editorially called "the Quayle gamble"), it did not seem to move much of the electorate.[33] Indeed, Republican leaders maintained that they were besieged in grocery stores and other places by citizens who were outraged over what they perceived as the shabby treatment Quayle had gotten at the hands of the national media.[34]

On election day a campaign that had long been over came to its official end. A final poll by the *State* newspaper had Bush leading Dukakis by nearly 20 points—55.2 percent to 36.1 percent, with 8.7 percent undecided.[35]

RESULTS AND ANALYSIS

The 1988 presidential contest was an election that, despite the Democrats' early hopes, in many ways simply repeated 1984; the Republicans easily and

Table 7.1

Results of 1984 South Carolina Presidential and Congressional Elections

Candidates	Percent of Vote	Vote Totals
President		
Bush (R)	61.5	606,443
Dukakis (D)	37.6	370,554
Paul (L)	0.5	4,935
Fulani (UC)	0.4	4,077
U.S. House of Representatives		
First District		
Ravenel (R)*	63.8	101,572
Tillman (D)	36.2	57,691
Second District		
Spence (R)*	52.8	94,960
Leventis (D)	46.7	83,978
Sommer (L)	0.6	1,061
Third District		
Derrick (D)*	53.7	89,071
Jordan (R)	45.6	75,571
Heaton (L)	0.7	1,183
Fourth District		
Patterson (D)*	52.2	90,234
White (R)	47.8	82,793
Fifth District		
Spratt (D)*	69.8	107,959
Carley (R)	30.2	46,622
Sixth District		
Tallon (D)*	76.1	120,719
Cunningham (R)	23.9	37,958

Key to symbols: * indicates incumbent; R denotes Republican; D denotes Democrat; L denotes Libertarian; UC denotes United Citizens party.

Source: Compiled by authors from data provided by the South Carolina State Election Commission (Columbia, South Carolina).

decisively carried the state at the presidential level, and the state's six U.S. Representatives—four Democrats and two Republicans—were all re-elected (see Table 7.1). Bush came very close to reaching the extraordinary majorities won by Reagan four years earlier as Bush carried the state by nearly 236,000 votes (compared with Reagan's 270,000), capturing almost 62 percent of the vote (compared with Reagan's nearly 64 percent).

The potential South Carolina electorate was not highly motivated in 1988, at least in terms of numbers. Just 38.9 percent of the voting age population voted in the presidential race; nationwide, only Georgia was lower, at 38.8.[36] If only registered voters are considered, however, the percentage of those voting rose to 72 percent.[37]

Analysis: The Presidential Race

South Carolina voters gave George Bush 61.5 percent of their votes, the highest percentage in the South (Florida was second in the South at 60.9 percent) and the fourth highest in the nation (Utah, New Hampshire, and Idaho led nationally).[38] The Republican ticket carried thirty-four of the state's forty-six counties.

Like Republican presidential candidates before him (stretching all the way back to the 1950s), George Bush showed his greatest strength in the state's Standard Metropolitan Statistical Areas (SMSAs), sweeping all 12 counties falling in the three urban corridors. In these 12 counties representing over 60 percent of all the votes cast in the state, Bush won 65.1 percent.[39] While Bush did well in all three urban corridors, he did best in the upcountry Greenville-Spartanburg corridor (67.9 percent), almost as well in the Columbia midlands corridor (64.0 percent), and somewhat less well in the Charleston lowcountry corridor (61.4 percent, see Table 7.2). The explanation for the variation in the Bush vote in the urban corridors lies largely in their variation in black voter registration (least in Greenville-Spartanburg and greatest in Charleston). In the rapidly growing suburban-rural county of Lexington, just outside the state capital of Columbia, Bush obtained an astonishing 77.9 percent of the vote. Lexington County had the fifth largest number of registered voters, only 7.2 percent of whom were black (as compared with about 27 percent statewide). The county has become the most consistently Republican county, not only in South Carolina, but in all five of the Deep South States.[40]

Exceptional Republican strength in the urban counties is confirmed by a look at Bush victories elsewhere in the state. In the twenty-two non-SMSA counties carried by Bush (which together constituted 29.4 percent of the statewide vote), he ran well at 60.0 percent, but still less strongly than in any of the urban corridors.

In contrast to Republican strength in the metropolitan areas, the 1988 election also extended a second trend, one emerging in the 1970s and relating to the increasing narrowness of Democratic support, at least in presidential elections. Like Walter Mondale before him, Michael Dukakis overwhelmingly carried the black vote while overwhelmingly losing the white vote. He carried only twelve of the state's counties, but these included all eleven black majority counties and an additional county (Marlboro) with a large black voter registration (40.9 percent). Unfortunately for Dukakis, the twelve counties together constituted only 10.4 percent of the total state vote, as all these counties are sparsely populated and rural (see Table 7.3). Although eleven of the twelve had majorities of registered black voters, in only five did blacks actually constitute a majority on Election Day; small percentages of additional (white) voters put Dukakis over the top in the other counties he won. While blacks constituted the Democratic base across the state, that base was diminished by blacks' lower turnout rates. While 26.7 percent of registered voters were black, they constituted only 23 percent of actual voters; black voter turnout (at 64 percent of registered voters)

Table 7.2

Bush Proportion of Vote, White Proportion of Vote, and County Proportion of Total State Vote in South Carolina's Three Urban Corridors in 1988 (in percent)

Corridor	Bush Vote	White Proportion of Vote*	Proportion of State Vote**
Lowcountry (Charleston) Urban Corridor			
Berkeley County	63.8	73.6	2.7
Charleston County	59.3	71.0	8.4
Dorchester County	66.4	77.3	2.3
(Corridor Average)	(61.4)	(72.6)	--
(Corridor Total)	--	--	(13.4)
Midlands (Columbia) Urban Corridor			
Aiken County	71.8	83.3	3.9
Florence County	60.5	70.1	3.3
Lexington County	77.9	93.9	5.4
Richland County	52.7	67.8	8.4
(Corridor Average)	(64.0)	(77.6)	--
(Corridor Total)	--	--	(21.0)
Upcountry (Greenville-Spartanburg) Urban Corridor			
Anderson County	67.6	89.0	3.9
Greenville County	70.8	87.6	9.6
Pickens County	73.6	95.3	2.4
Spartanburg County	63.2	84.9	6.5
York County	65.0	86.9	3.4
(Corridor Average)	(67.9)	(87.8)	--
(Corridor Total)	--	--	(25.8)
Average Bush Vote in Urban Corridors	65.1	--	--
Urban Corridor White Vote Proportion	--	80.8	--
Urban Corridor Proportion of Total State Vote	--	--	60.2

*White proportion of vote, 8 November 1988.
**Total county vote as percentage of total state vote.

Source: Calculated by authors from 1988 election statistics provided by the South Carolina State Election Commission (Columbia, South Carolina).

was 8 percent higher than in 1984, but it was still substantially less than white voter turnout (at 76 percent).[41]

In short, the Republican presidential vote tended to be white and urban/ suburban. The Dukakis vote tended to be black and rural. Additional evidence of the striking racial polarization in the state's presidential vote is provided by more detailed analysis at the precinct level. Examination of those precincts in the state's three most populous counties, Charleston, Richland (Columbia), and Greenville, which have 95 percent or more white voter registration or 95 percent or more black voter registration, helps to demonstrate the state's racial division (see Table 7.4). Dukakis won very nearly the entire vote in the seventeen over-

Table 7.3
Dukakis Proportion of Vote, Black Proportion of Vote, and County Proportion of Total State Vote in Counties Carried by Dukakis in 1988 (in percent)

County*	Dukakis Vote	Black Proportion of Vote**	Proportion of State Vote***
McCormick	59.1	51.2	0.3
Jasper	58.7	52.6	0.5
Fairfield	58.1	48.5	0.7
Allendale	57.7	52.5	0.3
Marlboro	57.3	37.8	0.7
Williamsburg	55.1	54.9	1.4
Hampton	54.5	46.9	0.7
Bamberg	53.9	47.8	0.5
Lee	53.8	50.4	0.7
Clarendon	53.5	47.9	1.0
Marion	52.8	43.9	1.0
Orangeburg	52.2	49.4	3.1
Dukakis Vote in Dukakis Counties	54.5	--	--
Dukakis Counties Black Vote Proportion	--	48.7	--
Dukakis Counties Proportion of Total State Vote	--	--	10.4

*In all counties listed (except for Marlboro) blacks had a majority in voter registrations. In Marlboro, black voter registration was 40 percent.

**Black proportion of vote, 8 November 1988.

***Total county vote as percentage of total state vote.

Source: Calculated by authors from 1988 election statistics provided by the South Carolina State Election Commission (Columbia, South Carolina).

whelmingly black precincts, varying only slightly among the three areas and never dropping below 95 percent. On the other hand, in the overwhelmingly white precincts, Bush won by huge margins—by nearly 80 percent to 20 percent in Charleston and Greenville, and by 72 percent to 28 percent in Richland. As in 1984, the Democratic ticket attracted the support of only about 20 percent of the white population statewide, possibly the worst showing among whites in any state in the country.[42] Indeed, if one assumes that the black vote in the heavily black counties carried by Dukakis was nearly unanimously his, Dukakis won several of those counties with 20 percent or more of the white vote, to be sure; but in some of those counties (such as Orangeburg), the Dukakis vote among whites may have slipped to as low as 7 or 8 percent (see Table 7.3).

Republican success and Democratic failure in the state stemmed not only from long-term trends but also from short-term factors as well. Bush was well known in the state (having visited a number of times and having won a primary in the state only a few months earlier), he was seen as the heir to a popular president

Table 7.4
Dukakis and Bush Vote in Predominantly White and Predominantly Black
Precincts in Charleston, Richland, and Greenville Counties in 1988 (in percent)*

County/Precincts**	Dukakis Vote	Bush Vote	(Total Vote in Selected Precincts***)
Charleston County			
White Precincts (25)	20.8	79.2	(21,649)
Black Precincts (6)	96.1	3.9	(2,707)
Richland County			
White Precincts (15)	27.8	72.2	(13,843)
Black Precincts (10)	95.2	4.8	(7,455)
Greenville County			
White Precincts (56)	20.5	79.5	(47,940)
Black Precincts (1)	96.4	3.6	(994)

*Precincts with voter registration either 95 percent or more white or 95 percent or more black.

**Number of precincts included in category indicated in parentheses.

***Two-party presidential vote only (minor party vote excluded).

Source: Calculated by authors from statistics provided by the South Carolina State Election Commission (Columbia, South Carolina).

to whom even white Democrats had given substantial support, he skillfully played on themes (defense, crime, and patriotism) that were seemingly tailor-made for a state like South Carolina, and his campaign was well organized across the state. His campaign themes—especially social issues with a high emotional content—were appealing, particularly to South Carolina's white males, introducing yet another variation on the "gender gap" that is periodically attributed to one or the other party: While women appeared to split nearly evenly (with a small margin for Bush), men supported Bush at about two to one.[43]

While the failure to make inroads among South Carolina blacks was disappointing for Republicans in 1988, it was hardly damaging to their presidential candidate, given the extraordinary support South Carolina whites have given to both Reagan and Bush. At other levels, however, the failure to attract black voters *is* significant as the state's Democrats retain enough support among those whites who simultaneously see themselves as "South Carolina Democrats" and as presidential Republicans to maintain their majority status in both the legislature and the various county courthouses around the state. On the other hand, the Democrat's failure to (again) attract white support much above 20 percent bodes ill, not only for future presidential contests, but also for their long-term vitality in state and local elections.

Analysis: The Congressional Elections

Other than the presidential race, no statewide races were held in South Carolina in 1988. Previous to the 1988 elections, the state's six seats in the U.S. House of Representatives were divided 4 to 2 between the parties (with Democrats in the majority), and of course, all six were on the ballot. While all the congressional seats featured incumbents seeking re-election, both parties had some hope of capturing a seat held by the other party. In the Second District, the Democrats hoped to unseat an incumbent Republican who was in poor health, and in the Fourth, Republicans expected to regain a seat that had been held by a Republican until the 1986 elections. However, by varying margins, all six incumbents were re-elected (see Table 7.1). The four Democrats bucked the Bush presidential tide, winning substantially more white votes in their districts than Dukakis won.

In the First District (Charleston County and all or part of six counties mainly west of Charleston), incumbent Republican Arthur Ravenel, Jr., was re-elected with 63.8 percent of the vote, easily defeating North Charleston lawyer Wheeler Tillman.[44] Ravenel, a moderate Republican, had become a favorite of the national media for his provocative, colorful, "down-home" comments about such things as using the Air Force to shoot down planes carrying drugs into the United States. Much better known than his underfinanced opponent, who had a difficult time finding an issue on which to challenge him, Ravenel took great pride in providing a high level of constituent service. An environmentalist, he obtained the endorsement of such groups as the Sierra Club, which was unusual for a Republican in South Carolina.[45]

In the Second District (Richland County, Lexington County, and three rural counties), nine-term Republican Congressman Floyd Spence was expected to retire at age sixty because of serious health problems (emphysema). A well-known, conservative banker-lawyer, Jim Leventis, filed for the Democratic nomination for what most observers expected to be an open seat, and one that Leventis would likely win. Spence, however, surprised nearly everyone by announcing for re-election in the spring, undergoing a rare double-lung transplant in May, taking a new bride in July, and campaigning for re-election in the fall. In the face of such extraordinary feats, even the well-financed and well-organized Leventis campaign was unable to prevail. Spence was re-elected with 52.8 percent of the vote, helped considerably by his better than two to one margin in heavily Republican Lexington County, his home county.

In the Third District (eight largely rural counties on the western border of the state), six-term incumbent Democrat Butler Derrick was re-elected but by a reduced margin (53.7 percent) from his previous races. He defeated Aiken physician and extremely conservative Republican Henry Jordan, who in 1986 had unsuccessfully sought the Republican nomination to run against Democratic Senator Hollings. Jordan had attempted to make an issue out of Derrick's sponsorship of a resolution changing the name of Clarks Hill Lake to Lake Thurmond (after Strom Thurmond), a move resisted by some, who thought it would injure the tourist business that was centered on the widely advertised Clarks Hill Lake.[46]

In the Fourth District (Greenville, Spartanburg, and Union Counties), Republicans hoped to defeat one-term incumbent Democrat Liz Patterson. Governor Campbell had held the seat until he successfully ran for governor in 1986, and Republicans saw it as one rightfully "belonging" to them, given Republican strength in the state's most affluent district.[47] Patterson, however, has excellent political instincts, carefully balancing issues important to her district (particularly those relating to fiscal responsibility) and national Democratic party politics. In defeating Greenville City Councilman Knox White, she won with 52.2 percent of the vote, the narrowest margin of any of the six house incumbents (Bush was simultaneously carrying the district with over 67 percent.) Republicans were greatly disappointed, as Governor Campbell had put his personal prestige on the line in the effort to recapture the seat, White had appeared to be an especially strong candidate, and only seven challengers nationally had spent more than White (who spent over $600,000 while Patterson spent nearly $1 million).[48]

In the Fifth District (nine mostly rural counties in the northern part of the state), incumbent Democrat John Spratt was easily re-elected to a fourth term with 69.8 percent of the vote. Without Republican opposition in 1984 and 1986, Spratt was opposed in 1988 by a political unknown, college professor Robert Carley.

In the Sixth District (ten counties in the northeast, including the state's tobacco-raising area as well as the Grand Strand beaches), incumbent Democrat Robin Tallon was re-elected to a third term, defeating Robert Cunningham, a retired newspaperman and former Central Intelligent Agency (CIA) officer. Aided by his base of black support in the state's most heavily black congressional district (about 40 percent), Tallon swamped his opponent with 76.1 percent of the vote, the largest margin in any of the House races.

In 1988, three of South Carolina's House races were typical of those nationally: Ravenel, Spratt, and Tallon raised campaign funds easily, defeated their opponents decisively, and finished the campaign with money left over for 1990. On the other hand, Derrick, Spence, and Patterson won by small margins, at least by the standards of House incumbents, and finished their campaigns in debt. All three in the latter group will likely face continued pressure, especially Patterson, whose success is something of an embarrassment for Governor Campbell and South Carolina native Lee Atwater, and whose defeat will likely be a high priority once again among both state and national Republicans.

CONCLUSION: SOUTH CAROLINA AND PARTISAN REALIGNMENT

Despite the early hopes of Democrats, the 1988 presidential election in South Carolina did not vary much in terms of outcome from the 1984 re-election of

the Reagan-Bush team. However, it did provide additional support for the five
trends noted earlier in this chapter. While Republican strength was evident across
the state, it was especially strong in the three urban corridors. Conversely,
Democratic presidential strength was confined to relatively sparsely populated
rural counties. Blacks, despite some effort on the part of South Carolina Republicans, remained nearly unanimously Democratic. Moreover, the 1988 contest
reinforced a party sorting that was already well underway in the state, rather
clearly delineating the state's parties ideologically between a conservative party
and a liberal party. Finally, many of the state's white voters continued to split
their ballots between Republicans at the presidential level and Democrats at the
congressional and state/local levels; indeed, in twenty-six of the forty-six counties, a majority of voters split their ballots between Bush for president and the
Democratic nominee for Congress (particularly in the Third, Fifth, and Sixth
districts, with incumbents favored in twenty-five of the twenty-six counties).[49]

Partisan politics in South Carolina continues to evolve, and it is not yet clear
that Republican ascendancy will go so far as to result in Republican domination
of the state's politics in the near term. With an electorate roughly divided into
thirds, both parties can now count on a hard core of supporters. For the Republicans, perhaps a little less than a third of the voters—almost all white—identify
with (and vote for) party candidates. A little more than a third of the voters
continue to support the Democratic party; while a majority of these are black,
white traditional Democrats and white liberals also contribute to the party's base.
The remaining third consists of generally conservative white Independents who
shift back and forth, depending on the candidates running and the offices sought.
The key to political office in South Carolina, therefore, turns on attracting these
voters who do not identify with either party, a goal that has generally eluded
the national Democratic party since the late 1960s. Despite their nonaligned
status, these Independents are not necessarily without long-term commitments,
particularly to specific candidates. Senator Thurmond, for example, seems in-
vulnerable to any kind of short- or long-term trend; indeed, in 1990 he was easily
re-elected to a seventh term at 88 years of age.

In 1986 the state elected as its governor a committed Republican, Carroll
Campbell, who was determined to build party strength in the state. An element
of the party's strategy has been to convince conservative Democratic officeholders that they could find a more hospitable home in the Republican party,
where they would not have to undergo a (Democratic) primary dominated by
generally liberal blacks and whites. In 1989, for example, the party convinced
five Democrats in the state legislature to make the shift, and Republicans will
likely continue to succeed in making at least some converts (but whether they
can do so on a wholesale basis remains to be seen). Governor Campbell, who
with some degree of personal political risk took on the role of southern chair of
the Bush campaign at a time when the election looked to be close and when the
South looked to be crucial to the Bush-Quayle ticket, has emerged as one of the
state's strongest political figures. He was decisively re-elected in 1990, as all

credible Democratic challengers declined to run.

Many of the state's Democrats, despairing of their repeated failures to win at the presidential level, express worry that state and local offices may be in jeopardy as well. Although the Democrats' strength has eroded clearly and substantially from that long period when they were effectively the only party in the state, the party is hardly on the ropes, as presidential coattails have proven to be notably short. After the 1988 elections, the party continued to dominate the state legislature even after the defections (34 to 12 in the Senate; 83 to 40 with one vacancy in the House).[50] In the courthouses around the state, Democrats continued to hold nearly three-quarters of the offices. The party also has no shortage of attractive candidates at all levels of power. For example, when Governor Campbell retires as governor, there are a number of potentially tough Democratic contenders; these include former Governor Richard Riley, Lieutenant Governor Nick Theodore, and Mayor of Charleston Joseph P. Riley, Jr. (no relation to Richard Riley). Mayor Riley in particular began to emerge in late 1989 when he exercised extraordinary personal leadership during the disastrous sweep of Hurricane Hugo across South Carolina in September.

Michael Dukakis did better than any Democratic presidential candidate (other than Jimmy Carter in 1976) since 1964—except in the South. That fact has encouraged some Democrats to look to the South for future presidential candidates, candidates attractive to white southern voters but credible elsewhere as well. Whether the party should pursue its own version of such a Southern Strategy (just as Republicans have done since 1964) by turning to Senator Lloyd Bentsen of Texas, Senator Sam Nunn of Georgia, or some other southerner remains a point of great contention within the national Democratic party. However, without a strategy of some type, it is clear that in South Carolina, Republicans will continue to dominate presidential contests. Whether that domination will in the long run be the catalyst that permits the party to dominate other races as well is still not clear. For the short term, though, the Democrats "must battle with independents and Republicans to win elections. . . . They will have to convince a skeptical majority of the fairness of their fiscal policies. If they do not, they can expect continued dealignment to result in the same partisan devastation for them as for Democratic presidential candidates."[51]

NOTES

1. "Teddy Dukakis" is a coinage by political scientists Earl Black and Merle Black, and used by them as early as March 1988. See their discussion in Chapter 14 of this volume.

2. Columbia *State,* May 22, 1988, 1-A.

3. For a detailed study of the 1984 presidential election in South Carolina, see Laurence W. Moreland, Robert P. Steed, and Tod A. Baker, "South Carolina," in *The 1984 Presidential Election in the South,* ed. Robert P. Steed, Laurence W. Moreland, and Tod A. Baker (New York: Praeger, 1986), 123–156.

4. Charleston *Evening Post,* July 22, 1988, 1-A.

5. This and the following paragraphs in this section are based on the following surveys of the state's recent electoral history: Moreland, Steed, and Baker, "South Carolina," in *The 1984 Presidential Election in the South*, 123–132; Cole Blease Graham, Jr., "Partisan Change in South Carolina," in *The South's New Politics: Realignment and Dealignment*, ed. Robert H. Swansbrough and David M. Brodsky (Columbia: University of South Carolina Press, 1988), 158–174; Donald L. Fowler, *Presidential Voting in South Carolina, 1948–1964* (Columbia: Bureau of Government Research and Service, University of South Carolina, 1966); V. O. Key, Jr., *Southern Politics in State and Nation* (New York: Knopf, 1949), 130–155; Chester Bain, "South Carolina: Partisan Prelude," in *The Changing Politics of the South*, ed. William C. Havard (Baton Rouge: Louisiana State University Press, 1972); William V. Moore, "Parties and Electoral Politics in South Carolina," in *Government in the Palmetto State*, ed. Luther F. Carter and David S. Mann (Columbia: Bureau of Government Research and Service, University of South Carolina, 1983), 45–60; Laurence W. Moreland, Robert P. Steed, and Tod A. Baker, "Regionalism in South Carolina Politics," in Carter and Mann, *Government in the Palmetto State*," 5–26.

6. Graham, "Partisan Change," 158. See also Key, *Southern Politics*, 131.

7. All 1986 election percentages cited here and below were calculated from official voting statistics provided by the South Carolina Election Commission, Columbia, S.C.

8. A listing of the Republican party's organized precincts in the state confirms that there is a dramatic fall-off in formal organization between the urban corridors and the state's rural counties.

9. Calculated from voter registration figures as of October 25, 1988, provided by the South Carolina Election Commission, Columbia, S.C.

10. From 1988 South Carolina Delegate Survey, conducted by the authors of this chapter.

11. Cited in Graham, "Partisan Change in South Carolina," 171.

12. Telephone interview (September 12, 1988).

13. Charleston *Evening Post*, July 21, 1988, 1-A. Some Jackson delegates, however, complained that the Hollings endorsement had come so late as to be meaningless, and therefore was an insult to them and the Jackson candidacy, particularly since Hollings had been less attentive on other occasions (Hollings had supported the candidacy of Robert Bork for the Supreme Court, for example). Four Jackson delegates did boycott a lavish conciliatory luncheon hosted by Hollings for Jackson delegates in Atlanta during the convention; for news accounts of the Hollings relationship with many of the state's black leaders, see Columbia *State*, July 11, 1988, 1-B, and July 20, 1988, 10-A.

14. Charleston *Evening Post*, July 21, 1988, 1-A.

15. Ibid.

16. Charleston *Evening Post*, July 25, 1988, 8-A.

17. Ibid.

18. Ibid. Edwards was subsequently defeated in his bid for re-election in 1988.

19. Ibid.

20. See Barbara S. Williams, "Dimensions," Charleston *News and Courier*, July 26, 1987, 12-A.

21. See the Charleston *News and Courier*, March 5, 1988, 5-B.

22. Unofficial returns reported in the Charleston *News and Courier*, March 6, 1986, 11-A.

23. Charleston *News and Courier*, July 24, 1988, 1-B. In their spring 1988 convention,

state Republicans got along harmoniously, unlike at their 1987 state convention. See "State GOP Puts Battles behind It," Charleston *News and Courier,* April 10, 1988, 1-B.

24. Barbara Williams, "What Rewards Await Campbell and Hartnett?" Charleston *Evening Post,* August 16, 1988, 1-A.

25. Charleston *News and Courier,* August 26, 1989, 1-B.

26. *New York Times,* June 18, 1988, 7.

27. Columbia *State,* July 22, 1988, 1-C. A few days later, the candidate's son, George Bush, Jr., visited Charleston, where he spoke to a Republican group including a small contingent of black businessmen (Charleston *News and Courier,* July 28, 1989, 8-A).

28. Columbia *State,* July 22, 1988, 2-C.

29. Columbia *State,* September 5, 1988, 1-A. In its front page story, the *State* opined that Quayle had been upstaged by the celebrity race car drivers and by Flat Nose, a tree-climbing dog that had been featured on television (NBC's "The Tonight Show with Johnny Carson").

30. Columbia *State,* September 11, 1988, 1-A.

31. *Charlotte Observer,* October 9, 1988, 1-D.

32. *Charlotte Observer,* October 9, 1988, 1-D. By early October, of course, Dukakis's strength was dropping all across the South. In early October, the *Atlanta Journal-Constitution* reported a South-wide margin for Bush of 12 points (*Atlanta Journal Constitution,* October 9, 1988, 1-A).

Early in the campaign, Riley had been confident that Dukakis would run a tough campaign. Noting that South Carolina native Lee Atwater was "purported to be a person who specializes in negative campaigns," he contended that "Dukakis is tough—he's not going to sit by and not fight back" (Columbia *State,* August 2, 1988, 1-A, 10-A).

33. Charleston *Evening Post,* August 17, 1988, 10-A.

34. Charleston *News and Courier,* September 1, 1988, 12-A. Republican State Representative Eugene Foxworth reported that "I have been accosted, almost assaulted by people in the grocery store fussing about what's taking place against Quayle." He noted that one woman was so upset that she almost hit him over the head with a bunch of carrots.

35. Columbia *State,* November 6, 1988, 1-A.

36. *Congressional Quarterly Weekly Report* (January 21, 1989): 2.

37. South Carolina State Election Commission, "South Carolina Voting History and Statistics, November 8, 1988, Statewide General Election," (Columbia, S.C.).

38. "Official 1988 Presidential Election Results," *1988 Congressional Quarterly Almanac* (Washington, D.C.: *Congressional Quarterly, Inc.,* 1989), 7-A.

39. All state election and registration statistics in this section are figures provided by, or are calculated from figures provided by, the South Carolina State Election Commission (Columbia, S.C.).

40. See Columbia *State,* October 30, 1988, 1-A, 15-A.

41. Black voter registration in the state for 1988 was down from 1984, when 27.9 percent of all registered voters were black. See "Drop in S.C. Black Vote Bodes Ill for Democrats," Columbia *State,* October 28, 1988, 1-C.

42. Moreland et al., "South Carolina," 145.

43. Pre-election survey reported in Columbia *State,* November 6, 1988, 1-A, 8-A. For a similar post-election analysis, see Columbia *State,* November 10, 1988, 1-A, 20-A.

44. All percentages relating to congressional elections calculated from statistics provided by the South Carolina State Election Commission (Columbia, S.C.).

45. Charleston *Evening Post,* October 12, 1988, 8-D.

46. See the *Charlotte Observer,* "What's in a Name? In S.C., Derrick Hopes It Isn't Votes," October 30, 1988, 3-B.

47. *South Carolina Statistical Abstract 1989* (Columbia: South Carolina Division of Research and Statistical Services, 1989), 169.

48. Charleston *News and Courier,* July 23, 1989, 11-A.

49. For an excellent short analysis of the 1988 election in South Carolina, see "Split Decision in South Carolina and the Nation," *The Carolina Report,* November 15, 1988.

50. The twelve Senate seats, however, offer the possibility of a "veto-proof" legislature in the event of vetoes by the state's Republican governor.

51. Graham, "Partisan Change," 174.

PART III

THE CAMPAIGN AND ITS
CONSEQUENCES: THE RIM SOUTH

8

Arkansas: Reluctant Republicans in Razorback Land

DIANE D. BLAIR

Long after most of the South had been conceded to Bush, Arkansas was still being characterized as too close to call, an anomaly that raises three questions. First, were predictions of a possible Democratic victory in Arkansas ever realistic; and if so, why? Second, to whatever extent Arkansas was correctly characterized as genuinely competitive in 1988, what combination of factors eventually placed it in the Republican column? Finally, what does this most recent Republican presidential victory portend for Arkansas' political future? To begin answering these questions, the 1988 campaign must first be placed in the context of Arkansas' developing political traditions.

INTRODUCTION: THE DEMOCRATIC TRADITION

Having resisted the lures of presidential Republicanism longer than any other southern state, Arkansas finally joined the Republican bandwagon with a flourish in 1972 (69 percent for Richard Nixon). Jimmy Carter carried Arkansas in 1976 by a margin (63 percent) larger than that in any state but his native Georgia, but then lost the state narrowly (47.5 percent to Ronald Reagan's 48.1 percent) in 1980. By 1984, however, Reagan was not just a slim preference but a resoundingly popular choice (61 percent) over Mondale. Indeed, the dimensions of Reagan's victory were so sweeping (sixty-five of Arkansas' seventy-five counties, all four congressional districts, and a plurality of nearly 200,000) that Republicanism generally seemed to have enhanced its hold on Arkansans' political affections, if not their offices. The systematic Republican campaign to convince Arkansans that national Democrats no longer represented their traditional values seemed to have been a significant component of Reagan's 1984 victory.[1] Early in the next election season of 1986, it appeared that the conversion campaign might have begun paying off below the presidential level.

For the first time in Arkansas history, there were more candidates in the Republican primary for the gubernatorial nomination than in the Democratic— a far cry from the recent past, when some Republican stalwart would be pressed into service as a sacrificial lamb. When Frank White triumphed over his three Republican opponents, and Bill Clinton easily defeated his two Democratic opponents (including Orval Faubus, who was making his third unsuccessful comeback bid), the stage was set for a highly combative third match between the two. Moreover, unlike their two previous encounters, this was a battle for Arkansas' first four-year gubernatorial term since Reconstruction (increased from two years by a constitutional amendment that was ratified by voters in 1984). The thrust of White's challenge was that Clinton was forcing the state (and its taxpayers) forward too quickly in order to advance Clinton's political fortunes, not the state's well-being. On a broad range of issues (school standards, spending, consolidation, taxes, abortion, and the appropriate role for the governor's wife), voters were offered a fairly clear choice between the options of governmental activism and social progressivism, and those of governmental restraint and social conservatism.

The U.S. Senate race in 1986 offered an even more clear-cut choice between the Republican right and the Democratic left. Republican challenger Asa Hutchinson, a graduate of Bob Jones University, a member of a fundamentalist church, a pro-life and scientific creationism activist, and a fiscal conservative and Reagan loyalist, carried the conservative standard. Incumbent Democrat Dale Bumpers, outspoken critic of the Strategic Defense Initiative, the MX Missile, and the B–1 Bomber; and an opponent of both the school prayer and balance-the-budget constitutional amendments, seemed like a prime target for charges that he had forgotten his roots in Arkansas traditionalism. Moreover, a parade of prominent Republicans came to remind Arkansas voters that a senator who "voted for the liberal Eastern establishment" and "85 to 95% of the time with ultra-liberal Ted Kennedy" was totally out of tune with Arkansas values.[2]

It was a valiant effort to wean Arkansas voters from their Democratic ways, but it was ultimately unsuccessful. Clinton was re-elected to his fourth gubernatorial term and by his highest margin ever (64 percent) over White. Bumpers was returned to the Senate with a 62 percent margin, better than his 59 percent victory in 1980. Moreover, in other state and county races, Democrats continued to win it all except in a few northwestern counties where Republicanism has gone beyond acceptability to advantageousness.

Arkansas "Almost-Rans"

Had either Bumpers or Clinton tossed his hat into the 1988 presidential ring, certainly this chapter, and perhaps this volume, would have recorded far different outcomes; and Arkansas citizens were tantalized for months by the hints that either Bumpers or Clinton would be on the national Democratic ticket. Bumpers, who had pondered the possibility of a presidential candidacy in both 1976 and 1980, did so again for 1988. One of his strongest supporters was Senator Paul Simon (who expressed the opinion that should Bumpers become a candidate, he would "have more support in the United States Senate than any other candidate").[3] However, on March 20, 1987, Bumpers emphatically withdrew himself from consideration.

Clinton examined the scene much more vigorously, sending operatives into a number of southern states to gauge the strength of the announced candidates' organizational and financial backing, and making speeches in Iowa and New Hampshire, and at numerous Democratic functions and fund-raisers elsewhere.[4] Clinton's potential presidential quest raised much more serious strategic problems than did Bumpers's: acute budgetary and other problems insured there would be constant charges of neglect if Clinton spent more time out of state than in; and though Lieutenant Governor Winston Bryant, who assumed the governorship immediately upon the Governor's absence, was reliable, the next in line of "succession" was definitely not. In fact, in a spring preview of possible disasters, Senate President Pro Tem Nick Wilson made twenty "gubernatorial" appointments and "demoted" the Governor's Chief of Staff during the brief absence of both Clinton and Bryant.

Despite these obvious obstacles, however, Clinton's exploratory operations were much more systematic and serious than those of Bumpers had ever been. Indeed, ten experienced presidential campaign activists (including Raymond Strother, Gary Hart's former media consultant) had gathered in Little Rock for what they presumed would be Clinton's presidential declaration when Clinton shocked them with the announcement that he would not run. Clinton's July 15 press conference emphasized the deleterious effects that prolonged absences would have on the Clintons' seven-year-old daughter Chelsea, and the battle fatigue brought on by having run fifteen campaigns in the last thirteen years. There was some speculation, as there had been with respect to Bumpers's decision, that the intense 1987 press interest in candidates' past personal lives was a contributing factor. For Arkansas, however, the bottom line was that all those among whom they eventually made their 1988 presidential choices were seen as less attractive than what might have been. In the week preceding Super Tuesday, *Arkansas Democrat* cartoonist Jon Kennedy captured the mood by depicting a reluctant Arkansas Democrat voter shuffling toward the Gore "Super-Dixie Bandwagon" while muttering to himself, "Shoulda been Dale . . . or Bill." On the other hand, the constant publicity about the possibility of an Arkansas

candidate on the national Democratic ticket may have been influential in re-
minding Arkansans that their most long-standing and prominent politicians and
traditions have been Democratic.[5]

Not-so-Super Tuesday

In the aftermath of the generally disastrous 1984 Arkansas experiment with a
caucus system, which had attracted only 22,202 participants as compared with
the nearly 450,000 Democrats who had participated in the 1980 presidential
primary, the state legislature mandated a return to the preferential primary in
1988, and also opted to join the other southern states in a common March 8
presidential primary date. The extent to which Super Tuesday generally did and
did not meet its advocates' and opponents' expectations has been and will be
explored extensively elsewhere.[6] Here it is only necessary to mention some
Arkansas-specific consequences of this experiment.

First, despite their late start while the possible favorite sons agonized over
their decisions, all the major Democratic and Republican candidates did have
some organization in place by election time, and all came personally to the state
to compete for its delegates. (The six major Democratic candidates logged in a
cumulative total of twenty visits, and the Republicans nine, though much of this
was "tarmac" time.) None of the candidates, however, seemed to truly catch
fire. Democratic activists dutifully attended cocktail parties and breakfasts, but
found the hopefuls sorely lacking in comparison with Arkansas' native talent.
(At a breakfast for Gore, for example, one attendant, dozing through the candidate's stock lines and wooden gestures, expressed doubt "that this guy ever
did drugs in college," and another noted the remarkable similarity between
Gore's voice and that of the computerized announcer at the Atlanta airport.)[7]
While most of the candidates had a respectable complement of Arkansas elected
officials heading or lending their names to their campaigns, none of those with
strong statewide organizations (namely, Bumpers, Clinton, or Pryor) attempted
to activate their campaign machinery in a particular candidate's behalf. Indeed,
it was widely observed that the peculiarly early March 8 date had a deadening
impact on interest and competition generally.

Much of this apathy was the inevitable by-product of the fact that, thanks to
the 1984 constitutional change, Arkansas' elected executives (most notably the
Governor) were not seeking nomination to another two-year term but were mid-
way in a four-year term; and with neither U.S. Senator up for re-election, there
simply were no attention-getting statewide seats at stake. Additionally, by combining the usual primaries with the presidential primary, decisions about running
and filing had to be made by late December, and other than incumbents, few
accepted the challenge. For state legislative seats, for example, only 14 House
and 2 Senate incumbents (out of a possible 117) drew primary opposition, leading
some to label Super Tuesday the "Incumbent Re-election Act." Furthermore,
only one of Arkansas' four incumbent Congressmen, Bill Alexander of the First

Table 8.1
Primary Voter Turnout in Presidential Election Years, 1976–1988

Year	Democratic Primary	Republican Primary
1976	525,968	22,797
1980	445,406	8,177
1984	492,321	19,040
1988	497,506	68,305

Source: Compiled by author from Arkansas Election Returns for years indicated.

District, drew opposition in the primary.

However, while the press periodically bemoaned the general apathy and the impossibility of campaigning Arkansas-style (with outdoor crowds gathered at barbecues and fish-fries) in January and February, Republicans started seeing the situation as a superb opportunity for increasing their numbers. By early 1988, State GOP Chairman Ed Bethune, who had originally expressed grave misgivings about Super Tuesday, had become its most enthusiastic state champion. Republican-sponsored radio and newspaper ads immediately prior to Super Tuesday attempted to persuade Arkansas voters that it was perfectly legal, in the absence of party registration, for anyone to vote in the Republican primary; and that most Arkansans would find a more comfortable ideological home there ("If you're just not interested in any of the Democratic candidates," one radio ad appealed, "and if you're fed up with higher taxes, liberal giveaways and backing down to the Soviets," you should be voting in the Republican primary). Whether the advertisements were successful, or (more likely) whether due to the absence of meaningful contests within the Democratic primary, many Arkansas voters were presented with their first opportunity to vote in the Republican primary without sacrificing their right to select most of their state and local officials, and turnout in the 1988 Republican primary reached new heights, as Table 8.1 indicates.[8]

Chairman Bethune's post-election claims that "we went through, we broke the sound barrier," and "we're on the move, we can't be written off anymore" were somewhat extravagant.[9] More than seven times as many voters chose the Democratic over the Republican primary. Reflecting the strongly regional strength of Arkansas Republicans, in thirty-one of Arkansas' Republican counties, fewer than 100 votes were cast in the Republican primary contest. Over half of those who did vote Republican did so in the northwestern Third Congressional District, which has kept Republican Congressman John Paul Hammerschmidt in the U.S. House since 1966. Moreover, in the central Second Congressional District, where Little Rock is located, Republican primary turnout was so sparse that it took only 6,648 votes to select Warren Carpenter as the Republican congressional nominee, giving embarrassed Republicans a candidate who claimed that he was being poisoned by death rays from the Reagan White

House.

One partisan pundit attempted to disparage the advantageousness of the out-come for Republicans, pointing out that Jackson got twice as many votes as did George Bush in Arkansas and, in fact, got more votes in Arkansas than all six Republicans combined; indeed, even "uncommitted" in the Democratic primary drew more votes than did Bush. This observer triumphantly concluded:

Perhaps the greatest irony was that right here, in one of the biggest notches in the Bible Belt, we still confound the experts. Gary Hart had some minor public relations problems, didn't campaign in Arkansas, and had no headquarters here. Pat Robertson practically lived here, had a paid staff, claimed an invisible army of new voters, and won several GOP straw votes. Gary Hart got more votes in Arkansas than did Pat Robertson. It *was* a Super Tuesday![10]

The fact remains, however, that while Republicans were showing an impres-sive tripling of their usual primary turnout, Democratic numbers stayed flat. Of even greater seeming consequence for the fall contest was the fact that Arkansas Republicans overwhelmingly demonstrated their preference for Bush (with 47 percent, compared to Dole's distant 26 percent, Robertson's 19 percent, and Kemp's 5 percent), who on Super Tuesday effectively became the party's nom-inee. In sharp contrast, Arkansas Democrats were showing a decided preference (37 percent) for neighboring Senator Albert Gore, who was soon to be eliminated from contention, and a relatively weak (19 percent) second preference for Du-kakis, who was to be their nominee. Furthermore, an important segment (17 percent) of Arkansas Democrats opted for Jackson, who was not to be on the ticket at all. While there were a few notable regional variations within the larger state pattern (Gephardt carried four counties on the Missouri border, for example, and Jackson carried ten counties with high black populations), both Bush and Gore carried all four of the state's congressional districts in the only displays of broad-based support. On balance, then, Super Tuesday was a net plus for Ar-kansas Republicans, and the subsequent nominating conventions did nothing to erase that advantage.

Arkansas and the Conventions

Both party's conventions came to upbeat conclusions with surprisingly inspi-rational acceptance speeches by the nominees following the tedium of most of what had preceded them. In Arkansas, as elsewhere, the choice of Senator Dan Quayle to run with Bush was a net negative, especially as seen in contrast to Dukakis's selection of neighboring-state Senator Lloyd Bentsen.[11] However, for most Arkansans, *the* convention story, in terms of salience, coverage, shock value, and reverberations throughout the fall campaign, was The Speech, as Clinton's speech nominating Dukakis came to be known.

After considerable speculation that either Bumpers or Clinton might be the vice presidential choice of Dukakis, and then speculation that either Bumpers or Clinton might be selected as the keynote orator (and disappointment on both counts), there was finally heartening news for Arkansas Democrats. First, it was announced that Lottie Shackelford, Little Rock's black woman mayor, had been selected to be one of the convention's four presiding chairs. For a state that still suffers from its identification with "Little Rock Central High," this very visible position for a much more accurate symbol of contemporary Arkansas was enthusiastically received.

Even more gratifying was the news that Governor Bill Clinton had been selected by Dukakis to give the only nominating speech. In the effusive words of the *Arkansas Gazette*:

Michael Dukakis deserves full credit for knowing where to look—Arkansas—when he needed someone of marvelous elocution to make his nominating speech. . . . Of the four sublime orators in the party—Clinton, U.S. Senator Dale Bumpers, Jesse Jackson and Governor Mario Cuomo—two are from Arkansas.[12]

On the evening of July 21, Arkansas delegates in the convention hall in Atlanta and Arkansans at home in front of their television sets eagerly awaited the reflected glory that would be theirs when Clinton demonstrated these oratorical gifts to the nation. Instead, to their acute dismay, The Speech was, in the words of the same newspaper which had dubbed him a "sublime orator," an "unmitigated disaster." A speech that was scheduled to last only fifteen minutes ran for what seemed an interminable thirty-two minutes, and was greeted with increasingly vocal disapproval by delegates and television newscasters alike. In a *Washington Post* story headlined "The Numb and the Restless," Tom Shales described "Windy Clinty's classic clinker" as having "calcified" the convention, while Jesse Jackson had "electrified" it; and Johnny Carson made a running gag about the "Arkansas windbag" for many nights running.[13]

Clinton's subsequent appearance on the "Johnny Carson Show," where he managed to display his saxophone-playing skills as well as his self-deprecating wit, turned Carson (and presumably Carson's audience) from critics to fans. Demonstrating the defensiveness that had made the speech itself so embarrassing, over one-fourth of the state's population (the highest ratings in the history of Arkansas television) watched their Governor redeem his and the state's reputation, and exulted in his success. There was, however, a strong undercurrent of suspicion as well as sorrow and shame.

After all, in the course of Clinton's fifteen campaigns for office and constant appearances around the state as Governor, most Arkansans had heard him speak numerous times; and while there were undoubtedly occasions when he was less than "sublime," few could remember him ever having given less than a good speech. Indeed, as one observer noted, "those of us in Arkansas have seen Clinton when we thought he could bring a crowd to its feet by reading a credit card application.'' In a state where politics is still intensely personal, and some-times paranoid, political attentives speculated endlessly on the possibilities of deliberate setup and sabotage. The bitterness of some Dukakis's operatives over Clinton's refusal to openly endorse Dukakis before the March 8 primary was remembered; and the facts that Dukakis floor operatives on the night of Clinton's speech had not dimmed the lights, as Clinton expected, and did nothing by way of crowd control when the speech, approved by Dukakis, so clearly turned out to be the wrong speech at the wrong time, were widely discussed and resented. Although the Atlanta convention had seemingly sidestepped some of the disasters of San Francisco, the flag-waving smoothness of the Republican convention, compared with the anguish and anger prompted by Clinton's appearance at the Democratic convention, provided another net plus for the Republicans.[14]

THE CAMPAIGN

Despite these setbacks for Dukakis and the Democrats, the fall campaign— at least until the time of the second presidential debate—was waged as though Arkansas were genuinely up for grabs. Commentary in the national press con-sistently described Arkansas as a toss-up, as being winnable by either side but certain for neither, and these estimates were echoed by most of the state press as well.[15]

Reinforcing the impressionistic accuracy of these analyses was the unusual frequency with which Dukakis, Bentsen, Bush, and Quayle all personally came to campaign in the state. Counting only those appearances by the candidates themselves (and not the even more frequent presence of spouses and surrogates), by campaign's end, Dukakis had been to the state three times, Bentsen six, Bush once, and Quayle twice, which figures out at more than two personal appearances per each of Arkansas' six electoral votes. Clearly, Arkansas was seen by both camps as a state that could and must be contested for.

With no Arkansas statewide seats at stake, there was little professional polling, and therefore, these early general estimates are somewhat difficult to evaluate. However, a September 27 poll done for a constitutional ballot issue indicated that Bush and Dukakis were at a dead heat with 44 percent each and the rest undecided. On October 6, Republican Chairman Ed Bethune revealed that ''three weeks ago'' a poll had indicated that the race was a toss-up in Arkansas; and returning from a Republican Southern Strategy session several days later, he quoted Lee Atwater to the effect that ''the state he has historically worried about was Arkansas.''[16]

On the Democratic side, a mail survey of the state's seventy-five Democratic County Chairs, sent out on September 22 and returned over the course of the next three weeks, further substantiated the general impression that the Democratic ticket had a stronger chance of carrying Arkansas in 1988 than it had in 1984.[17] Of the fifty-one chairs who responded, only two thought Dukakis was running worse than had Mondale in 1984, six said about the same, and the other forty-three said better—twenty-four said marginally better and nineteen considerably better. The chair's responses indicated that the ticket did have problems. Asked whether they had been hearing in their counties any items on a checklist of criticisms, they produced the following affirmatives: will probably raise taxes (thirty-nine); will be "soft" on defense (twenty-six); has given in too much to Jesse Jackson (seventeen); opposed the Pledge of Allegiance (twenty-five). Furthermore, when asked to identify any other negative comments or criticisms they had been hearing, none of the chairs gave an early indication that Dukakis's position on gun control (even before the National Rifle Association began its anti-Dukakis commercials) was beginning to create problems; eight indicated Dukakis's pro-abortion position was not going down well in their counties; and ten simply noted that area voters were concerned that the candidate was just too liberal.

Clearly, from the very beginning there were misgivings about the ability to "sell" Dukakis in Arkansas. However, when interviewed on October 12, Clinton insisted that even though Bush's relentless attacks on Dukakis had "turned him into an alien in the eyes of Arkansas and the South," it was still too early for Democrats to write off the state.[18] Since by this time Clinton had been named one of Dukakis's twelve national campaign chairs, his assessment might be discounted. There were, however, several factors that seemed capable of drawing Arkansas back into the Democratic presidential column.

The Democratic Draws

One factor making the Dukakis candidacy appear stronger than Mondale's was the readiness with which almost all of Arkansas' elected officials embraced it. Clinton's enthusiastic backing was clearly a plus in Arkansas: erasing (or at least easing) the doubts about possible Dukakis duplicity in the disaster at Atlanta, giving the Dukakis organization access to the best lists (in terms of both workers and contributors) in Arkansas, and especially making available to the national campaign the extraordinary rapport with Arkansas' black voters for which Clinton is legendary. In contrast to 1980, when Bumpers had his own campaign for re-election and wisely stayed somewhat aloof, and 1984 when Senator David Pryor did likewise, both Senators made numerous appearances with and for the national ticket, attempting to transfer the Arkansas imprimatur to it. Congressman Beryl Anthony, Chairman of the Democratic Congressional Campaign Committee (and originally a Gephardt supporter) actively stumped for the ticket, as did Congressman Bill Alexander. The distinctive case of Second District Congressman Tommy Robinson will be discussed below. With that singular exception, all Arkansas officialdom, including the Lieutenant Governor, who chaired Dukakis' Arkansas campaign, all other elected executives, state legislators, county judges, and sheriffs, dutifully appeared with and spoke in the ticket's behalf.

Of course, the Bush campaign had a popular and politically skillful elected official at its helm as well: Congressman John Paul Hammerschmidt, who had entered the House with Bush in 1966 and maintained a close personal friendship. However, Hammerschmidt's influence, while strong in the Republican Third District, could not be equated with that of Arkansas' Democratic Big Three (Clinton, Bumpers, and Pryor), all of whom, in an October poll, had strong approval ratings from Arkansas voters (of 62 percent, 63 percent, and 59 percent, respectively).[19] The fact that the Big Three were free to campaign for Dukakis because they were not fighting for their own offices had a decided downside as well: Their faithful followings would not necessarily be turning out in the usual large numbers, an especially worrisome problem insofar as black voters were concerned. However, the larger point here is that the state's most successful politicians (again with the notable exception of Congressman Tommy Robinson) all seemed comfortable with and supportive of their Democratic party, thereby reinforcing the traditions of most Arkansas voters.

Contemporary demographics also strengthened Democratic chances. While Arkansas has of course participated in the general modernization and "nationalization" of the South in recent decades, it remains one of the poorest and most rural states, with smaller proportions of those populations (urban and metropolitan; middle-class and better educated; and those in managerial, technical, and service occupations) who are the cutting edge of Republican organization and growth elsewhere in the South. In-migration has helped to swell Republican ranks, especially because it has been concentrated in the Arkansas uplands where Republicans have maintained a small base since the Civil War, but many of those moving into Arkansas have previous Arkansas ties, including an apparent tie to Democrats at sub-presidential levels. Blacks now constitute 14.6 percent of the state's population, and a slightly smaller percentage of the registered voters, obviously a minority. However, with overwhelming support from the black community, which has tended to vote in monolithic fashion for Democrats, candidates need obtain little more than one-third of the white vote to win a statewide race. The black population appears to be sizeable enough to be politically influential, but not so sizeable that its visible strength has frightened off all the state's traditional white Democrats.[20]

Economics as well as demographics seemed to favor Democrats in 1988. The combination of years of sagging farm prices, unemployment rates consistently higher than the national average, low oil prices and cheap Canadian timber imports, and the loss of thousands of low-wage, low-skill manufacturing jobs to plants overseas, meant more voters could better relate to Dukakis's expressions of economic anxiety than to Bush's boasts about a boom that few had yet experienced. In the state's urban center and in some prosperous pockets around the state there was economic vitality; but overall, per capita income in Arkansas, after years of steady growth relative to the national average, was on the relative decline.

There was an additional reason, absolutely unique to Arkansas, that gave Democrats reason to hope and Republicans reason to emphasize the ease and importance of absentee voting. Because of the unusual lateness of the November

Table 8.2
Expressed Voter Preferences in Arkansas, October 1988 (in percent)

Poll	Poll Date	Bush	Dukakis	Undecided	(N)
Mason-Dixon Research	October 10-11	47	41	12	(826)
Center for Research & Public Policy	October 14-19	54	32	14	(394)
Opinion Research Associates	October 24-26	48	32	20	(452)
Mason-Dixon Research	October 26-28	49	40	10	(809)

Source: Compiled by the author from polls published in Arkansas Democrat and Arkansas Gazette.

8 Election Day in 1988, it fell during the first week of deer hunting season, when it was estimated that 250,000 to 300,000 avid Arkansans (and surely most of them no friends of "anti-gun" Dukakis) would be in the woods instead of at their polling places on November 8.

The Republican Advantage: Arkansas Iconography

Whatever advantages Democrats brought into the 1988 campaign were soon submerged in a sea of negative imagery. By early October, the signs of another Republican presidential victory in Arkansas were evident, as Table 8.2 demonstrates. Bush surged immediately after the second presidential debate and dropped thereafter; but he never lost his "plurality" in the preference polls.

There is little mystery regarding the reasons for these attitudes and, ultimately, votes. What happened in Arkansas differs little from what happened in the rest of the South; indeed, from what happened in 1984. One analysis of the 1984 presidential race in Arkansas focused on the fact that whereas Democrats came to the state espousing a broad spectrum of of initiatives, "all Republican speakers dealt in some fashion with the same trinity of themes: We will not raise taxes; we will stand up to our enemies abroad; the Democratic Party has lurched to the left and abandoned its traditional constituency."[21]

With minimal variation, the same trinity of themes provided the campaign focus, and the menu for success, again in 1988. The first of these themes, the oft-repeated "Read my lips, no new taxes," needs no elaboration. The interesting Arkansas variation in 1988 stems from the publicity and plaudits that Senator David Pryor had received all year in Arkansas for his proposed populistic Tax-payers Bill of Rights, to protect citizens against unfair harassment by the Internal Revenue Service. While Pryor did "everything I know to do with the Dukakis campaign to sensitize him to this issue," it was Bush who gave the plan his ringing endorsement in a Little Rock speech on October 6, while ridiculing the

Dukakis plan for bringing the budget under control by "creating an auditor's army of IRS agents to squeeze another $35 billion out of the American tax-payers."[22]

On the second theme of a strong defense, Bush warned his Little Rock listeners that the country could not "gamble on another unknown liberal governor who would be willing to deal with the Soviet Union from a position of weakness;" and later, in Little Rock, President Reagan accused Dukakis of backing "a weak-kneed defense policy that only McGovern could love." Republican Chairman Bethune repeatedly reminded audiences that "under Carter and the liberals, our military was weak and morale was very low," and Marvin Bush, son of the Vice President, added his own disparaging touch: "My dad has experience. So does Dukakis. He's eaten breakfast at the International House of Pancakes."[23]

Above all, the Republicans used every appearance and occasion, every mailing and sound bite, to wrap the liberal label around the national ticket. In 1984, the leftist tag had something of a special interest and San Francisco flavor—labor and the National Education Association (NEA), gays and feminists; in 1988 the charges had a more Massachusetts flavor—big-spending, welfare-loving, criminal-coddling. What distinguished the 1988 from the 1984 effort most of all, however, was the specificity of the liberal charges, tied this time to Willie Horton and furloughs for criminals, to the Pledge of Allegiance and Dukakis's membership in the ACLU, to Dukakis's opposition to the death penalty, and, perhaps most critically, to Dukakis's much-discussed position with respect to gun control. It is impossible to overemphasize how quickly the stories spread that Dukakis wanted to confiscate all personally owned guns, how rapidly the bumper stickers appeared saying "Defend Firearms, Defeat Dukakis," and how devastatingly this damaged Dukakis in precisely those rural and small-town constituencies who have been the backbone of what is left of "Yellow Dog" Democracy.

While traditional Democrats in 1984 might have been made to feel vaguely uncomfortable with Mondale because of his platform, his running mate, and his organizational backing, it was Dukakis himself who came to be portrayed in 1988 as the epitome of liberalism, which in turn came to be spoken of in tones usually reserved for Satanism. Bethune solemnly and repeatedly proclaimed that "I have never met a person in my whole life who is more liberal," and went on to elaborate that "Michael Dukakis is a screeching liberal and Lloyd Bentsen, his running mate, is his fig leaf." Neil Bush, another of George Bush's sons, warned that Dukakis had "a radical leftist agenda" and would lead the country "down a new path of radical change." Moreover, President Reagan himself, in his October 27 Little Rock rally, used "liberal," "liberalism," and "left-wing," references fourteen times in seventeen minutes, concluding—should anyone have missed the point—that the Democratic leadership "can only be described by the dreaded L-word—liberal, liberal, liberal."[24]

The Democrats were not entirely passive as this Arkansas-unattractive image was being fashioned. They attempted to invoke symbols and emblems, like the

Arkansas Razorbacks and Harry Truman, with assumed appeal. Consistently, however, they were one-upped by the Republicans.

Like all political visitors to Arkansas, the 1988 presidential campaigners paid homage to the fighting Razorbacks, totem of the University of Arkansas athletic teams. Appearing at a campus rally during the traditional Beat Texas week, for example, Bentsen suggested that the Democratic party must be unified indeed "if a Texan can be here three days before the game saying nice things about Arkansas." Earlier in the week, Bush had begun his rally remarks in Little Rock by mentioning the university's rout of Texas Christian University the previous week, and deliberately provoked a round of ecstatic hog calling by asking the rhetorical question; "How about the way those Hogs are doing?" Both were outdone, however, by the Gipper, Ronald Reagan himself. Appearing before twenty thousand ecstatic Arkansans ten days before the election, he began by noting that Arkansas has some of the greatest college football teams in the United States, cheerfully accepted a T-shirt proclaiming "I'm A Bush Hog," and even uttered the inspirational (to Arkansas ears) words, "Hey pigs, sooie."[25]

Dukakis officially opened his Arkansas campaign with a well-executed whistle-stop in Walnut Ridge in late August. Despite stormy weather, between three and five thousand people waited to greet him, and heard Dukakis remind them that he, like Harry Truman, was a son of small-town America; and that he, like Truman, could stage a successful campaign, in the interests of the average American family, by train. Again, however, it was Reagan who had the last word, proclaiming, on his late-October campaign swing, that Truman was "the true father of today's Republican party."[26]

If one were looking for the precise imagery to capture what went right for the Republican ticket in Arkansas in 1988, and what went wrong for the Democrats, the symbols surrounding Bush's October 6 Little Rock rally serve nicely. Attempting to steal some of Bush's media attention, a Democratic press conference was held at party headquarters hours before Bush's arrival, at which four people— a blind woman, a mother, a veteran, and a sheriff— explained how much worse off they were under the Reagan administration, and how little Bush and Quayle seemed to care about their respective plights. Within hours, these pleas for sensitivity and mercy, and reminders of need and pain, were followed by a wholly upbeat, colorful, and cheerful Bush rally, perfectly staged and executed at the downtown MainStreet Mall, complete with flags, cheerleaders, bands, hog calls, and peppy punch lines—about standing up to the Soviet Union, watching your wallet, and protecting the right to bear arms. Rounding out the day's imagery, the *Arkansas Democrat* write-up noted that

Before the speech, about 25 supporters of the Massachusetts governor gathered at Urbi Et Orbi, an art gallery in the MainStreet Mall. They sipped white wine while placing Dukakis-Bentsen posters in the windows facing the Metrocentre Mall. A dalmation wore a collar made out of Dukakis bumper stickers.[27]

It seems safe to assume that, in 1988 in Arkansas, there were more flag lovers, football enthusiasts, and gun owners than art collectors and white-wine sippers.

Arkansas' own politicians attempted to deride the Republican's negative iconography. "Take 'Kennedy' and 'liberal' out of the Republican's vocabulary and he gets lockjaw," Bumpers claimed. Clinton gave his own version of the Bush campaign collapsed into a single statement, as follows:

Look, whatever you think of me, you have to vote for me for president because you can't vote for that other guy because, after all, he doesn't like to say the Pledge of Allegiance and he loves to turn criminals loose. And, after he turns them loose, while they're on their way to your house to mug you, he's going to come take your gun away so you can't defend yourself. And after they mug you, he's going to make sure that they're defended in court by the ACLU. And, while the trial's going on, if you've got anything left, he's going to give it away to the communists."[28]

Bumpers and Clinton always provoked appreciative cheers and laughter with such remarks, but what surrogates could say in Dukakis's defense needed to be effectively conveyed by the candidate himself, and it never was. With increasingly evident exasperation, the Big Three began to privately, and then publicly, acknowledge that Dukakis's inexplicable failure to dispel the damaging impressions being created was making it impossible for them to carry the Democratic standard on his behalf.[29]

In a state where school prayer and the death penalty are so universally supported as to not even be controversial, and where a truck without a gun rack is a rare sight indeed, the Republican campaign portraying Dukakis as being "soft on crime, weak on defense, naive on foreign policy, big on taxes, and rejecting traditional family values" was precisely on target. Thus, for the third time in a row, the Republican presidential ticket carried Arkansas.[30]

RESULTS AND ANALYSIS: DÉJÀ VU ALL OVER AGAIN

While Bush's final 56.3 percent victory margin in Arkansas was better than his national margin of 53.9 percent, it was a less impressive margin than that in the South generally (58.5 percent) and considerably less impressive than Reagan's winning margin of 61.2 percent in 1984. Dukakis carried twenty-three of Arkansas' seventy-five counties, whereas Mondale had carried only ten; and Bush's plurality of 117,341 was substantially less than Reagan's 196,128.

Whether it was a general lack of enthusiasm for the presidential candidates (in a late October poll, 40 percent of Arkansas' potential voters expressed unhappiness with the choices) or the absence of other meaningful contests on the ballot, Arkansas' voting turnout, which had exceeded that of the nation in 1984 (52.5 percent of the VAP compared to 51.4 percent of the national VAP) dropped below the national average (44.2 percent) in Arkansas compared to 49.1 percent of the VAP nationally in 1988. Turnout might have been lower still had not the

Table 8.3

Simple Correlation Coefficients (Pearson's r) between the 1984 Reagan Vote, the 1988 Bush Vote, and Selected Variables

Variables	1984 Vote for Reagan	1988 Vote for Bush
Demographic Variables		
Percent population growth, 1970-80	.5749	.5574
Percent black	-.6591	-.5532
Percent population born in state	-.5627	-.4976
Percent persons living below poverty level	-.5643	-.5001
Percent urban	-.0650	-.0506
Electoral Variables		
Percent Republican pres. vote, 1960	.6233	.5630
Percent Republican pres. vote, 1968	.6697	.6290
Percent Republican pres. vote, 1980	.8356	.7680
Percent Republican U.S. Senate vote, 1984	.9049	.8649
Percent Republican gubernatorial vote, 1984	.8248	.7664
Percent Democratic U.S. Senate vote, 1986	-.8294	-.8312
Percent Republican pres. vote, 1984		.9072
Percent Jackson vote, 1988 Dem. primary		-.5178
Percent Dukakis vote, 1988 Dem. primary		.5205
Percent Gore vote, 1988 Dem. primary		.0869

Source: Coded, compiled, and analyzed by the author with the assistance of Kimberly Johnson.

efforts to remind deer hunters to vote before they hunted produced unprecedented levels of absentee voting.[31]

The basic components of Republican victory in 1988 were much the same as those in 1984. Both the demographic data in public opinion polls and the correlations displayed in Table 8.3 suggest that Bush did better with the higher income and better educated voters than he did with less educated and less affluent Arkansans. Bush's strongest counties were the more prosperous growth counties; Dukakis' strongest counties were those with larger numbers of blacks, native Arkansans, and those living in poverty. The average October unemployment rate in Dukakis's twenty-three counties was 9.6 percent, compared to the state average of 6.7 percent.[32]

Probably the best news for Republicans in the 1988 Arkansas victory was that, as in 1984, the strongest support came from the youngest voters: According to a late October Opinion Research Associates poll, 63 percent of those under thirty-five favored Bush, compared with 52 percent of those aged thirty-five to sixty-four, and only 31 percent of those sixty-five and above.[33] The increasingly strong correlations between Republican votes for all major offices is another sign of a stable, rather than totally episodic, Republican vote in Arkansas. The correlations in Table 8.3 also suggest, as was indicated earlier, that the national Democratic party nominated the candidate least likely to appeal to Arkansas Democrats.

Especially in view of that fact, Republicans might be disheartened that Dukakis did win back some of the voters that Mondale had lost. According to one late October poll, only 7 percent of those who had voted for Mondale were planning to vote for Bush, whereas 16 percent of those who had voted for Reagan were planning to vote for Dukakis.[34] Furthermore, Bush's victory generated no significant Republican breakthroughs below the presidential level. In the state's most populous Pulaski County, two open legislative seats were won by Republicans, but this left Republican state legislative strength at minimal levels: four out of thirty-five in the Senate, eleven out of 100 in the House. Republicans won seven of eleven local races in White County, home of Republican Chairman Bethune and also home to very conservative Harding College. The state's most northwestern and most Republican Benton County continued to eliminate all Democrats from office (only two are left), and in its neighbor, Washington County, some Democratic incumbents fought off challenges by margins that will encourage rather than discourage future contests.

For the most part, however, as previous analyses of the contemporary political patterns in Arkansas have emphasized, Republican strength is still mostly confined to the Ozark uplands and some of the more prosperous precincts in urban areas.[35] The maps of counties carried by the candidates in Figure 8.1, and of Bush's and Dukakis's strongest counties in Figure 8.2, simply confirm these long-standing regional variations: strength for the Republicans in the northern and western Third Congressional District, where history, in-migration, and prosperity uniquely combine to Republican advantage; strength for the Democrats in the delta lowlands, where poverty is greatest, black populations most numerous, and traditions strongest. Indeed, while elsewhere in the South it was estimated that only 32 percent of white voters supported Dukakis, he carried some east Arkansas counties (Clay and Fulton) with literally no black population, and some (Randolph and Poinsett) where the black population is minimal.

One small-town newspaper editor lamented how hard it was becoming to be a Democrat when candidates like Dukakis kept winning the party's nomination:

There aren't enough wide-eyed liberals who actually believe those outrageous plans of the new Democrats to get anybody elected custodian of the White House john, let alone the presidency. . . . The liberal Democrats are losing a large chunk of their voting support. That train has done left the good old boys at the station.[36]

On the other hand, it is hard to imagine the "good old boys" feeling comfortable at the 1988 Bush victory celebration, which was hosted by Bush campaign co-chair Mary Anne Stephens and her husband Jack, a multimillionaire investment banker, and where the offerings included, "Oysters Rockefeller, an international cheese tray and smoked salmon, plus lamb chops and Shrimp Provencal cooked tableside by white-coated chefs."[37]

A recent analysis of partisan realignment and dealignment in Arkansas concluded that Arkansans still have a standing decision to be Democrats, although

Figure 8.1
Counties Carried by Presidential Candidates, 1984 and 1988

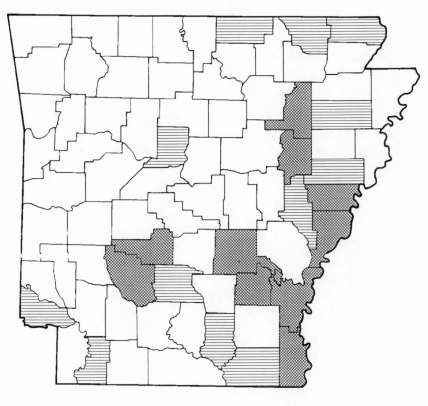

☐ Carried by Bush, 1988

▤ Carried by Dukakis, 1988

▨ Carried by Dukakis, 1988
and Mondale, 1984

"now that Republican candidates are generally considered to be at least potentially palatable items on the election menu, the Democratic party is simply
standing on less firm ground."[38] In 1988, Republicans successfully portrayed
Dukakis as totally unpalatable to Arkansas tastes, but the Democratic offerings
will probably still get first consideration.

Figure 8.2
Candidates' Strongest Counties, 1988, by Congressional District

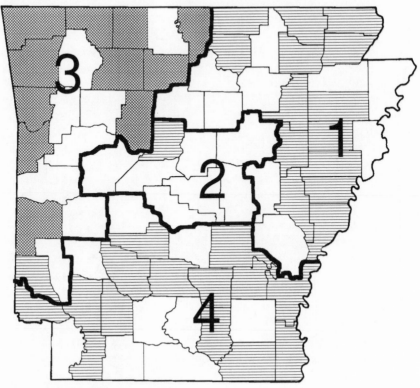

Bush 5% or more above
his state average

Dukakis 5% or more
above his state average

Source: Prepared by author.

CONCLUSION

By reinforcing what has become a pattern of presidential Republicanism, the
1988 election continued to weaken long-standing Democratic ties and traditions.
However, no major state offices changed hands, nor need most Democratic
officials (outside the Ozark uplands) feel threatened in the near future. Clinton's
close association with the Dukakis campaign probably did him less damage than
did legislators' professed belief that the evident popularity of Bush's ''no new
taxes'' pledge made Clinton's ambitious $211 million revenue-raising scheme
for educational and economic improvements political poison. Of equal practical

effect, it is possible that had Clinton spent more time campaigning for the proposed Fair Tax Amendment (which would have made it constitutionally easier to raise most taxes, but which was defeated) and less time on the Dukakis campaign, his 1989 legislative program might have had a better chance for success.

Perhaps above all, what 1988 demonstrated was the uncanny ability of maverick Congressman Tommy Robinson, from Arkansas' Second Congressional District (Little Rock and surrounding suburban and rural counties) to align himself with Arkansas sentiments. Robinson was first elected in 1984 after extremely colorful and controversial service as Pulaski County Sheriff which kept him constantly on camera.

Given Robinson's affiliation with the Boll Weevils, it surprised no one that he was the only Democratic member of Arkansas' congressional delegation not named a super delegate. Undaunted, Robinson successfully sought election by the state Democratic convention as a state official pledged to Gore; but he was elected only after a challenge brought by those who wanted to punish Robinson for having weeks previously told a Little Rock peace activist to take her anti-MX petitions and "stick 'em where the sun don't shine." Later, at the national Democratic convention, when the other Gore delegates dutifully switched to Dukakis for a final show of unity, Robinson switched to Jackson, claiming that Jesse's speech "had touched my soul." He indicated that he would vote for Dukakis, but "I'll have to hold my nose. He needs some good old boys giving him the other side of the story."[39]

Robinson's September newsletter to constituents had a front-page picture of Dukakis, but throughout the fall he expressed highly critical opinions to the effect that Dukakis should spend less time in Texas and California speaking Spanish and more time in "states like Arkansas speaking words we can understand"; that, "what has played for Dukakis in ethnic neighborhoods in New York and Boston won't play in places such as Lonoke and Searcy"; and that Dukakis was not welcome in Jacksonville, home of Little Rock Air Force Base and a finalist as a potential MX garrison. Finally, in an October 26 speech to the Arkansas Hospitality Association, Robinson stated, "I'm an Arkansas Democrat. There is a distinct difference between an Arkansas Democrat and a national Democrat"; and flatly declined to endorse the national ticket. Advertising himself as an "independent voice in Washington," Robinson easily defeated Republican Warren Carpenter with 87 percent of the vote.[40]

Had Dukakis won the presidency, there is a strong likelihood that Clinton's next career step would have been in the cabinet. With Bush in the White House, and Clinton pledged not to challenge Pryor in 1990, his attention increasingly turned to another bid for the governorship. When, in the week immediately after the election, Robinson strongly intimated that he might be looking at the governorship as well, anticipatory anguish rippled through Arkansas Democrats. Conceivably, Robinson could switch to the Republican party, secure the nomination almost without contest, and proceed to a fall blood bath against Clinton.

Furthermore, the earth could be scorched even sooner, in a raucous Democratic primary such as the state had not witnessed in years. The 1988 presidential election created relatively little interest in Arkansas, and had no immediate impact on the state's political infrastructure. It could, however, be a prelude to a race in which the two principals chose decidedly different paths in the 1988 contest, and that race would have profound portent for Arkansas' political future.

Postscript: On July 28, 1989, Congressman Tommy Robinson, standing by President Bush's side at the White House, announced his decision to switch to the Republican party. ''The hard fact is,'' he said, ''that there is and will be no room for conservative southern Democrats in today's National Democratic Party.''

NOTES

1. For details on the attempts to dealign Democrats in Arkansas in 1984, see Diane D. Blair, ''Arkansas,'' in Robert P. Steed, Laurence W. Moreland, and Tod A. Baker, eds., *The 1984 Presidential Election in the South* (New York: Praeger, 1986), 192–194.

2. Citations and details on the 1986 elections in Arkansas in Diane D. Blair, *Arkansas Politics and Government: Do the People Rule?* (Lincoln: University of Nebraska Press, 1988), 272–280.

3. Senator Simon quoted by Carol Matlack, ''Bumpers Keeps Quiet on Presidential Plans,'' *Arkansas Gazette,* January 27, 1987, 6A.

4. See, for example, stories in the *Wall Street Journal,* April 28, 1987, 60; *New York Times,* May 31, 1987, 28; and *Washington Post,* June 8, 1987, 3A.

5. For extensive coverage and analysis of Clinton's withdrawal, see numerous stories in the *Arkansas Democrat* and *Arkansas Gazette,* July 16 and 17, 1987; Kennedy's cartoon appeared on March 4, 1988, 6B.

6. See, for example, Charles D. Hadley and Harold W. Stanley, ''An Analysis of Super Tuesday: Intentions, Results, and Implications'' (Paper delivered at the 1988 annual meeting of the Midwest Political Science Association, Washington, D.C., April 14–16, 1988).

7. Remarks overheard by the author at the Washington County Democratic breakfast for Senator Gore, December 17, 1987, Fayetteville, Ark.

8. For Bethune's changing position, see *Arkansas Gazette,* December 15, 1986, 9A; and February 27, 1988, 10A. Text from radio ad broadcast on KEZA, Fayetteville, March 7, 1988, and in *Springdale News,* March 6, 1988, 6D.

9. Bethune quoted in *Arkansas Democrat,* March 10 1988, B1.

10. Steve Smith, ''A few Alibis and Retrospectives on the South's Super Tuesday,'' *Arkansas Gazette,* March 15, 1988, 11A.

11. Polls in the *Arkansas Democrat,* October 14, 1988, 1A; and in an October 28 AETN press release, showed most Arkansas voters thought Quayle was unqualified, and had Bentsen been the Democratic nominee, he would have outpolled Bush, 42 to 38 percent, with 20 percent undecided.

12. Editorial, ''Who Else for the Nominating Speech?'' July 9, 1988.

13. For these quotes and many additional columns and analyses regarding The Speech, see the *Arkansas Gazette* and the *Arkansas Democrat,* July 22 and 23, 1988.

14. Quotation from Tom Welch, ''Dukakis Staff at Fault in Clinton's Debacle,''

Arkansas Gazette, July 30, 1988, 1A. The widespread suspicions of sabotage were confirmed by Governor's Clinton's Chief of Staff, Betsey Wright, in a telephone conversation, August 26, 1988.

15. See, for example, the *Congressional Quarterly* analysis cited in the *Arkansas Democrat,* July 23, 1988, 6B; the *Washington Post* estimate cited in the *Springdale News,* October 19, 1988, 5A; and R. W. Apple's analysis in the *New York Times,* October 13, 1988, 12A. See also John Brummett in the *Arkansas Gazette,* August 27, 1988, 1B. On the other hand, by October 12, John Robert Starr of the *Arkansas Democrat* estimated that Bush was "comfortably ahead, and will be further ahead by Election Day," quoted in the *New York Times,* October 13, 1988, 12A.

16. September 27 poll done by Public Opinion Research and made available to the author in Little Rock on October 7; Bethune quoted in *Arkansas Gazette,* October 7, 1988, 12A; and in *Arkansas Democrat,* October 11, 1988, 1B.

17. Mail survey constructed and conducted by the author. Tabulated responses in the author's possession.

18. Clinton quoted by R. W. Apple, "Bush Has a Slight Lead in Arkansas," *New York Times,* October 13, 1988, 12A.

19. Approval ratings in the *Arkansas Democrat,* October 15, 1988, 10A.

20. For discussion of the impact of these factors in the South generally, and why they suggest less Republican growth in Arkansas than elsewhere, see Earl Black and Merle Black, *Politics and Society in the South* (Cambridge, Mass.: Harvard University Press, 1987), 264–275, 308–316. For a more extensive discussion of contemporary demographics and politics in Arkansas, see Blair, *Arkansas Politics and Government,* 71–87, 265–267.

21. Blair, "Arkansas," 193.

22. Pryor quoted in *Arkansas Gazette,* October 8, 1988, 3A; Bush quoted in *Arkansas Gazette,* October 7, 1988, 12A.

23. Bush quoted in *Arkansas Gazette,* October 7, 1988, 7A; Reagan quoted in *Arkansas Democrat,* October 28, 1988, 10A; Bethune quoted in *Hot Springs Sentinel-Record,* August 26, 1988, 1A, 9A; Marvin Bush quoted in *Arkansas Democrat,* September 29, 1988, 1B.

24. Bethune quoted in *Arkansas Democrat,* October 28, 1988, 10A, and in *Hot Springs Sentinel Record,* August 26, 1988, 1A; Neil Bush quoted in *Arkansas Gazette,* October 20, 1988, 1B; Reagan quoted in *Arkansas Democrat,* October 28, 1988, 10A.

25. Bentsen quoted in *Springdale News,* October 13, 1988, 1A; Bush quoted in *Arkansas Gazette,* October 7, 1988, 1A; Reagan quoted in *Arkansas Democrat,* October 28, 1988, 1A, 10A, and in *Arkansas Gazette,* October 28, 1988, 1A, 4A.

26. Dukakis quoted in *Arkansas Democrat,* August 20, 1988, 1A; Reagan quoted in *Arkansas Democrat,* October 28, 1988, 10A.

27. The day's events described in *Arkansas Gazette,* October 7, 1988, 1A, 7B, 10B; and *Arkansas Democrat,* October 7, 1988, 1A, 8A.

28. Bumpers quoted in *Arkansas Gazette,* August 16, 1988, 8A; Clinton quoted in *Springdale News,* October 28, 1988, 1A.

29. See, for example, Bumpers's admission that Dukakis was his "own biggest handicap," *Arkansas Democrat,* November 5, 1988, 4B; and Clinton's similar criticisms in *Arkansas Democrat,* October 11, 1988, 1B; October 19, 1988, 8A; and October 25, 1988, 1B.

30. For Arkansans' views on school prayer, capital punishment, and gun control, see

"Comprehensive Social Survey of Arkansas, Part V," prepared by William D. Mangold, University of Arkansas Sociology Department, July 27, 1987. Quotation from Republican campaign circular mailed to Arkansas registered voters, in the author's possession.

31. Exact absentee voting figures are not compiled statewide by the Secretary of State's office, but according to Elizabeth Spencer of the State Auditor's office, based on their communications with all county clerks, the amount of absentee voting was "unprecedented."

32. Demographic and electoral variables compiled by author from a variety of sources on all seventy-five Arkansas counties, and analyzed using Pearson's correlation coefficients.

33. "Survey Produces Interesting Statistics on Presidential Race," October 28, 1988, press release from Arkansas Educational Television Network.

34. Poll conducted by the Center for Research and Public Policy at the University of Arkansas at Little Rock for the *Arkansas Gazette* and published in the *Gazette,* October 23, 1988, 1A, 15A.

35. For extensive discussion of these regional patterns, see Blair, *Arkansas Politics and Government,* 61–87; and Blair, "Arkansas," 196–206.

36. Tom Larimer in *Arkansas Gazette,* November 20, 1988, 6C.

37. *Arkansas Democrat,* November 9, 1988, 10A.

38. Diane D. Blair and Robert L. Savage, "The Appearances of Realignment and Dealignment in Arkansas," in Robert H. Swansbrough and David M. Brodsky, eds., *The South's New Politics: Realignment and Dealignment* (Columbia: University of South Carolina Press, 1988), 139.

39. Robinson quoted in *Arkansas Gazette,* May 15, 1988, 1A; and in *Northwest Arkansas Times,* July 21, 1988, 1A.

40. Quotations from *Arkansas Democrat,* July 27, 1988, 8A; September 22, 1988, 4B; October 15, 1988, 4B; and October 27, 1988, 3B.

9

Florida: The Republican Surge Continues

WILLIAM E. HULBARY, ANNE E. KELLEY, AND
LEWIS BOWMAN

The Republicans' strategy of targeting Florida as an area of particular hope and effort in 1988 bore fruit.[1] Bush swept Dukakis in Florida. It was never a contest, as Bush rolled up a winning margin of 22 percentage points to keep Florida in the forefront of the Sun Belt's expanding presidential electoral base.[2] Bush received 61 percent of the vote—above Reagan's 56 percent in 1980 and not far below the latter's 65 percent in 1984. Republicans also took a U.S. Senate set away from the Democrats, captured significant statewide cabinet offices for the first time, and increased their threat to continuing Democratic control of the state legislature and local governmental offices.

Since the 1950s, Republican presidential candidates have done well in Florida. Being a leader in the Republican renaissance in the South has become part of Florida's evolving megastate image. As one commentator noted, "Florida . . . has become an almost impregnable Republican bastion in presidential elections."[3] Florida produced the largest, or nearly the largest, victory margin for every Republican presidential candidate throughout the 1970s and 1980s. The 1988 Florida elections give considerable insight into the post–World War II success of Republicanism and Republican presidential candidates, both in Florida and throughout the South.

RECENT POLITICS

From 1952 through 1984, Republican presidential candidates won seven of nine presidential elections. During this period the state escaped one-partyism and became a competitive two-party state in presidential politics. As early as 1960, Florida's "solid Democratic South" image was changing. That year, while Richard Nixon captured the state's electoral vote for President, Democratic nominees for Governor and cabinet campaigned as the "Florida Democratic party," separating themselves from the national Democratic party ticket.[4]

In the last twenty-five years, Florida also has: (1) elected three Republican U.S. Senators; (2) increased the proportion of Republicans in its congressional delegation (from three of fifteen members in 1979 to seven of nineteen in 1986); (3) elected Republican governors Claude R. Kirk, Jr., and Bob Martinez; (4) elected a legislature with sufficient GOP strength to sustain a Republican governor's veto; and (5) increased the proportion of Republicans in both Houses of the State Legislature. The GOP also won local elections regularly in several populous counties, including Dade, Broward, Palm Beach, Sarasota, Orange, and Pinellas. For some offices the growth in Republican success has been sporadic, but the long-term trend over the period indicates growing Republican success in state and local as well as national elections.

Shifting Partisanship and Voter Registration

A more competitive Republican party in Florida has increased Republican voter registration and made Republican registration data more congruent with the reality of partisanship.[5] Over the past twenty years, the Republicans leaped from a little over a half million registrants to well over two million, and gained more than five times as many registered voters as the Democrats in the past decade.[6] In the 1988 general election, 93 percent of all registered voters were registered as members of the two major parties; of these, 58 percent were registered Democrats and 42 percent were registered Republicans.[7]

Floridians also have been shifting their party identifications from the Democratic to the Republican party, resulting in a net gain for the Republicans.[8] From 1979 through 1986, the percentage of voters identifying with the Republicans rose from 26 percent to 38 percent, while the percentage identifying with the Democrats fell from 45 percent to 32 percent. Independents remained relatively steady at 29 to 30 percent. Republican gains were greatest among whites, the new residents in the state, and the young (18 to 29 years old). This argues that if the young continue to show Republican leanings, and if the newcomers continue to bring their Republicanism with them, the state will continue moving in a Republican direction.[9]

The emerging Republicanism evident in voter registration and party identification is associated with political ideology as well. A sizeable minority of voters with Democratic party loyalties or voter registration are political conservatives who are less than happy with the more liberal orientation of others in their party. As a more homogeneous and conservative Republican party becomes stronger and more successful, conservative Democrats gradually are switching their party loyalties and voter registration to the Republican party. This phenomenon is occurring among both party activists and rank and file voters in Florida.[10]

Social and Economic Changes

To the extent that Republicanism is growing in the more populated areas in south and central Florida, it is probably associated with two demographic factors. First, the more populous areas in south and central Florida have been especially attractive to northern retirees—many of whom were formerly professionals, managers, and administrators, and tend to be Republican, affluent, and politically conservative.[11] Second, central and south Florida have experienced sizeable growth in service, light manufacturing, and "high-tech" industries that require more highly skilled, white-collar workers. Workers in these industries tend to be more politically conservative and more Republican.

THE PRIMARIES

Presidential Primaries

As early as January 1988, the Florida Newspaper poll reported that George Bush was the overwhelming favorite among the Republicans seeking the nomination and that Michael Dukakis was leading among the Democrats.[12] Both candidates won Florida's Super Tuesday primaries in their respective parties— Bush with a sweeping majority among Republicans, and Dukakis with only a modest plurality among the splintered Democrats.

Republican. The groundwork for George Bush's nomination and general election victories in Florida was laid well before the primary. Prominent state Republican politicians struggled to be in the forefront of the Bush campaign. Five of Florida's seven Republican congressmen joined his campaign as early as 1987.[13] Governor Bob Martinez served as Bush's Florida campaign chairman as well as his national campaign co-chairman. Jeb Bush— George's son and a highly visible Republican party official holding statewide appointive office—played a prominent role in developing a campaign organization for his father.[14]

George Bush won sixty-four of Florida's sixty-seven counties in the Republican primary. The other three counties, all in the panhandle, went to Pat Robertson. ABC exit polls showed Bush was favored by Republican primary voters of all ages and incomes.[15] Bush took 62.1 percent of the Republican vote in the primary; the only other candidates with any appreciable portion of the primary vote were Dole (21.2 percent) and Robertson (10.6 percent).[16]

Democratic. Dukakis invested heavily in the Florida primary, using about twenty paid staffers compared to only ten in the October general election campaign. His campaign targeted groups viewed as particularly likely to support him, particularly north-easterners and Jews in southern Florida.[17] Dukakis won thirty-nine of Florida's sixty-seven counties, receiving most of his support in central and south Florida, yet he got only 40.9 percent of the vote, while Jackson (20 percent), Gore (12.7 percent), and Gephardt (14.4 percent) each received more than 10 percent.[18] The runner-up, Jackson, took three congressional districts, each with 22–25 percent black population.

Compared to the Republican primary, the Democratic primary vote was more splintered. Dukakis's inability to dominate the primary was a sign of the difficulties he would face in Florida later, during the general election campaign. Despite early success with selected groups, Dukakis was a candidate who had difficulty appealing to a broad constituency in a state that in 1984 gave Ronald Reagan a larger majority than any southern state.

Other Primaries

Factionalism appeared in Democratic primaries for other offices as well. As a dominant majority party without significant opposition during most of the post–World War II era, the Democratic party has had splintered leadership, factional divisions, and inconsistent policy direction. This continuing problem was clear in 1988 in the nominations for the U.S. Senate seat and for other statewide offices.[19] In 1988, the Democrats did move more effectively to ameliorate this problem. Moreover, there were signs that the narrowing of the Democratic coalition and broadening of the Republican coalition had gradually produced some factional problems among Republicans. However, Republicans traditionally seem to handle these factional problems better than the Democrats. The 1988 U.S. Senate race is a good example of these factional problems in both parties. However, the Republicans were more successful in controlling the damage of their primary battle.

Nearly a year before the election, Republican Congressman Connie Mack announced he would run against the Democratic incumbent Senator Lawton Chiles. The National Republican Senatorial Committee and other Republican sources, anxious to challenge for the seat, promised considerable help. Later, in December 1987, Chiles announced summarily that he would not be a candidate for re-election. Predictably, the Democrats looked in several directions at once. Five-term Democrat Dan Mica, representing the Fourteenth Congressional District on Florida's southeast coast, announced for the office. Congressman Buddy MacKay (D) of Ocala and others talked of entering the primary. Then Reubin Askew entered the race, abandoning political retirement again. His legendary status in recent Florida politics tended to drive both Democratic and Republican candidates from the field.[20] Askew became a favorite to win the primary and the general election, but in the late spring,

Askew tired of the campaign and announced he was withdrawing because he did not like fund-raising.

Much to the Republicans' delight, the political gyrations of Chiles and Askew forced the Democrats into one of their customary divisive primaries. Insurance Commissioner Bill Gunter, Representative Buddy MacKay, State Senator Pat Frank, and Representative Dan Mica became the major Democratic protagonists. Though each had political strengths, Gunter was viewed as the front-runner, and the other three candidates spent much time attacking him.

Gunter and MacKay finished first and second in the September 6 Democratic primary. MacKay won the October 4 runoff, and Gunter immediately endorsed him in an effort to contain the damages from the contentious primary battle and pull the party back together. The primary was hard-fought. Gunter accused MacKay of inadequate support for Social Security and Israel; MacKay accused Gunter of lacking integrity and misrepresenting his position on Social Security and Middle Eastern policy.

With Chiles and Askew out of the race and no clear Democratic front-runner for the Senate nomination, the Republican chances of winning improved markedly. Mack's early start gave him advantages in fund-raising and setting up an effective organization.[21] Throughout his long campaign, Mack repeatedly stressed the theme that the Republican party must reward him with the Senate nomination because he was willing to challenge Chiles when the Republican hopes for winning this seat were low. These efforts apparently discouraged several other prominent Republicans that had been mentioned as possible competitors for Mack (including Congressman Bill McCollum, former Senator Paula Hawkins, and Jeb Bush, who was Secretary of the Florida Department of Commerce at that time and a son of George Bush).

Ultimately, only Robert Merkle challenged Mack for the nomination. Merkle, a former U.S. Attorney, walked out of a federal courtroom and directly into the primary campaign seventy days before the primary. He had no organization or funds to speak of, but he had the advantage of a very charismatic persona, the publicity of being a former All-American fullback at Notre Dame, and more immediately, the publicity of just having convicted a major Colombian drug figure in federal court in Jacksonville.

In an effort to enforce "party discipline," party officials made every effort to keep Merkle from entering the race. Failing that, they worked hard and successfully at cutting him off from funds and organization. Merkle, in turn, attacked Mack as a "packaged product and a political chameleon."[22] It appeared that Merkle damaged Mack politically during the weeks just prior to the September 6 primary. Almost without resources and never close to winning the primary, Merkle still got almost 40 percent of the primary vote, and demonstrated that Mack was vulnerable to attacks on his image and record. This may have actually helped the Mack organization in the ensuing general election by alerting them to potential problems facing their candidate in time to develop a strategy to deal with the problems.

THE GENERAL ELECTION CAMPAIGNS

The Presidential Campaign

Republicans. Following the nominating conventions in August, a Gallup survey in Florida reported that Bush held a 2 percentage point lead over Dukakis.[23] By late September, Bush had strengthened this lead to 17 percentage points, and the Dukakis national campaign began reassigning resources from Florida to other states. Paul Pezzella, the Florida coordinator for the Dukakis campaign, said at this point, "Although the polls are not encouraging, we have felt from day one that this is not an easy state for us."[24]

The perception of Florida as a safe state for the Republicans discouraged both candidates from visiting and discussing the issues. After the conventions, each presidential candidate visited the state only once to campaign. Bush's organization used extensive paid advertisements focusing on such issues as child care, health care, and education.

Twenty-two Florida newspapers endorsed Bush; only seven endorsed Dukakis.[25] In endorsing Bush, the *Tampa Tribune* urged its readers" to consider the central facts of this election year—not only peace and prosperity, but the mainstream values and vast experience of the Republican candidate."[26] The *Miami Herald* stressed other issues in endorsing Bush: "Mr. Bush emerges as a seasoned leader with growth potential while Mr. Dukakis is ever the earnest technocrat. The nation doesn't need an ill-defined iceman; it needs a president."[27]

Democrats. The vice presidential candidate, Lloyd Bentsen, and Senator Lawton Chiles campaigned in the state in September. They stressed traditional Democrats issues such as fair trade, equal educational opportunities, fairness, and the acceptance of diversity.

One of the few newspapers in the state endorsing Dukakis, the *Tallahassee Democrat,* supported him in order to oppose the policies of the Reagan years. The paper was concerned about the deficit and about finding new directions for the country. They argued this could hardly be accomplished if President Reagan's vice president were elevated to the presidency. It wrote: "By electing Dukakis, voters can steer away from the affable-monarch model of government of the Reagan administration to one of compassionate competency and focused strength, to a government that plays fair instead of favorites."[28]

Jesse Jackson's supporters splintered after the Democratic National Convention. Some felt the Dukakis campaign was not emphasizing the Jackson issues as promised; others felt the Democrats were primarily seeking the Reagan Democrats. In the face of these controversies, black leaders resolved some of the dilemma by focusing on support for Representative Buddy MacKay in his campaign for the U.S. Senate.[29]

As early as October, the director, the political coordinator, and up to eight other members of Dukakis's Florida organization were transferred to Illinois.[30] Even though Dukakis made more of an effort in Florida in 1988 than Mondale had in 1984, some observers argue that, given contemporary Florida politics, Democratic presidential candidates are behind from the beginning. They give four reasons for this: (1) the state has become very accustomed to landslide victories for Republican candidates over a thirty-two-year period; (2) the citizens of the state are very mobile, not very interested in politics, politically uninvolved, and hence prime targets for the special influence of television in campaigns; (3) the television market is very diverse and broadly dispersed, creating extra demands on scarce resources if the market is to be exploited well; and (4) the state is very conservative because of selective migration into the state and because of the continuance of the underlying conservatism from the southern Cracker heritage of Florida and south Georgia.[31]

Other Campaigns

The campaign for the U.S. Senate seemed to be the other Florida 1988 election with the potential for the most effect on the presidential race, and vice versa. Both campaigns dealt with many of the same issues and were structured along fairly similar ideological lines.

From the beginning, regardless of the opposition, the main strategy of the Mack organization was to label the Democratic candidate a liberal. Whatever else the Republicans had learned from President Reagan, they had learned very well that charging an opponent with being a liberal plays well for Republicans, particularly in Florida. Askew entered the primary, talking about his "Crusade for Tomorrow" and how it would help reduce the federal budget deficit. Soon Mack attacked this and other aspects of Askew's liberal image, saying, "The days of Reubin Askew–style tax and spend government is over."[32] Even while his eventual Democratic opponent, Buddy MacKay, was still campaigning in the Democratic primary, Mack's organization launched a $100,000 television blitz, running a ten-second commercial that ended with the line, "Hey Buddy, you're too liberal!" Mack followed up on this theme during the general election by declaring MacKay to be one of the most liberal members of Congress and the most liberal member from Florida.[33] During the general election campaign, Mack repeatedly tried to tie his campaign to that of Bush and MacKay's to that of Dukakis in order to stress the liberal ties of his opponent.[34] He made a constant effort to tie himself to Ronald Reagan's conservatism, and his campaign utilized both Reagan and Oliver North (a hero to the Republican right because of his activities related to providing aid to the Contras in Nicaragua) to assist in fundraising in the state.

WINNERS AND LOSERS

National Offices

Unlike in many other states, no data indicate that Dukakis was ever ahead in Florida. He lost by a larger margin in Florida (22 percentage points) than he did in most other southern states. Nationally, voters in only four states—Utah, New Hampshire, Idaho, and South Carolina—cast a larger percentage of their ballots for Bush.[35]

The congressional results in Florida produced major changes. The Republicans regained a Senate seat to replace the one they had lost in 1986. They also gained two House seats, giving Florida's House delegation a nearly even partisan split with a slight edge to the Democrats—ten Democrats and nine Republicans. (By February 1989 this had changed to a Republican advantage—ten Republicans and nine Democrats—when Bill Grant, who represents Florida's Second Congressional District, located in the panhandle, switched to the Republican party.)

The U.S. Senate. In winning the Senate seat vacated by Democratic Senator Lawton Chiles, Republican Connie Mack's campaign theme was "less taxing, less spending, less government and more freedom."[36] Apparently this neo-populist cry so popular with the political right in Florida, plus Mack's ability to use television effectively and to define the election as a contest between a liberal and conservative, were enough to beat Buddy MacKay, one of the most respected legislators in Florida history.

The contest was one of the closest elections in Florida history, and the official designation of a winner did not occur until several days after the election. The final narrow margin for the winner was in part determined by absentee ballots and by a quirk of ballot placement that caused substantial numbers of votes to skip the Senate race as they marked their ballots.[37] This latter problem occurred in several key large counties where MacKay normally would have received a disproportionate number of the unmarked ballots.

The U.S. House. The Republicans' gradual accumulation of Florida's House seats continued in 1988. They picked up two seats, in each case an outcome that most observers would have doubted possible only a few months before the election.

Republican Cliff Stearns won the open seat in Florida's Sixth District that MacKay had vacated in order to run for the Senate. Stearns had no political experience, yet he won by 53 to 47 percent. He actually took advantage of his inexperience by campaigning heavily on the claim that there was a need for a "citizen" congressman to go to Washington to reform Congress. His opponent, Florida House Speaker Jon Mills (D), was an overwhelming favorite but was tagged early as a liberal who had supported an unpopular tax while in the legislature. As Stearns's campaign manager said, "We feel like Mr. Mills is a traditional tax-and-spend liberal; he's got his own brand of Dukak-enomics."[38] Compounding his campaign problems, the Democratic candidate apparently ran a rather complacent campaign.

Incumbent Democrat Bill Chappell, Jr., lost Florida's Fifth Congressional District to Republican Craig T. James by a few hundred votes. Chappell had been in Congress for twenty years and was chair of the House Defense Appropriations Committee. This post had made him unbeatable in recent elections because of the high visibility it gave Florida in attracting defense dollars. His strength in earlier elections, however, contributed to his defeat in 1988 because of Chappell's link to the ongoing federal probe into bribery and rigging bids for national defense procurement contracts.

Republican Craig James made ethics the major campaign issue. It caught on with the public, and the election resulted in a virtual tie. The Florida Supreme Court eventually had to settle procedural issues that Chappell had raised in the recount and declared James the winner several weeks after the election.

Other Results

Cabinet Races. In the past, the Republican party's nominees for statewide cabinet posts have not been successful. In 1988 they won the races for Secretary of State and Commissioner of Insurance and Treasury. With these new members and the Republican Governor (who also serves in the cabinet), the Florida Cabinet now has three Republicans, an unprecedented number in the twentieth century. In two years the Democrats have dropped from total control of the cabinet to a slight four to three lead.

Legislative Races. The Republicans picked up two seats in each house of the state legislature. In partisan terms these are not big gains for the Republicans. The election results still leave the Democrats with a 73 to 47 margin in the Florida House and a 23 to 17 margin in the Florida Senate. However, the Democratic losses are greater than these numbers alone indicate. Several key Democratic state legislators were lost, either through losses to Republicans or because they left the legislature to run for other state offices.

HOW THEY WON

NBC's exit polls in Florida showed that Bush and Quayle did well among most groups.[39] They received 64 percent of the vote from those eighteen to thirty-four years old, and 55 percent from those sixty-five or older. The Hispanic vote went Republican by a 2 to 1 margin. Those earning more than twenty thousand dollars per year voted disproportionately for the Bush/Quayle ticket as well. A majority of men and women voted for the Republicans, as did a majority of independents and nineteen out of every twenty Republicans. Dukakis did well only among blacks and Democrats; he got the votes of over 90 percent of the former and about 80 percent of the latter.

Election Trends in the 1980s

The 1988 electoral success of George Bush and Connie Mack in Florida was only the most recent manifestation of growing Republican electoral strength statewide. The 1980s provide several other examples of Republican electoral success in high-visibility statewide elections as well as presidential races—Ron-

Table 9.1

Florida's 1988 Presidential and Senatorial Elections: Correlations between County Vote Percentages and Selected Political and Demographic Variables

Political and Demographic Variables	Percent of Vote for Bush	Mack
Recent Statewide Elections		
President: percent of 1984 vote for Reagan	.94*	.83*
percent of 1980 vote for Reagan	.54*	.77*
Senate: percent of 1988 vote for Mack	.81*	--
percent of 1986 vote for Hawkins	.72*	.84*
percent of 1982 vote for Chiles	-.42*	-.68*
percent of 1980 vote for Hawkins	.29**	.63*
Governor: percent of 1986 vote for Martinez	.82*	.72*
percent of 1982 vote for Graham	-.29**	-.54*
Voter Registration and Turnout		
Percent registered Republican, 1988	.21***	.51*
Change in percent registered Republican, 1980-88	.30**	.48*
Change in percent registered Republican, 1986-88	.37*	.48*
Voter turnout (percent voting of those registered), 1988	.19	.30*
Income		
Per capita income, 1987	.08	.37*
Percent change in per capita income, 1982-87	-.07	.14
Race		
Nonwhite percent of population, 1986	-.44*	-.42*
Blacks as percentage of registered voters, 1988	-.47*	-.45*
Blacks as percentage of registered Democrats, 1988	-.49*	-.37*
Age		
Percent of population aged 65 or older, 1986	-.18	.02
Percent of population aged 18-44, 1986	.10	-.01
Urbanization		
County population, 1987	-.29**	.01
County population density (persons/square mile), 1986	-.19	.04
Population Change and Migration		
Percent change in population, 1982-1987	.31**	.43*
Percent change in population due to migration, 1980-86	.16	.33**
Percent change in size of labor force, 1981-1986	.27***	.39*

Note: Table entries are Pearson correlation coefficients. Percentage of the major party vote received by the indicated candidate was used in all elections. The units of analysis are Florida's 67 counties.

*Significant at the .001 level.
**Significant at the .01 level.
***Significant at the .05 level.

Source: Compiled by authors.

ald Reagan's victories in Florida in 1980 and 1984, Paula Hawkins's election to the U.S. Senate in 1980; and Bob Martinez's election as Governor in 1986. If we look at the correlations between the county-by-county vote percentages for Bush and Mack and the vote for these other elections, we can see that all are closely associated—at the presidential level and in contests for Governor and U.S. Senator (see Table 9.1).

The correlations with the Bush vote are quite strong, especially in the 1984–1988 period. Counties that supported Reagan most strongly in 1980 and 1984 also gave the strongest support to Bush in 1988. Similarly, counties that gave Bush the most support also gave more support to Connie Mack in his 1988 Senate race and to Martinez in his 1986 gubernatorial race. Although Paula Hawkins lost in her 1986 re-election campaign for the Senate, the correlation between her support in 1986 and Bush's support in 1988 is also quite strong.

The correlations between Connie Mack's victory in Florida's 1988 Senate race and other statewide elections in the 1980s are as strong as comparable correlations with the Bush vote (Table 9.1). Mack's statewide victory margin was much narrower than Bush's; Mack received only 50.4 percent of the vote compared to Bush's 61.2 percent. However, Mack and Bush's victories in 1988 were not isolated, idiosyncratic events. Instead, they should be viewed as two additional indicators (among many) of the pervasive strength of Republicanism in Florida in the 1980s.

Voter Registration

Partisan voter registration is another indicator of electoral strength. Throughout the 1980s, Republican voter registration has been increasing slightly more than 1 percent a year, while Democratic voter registration has been declining by a similar amount. By 1988 the Democrats still held a slight edge—58 to 42 percent—among those registered with the two major parties, but these figures probably underestimate the strength of Republican party loyalties in the electorate. In Florida as in other southern states, many registered Democrats are ''crossover voters'' who abandon their party and vote Republican in presidential elections and (though less frequently) in other elections as well. Consequently, partisan voter registration is a less than perfect measure of underlying party loyalties. Recent sample surveys of the Florida electorate probably provide a more accurate indicator, and these suggest a fairly even split in party loyalty.[40]

In view of the growth in Republican voter registration, we examined the association between the vote for Bush in 1988 and the percentage of registered Republicans (Table 9.1). The correlation was quite small (.21) and barely achieved statistical significance. However, when we examined correlations between the vote for Bush and the growth in the percent of registered Republicans during the 1980s, the correlation was stronger (.31 and .37). Those counties that had larger increases in the percent of registered Republicans also tended to give a larger percentage of their votes to Bush. Republican voter registration in 1988 was not a very accurate indicator of Bush's electoral strength in Florida. However, the increase in Republican voter registration is not without consequence. It is a further manifestation of growing Republican electoral strength, and at least a partial indicator of likely Republican electoral success.

The association between Republican voter registration and the Mack vote resembled the comparable correlations for the Bush vote. The Mack vote was more strongly correlated with the percent of registered Republicans and with growth in that percentage during the 1980s. Mack's vote appeared to be more a straight party vote with less crossover voting. If that is so, the U.S. Senate election more closely reflects the underlying distribution of partisanship in Florida's electorate. Furthermore, the close Mack-Mackay contest suggests a nearly equal partisan balance in the Florida electorate—a highly competitive, two-party electoral system. Such a conclusion is consistent with recent sample surveys of party identification in Florida.[41]

Voter Turnout

Florida typically is a low-turnout state, and 1988 was no exception. Only South Carolina, Georgia, and the District of Columbia had lower voter turnouts than Florida.[42] Among the estimated 9,309,238 persons eligible to vote in Florida's 1988 general election, only about 46 percent cast presidential ballots.[43] Less than two-thirds of eligible voters were registered to vote, and only 71 percent of registered voters voted in the presidential election. Since the 1960s, turnout in Florida's presidential elections has been around 75 percent of registered voters, so turnout in 1988 was fairly low even when compared to other recent presidential elections.

At first glance, the level of voter turnout appears to have little to do with Bush's victory margin in Florida (see Table 10.1).[44] Bush did just as well in counties with low voter turnout as in counties with high turnout. However, we believe that the low correlation between voter turnout and support for Bush is incomplete and perhaps misleading evidence of the importance of turnout in Bush's victory margin.[45] Our data indicate that voter turnout was lower in those counties: (1) that were less affluent; (2) where a larger proportion of the population was nonwhite; and (3) where a lower percentage of registered voters were Republicans. This also suggests that counties with characteristics indicating a higher proportion of likely Democratic voters (lower income, more nonwhite, fewer registered Republicans) generally had lower voter turnout as well. We believe that the absence of a vigorous Dukakis campaign in part explains the low turnout in Florida. Also, we believe the lower turnout—especially in those counties with a greater percentage of likely Democratic voters—added to Bush's margin of victory.

Compared to the Bush vote, Connie Mack's margin of victory was associated more closely with voter turnout. In Mack's election, turnout also was lower in counties with a greater percentage of likely Democratic voters—counties with a smaller percentage of registered Republicans, lower per capita income, and proportionately more nonwhites. Consequently, we believe that lower turnout played an even bigger role in Mack's victory than in that of Bush. We also believe that Mack's election more accurately reflects the general association between turnout and Republican electoral strength in the Florida.

Regionalism and Political Conservatism

In analyzing the distribution of Republican electoral strength we divided Florida into three regions: north, central/southwest, and southeast.[46] Compared to the rest of Florida, north Florida's political culture is closer to the conservative Democratic tradition of the Deep South, and has been changing in similar ways. The region has the largest proportion of native white southerners in the state, and generally is considered one of the state's most politically conservative regions. In the past, north Florida also had strong Democratic party ties and a substantial majority of registered Democratic voters, but their willingness to vote a straight party ticket has declined. Though north Florida's voters often vote Democratic in state and local elections, they have regularly voted for Republican presidential candidates since the 1960s. They also have voted for some Republicans at the state and local level when forced to choose between a Republican and a Democrat they viewed as too liberal. If dealignment means decreasing or low levels of partisan loyalty in voting and greater emphasis on candidates than parties, then in this respect, north Florida is experiencing dealignment.[47]

In the other two regions of Florida, partisan and ideological differences are more like those in northern states. Rapid economic development and substantial migration into central and south Florida have made these areas less uniquely "southern" and more like the rest of the nation. Southeast Florida is the most politically liberal region of the state. Although registered Republicans are a strong minority and quite competitive in many parts of southeast Florida, the region is generally Democratic. In contrast, central/southwest Florida is the area where Republicans have the greatest electoral strength. The area also tends to be fairly conservative—more like north Florida in political ideology.

Bush's 1988 Florida victory exemplifies these regional differences. Not surprisingly he carried central/southwest Florida with 64 percent of the vote. In this area, the proportions of registered Democrats (46.9 percent) and Republicans (45.9 percent) are about equal. In north Florida, Bush's margin of victory (64.7 percent) was about the same as in central/southwest Florida, but registered Democrats (66.7 percent) far outnumber registered Republicans (28.4 percent). In contrast to both the other two regions, southeast Florida gave Bush a smaller margin of victory (only 55.2 percent—very close to nationwide results). Registered Democrats (54.2 percent) in southeast Florida are more numerous than registered Republicans (37.6 percent), but the difference is much smaller than in north Florida and closer to the even balance in central/southwest Florida.

These figures show that Bush won in all three regions of Florida. Moreover, his margin of victory in each region was much greater than one would expect on the basis of partisan voter registration. This was especially true in north Florida, where the percentage of the vote for Bush was more than twice as large as the percent of registered Republicans—a difference of 36 percent. In the two south Florida regions, this difference was about 18 percent in each region. Lower voter turnout could explain some of the margin of victory, but Bush's winning margin also was enhanced by substantial numbers of Democrats who abandoned their party and voted for Bush. This crossover vote appears to have been especially large in north Florida, and reflects the rejection by conservative Democrats of a Dukakis image that was too liberal—a theme stressed again and again in Republican campaign advertising throughout the state.

Connie Mack's vote margin was consistently smaller than Bush's in all three regions of Florida, but in other respects the regional distribution of the Mack and Bush votes was similar. In central/southwest Florida (where Republicans are strongest) and north Florida (a conservative Democratic area), Mack ran about 12 percentage points behind George Bush; yet Mack still won in both areas with 52 percent of the vote. In southeast Florida—the most liberal area of the state—Mack actually lost, receiving 46.5 percent of the vote to Mackay's 53.5 percent. Mack's loss in southeast Florida was close and was sufficiently offset by his victory margin in the other two regions to give him a narrow winning margin statewide.

Race

In 1988, the Florida electorate divided along racial lines in much the same way as other southern states; the racial composition of Florida's counties was closely associated with the margin of victory. Both Bush and Mack received a smaller percentage of the vote in counties with a larger percentage of nonwhites and in counties where blacks constituted a larger percentage of registered voters and registered Democrats. Although Florida has a rather small proportion of nonwhites when compared to other southern states—only 14.6 percent—racial differences still played an important role in the 1988 vote. The correlations of vote margin with race were larger—at least as large, or larger than, the correlations with other social, economic, and demographic characteristics (Table 9.1).

The elections of George Bush and Connie Mack show the importance of racial divisions in Florida's electorate, and the convergence of racial and partisan divisions. The results are consistent with several recent studies of partisan change in Florida and the South.[48] Southern blacks show continued loyalty to the Democratic party. In contrast, white northerners migrating south and native white southerners, whether young or old, have become more Republican and Independent and less Democratic in their party loyalties.

Income and Affluence

Income and affluence played a larger role in Mack's victory than in that of Bush (Table 9.1). Bush did nearly as well in less affluent counties as he did in more affluent counties. In contrast, Mack did less well in lower income counties and better in more affluent counties. Unlike the presidential election, Florida's Senate race revealed a clear partisan electoral division based on income and affluence.

Age

Age was weakly correlated with Bush's margin of victory and not correlated at all with Mack's vote margin (Table 9.1). Mack did equally well in counties with a greater percentage aged sixty-five and over and counties with a greater percentage aged eighteen to forty-four. In contrast, Bush's vote margin was slightly higher in counties with a larger percentage of persons aged sixty-five or more and slightly smaller in counties with proportionately more younger voters (aged eighteen to forty-four). This suggests that younger voters tended to vote more Republican, and older voters, more Democratic—a result consistent with findings showing Reagan's attraction of the young during the 1980s.

Urbanization, Population Change, and Migration

During the 1980s, Florida experienced considerable population growth and migration into the state, and these factors were associated with Bush's margin of victory. The correlation between population size and Bush vote was negative and moderately large; the correlation between population density (people per square mile) and Bush vote was smaller but also negative (Table 9.1). This indicates that Bush did less well in the larger, densely populated urban counties than in the small- to medium-sized counties.

In contrast, measures of population change and growth indicate a moderately strong and positive correlation with Bush's victory margin. The Bush vote was proportionately greater in counties experiencing more growth from 1982 to 1987, and in counties with larger percentage increases in the size of the labor force and larger percentage increases from migration. Population growth enhanced Bush's winning margin. In part, this may be due to in-migration of Republican voters, but the correlation of Bush's vote with migration is smaller than with the other measures of population growth. We believe that growth in general, and the prosperity and economic development usually associated with it, also contributed to Bush's victory.

The vote for Connie Mack was not associated with urbanization; Mack did equally well in larger, densely populated counties and smaller, more sparsely populated counties. Like the Bush vote, however, the Mack vote revealed a partisan division based on population growth and migration. Mack received a greater percentage of the vote in those counties where: (1) population growth was greatest between 1982 and 1987; (2) migration into the state was greatest between 1980 and 1986; and (3) increases in the size of the labor force were greatest between 1981 and 1986. These factors were also important in Bush's victory, but based on the size of the correlations, they were more critical in Mack's election (Table 9.1). In both elections, but especially in Mack's, Republican candidates were beneficiaries of population growth, migration, and the associated economic growth, development, and prosperity that occurred in Florida during the 1980s. Assuming that these demographic and economic trends continue, the future of the Republican party in Florida appears to be quite promising.

SUMMARY

Immediately following the election, the political director of the state Republican Party said, "We've never been able to help our candidates like we did this year."[49] Florida has become a major state in the national Republican party's strategy; the party is willing to support candidates at every level in the state because Florida has become fertile Republican political ground. For a generation, Florida has been a dependable state for Republicans in presidential elections. Recently it has given many indications of being a competitive state for Republicans in many statewide and congressional races. Tradition, a dearth of attractive candidates, personal attachments to preponderantly Democratic incumbents and politicians—these and other factors have made the development of two-partyism slower in state legislative and local elections. However, even at these levels, the 1988 election continued the gradual process of evolving two-partyism in Florida.

NOTES

1. See the discussion in "Republican Hope in Florida," *The Economist*, October 29, 1989, 28.
2. See "From Ike to Reagan: The Changing Republican Base," *Congressional Quarterly Weekly Report* (August 20, 1988): 2312.
3. Mark Gersh, who was quoted in Paul Taylor, "Must the Democrats Look South to Find 270 Electoral Votes?" *Washington Post National Weekly Edition*, May 9–15, 1988, 13.
4. Allen Morris, ed., *The Florida Handbook, 1979–80* (Tallahassee: Peninsular Publishing Co., 1980), p. 469ff. For general background in the state's politics, political parties, and elections, see Manning Dauer, ed., *Florida's Politics and Government*, 2d ed. (Gainesville: University Presses of Florida, 1984), chs. 3–5.
5. It is likely that Republican voter registration data often have *underestimated* Republican partisanship in Florida. For years in Florida, as in the South generally, the candidate who won the Democratic party primary was virtually guaranteed victory in the general election. Many Independents and Republicans often registered as Democrats to vote in the Democratic primaries in order for their votes to play a meaningful role in elections.
6. This is based on a report of the University of Florida's Bureau of Economic and Business Research which was reported in the *St. Petersburg Times*, August 5, 1988, 2B.
7. Florida Department of State, Division of Elections, *Official General Election Returns: November 8, 1988* (Tallahassee: Florida Department of State, 1988), 1–2.
8. See the studies of the Survey Research Center at Florida State University: Suzanne L. Parker, "Are Party Loyalties Shifting in Florida?" *Florida Public Opinion* (Winter 1985): 17–19; and Suzanne L. Parker, "Shifting Party Tides in Florida," in Robert H. Swansbrough and David M. Brodsky, eds., *The South's New Politics* (Columbia: Uni-

versity of South Carolina Press, 1988), ch. 3.

9. Parker warned, however, that this is not as certain as some would assume because the popularity of Ronald Reagan is one powerful explanation for the change in party identification toward the Republican advantage during the period (see Parker, "Shifting Party Tides," pp. 32–34). Others have played down the Reagan explanation and interpreted the changes in party identification as the initiation of party realignment in Florida. For example, see Paul Allen Beck, "Realignment Begins? The Republican Surge in Florida," *American Politics Quarterly* 10 (1982): 421–438.

10. In a study of this "party sorting," we found precinct committeepersons making their political ideology more congruent with their political party affiliation by switching in both directions. The process was being utilized disproportionately, however, by the conservative Democrats, who were switching to the Republican party. See Lewis Bowman, William E. Hulbary, and Anne E. Kelley, "Party Sorting at the Grassroots: Stable Partisans and Party Changers among Florida's Precinct Officials," in Robert P. Steed, Laurence W. Moreland, and Tod A. Baker, eds., *The Disappearing South?* (Tuscaloosa: University of Alabama Press, 1989), ch. 4.

11. For a discussion of how this evolved, see Peter D. Klingman, *Never Die nor Surrender: A History of the Republican Party in Florida, 1867–1970* (Gainesville: University Presses of Florida, 1984), 157.

12. Reported in the *St. Petersburg Times*, January 31, 1988, sec. B.

13. These events were reported in articles in the *Tampa Tribune*, July 16, 1987.

14. A Kemp supporter alleged that the Republicans' favoritism toward Bush went so far that a straw ballot for Republican presidential candidates at the state Republican convention was being rigged to assure that Bush would be the winner.

15. Reported in the *Miami Herald*, March 9, 1988, 15.

16. *Congressional Quarterly Weekly Report* (August 13, 1988): 2254.

17. *Tampa Tribune*, October 24, 1988, 1A.

18. *Congressional Quarterly Weekly Report* (July 9, 1988): 1893–1894.

19. Aside from the Senate race, the Democrats also faced serious primary battles and their aftereffects in primary elections for Insurance Commissioner and Secretary of State. The Democrats lost both these offices in the general election.

20. For a detailed account of Askew's strengths and weakness as a candidate for this post, as well as a general discussion of the Senate campaign in the early stages of 1988 for both parties, see "Senate: Askew II," *Congressional Quarterly Weekly Report* (February 27, 1988): 405–406.

21. From early in the primary process, Mack reportedly had the help of national and state Republican leaders in seeking to block other candidates. See the account in the *Congressional Quarterly Weekly Report* (February 27, 1988): 406.

22. "Senate: Prime Time," *Congressional Quarterly Weekly Report* (October 15, 1988): 2889.

23. Reported in the *Orlando Sentinel*, August 5, 1988, 1.

24. Quoted in the *Tampa Tribune*, October 1, 1988.

25. According to a count reported in the *Tampa Tribune*, November 7, 1988, 1B.

26. Quoted in the *Tampa Tribune*, November 6, 1988, sec. E.

27. Quoted in the *Tampa Tribune*, October 31, 1988, 4B.

28. Quoted in the *Tampa Tribune*, October 31, 1988, 4B.

29. Reported in the *St. Petersburg Times*, October 16, 1988, 6B.

30. Reported in the *St. Petersburg Times*, October 6, 1988.

31. Jack W. Germond and Jules Witcover, "Candidates Ignore Florida's Voters," *St. Petersburg Times*, October 8, 1988, 14A.

32. *Tampa Tribune*, December 22, 1987, 4B.

33. *Tampa Tribune*, October 6, 1988, 4B.

34. *Tampa Tribune*, November 2, 1988, 1B.

35. "Official 1988 Presidential Election Results," *Congressional Quarterly Weekly Report* (January 21, 1989): 139.

36. "Profiles of the Incoming Senate Freshmen," *Congressional Quarterly Weekly Report* (November 12, 1988): 3259.

37. The Republicans' special effort in seeking absentee voters may suffice for an explanation of much of Mack's margin of victory. The party sent out a million-piece mailing to generate support among absentee voters. Mack eventually received enough support from the 135,000 absentee ballots cast to give him a 33,612 vote margin over MacKay. See the story in the *Orlando Sentinel*, November 12, 1988, sec. D.

38. Quoted in the *St. Petersburg Times*, November 10, 1988, 1B.

39. *Orlando Sentinel*, November 9, 1988, sec. A.

40. Suzanne L. Parker, "How Strong is Republicanism in Florida?" *Florida Public Opinion* (Winter 1988): 13–19.

41. See Parker, "Are Party Loyalties Shifting in Florida?"; Parker, "Shifting Party Tides in Florida"; and Parker, "How Strong is Republicanism in Florida?"

42. "Those Who Chose to Vote," *New York Times*, November 10, 1988, 18.

43. These and subsequent data on turnout were compiled from various sources. See Bureau of Economic and Business Research, the University of Florida, *Population Program Population Studies*, June 1988, Bulletin No. 85–86, in *Economic Leaflets* 47 (July 1988); Florida Department of State, *Official General Election Returns: November 8, 1988*; and unpublished data and pamphlets from the Florida Department of State, Division of Elections.

44. We measured turnout as the percent of registered voters who voted in the election. As a second measure, we also calculated turnout as a percentage of the estimated 1988 voting age population who voted. Correlations with this second measure of turnout are not reported here because 1988 voting age population estimates are less reliable figures than the number of registered voters, particularly in a state like Florida which is experiencing rapid population growth. Note, however, that turnout relative to the voting age population yielded correlations similar to the correlations with turnout as a percentage of registered voters.

45. Aggregate county data cannot provide clear, unambiguous evidence on this issue. Survey data would be more desirable, but even individual-level survey data cannot tell us, except hypothetically, how nonvoters would have voted if they did in fact vote. Nonetheless, it is generally believed that low turnout aids Republican candidates and hurts Democrats. Democratic constituencies tend to be less well educated, less affluent, and nonwhite when compared to Republicans. These "Democratic" characteristics also are associated with nonvoting, and in part account for lower voter turnout among Democratic partisans. When voter turnout is high it is because more potential voters or "marginal voters" actually do vote. These marginal voters are more likely to vote Democratic when they do vote, and consequently, Democratic candidates benefit when turnout is higher.

46. Our definition is virtually identical to that specified in Parker, "Are Party Loyalties Shifting in Florida?" North Florida includes those counties north and west of Orlando

and Daytona Beach. Central/southwest includes those counties from Naples up the west coast to Tampa, plus those in central Florida in the triangle formed by Tampa, Daytona Beach, and Vero Beach. The remainder of the counties along the southeast coast and around to Key West are included in southeast Florida.

47. See Harold W. Stanley, ''Southern Partisan Changes: Dealignment, Realignment, or Both?'' *Journal of Politics* 50 (February 1988): 64–88.

48. Parker, ''How Strong is Republicanism in Florida?''; Stanley, ''Southern Partisan Changes.''

49. Quoted in the *St. Petersburg Times,* November 10, 1988, 5B.

10

North Carolina: The Confluence of National, Regional, and State Forces

CHARLES L. PRYSBY

INTRODUCTION

The 1988 elections in North Carolina were acted out against a backdrop of over two decades of political change. The most salient feature of this transformation was the growth of the Republican party. Republican successes at the top of the ticket made North Carolina a genuinely competitive two-party state for the high-visibility offices, and while the Democratic party was more secure further down the ballot, even here Republicans had made significant gains by the late 1980s. Concomitant with this partisan realignment were significant social and economic developments, which in turn had important political ramifications.

Republican Growth

Growing Republicanism appeared earliest and was most pronounced in presidential elections. Four of the five presidential elections preceding 1988 were won by the Republican candidate. Only in 1976, with southerner Jimmy Carter heading the ticket, did the state go Democratic in the presidential election. This twenty-year period of Republican success was in striking contrast to the previous decades, which were characterized by a clear and consistent Democratic advantage in presidential elections.

Below the presidential contest, Republican advances were less thorough and more uneven. Congressional elections displayed a pattern of surge and decline that paralleled presidential successes. Four of the eleven U.S. House seats were captured by Republicans in 1972 and 1980, but in both cases ebbing Republican strength in the following off-year elections reduced the seats held to two. A high-water mark of five Republican seats occurred in 1984, but the familiar drop-off resulted in only three Republican seats after 1986. The inability of Republicans to win a majority of U.S. House seats indicates the difficulty of quickly translating success at the top of the ticket into victories in other races.

On the other hand, U.S. Senate elections proved to be a more favorable hunting ground for Republicans. The first breakthrough came in 1972, when Jesse Helms became the first Republican senator from North Carolina in the twentieth century. He was re-elected in 1978 and 1984, the latter year being that of the bitter, expensive, and infamous race against former Governor Jim Hunt. A second Republican senator, John East, was elected in 1980, but the Democrats recaptured this seat in 1986. In that election, a united Democratic party supported Terry Sanford, while the Republican candidate, James Broyhill, had the burden of a divisive primary battle against a candidate supported by Helms's Congressional Club.

Elections for the state offices displayed patterns similar to those for congressional elections. Republican successes were concentrated at the top of the ticket, and were greatest in the presidential years, when the state went Republican. Gubernatorial victories in 1972 and 1984 were two of the jewels in the Republican crown. Democratic domination remained further down the ballot even into the mid-1980s, as Republicans failed to win any statewide race below Governor, and never moved beyond being a distinct minority in both houses of the state legislature. Even here, however, emerging Republican strength was reflected in a growing competitiveness in these elections, at least in terms of the closeness of the vote, if not actual victory.

The growth of the Republican vote reflected shifting party loyalties among the voters. Party registration figures only imperfectly capture these shifting sentiments. In 1968, registered Republicans were only 22 percent of the total.[1] Twenty years later, this figure had increased to almost 30 percent, a sizeable increase in proportional terms but still quite a minority of the electorate. However, more than 30 percent of the electorate considered themselves Republicans when it came to party identification. Data on party identification are not available for every year, but good measures exist for 1968 and 1986.[2] These data show that Republican identifiers of all types (including Independents who lean to the Republicans) represented 37 percent of the electorate in 1986, as compared to 27 percent in 1968. Democratic identifiers declined from 68 percent in 1968 to 58 percent in 1986 (pure Independents were 5 percent in both years). Moreover, Republican identifiers were an even higher percentage of actual voters, as they were more likely to register and go to the polls.

This recent pattern of party growth gave Republicans reason to be optimistic about their prospects in 1988. Encouraged by successes in 1980 and 1984, they anticipated retaining the governorship, adding congressional seats, and making further inroads into state government. However, Democrats also had reasons to be hopeful. Party leaders felt that Sanford's victory in the 1986 Senate election proved that the party was still able to win a high-visibility statewide election, even against a relatively well-financed and respected Republican opponent. Moreover, in 1986, the Democrats also retained all the U.S. House seats they held and captured two Republican seats, suggesting to some that the impact of the Reagan era on state politics was waning.

State, Region, and Nation

Growing Republicanism in North Carolina must be viewed within the context of the region and the nation. Partisan shifts within the state in large part reflect a combination of southern and national change rather than factors unique to North Carolina. Overlaying these political patterns will allow us to see the shifting nature of North Carolina electoral politics from a broader perspective.

Developments in North Carolina paralleled the realignment of southern politics, a transformation that began with the turmoil of the 1950s and 1960s and surged forward in the 1970s and 1980s.[3] Republican gains in North Carolina followed the pattern typical in the South, especially in rim states. Increases were registered first at the presidential level, as early as the 1950s, and then somewhat later in gubernatorial and congressional elections. A period of slow growth in sub-presidential races that began in the 1960s came to a peak of 1972, subsided during the remainder of the decade with the impact of Watergate and Jimmy Carter's 1976 campaign, rose to a peak again in 1980, and remained fairly steady through the mid-1980s.

Similarities between North Carolina and the South as a whole were not restricted to election outcomes. The sources, patterns, and dynamics of electoral behavior also were similar. In North Carolina, as in other southern states, Republican votes were drawn very heavily from conservative whites, a group that had been strongly Democratic in the past.[4] The exodus of whites from the Democratic party, coupled with the effective enfranchisement of blacks following the 1965 Voting Rights Act, substantially changed the composition of the Democratic coalition. In the post–civil rights South, Democratic victory hinged on a coalition of whites and blacks.[5] By 1984, blacks accounted for 19 percent of the registered voters in North Carolina, leading to a calculation that a Democratic candidate would win if he carried over 40 percent of the white vote and nearly all of the black vote.[6] While racial politics added a dimension that was not present in many non-southern states (at least not to the same degree), in other ways there was a growing congruence between southern and northern patterns. For example, modest class cleavages emerged among whites in the South, and by the 1980s there was little difference between the two regions on this dimension.[7]

While much of this transformation of southern politics is properly understood in terms of factors peculiar to the region, there is a national dimension as well, especially during the 1980s. This is most evident in presidential elections. The increases and decreases in the Republican share of the vote in recent presidential races display a similar pattern for North Carolina, the South, and the nation. Ronald Reagan's victories in North Carolina were much more a reflection of his national strength than a disproportionate appeal to North Carolinians in particular or southerners in general. In 1980, Reagan's share of the vote in North Carolina was only 1 percentage point different from his national vote, and there was only a 3 point difference in 1984. Similarly, shifts in the results of congressional elections in North Carolina followed the oscillations of the national congressional vote, except that North Carolina had a much higher proportion of marginal seats that shifted back and forth between the parties. During the 1970s and 1980s, five of the eleven House seats switched partisan hands, with three of them doing so twice or more.

The link between national political forces and North Carolina election results provided reasons for both state parties to be hopeful during the spring of 1988 about their prospects for the general election that fall. North Carolina Republicans were encouraged by the effective nomination campaign of George Bush, especially his strong showing in the South on Super Tuesday. Even if Bush might have troubles in the general election, he could be expected to run better in the South than nationally, and thus would still be likely to carry North Carolina.

North Carolina Democrats were less pleased with their apparent nominee, Michael Dukakis. Like other southern Democrats, they had hoped that Super Tuesday would help nominate a southerner, or at least a candidate who would be particularly appealing in the South. Despite this disappointment, North Carolina Democrats were optimistic that Bush would be a weak candidate and would not be able to generate the enthusiasm that Reagan had generated. Even if Dukakis ran less well in North Carolina than nationally, he might still carry the state if his overall strength were great enough.

Social and Economic Forces

The Republican growth of the 1970s and 1980s occurred alongside significant social and economic changes in North Carolina. During this period, family income in the state increased significantly, both in absolute terms and relative to national levels. Median family income in North Carolina during the 1970s jumped from 81 percent to 84 percent of the national figure.[8] The same phenomenon was occurring elsewhere in the South, and overall regional disparities in income were far less by 1980 than they had been just a few decades ago.[9]

Economically, North Carolina was characterized by having a high proportion of its workers in manufacturing. Data from the mid-1980s indicate that 30 percent of the state's labor force was in the manufacturing sector, compared to only 19 percent nationally.[10] Moreover, if we look at a broader industrial sector—which includes manufacturing, transportation, utilities, and construction—this accounts for 41 percent of the North Carolina labor force versus 29 percent nationally.[11] However, manufacturing in North Carolina was not characterized by high-paying jobs, as in some northern industrial states. The typical North Carolina industrial worker was in a fairly low-paying job, such as in the textile industry, which is one of the most important industries in the state. The rate of unionization in the state also was extremely low. Thus, while North Carolina had advanced considerably in recent decades, and while there were examples of high-technology industry (such as in the Research Triangle Park area), the state was still highly dependent on the economic health of some older and potentially vulnerable industries.

Economic growth was associated with the growing urbanization of the state, but while areas such as Charlotte and Raleigh-Durham did undergo periods of rapid growth, North Carolina overall remained a fairly rural state in which small towns and cities were very important. In 1986, only 55 percent of North Carolinians lived in a metropolitan area, compared with a national figure of 77 percent.[12] The relatively high proportion of the labor force in manufacturing and the relatively low proportion of the population in metropolitan areas might appear to be an unlikely combination, but the character of the manufacturing accounts for this. Textile plants, for example, are frequently found in small cities rather than large metropolitan areas.

On one economic aspect, North Carolina ranked far ahead of the country as a whole. Unemployment throughout the 1980s was lower in the state than nationally, sometimes by close to 2 percentage points. In October 1987, for example, the North Carolina unemployment rate was 3.9 percent, while the national rate was 5.8 percent.[13] This relatively low unemployment rate was one of the factors that encouraged Republicans, who felt that their election chances depended in part on favorable perceptions of the economic performance of the Reagan-Bush administration.

THE CAMPAIGN

As we have suggested above, both parties in the state had reasons to be optimistic about their election possibilities in 1988. The continued popularity of Ronald Reagan in the final year of his administration, the southern appeal of George Bush, and the relatively low unemployment rate (both nationally and in the state) were factors that suggested a favorable year for Republicans overall. Additionally, an incumbent Republican governor was running for re-election for the first time ever. Prior to the 1980s, governors were prohibited from running for re-election, so Republican James Holshouser, who was elected in 1972, had left office after his four-year term expired.

Democrats had their reasons to be optimistic as they approached the 1988 elections. Believing that national circumstances were more favorable than in the previous two presidential election years, and hoping that Bush would prove to be a weak candidate, the Democratic party anticipated at least retaining the offices they already had, if not capturing the governorship or a congressional seat. Furthermore, the party had avoided a divisive primary for key offices, unlike the situation in some past years. Bitter primary fights for the gubernatorial nomination had hampered Democratic chances in 1972 and 1984, for example. However, in 1988 the party united very early behind Lieutenant Governor Bob Jordan as their gubernatorial nominee, and a very competitive primary battle for Lieutenant Governor ended in a relatively harmonious fashion.

Events during the summer of 1988 reinforced these Democratic hopes. Most important was Dukakis's choice of Texas Senator Lloyd Bentsen as his running mate. The symbolic nature of this choice to southern Democrats stood in stark contrast to the selection of Geraldine Ferraro by Walter Mondale in 1984. A harmonious Democratic convention, marked by a rapprochement between Dukakis and Jesse Jackson, also was a favorable development. Finally, the selection of Dan Quayle as the Republican vice presidential nominee was followed almost immediately by an explosion of negative news stories about his past behavior and lack of qualifications, much to the glee of Democrats.

For many observers, the 1988 elections were a key to the future direction of state politics. Possibly, 1988 might be similar to 1976, a year in which Democrats recaptured some of the offices lost in 1972. Alternatively, 1988 might represent a continuation or even an acceleration of trends that took place during the Reagan years. This latter outcome would signify a further realignment of partisan forces within the state.

The Presidential Election

Early public opinion polls indicated a close presidential election in North Carolina. An August poll by the *Greensboro News and Record* had Bush and Dukakis virtually even.[14] Early September polls by the *Charlotte Observer* and the *Raleigh News and Observer* also showed the race to be a dead heat.[15] For Bush, this situation represented an improvement over his earlier position, as a June poll had him down by 6 points in the state.[16]

Observers also felt that the election would be close because the Dukakis campaign had targeted North Carolina as one of the states that could be won. Unlike some other southern states such as South Carolina, the Democrats were willing to commit time and resources to North Carolina. Even when the Dukakis campaign scaled back its efforts in several southern states in late September, North Carolina remained on the active list.[17] Near the end of the campaign North Carolina was dropped as a target state, but for most of the campaign it did receive substantial Democratic attention.[18]

The Dukakis campaign in North Carolina was a coordinated effort with the state Democratic Party. The "Victory '88" campaign received about $500,000 in soft money from the national party.[19] This money was used to fund a significant grass-roots organization involving over 100 paid workers.[20] Phone banks were established in sixty-five counties, and over 200,000 households in targeted precincts were contacted.[21] Follow-up mailings were sent, with the content of the information matched to the concerns of the contacted individual. Media buys also were made in North Carolina by the Dukakis campaign. As late as early October, the campaign purchased substantial local television time to run political advertisements.[22] Of course, most of the television advertisements that North Carolinians saw were national network ones, but the local media buys supplemented the national effort.

The Republicans also formed a coordinated "Victory '88" campaign, and they channeled a similar amount of money (about $700,000) into party activities.[23] The Republican effort relied less on the grass-roots approach of the Democrats (fewer than ten paid staffers were on the payroll).[24] Instead, they emphasized a more sophisticated approach in terms of campaign technology, hiring professional polling and mailing organizations to carry out their activities.[25] Still, the Republican Victory '88 activities were similar to the Democratic ones. Telephone surveys to determine potential Republican supporters, especially among registered Democrats in key precincts, were a key element of the GOP strategy. Mass mailings also were important. Like the Democrats, Republicans were concerned with "get-out-the-vote" activities. Additionally, the Republicans put a particular stress on the casting of an absentee ballot by individuals who could not go to the polls in person on election day.[26] This Republican emphasis probably reflected the belief that absentee ballot voters are disproportionately Republican.

The Republican candidates made several visits to the state. Bush appeared three times, and Quayle twice. Additionally, there were probably around twenty visits by campaign surrogates, including an appearance by President Ronald Reagan.[27] The Democratic candidates also targeted the state, with Dukakis and Bentsen each making two trips to North Carolina, and numerous visits by Democratic campaign surrogates, including Jesse Jackson, were scheduled. Notably, state and local Democratic leaders did not attempt to avoid campaigning with Dukakis or Bentsen, unlike the situation in 1984.

The most important trip that the presidential candidates made to the state was for the first debate, which was held September 25 in Winston-Salem. While this was truly a national event, and not a local one, the presence of such an event in the state did generate considerable local media coverage, particularly in the Piedmont Triad area. The debate did not produce a clear winner, although neither candidate hesitated to claim a decisive victory. The fairly even outcome was in reality more favorable to Bush, as he had moved ahead in the polls by this time and needed only to maintain his lead to secure his election.

The points emphasized by the candidates in their trips to the state and the messages stressed in the mass mailings and media advertisements directed at North Carolinians did not differ markedly from the national campaign themes. The Bush campaign attacked Dukakis for being too liberal, hammering particularly on the idea that he was soft on crime (the Massachusetts prison furlough issue being used effectively on this point), weak on national defense, and generally out of step with mainstream American values (Governor Dukakis's lack of support for a bill to require the recitation of the Pledge of Allegiance in Massachusetts public schools was one example stressed by Republicans).

As an example of Republican campaign strategy, Dan Quayle suggested in a visit to Asheville that Dukakis could be called "Mr. Weak-on-Defense" or "Mr. Soft-on-Crime."[28] Similarly, Ronald Reagan attacked Democrats during his visit to the state, claiming that they were "liberal, liberal, liberal," and stressing such issues as the Pledge of Allegiance, the prison furlough question, and the death penalty.[29] Moreover, a GOP mass mailing to all Republican households (about 580,000) before the election, in the form of a letter from Governor Jim Martin urging supporters to go to the polls, stressed the dangers of "tax and tax, spend and spend policies of the Democrats under Mike Dukakis," "unilateral disarmament," and "liberal social programs [that] would threaten the strength of the family."[30] All this was very similar to the campaign messages that were being disseminated nationally.

The Democratic campaign in North Carolina also reflected its national characteristics. Whereas the Republicans ran a very sophisticated and efficient presidential campaign, directed by experienced professionals, the Dukakis campaign appeared disorganized, unfocused, and amateurish. Democratic leaders in the state were both upset with the negative tone of the Bush campaign and frustrated by the inability of the Dukakis campaign to mount a forceful rebuttal and counterattack.[31] There were, of course, some themes discernible in the Dukakis campaign, even if they were unclear to many voters, such as criticisms of the Reagan administration for selling arms to Iran or creating monstrous budget deficits. Moreover, there were some attempts to focus on issues of particular concern to the state, as when Dukakis criticized Reagan's veto of the textile import bill during a visit to Asheville.[32] Overall, however, the Democratic campaign was ineffective both in responding to the Republican charges and defining salient ideas that aroused the electorate.

One interesting difference between the two campaigns was in the role of the vice presidential candidates. The Democrats stressed Bentsen's being on the ticket, almost always referring to the Dukakis-Bentsen team. Republicans, on the other hand, usually referred simply to Bush and generally gave Quayle a lower profile in the campaign. These differences stem from the factors discussed earlier, reinforced by poll results, which indicated that North Carolinians had quite different attitudes toward the two vice presidential candidates. One media poll reported that 34 percent of the electorate felt that Quayle was not qualified to be President, while only 8 percent felt that way about Bentsen.[33] How much effect evaluations of the vice presidential candidates had on the presidential vote is uncertain, but what influence was present undoubtedly worked to the advantage of the Democrats.

The overall superiority of the Bush campaign, both nationally and in the state, began to have an effect on voter intentions in September. By late September, Bush had moved out to a clear advantage, and in mid-October he had a double-digit lead.[34] Near the end, Dukakis began to campaign more effectively, but it was too little, too late. Bush held a comfortable 10 point lead in the media polls that were reported on the eve of the election.[35]

Congressional and State Elections

Important campaigns were occurring below the presidential race, in part because North Carolina state elections coincide with presidential elections, unlike the situation in most states. The gubernatorial election drew considerable attention. Republican incumbent Jim Martin appeared to have several significant advantages besides simply being the incumbent, including very favorable job performance approval ratings.[36] Nevertheless, the Democrats put a major emphasis on this race. The result was a very visible campaign. Both candidates spent heavily, around $5 million each.[37]

Not surprisingly, Martin's campaign stressed the accomplishments of the past four years and argued that the state was in excellent shape. The Republicans also attempted to label the Democrat, Bob Jordan, as a politician who was lacking in openness and trust. Jordan attacked Martin for being an ineffective and uninvolved governor. One controversial Jordan television advertisement showed a group of monkeys playing on a desk with papers as a way of portraying the Martin administration as bunglers when it came to budget construction. While Jordan's attacks may have had some effect, media polls indicated that Martin maintained a fairly comfortable lead throughout the campaign. *Charlotte Observer* polls, for example, reported an 8 point lead for Martin in mid-September, a 13 point lead in mid-October, and a 12 point lead just before the election.[38]

Republicans were not content to simply retain the governorship; they had their eyes on the election for Lieutenant Governor. The nomination of Jim Gardner, a former member of the U.S. House, gave the Republicans a candidate with significant name recognition in this race. The Democratic candidate, State Legislator Tony Rand, was less well known, although he gained some name recognition as a result of a well-publicized primary battle for the nomination.

State legislative races also were the focus of GOP efforts. The state Republican Party earmarked $160,000 to help out candidates in targeted legislative districts, and made available other support, such as research.[39] In part, Republican hopes were based on the belief that many voters held negative perceptions of the existing legislature, especially regarding the lack of openness and abuse of power by some of the leaders.

Several congressional races were expected to be extremely competitive as well. In the spring, the national Republican party identified four districts where incumbent Democrats were vulnerable (the Fourth, Fifth, Eighth, and Eleventh districts), and planned to pump $700,000 into the state to support Republican challengers.[40] The Democrats not only intended to defend those seats, but also to mount a significant challenge against the Republican incumbent in the Sixth District, who had won by less than 100 votes in 1986. The competitiveness of these congressional campaigns was reflected in the campaign expenditures. In the Fourth, Fifth, Sixth, and Eleventh districts, the incumbent and the challenger each spent over $400,000.[41]

RESULTS AND ANALYSIS

The 1988 elections in North Carolina may have been exciting to political analysts, but they did not attract many voters to the polls. A dismal 43 percent of those over the age of eighteen cast a ballot, making North Carolina one of the worst states in the nation for voter turnout.[42] Nationally, slightly over 50 percent of the voting age population voted, which was the lowest turnout rate in over sixty years.[43] Many reasons might be given to explain the low turnout, including the issue-less and negative presidential campaign, but it is interesting to note that the decline in turnout from 1984 to 1988 was significantly greater in North Carolina than nationally.[44]

Election Results

George Bush carried North Carolina fairly easily, winning 58 percent of the vote. His share of the vote in the state was about 4 points higher than his national total, a differential that was very similar to that of 1984. Bush's victory was no surprise, as polls had predicted his election well before Election Day. The re-election of Governor Martin was no surprise either. His 56 percent of the vote was a slight improvement over his 1984 vote.

More surprising were Republican victories further down the ballot. Gardner won a very close race for Lieutenant Governor, with a winning margin of less than 30,000 votes out of over two million cast. Democrats won the remaining statewide races, but Republicans were very competitive in several cases. In five of the eight elections for Council of State offices, the Republican candidate received at least 46 percent of the vote. Republican gains also were registered in state legislative races. The GOP went from thirty-six to forty-six seats in the North Carolina House and from ten to thirteen seats in the Senate.[45]

The 1988 elections proved to have an enormous impact on the North Carolina General Assembly when it convened in January. In the House, the Republican minority combined with disgruntled Democrats to oust a powerful and autocratic Speaker and replace him with a maverick Democrat. As part of the coalition bargain, Republican legislators received a sizeable number of subcommittee chairs. On the Senate side, the Democratic majority stripped the Lieutenant Governor of many powers that had been allocated to him by Senate rules, such as the appointment of committee chairs.

The Republican successes in state races were not matched by gains in congressional races. Republicans failed to add a single U.S. House seat to their total of three, as all eleven incumbents were re-elected. The lack of significant presidential coattails in the congressional races in the state reflected a similar pattern at the national level. While none of the North Carolina Republican challengers won, in three districts they received a very competitive share of the vote—47 percent in the Fifth District, 49 percent in the Eighth District, and almost 50 percent in the Eleventh District.[46]

Voting Patterns

Some fairly clear sources of voting behavior existed in 1988. Relying largely on exit polls carried out in North Carolina by CBS and NBC, supplemented with pre-election polls by the major newspapers in the state, we can examine some of the correlates of the presidential and gubernatorial vote.

Table 10.1 contains data on the relationship between a variety of social factors and voting behavior. The NBC exit poll data are reported, rather than those of CBS, because the NBC poll interviewed a larger number of respondents (approximately 2,500 compared to 1,500). However, the patterns in the NBC data do not differ substantially from the CBS data or from the newspaper pre-election polls.

The greatest difference is on race, as we would expect. This overwhelming support of blacks for the Democratic candidates is similar to the pattern in earlier years in the state and to national patterns.[47] The significant fact is that the Democratic candidates for President and Governor were unable to win the support of more than one-third of the white voters in the state, far less than the approximately 40 percent needed for election.

We also would expect Republicans to do better among voters with higher socioeconomic status (SES). The data are inconsistent on this point, however. Clear and consistent differences do exist for income, but the patterns for education and occupation are neither, although it is true that those in the bottom category of occupation and education are always the most Democratic. Some of the relationship between SES and voting may be due to the confounding effect of race, but looking at whites only (a breakdown available in the CBS data) still reveals an impact, especially for income. National exit poll data suggest that SES as a whole was a little more important in structuring the vote nationally than in North Carolina.[48]

Gender differences were large, both relative to past patterns in the state and to national patterns in 1988.[49] Age differences also were significant, with the Republicans doing better among the young, a pattern that does not appear to have been present nationally in the presidential election.[50]

The vote in the state also displayed some important regional variations. Bush did best in the western part of the state, where he received 62 percent of the vote, and worst in the east, where he won 54 percent.[51] In the central Piedmont, Bush did less well in the five metropolitan counties (the counties containing Charlotte, Raleigh, Greensboro, Winston-Salem, and Durham) than in the remainder of the Piedmont. Some of these regional patterns are due to racial

Table 10.1

Presidential and Gubernatorial Vote by Selected Social and Demographic Characteristics (in percent)*

Characteristic	Presidential Vote for Bush	Gubernatorial Vote for Martin
Race		
White	68	66
Black	8	11
Income		
Less than 20,000	42	43
$20,000 - 50,000	61	59
More than $50,000	68	68
Occupation		
Blue collar	60	56
White collar	63	65
Professional	61	61
Education		
Less than high school graduate	51	55
High school graduate	64	61
College	60	58
Graduate/professional work	52	55
Gender		
Male	63	62
Female	53	54
Age		
18-24	65	63
25-49	59	59
50-64	56	56
65+	52	52
Religion		
Protestant	65	63
Catholic	48	55

*Figures reported are percentages for the Republican candidates.

Source: NBC exit poll (N=2516).

differences; blacks are most prevalent in the eastern part of the state and least prevalent in the west.

Perhaps more important than the social correlates of the vote are the attitudinal sources of voting behavior. Table 10.2 presents data for three basic factors. The data for party identification indicate that Bush and Martin put together their winning coalitions in much the same fashion, holding nearly all Republicans, adding a very substantial majority of Independents, and including a modest minority of Democrats.

Going beyond party identification, we see that, as expected, both Bush and Martin did much better among conservatives than among liberals. Unfortunately, the limited polling data available for North Carolina did not permit a detailed

Table 10.2
Presidential and Gubernatorial Vote by Selected Political Attitudes and Orientations (in percent)

Characteristic	Presidential Vote for Bush	Gubernatorial Vote for Martin
Party Identification		
Republican	94	93
Independent	70	69
Democrat	18	18
Ideology		
Conservative	83	82
Moderate	49	47
Liberal	27	33
Reagan Performance		
Approve	86	NA
Disapprove	9	NA

*Figures reported are percentages for the Republican candidates.

Source: Compiled by author from NBC exit poll (N=2516) and CBS exit poll (N=1503).

discussion of the role of specific issues in voting behavior, so we cannot be very thorough or precise on this point. The data that are available indicate that Bush was viewed by the electorate as more likely than Dukakis to maintain a strong defense, deal effectively with the Soviet Union, and prevent an increase in taxes. Dukakis scored better on protecting the environment and protecting civil rights.[52]

More important than ideology or specific issues are retrospective evaluations of the performance of the Reagan administration. Table 10.2 contains one item, evaluation of Reagan's job performance, which is highly related to presidential vote. Other items in exit or pre-election polls also indicate that feelings about administration performance, especially concerning the economy, played a big role in the election. Dukakis did very well among voters who expressed significant concerns about the health of the economy, but the majority of voters were more favorable in their view of economic performance.[53] The available survey data show that Dukakis was unable to convince North Carolinians that he would be better able than Bush to manage the economy. The two candidates were rated evenly on reducing the federal budget deficit and on providing jobs for American workers.[54]

Almost no data are available on how the electorate viewed the personal characteristics of the two candidates. Since such factors normally play a strong role in a presidential election, the lack of data is most unfortunate. Pre-election survey data do suggest that Bush was seen as more likely to provide strong leadership, which is one important factor.[55] Beyond that we can only speculate, but some observers felt that the negative tone of the campaign left many voters with a fairly negative view of both candidates.

CONCLUSION

Nineteen eighty-eight was an important year for the future of electoral politics in North Carolina. The extent of Republican victories in state elections indicates that the state is moving at a fairly rapid pace toward a truly competitive two-party system. Not only did the GOP consolidate and extend the gains made by the party during the Reagan years, but it did so in a year in which the Democrats were reasonably unified and well financed. Even the failure of the Republicans to gain a single congressional seat does not greatly diminish the gains that were made. There were no open seats in 1988, and congressional incumbents are very difficult to unseat, recent North Carolina history notwithstanding. The closeness of the vote in several of the congressional elections suggests that Republicans would have a good chance of winning some seats when current incumbents leave office. However, one important qualification should be placed on the Republican success. North Carolina Republicans once again had the advantage of a winning presidential candidate at the top of the ticket. The unanswered question is whether Republicans will be able to maintain and develop their strength if the nation enters a period that is not marked by Republican domination of presidential elections. The future of North Carolina politics probably hinges on the direction of national politics.

ACKNOWLEDGMENTS

I wish to express my appreciation to several individuals who assisted in the writing of this article. Tim Storey was an excellent research assistant. Josh Collett, CBS; Mary Ann Campbell, NBC; and Seth Effron, *Greensboro News and Record*, made available the results of exit or pre-election polls, which were essential for determining the sources of party support. Ken Eudy, North Carolina Democratic Party Executive Director; Jack Hawke, North Carolina Republican Party Chairman; William Graham, North Carolina Bush Campaign Chairman; and Jim Van Hecke, North Carolina Democratic Party Chairman, graciously shared invaluable information and insights with me. Whatever errors of fact or interpretation remain are my responsibility.

NOTES

1. Calculated from figures supplied by the North Carolina Board of Elections.
2. Jack D. Fleer, Roger C. Lowery, and Charles L. Prysby, "Political Change in North Carolina," in *The South's New Politics: Realignment and Dealignment*, ed. Robert H. Swansbrough and David M. Brodsky (Columbia: University of South Carolina Press, 1988), 97.
3. For detailed discussions of this change, see Jack Bass and Walter DeVries, *The Transformation of Southern Politics* (New York: Basic Books, 1976); Earl Black and

Merle Black, *Politics and Society in the South* (Cambridge, Mass.: Harvard University Press, 1987); and Alexander P. Lamis, *The Two-Party South* (New York: Oxford University Press, 1984).

4. Fleer, Lowery, and Prysby, "Political Change in North Carolina."

5. See Lamis, *The Two-Party South*, for an extensive discussion of this theme.

6. Charles L. Prysby and E. Lee Bernick, "The Impact of the Jackson Candidacy on the Democratic Party in North Carolina" (Paper delivered at the 1986 Meeting of the North Carolina Political Science Association, Mars Hill, N.C.).

7. Charles L. Prysby, "The Structure of Southern Electoral Behavior," *American Politics Quarterly* 17 (April 1989): 163–180.

8. U.S. Bureau of the Census, *Statistical Abstract of the United States, 1988*, 108th ed. (Washington, D.C.: U.S. Government Printing Office, 1987).

9. "Social Indicators," *Public Opinion* 11 (November/December 1988): 16.

10. U.S. Census Bureau, *Statistical Abstract*, 386.

11. Ibid.

12. Ibid., 27.

13. U.S. Bureau of Labor Statistics, *Employment and Earnings* 35 (December 1988): 115.

14. *Greensboro News and Record*, September 24, 1988, A1.

15. *Charlotte Observer*, September 17, 1988, A1; *Raleigh News and Observer*, September 21, 1988, A1.

16. *Charlotte Observer*, June 5, 1988, A1.

17. *Charlotte Observer*, September 28, 1988, A1.

18. Interview with Jim Van Hecke, Greensboro, December 14, 1988.

19. Ibid.

20. Interview with Ken Eudy, Raleigh, December 21, 1988.

21. Ibid.

22. *Raleigh News and Observer*, October 4, 1988, A1.

23. Interview with William Graham, Raleigh, December 21, 1988.

24. Ibid.

25. Interview with Jack Hawke, Raleigh, December 12, 1988.

26. Ibid.

27. Interview with Graham.

28. *Charlotte Observer*, October 8, 1988, A1.

29. *Charlotte Observer*, October 22, 1988, A1; *Raleigh News and Observer*, October 22, 1988, A1.

30. Republican Party campaign mailing.

31. *Raleigh News and Observer*, November 4, 1988, A1.

32. *Charlotte Observer*, October 8, 1988, A1.

33. *Charlotte Observer*, October 15, 1988, A4.

34. *Greensboro News and Record*, September 24, 1988, A1; *Charlotte Observer*, October 15, 1988, A1.

35. *Raleigh News and Observer*, November 5, 1988, A1.

36. *Greensboro News and Record*, October 30, 1988, A1; *Raleigh News and Observer*, March 6, 1988, A1.

37. Interviews with Eudy, Hawke.

38. *Charlotte Observer*, September 18, 1988, A1; October 16, 1988, A1; November 4, 1988, A1.

39. Interview with Hawke.

40. *Raleigh News and Observer*, March 15, 1988, A1.

41. Campaign finance reports filed with the North Carolina Board of Elections.

42. Data provided by the Committee for the Study of the American Electorate (CSAE), Washington, D.C.

43. Ibid.

44. Ibid.

45. All election results were calculated from data provided by the North Carolina Board of Elections.

46. Ibid.

47. Jack Fleer, "North Carolina," in *The 1984 Presidential Election in the South*, ed. Robert P. Steed, Laurence W. Moreland, and Tod A. Baker (New York: Praeger, 1985), 265; Fleer, Lowery, and Prysby, "Political Change in North Carolina"; 1988 national exit poll data supplied by NBC.

48. Ibid.

49. Fleer, "North Carolina"; Fleer, Lowery, and Prysby, "Political Change in North Carolina"; NBC exit poll data.

50. Ibid.

51. Calculated from data provided by the North Carolina Board of Elections.

52. Mason-Dixon telephone poll of North Carolina, conducted for the *Greensboro News and Record*, September 17–19, 1988.

53. 1988 North Carolina exit poll data supplied by CBS.

54. Mason-Dixon poll.

55. Ibid.

11

Tennessee: A House Divided

DAVID M. BRODSKY AND ROBERT H. SWANSBROUGH

INTRODUCTION: PARTY COMPETITION—
NOT COMPLACENCY

An Early Inroad in the Solid South

Observers often identify Tennessee as one of the first southern states to develop a competitive party system. The roots of the Volunteer State's Republican party grew from east Tennessee's opposition to secession from the Union. In two 1861 ballots, the mountainous east Tennessee region voted against secession, while slave-owning west and middle Tennessee backed the Confederacy. Tennessee's voting patterns over the years usually reflected these three grand divisions, with Democrats controlling the state's politics from their historic strongholds in west and middle Tennessee.

Since the Civil War, Tennessee's eastern counties have maintained their GOP loyalties, despite their inability to win statewide offices against the entrenched Democratic party. Republicans monopolized east Tennessee's local offices and regularly sent congressional representatives to Washington; between 1947 and 1952, two Tennessee Republicans occupied the only House seats in the South's 105 member congressional delegation.[1] The state's GOP leaders acquired influence primarily through alliances with the competing Democratic factions, such as Ed Crump's Memphis-based political "machine."

A Partisan Rollercoaster

The 1963 death of Senator Estes Kefauver seemed to mark the waning of the Democratic party's domination of the Volunteer State.[2] Although President Lyndon Johnson carried Tennessee in the 1964 election, Senator Barry Goldwater's candidacy and his outspoken criticism of the 1964 Civil Rights Act attracted conservative Democrats to the GOP's candidates. Republican Howard Baker won his Senate seat in 1966, and four years later Bill Brock captured Senator Al Gore's office. The year 1970 represents the zenith of Republican electoral success: Winfield Dunn became Tennessee's fourth GOP governor, Baker and Brock held the Senate seats, and Republicans comprised four of Tennessee's nine-member congressional delegation. Democratic factional strife, personality-centered politics, weak party organization, and scandals contributed to the party's eclipse.

Between 1968 and 1984, the Democrats lost five out of six presidential contests in Tennessee, only breaking the trend with Jimmy Carter's victory. However, the Democrats recovered other political offices. Carter's 1976 coattails helped Jim Sasser capture Senator Brock's seat for the Democrats; six years later, Sasser demolished his GOP challenger, Congressman Robin Beard. Upon Howard Baker's 1984 retirement, U.S. Representative Al Gore, Jr., moved into the Senate chamber, where his father had once represented Tennessee, by soundly defeating Republican State Senator Victor Ashe. Although the Democrats reoccupied the Governor's Mansion with the 1974 win of Ray Blanton, the scandals surrounding the Blanton administration contributed to Republican Lamar Alexander's 1978 election. Alexander easily won re-election to a second term in 1982.

House Speaker Ned McWherter's 1986 gubernatorial defeat of ex-governor Dunn symbolized the recovery of Tennessee's Democratic party. In 1986 McWherter became governor, Sasser and Gore sat in the U.S. Senate, and Democrats enjoyed a six to three majority in Tennessee's congressional delegation as well as hefty majorities in the General Assembly's Senate (23 to 10) and House (61 to 38). Tennesseans appeared to reject the Democrats' presidential nominees as too liberal, but local issues, strong candidates, the power of incumbency, and traditional loyalties allowed the Democratic party to regain its commanding role in Tennessee's politics. Nevertheless, weakening regional partisanship, ticket splitting, and television dramatically changed the style of the Volunteer State's politics.

Regional Defections and Ticket Splitting

West Tennessee no longer represents a secure Democratic base. Populous Shelby County, with Memphis's large concentration of black voters, remains most firmly in the Democratic camp. However, the GOP suburbs surrounding Memphis and conservative rural white Democrats in the old cotton belt often join in supporting Republican candidates. Between 1970 and 1986, west Tennesseans cast a plurality of their vote for GOP presidential, gubernatorial and senate candidates in seven out of fifteen races.

Today, middle Tennessee, anchored by Nashville, stands out as the Democrats' key bastion, although even this traditionally Democratic region abandons some of the party's nominees. In six out of fifteen statewide electoral contests from 1970 to 1986, the Republican candidates won a majority of middle Tennessee votes.

The erosion of historic partisan bonds has also undermined the GOP's east Tennessee heartland. In 1982 and 1984, the region's Republicans cast a plurality of their ballots for the Democratic party's Senate candidates, and gave President Gerald Ford a very narrow victory over Jimmy Carter in 1976. Governor McWherter carried the hard-core Republican First Congressional District in 1986, largely because of lingering resentments over Dunn's policies during his 1970–1974 administration. According to McWherter's 1986 campaign manager, Jim Hall, their east Tennessee strategy concentrated on the bitter memories of Dunn's failure to establish a medical school at East Tennessee State University, his abandonment of a prison in Moristown, and the former governor's inaction on a "bloody" stretch of highway in this GOP area.[3]

In comparing the results of two post-presidential election surveys, the authors found that Democratic party identification in the Volunteer State fell 10 points between 1981 and 1985 from 42 to 32 percent, while Republican identifiers rose from 25 to 29 percent. The proportion of Tennesseans calling themselves Independents increased to 39 percent, comprising a plurality of the 1985 sample. The study disclosed that whites, higher income respondents, voters between ages thirty and fifty-four, and Tennesseans who dealigned from a major party to become Independents tended to split their ballots. The authors concluded that dealignment—not realignment—best characterized the contemporary period of Tennessee politics.[4] Anne Hopkins, William Lyons, and Steve Metcalf also highlighted Tennessee's new era of "more complex regionalism," while not discerning a clear realignment to the Republican party.[5]

THE CAMPAIGNS: TARGETING SWING VOTERS

Mirror-Image Strategies

The 1988 presidential race began in the Volunteer State with strategists in the Dukakis and Bush camps following traditional Tennessee political wisdom. Both campaigns recognized the historic voting patterns of Tennessee's three grand divisions. Dukakis's state coordinator, Peter Goelz, declared, "We've got to minimize their [Bush campaign] margins in East Tennessee, rack up a win in Middle Tennessee and rural West [Tennessee], then bang it home in Memphis."[6] Goelz admitted that this approach conceded most of East Tennessee to George Bush. "We had to go where our votes are. . . . It's reality that the national ticket is not going to carry Chattanooga. The national ticket is not going to carry Knoxville.''

Bush's state campaign director, Stephanie Chivers, acknowledged a similar geopolitical strategy—but in reverse. "Our game plan mirror images their game plan. . . . We've got to win big in East [Tennessee], break even in Middle [Tennessee], do what damage we can in rural West [Tennessee] and then carry the Republican boxes in Shelby [County].''[7] Chivers expressed the conventional belief that statewide GOP candidates needed to build a 125,000 vote margin in east Tennessee to win, since their vote advantage dwindles as the electoral wave rolls through middle Tennessee's counties to west Tennessee.

The state's GOP strategists carefully targeted Reagan Democrats to forge a winning coalition. Chivers explained, "We figured . . . that the swing vote is out in those rural areas in Middle and West Tennessee among those Reagan Democrats. . . . The urban areas will probably break the way they always do, so we've got to get the vote in the rural areas. We're focusing on things like gun control, prison furloughs and higher taxes—they're what hits home with these people.''[8] Thomas (Tommy) A. Hopper, political director of Tennessee's Republican party, explained that Reagan Democrat counties were identified as those that cast at least 60 percent of their 1984 ballots for President Reagan and 60 percent for Democratic Senator Al Gore.[9]

A Jump-Start Attack

After the August Republican convention, Tennessee's GOP Chairman Jim Henry called Tennessee "a swing state.''[10] The Bush campaign enjoyed an organizational advantage in the fall because of the Republican party's Super Tuesday primary competition in Tennessee. Former Tennessee Senator Bill Brock served as Senator Bob Dole's national campaign chairman. Brock's Tennessee ties allowed him to organizationally challenge Bush in the Volunteer State, compelling the Bush forces to develop a strong Tennessee effort. Chivers acknowledged that the county-by-county organization Bush created for super Tuesday gave the state GOP an advantage in the general election. Nevertheless, Chivers acknowledged how a lack of enthusiasm impeded the recruitment of volunteers. "Beyond a core group, it's been harder to get folks than normally.''[11]

The GOP's Victory '88 Committee established a fund-raising goal of $750,000, spending about $600,000 in the 1988 general election. The Bush campaign employed a slim field organization of five people (Tennesseans) paid by Victory '88; Hopper and Chivers, both Tennessee residents, received their salaries from the Bush payroll.

The Bush team relied extensively on direct mailings and flyers to contrast the records of George Bush and Michael Dukakis. A black-and-white brochure, featuring a sneering picture of Dukakis on the cover, provoked the greatest controversy. The headline declared, "Michael Dukakis says he will do for America what he has done for Massachusetts. THREAT . . . OR PROMISE?'' The mailing featured a picture of Willie Horton and a description of his crimes while released under Governor Dukakis's furlough program. Governor Ned McWherter declared he was "shocked, appalled and amazed" at the GOP brochure, while Hopper defended it as "totally factual."[12] About 320,000 copies were mailed to the targeted rural counties and about twenty "Reagan Democrat" precincts in each urban area, according to Hopper. Manifesting a similar tactic, Republican flyers blasting Dukakis's positions on gun control and crime closed with a large, bold-print warning, "Michael Dukakis: Too liberal for Tennessee."

Always Playing Catch-Up

Democratic leaders viewed Tennessee as one of Dukakis's winnable southern states after their successful July convention. However, the Massachusetts governor de facto Super Tuesday concession of Tennessee to favorite son Al Gore meant Dukakis lacked an organization in the state for the fall campaign. Furthermore, many of the state's black leaders—Dukakis's strongest potential base—stood aloof from the Democratic presidential campaign because of perceived slights to Jackson at the convention.

Shortly after the July Democratic convention, Dukakis's national campaign staff tapped Peter Goelz, an experienced Democratic politician from Kansas City, Missouri, to serve as its Tennessee political director. However, because of personal reasons, he did not arrive in Tennessee until late in August. Since Goelz had little knowledge of Tennessee politics, familiarization and introductions consumed additional critical time. Moreover, the national staff made no effort to have Governor McWherter "take the state and run it," according to the governor's Executive Assistant, Jim Hall.[13]

The Dukakis effort in Tennessee stressed a field organization to get out the traditional Democratic vote, but since Dukakis did not air any television ads in Tennessee during the primary or visit the state, he never established a positive identity in Tennessee. The campaign employed a total of twenty individuals, many with little political experience; fifteen were from Tennessee. Republican leaders like Hopper gleefully pointed out that the three highest Dukakis campaign officials in Tennessee were all "outsiders."

Some party officials, like Eugene (Chip) Forrester, Executive Director of Tennessee's Democratic party, fault the Dukakis campaign's failure to effectively utilize Governor Ned McWherter, who enjoyed great popularity in the pivotal rural counties.[14] McWherter's aide Jim Hall revealed that an advertising agency filmed endorsements of Dukakis by McWherter and the other southern governors attending the August 7–8 National Governors' Conference in Cincinnati, yet despite having McWherter's endorsement "in the can," the Dukakis campaign never aired the spot in Tennessee.

While at the National Governors' Conference, McWherter privately advised Dukakis to develop a "message for people in rural areas and small towns," which had been overlooked by the Reagan administration's policies.[15] As Gore's southern campaign chairman, the Tennessee Governor's colorful instructions on how to mobilize the South's rural vote for the Super Tuesday contest earlier achieved national attention. Saying some folks considered him a little "redneckish," McWherter advised, "You just got to get with those rednecks and wake 'em up. Crank 'em up and get 'em going."[16]

Courting Reagan Democrats

Tommy Hopper feels the targeted visits of George Bush, vice presidential nominee Dan Quayle, and Republican surrogates represented a key component in the GOP's Tennessee victory. Vice President Bush spoke at Middle Tennessee State University on August 29, followed by a fund-raiser in Nashville. During that visit Bush hit Dukakis for his stands on defense, taxes, school prayer, the Pledge of Allegiance, and the Massachusetts furlough program.[17] On September 26, the day after the first presidential debate, Bush and Quayle appeared together in Jackson, speaking to a crowd of 12,000 west Tennesseans. The GOP strategists purposely scheduled Bush's only Tennessee visits in the two Democratic regional strongholds; only Quayle, who made five visits, stumped in Republican east Tennessee. Childers explained, "We wanted him [Bush] in there with the Reagan/McWherter Democrats."[18]

The Bush strategists sent surrogates to small towns and medium-sized cities to break the Democrats' traditional rural white and urban black coalition. Senator Strom Thurmond campaigned in nine counties in West Tennessee, and Representative Bob Dorn (CA) stumped in rural conservative areas. Barbara Bush, Marilyn Quayle, George Bush, Jr., and Marvin Bush all paid visits to Tennessee. Former Marine Commandant General P. X. Kelley declared in the Volunteer State, "Michael Dukakis is anti-military."[19]

Uncomfortable Allies

Governor Dukakis traveled to Nashville to receive the endorsements of Governor McWherter and Senator Gore shortly after locking up the Democratic nomination. Reporters querried McWherter about his earlier statement that "on many issues [Dukakis] is more liberal that I'm comfortable with." Declaring his total support and endorsement of the Massachusetts governor, McWherter replied that Ronald Reagan was too liberal for him on the national debt. The Tennessee governor admitted that he disagreed with Dukakis on some "emotional issues," like capital punishment, which he felt should not arise in a national campaign.[20]

Michael and Kitty Dukakis attended the Wilson County Fair with Governor McWherter, Senator Sasser, and Senator Gore. McWherter introduced the Democratic presidential nominee, emphasizing that Dukakis "supports the programs that we need in this county and state and this country."[21] Accompanied by black Representative Harold Ford and Shelby County Mayor Bill Morris, Dukakis called for "breaking the back of apartheid in South Africa" at a late-evening Memphis meeting.[22] The next day, Governor Dukakis visited a computer class at the State Technical Institute at Memphis to stress his national theme, "Making America First," and Kitty Dukakis stopped briefly in Memphis on October 22 to address Democratic workers.

Vice presidential nominee Lloyd Bentsen shook hands at the Gibson County Fair and campaigned in west Tennessee with Governor McWherter and retiring Congressman Ed Jones in late August, defending Dukakis's patriotism and position on gun control. Senator Bentsen also attended the September 28 fundraiser at the Governor's Mansion, a mid-September Democratic fund-raiser in Memphis, and a September 16 Tri-State breakfast.

One week before the election, Governor McWherter called Dukakis the underdog in the Tennessee race; "If the election were held tomorrow, I've got to say that Bush would carry the state."[23] He assailed the failure of Dukakis's staff to recognize the problems that the Democratic nominee's positions on gun control, prison furloughs and defense issues represented in the South and West. A week later McWherter again criticized the judgment of Dukakis's "eastern strategists," although he lauded Dukakis's final give-em-hell campaign effort.

Senator Gore campaigned vigorously for the Dukakis-Bentsen ticket. He launched stinging counterattacks at some of the Bush camp's negative tactics, such as on the Pledge of Allegiance issue: "I served in Vietnam, and a lot of my friends came home in coffins covered by the flag. Nobody asked if they were Democrats or Republicans before they put that flag on the coffin."[24] The Tennessee senator labeled Vice President Bush a "back door fixer" for secretly engineering the dilution of pollution controls.[25] However, Gore also criticized the subtlety of the "Bush media handlers" ad produced by Dukakis's consultants as "too much inside baseball." On the eve of the election, Gore led prominent Tennessee Democratic officeholders across the state in a final push for a Dukakis victory. Mar Gearan, a Dukakis spokesman, lauded Senator Gore's efforts. "He's a great communicator. He's effective at articulating the agenda and how very high the stakes are in this election."[26]

Senator Gore demonstrated his party loyalty, gained considerable national exposure, and collected valuable political IOUs by his 1988 efforts to help elect Governor Dukakis and other Democratic officeholders. After Congress adjourned, Gore campaigned in about thirty states.[27] He spoke on behalf of Dukakis—or defended him—on "Meet the Press," "Face the Nation," "This Week with David Brinkley," "McNeil-Lehrer Newshour," and the Cable News Network. In mid-October, Gore strode into a luncheon with reporters wearing a white lab coat bearing the name tag, "Doctor of Spin."[28] Texas House Speaker Gib Lewis invited the Tennessee Senator to help campaign in ten of the closest Texas legislative races. Gore also attended a September 27 fund-raiser for Mayor James Donchess, a New Hampshire candidate for Congress. After Bush's victory, Senator Gore told skeptical reporters, "I have no plans to run again for President."[29]

Shoot the Messenger

The presidential polls in the general election brought little good news to the Democrats. The *Atlanta Journal and Constitution* presidential survey, conducted October 1–7 in fifteen southern and border states, placed the Democratic party in a defensive stance. The October 9 published results disclosed that Bush enjoyed a 10 point lead in Tennessee, Georgia, North Carolina, Kentucky and Arkansas—five states that had been considered competitive only two weeks prior.

Mason-Dixon Opinion Research conducted several Tennessee Polls for television stations and newspapers in the state. In its October 3–5 survey of 829 Tennessee registered voters, the Bush-Quayle ticket enjoyed a 46 to 41 percent lead over Dukakis-Bentsen, with 13 percent undecided. The Bush-Quayle team received the most (52–39 percent) support in Republican east Tennessee, but also won plurality support in middle (44–40 percent) and west Tennessee (45–42 percent). Among the "swing voters" who voted for President Reagan in 1984 and Governor McWherter in 1986, a majority (52 percent) favored Bush-Quayle over Dukakis-Bentsen (32 percent). The Mason-Dixon Tennessee Poll also disclosed the excellent/good job performance ratings of Senator Gore (79 percent), governor McWherter (64 percent), and Senator Sasser (60 percent).

Mason-Dixon again went into the field October 26–28, to interview 813 likely Tennessee voters. This statewide poll found the Bush-Quayle lead growing (51 percent) over the Dukakis-Bentsen ticket (41 percent). Dukakis suffered from a 41 percent unfavorable/42 percent favorable name recognition, compared with Bush's 30 percent unfavorable/50 percent favorable recognition. Men and younger voters expressed the warmest support for the Bush-Quayle team.

The *Atlanta Journal and Constitution* published on November 6 a survey of eight southern and border states, which showed Bush with a 14 point overall advantage. Its Tennessee results revealed that George Bush (49 percent) enjoyed a 12 point margin over Michael Dukakis (37 percent) in the Volunteer State. However, their subsequent tracking poll conducted over the weekend prior to the November 8 election showed Bush's lead in the eight states falling to 10 points, a decline that the newspaper attributed to a resurrection of Democratic party loyalties.

The Power of the Press

George Bush won the contest for major newspaper endorsements in Tennessee. The *Commercial Appeal* in Memphis endorsed the Republican nominee and labeled Dukakis as "one of the least prepared candidates for president in recent years," with less national and foreign policy experience than Jimmy Carter in 1976.[30] The *Knoxville News-Sentinel* endorsed Bush as the more qualified candidate, conceding that Dukakis had a "perfect right to be a liberal and a dove."[31] The conservative *Chattanooga News-Free Press* blasted Dukakis's liberal policies.

The *Tennessean* in Nashville extended Dukakis a weak endorsement, criticizing him as a "mediocre candidate" for not responding aggressively to Bush's Pledge of Allegiance attack and ACLU charges. Dukakis's problem, the paper assured readers, consisted of "image—not of ability or integrity."[32] When Dukakis began swinging at Bush during the campaign's final weeks, the *Tennessean* praised him for finally "acting like a candidate," lauding the Democratic nominee's new "give-em-hell" style. The *Chattanooga Times* handed Dukakis a solid endorsement: "Mr. Dukakis offers this country honest, principled leadership and a managerial competence that will steer us clear of the pitfalls explored along the careless course set by the present administration."[33]

A Senate Mismatch

Tennessee's senior U.S. senator, Jim Sasser, first won his seat by defeating incumbent Republican Bill Brock in 1976 and then demolished his 1982 challenger, Congressman Robin Beard, with a 62 to 38 percent victory. In twelve years he moved up the Senate seniority ladder. Sasser quietly followed the Senate's norms to gain entrance to its inner circle. "I think you get more accomplished by not being overly visible. When you develop a profile early, that raises some eyebrows. If you grow into that visibility by doing your job properly, people expect that."[34] During the 1988 campaign, Sasser emphasized that his re-election would make him the first Tennessean to chair a major Senate Committee in forty years—the Senate Budget Committee.

Sasser's re-election strategy concentrated very early on raising sufficient funds to discourage any significant GOP threat. Doug Hall, the Senator's administrative assistant, acknowledged that Sasser raised $1.5 million in 1987 to ward off "significant" opposition.[35] Sasser chose to generally ignore his Republican opponent, tending to Senate business while his campaign staff answered Bill Anderson's attacks.

Following the conventional wisdom of denying a platform to a weak challenger, Sasser rejected Anderson's call for six televised debates around the state, finally agreeing to one debate in Nashville. The *Commercial Appeal* editorially chastised Sasser for refusing to debate in Memphis, starkly displaying the Volunteer State's long-standing regional rivalries. Nashville, the paper argued, represented "a middle-of-the-road establishment capitol, run by people who find comfort in the thought that they're always going to get more than their share of the pie. . . . It only makes sense to figure that Sasser feels at home there."[36]

Bill Anderson began raising funds in 1985 for what he thought would be an open congressional seat. However, longtime First District Representative Jimmy Quillen ran for re-election in 1988 and resented Anderson's efforts to encourage his retirement. After shifting his candidacy to the Senate, Anderson sought to build name recognition for his campaign by working at a series of jobs throughout the state to get "in touch" with average Tennesseans.

Anderson initially offered a progressive Republican program, calling for day care tax credits, environmental enforcement, and the improving of employee productivity through stock ownership. Anderson switched his tactics in October and began attacking Sasser's acceptance of PAC money, using a series of news conferences in swings through Knoxville, Chattanooga, Nashville, Memphis, and the Tri-Cities to gain free publicity for his struggling campaign. Anderson claimed that Sasser's acceptance of PAC money represented a "senator for sale."[37] The Republican challenger also criticized Sasser's acceptance of honorariums, which "averaged over $27,000 in each of the [last] eight years."[38]

Sasser waited until the campaign's only debate in mid-October to personally respond to Anderson's charges. Sasser startled Anderson by unveiling an estimate of the costs of Anderson's proposed programs calculated by Fiscal Planning Services, a Washington firm commissioned by the Sasser campaign. Sasser declared Anderson's programs would cost $152 billion, requiring either a massive tax hike or a massive deficit. The Democratic senator stated that Anderson did not honestly oppose Sasser's PAC contributions, but that rather, "his objection is he doesn't get as much as me."[39] Sasser also hit Anderson for his opposition to raising the minimum wage, "It takes more than wearing a green shirt and working in a sausage plant to be a friend of the working man."[40]

Anderson continued to hit Sasser's PAC contributions after the debate, declaring the incumbent's "sweet tooth for sugar PAC monies [$14,500] is shameful."[41] A Sasser television commercial aired in East Tennessee underscored the cost of the sixty-seven programs Anderson proposed with the question, "Can we afford Bill Anderson's inexperience?"[42] Anderson tartly replied, "Being called a big spender by Jim Sasser is like being called ugly by a possum."

In the four major metropolitan areas, only the conservative *Chattanooga News-Free Press* endorsed Anderson, blasting the "very liberal record" of Sasser and the Democratic Senator's support of Governor Dukakis.[43] Even the usually Republican *Knoxville News-Sentinel* urged Sasser's re-election to retain the benefit of his "seniority and clout."[44]

An early October Mason-Dixon Tennessee Poll found Senator Sasser commanding a 62 to 27 percent lead over Anderson. Its October 26–28 statewide survey noted that Sasser's margin rose to a 65 to 26 percent advantage over his GOP foe. After the election, Anderson said his private polls revealed that "one out of three Tennesseans had not yet identified who I was and what my message means."[45] Tennessee Republican consultant Tom Ingram offered a succinct overview of the Senate race. "Sasser mounted an early, aggressive and effective campaign, and he never gave Anderson a chance to get off the ground. . . . [Anderson's] got no resources."[46]

Combat, Not Succession

In 1988, strategists from both national parties evaluated Tennessee's two open House seats for possible partisan gains; one resulted from the death of GOP Congressman John Duncan in the Second District and the other stemmed from the retirement of Democrat Ed Jones in the Eighth District. The examination of the traditional Democratic voting patterns in the Eighth District discouraged a major GOP effort. Instead, the Republican Congressional Campaign Committee assessed Democratic Congresswoman Marilyn Lloyd's narrow wins in 1984 and 1986, combined with her announcement in 1987 of plans to retire—and then her January 1988 decision to seek re-election—as an opportunity to recapture the Third District.

Observers expected John (Jimmy) Duncan, Jr., to easily slip into his father's congressional seat because no Democrat had represented the Second District in 130 years. However, Dudley Taylor resigned as Governor McWherter's Commissioner of Revenue to run a spirited race. Jimmy Duncan initially avoided the press and ran his campaign without consultants or a press secretary, refusing Taylor's demands for debates. Duncan felt such a low-key approach, augmented with person-to-person campaigning, would safeguard a 69 to 14 percent advantage over Taylor in Duncan's early-September survey.[47]

Taylor hired professional consultants and ran a very aggressive campaign. His advisors convinced Taylor to shave off his beard, revealing the facial scars he had received when the Marine helicopter he piloted in Vietnam was shot down. Although Taylor did not contrast his 330 combat missions to Jimmy Duncan's Vietnam-era service in the National Guard, the media's intense scrutiny of Dan Quayle's use of family influence to enter the National Guard made such comparisons inevitable.

The Democratic nominee claimed that Duncan hid "behind the media image of his father" in an attempt to inherit the office. He attacked Duncan's ties to C. H. Butcher, Jr.'s, banking scandal, especially Jimmy Duncan's involvement in the failed Knoxville Federal Savings and Loan. One hard-hitting television ad showed side-by-side pictures of Jimmy Duncan and C. H. Butcher, Jr.—who was wearing handcuffs. Another television spot blasted Criminal Court Judge Jimmy Duncan for writing a request on his letterhead to an Atlanta federal judge to grant probation to a black Knoxville businessman convicted of buying cocaine.

Taylor's mid-October release of a Hickman-Maslin poll electrified the race with its finding that Duncan's share of the potential vote had shrunk to 49 percent, with Taylor closing fast at 41 percent.[48] The rapidly changing nature of the contest even caught the attention of the *Washington Post*, galvanizing worried GOP leaders to pressure Duncan to hire Nashville's Ingram Group to serve as consultants and to produce television ads.

Taylor's campaign, bolstered by the publicized tightening of the race, kept the pressure on Duncan for having "lied" about his ties to C. H. Butcher, Jr. The Democratic candidate defended his tough television ads: "Personal integrity and personal judgment are issues in any campaign."[49] No longer able to ignore Taylor, Duncan charged that his Democratic opponent had resorted to "negative personal attacks and outright lies against me and my family."[50] In the general election Duncan won the endorsement of the *Knoxville News-Sentinel*, but Knoxville's *Journal* refused to endorse either man.

Attack, Counterattack

GOP nominee Harold Coker appeared to represent a major threat to Congresswoman Lloyd's 1988 re-election bid because he served as a Hamilton County Commissioner and had previously headed the Hamilton County Republican party; Hamilton County comprises over half the Third District's voters and includes its three major television stations. Coker flayed Lloyd for abandoning the House Public Works Committee, which oversees the Tennessee Valley Authority (TVA), to accept a seat on the Armed Services Committee. He charged that Lloyd—and not the district—benefited from the switch, since she received 96 percent of her 1987 honorariums ($27,000) from defense groups.

Lloyd quickly countered Coker's charges with her own attack, a pattern she successfully followed throughout the campaign. She accused Coker of embracing a "double standard" on honorariums, due to his failure to criticize Republicans Dan Quayle, Howard Baker, and Jack Kemp for also accepting them. Lloyd also challenged Coker to disclose his tire company's financial records. Coker's tough television and radio ads asserted that the Third District suffered from the largest 1987 decrease in federal funding among Tennessee's nine congressional districts, proving the ineffectiveness of the Democratic incumbent. Lloyd then turned the heat on Coker with her own television ad charge, "Why can't Harold Coker tell the truth?"

The two congressional candidates finally agreed to one televised debate, scheduled October 23 in Chattanooga. A Mason-Dixon Third District survey for WDEF-TV and the *Chattanooga Times* found that among respondents who watched the debate, 41 percent picked Lloyd as the winner and 13 percent felt Coker had won.[51] The congressional poll also concluded that Lloyd led Coker with a 54 to 34 percent advantage. Nearly half the respondents labeled the Third District campaign as too negative, with nearly two-thirds opposing Coker's negative ads. A subsequent November 2–3 Mason-Dixon poll indicated that a quarter of Bush's voters said they planned to split their ballots to support Lloyd. Coker received a 36 percent unfavorable recognition, compared with Lloyd's 17 percent negative rating. After the election, Coker acknowledged that his hard-hitting ads had backfired: "Unfortunately, we were perceived as being negative."[52]

RESULTS: A TICKET-SPLITTING TREND

Trouble at the Top

The 1988 presidential election results in Tennessee marked another in a string of Republican successes dating from 1952, and interrupted only by Lyndon Johnson in 1964 and Jimmy Carter in 1976 (Figure 11.1). George Bush duplicated Ronald Reagan's 1984 victory by capturing 57.9 percent of the popular vote compared to the 57.8 percent share rolled up by Reagan in 1984. Like his

Figure 11.1
Democratic Percent of Two-Party Vote

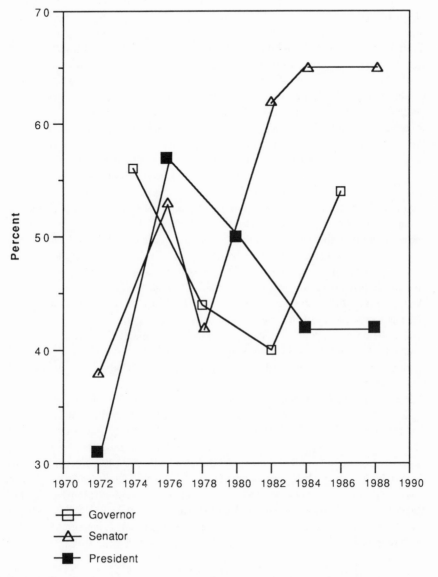

Source: Compiled from certified election returns and the *Tennessee Bluebook*, 1971–1972 to 1985–1986.

predecessor, Bush did well in each of Tennessee's three grand divisions, gaining 53 percent of the vote in west Tennessee, 55 percent in traditionally Democratic middle Tennessee and 65 percent in east Tennessee, the Republican party's historical mountain stronghold.

An examination of the county-by-county election returns reaffirms the extent of Bush's victory.[53] The Republican ticket carried seventy-three of Tennessee's ninety-five counties, including the state's four most populous counties, west Tennessee's Shelby (Memphis), middle Tennessee's Davidson (Nashville), and east Tennessee's Knox (Knoxville) and Hamilton (Chattanooga). Moreover, the Bush/Quayle ticket swept all thirty-three counties in Republican east Tennessee, captured 18 of 21 (81 percent) west Tennessee counties, and took 23 of 41 (56 percent) counties in Democratic Middle Tennessee. In comparison, the 1984 Reagan/Bush team claimed all the counties in the eastern region, won 16 of 21 (76 percent) west Tennessee counties, and recorded victories in 23 of 41 (59 percent) middle Tennessee counties. Thus, the Republican presidential candidate's performance in 1988 matched that of 1984 in east Tennessee, and showed a slight gain in the west and a minimal decline in middle Tennessee.

On the Democratic side, Dukakis and Bentsen repeated the 1984 ticket's failure to carry a single metropolitan area in the state. Indeed, the Democratic contenders found their strength confined to twenty-two rural counties, eighteen from middle Tennessee and four from the state's western grand division. Mondale and Ferraro carried twenty-three counties, including eighteen from middle Tennessee and five from west Tennessee. More important, although both parties experienced a decline from 1984 in the number of votes received by their presidential tickets, the Democratic vote in the four major metropolitan counties fell by 6 percent, with a 10 percent decline in Shelby County's (Memphis) Democratic vote. In contrast, the Republican vote dropped by just under 4 percent across the four counties, with the largest declines occurring in Shelby County (7 percent) and Knox County (5 percent).

Preliminary results from the NBC News Tennessee Exit Poll shed additional light on the composition of George Bush's winning electoral coalition in the Volunteer State.[54] The Bush/Quayle ticket received majority support from most voter subgroups. Blacks (13 percent), self-identified Democrats (13 percent), liberals (25 percent), voters with incomes below $20,000 (40 percent), respondents with less than a high school education (40 percent), and members of union households (47 percent) gave less support than other voter subgroups to the Republican candidates. Despite its obvious successes, the 1988 ticket did less well than Reagan and Bush among males (down 4 percent), eighteen to twenty-four-year-olds (down 5 percent), and voters age sixty-five and older (down 4 percent).

The presidential vote failed to confirm Republican hopes for a continuing realignment based on Ronald Reagan's popularity among Democratic identifiers. Eighty-seven percent of Democratic partisans voted for Dukakis and Bentsen. More important, the Bush/Quayle tandem held only 43 percent of so-called

"Reagan Democrats," Democratic identifiers who reported voting for Ronald Reagan and George Bush in 1984.

The exit poll results indicate that Dukakis and Bentsen did very well among self-identified Democrats, gaining 87 percent of their votes, and captured a 57 percent majority among "Reagan Democrats." The Democratic hopefuls fared poorly with independent voters, receiving only 22 percent of their votes. Although 87 percent of blacks reported voting for Dukakis and Bentsen, the diminished turnout in Tennessee's major metropolitan areas suggests either a lack of enthusiasm for the ticket or a negative reaction to the perceived mistreatment of Jesse Jackson.

A Senate Landslide

In 1984 enough Tennessee voters split their tickets to give overwhelming victories to Republican Ronald Reagan and Democratic Senate hopeful, Albert Gore, Jr. The results of the 1988 senate contest between a two-term incumbent Democrat, Jim Sasser, and his Republican challenger, Bill Anderson, demonstrate that a substantial proportion of the Volunteer State's electorate remains willing to cross party lines. While Gore received almost 61 percent of the vote and won majorities in 86 percent of Tennessee's counties in 1984, Sasser carried all but one county and captured 65 percent of the votes cast in 1988.

Senator Sasser performed well in each of Tennessee's three grand divisions. In the traditionally Republican eastern portion of the state, he received 58 percent of the vote. Sasser's share of the vote surpassed (by 8 points) Gore's showing in 1984 and gained 2 points on his own 1982 performance against former U.S. Representative Robin Beard (from west Tennessee).

Sasser's 1988 performance in west Tennessee (71 percent of the vote) also exceeded Gore's share (61 percent) of the 1984 vote and his own vote totals in 1982 (64 percent). Only in middle Tennessee, Gore's home region, did Sasser fail to improve on the junior Senator's 1984 share of the vote. Nevertheless, he still captured a substantial 68 percent of the votes cast, a slight improvement over his 1982 (67 percent) performance in the Democratic center of the state.

The NBC News Tennessee Exit Poll preliminary results indicate that Sasser carried a majority of all but two voter groups, self-identified Republicans, 73 percent of whom voted for Anderson, and self-described conservatives, 59 percent of whom marked their ballots for the Republican challenger. The exit poll results also show that Sasser did well among the voter groups important to the Democratic party's future prospects in Tennessee. Substantial majorities of "Reagan Democrats" (90 percent), younger voters (73 percent), and Independents (58 percent) supported Sasser, findings that offer additional evidence that the long run of Republican successes at the presidential level has not yet produced a realignment in the Volunteer State.

Traditional Loyalties Firm at Lower Offices

The conventional wisdom regarding the congressional races in Tennessee offered little prospect for change. Despite the vacant seats resulting from the retirement of Democrat Ed Jones and the death of Republican John Duncan, most political observers thought neither seat would change hands. Indeed, Republican John (Jimmy) Duncan, Jr., and Democrat John Tanner expected only token opposition in their bids to capture the Second and Eighth District seats, respectively. However, Republican challenger Harold Coker had high hopes of recapturing the Third District seat held by Marilyn Lloyd, and knowledgeable partisans on both sides of the fence expected a close race.

The election results for the most part confirmed the conventional wisdom. The Democrats retained their six to three advantage in Tennessee's congressional delegation. The Republicans failed to challenge the Democratic incumbents in the Fourth, Fifth, and Ninth districts, and mounted only token opposition in the Sixth. The GOP incumbents in the First and Seventh districts each gained 80 percent of the vote in defeating their Democratic opponents. Democrat Tanner, seeking to replace the retiring Democrat Ed Jones, easily carried the Eighth District with 62 percent of the vote. The contests in the Second and Third Districts, however, confounded expectations. Democrat Dudley Taylor's aggressive campaign in the Second District earned him 44 percent of the vote, an exceptional performance in a solidly Republican district, and in the Third District, Democrat Marilyn Lloyd, aided by her willingness to carry the fight to challenger Harold Coker, achieved victory by her widest margin (57 percent to 43 percent) since 1982.

The partisan balance of the Tennessee General Assembly remained solidly Democratic in the aftermath of the 1988 elections. The results gave the Democrats a 57 to 42 seat margin in the House of Representatives and a 21 to 12 seat advantage in the State Senate. The distribution of seats in the new General Assembly thus reflects a slight improvement in the Republicans' relative position, with a gain of two seats in the House and one seat in the Senate.

CONCLUSIONS

The 1988 election offers a series of mixed messages for political party strategists and students of Tennessee politics. Despite the disappointing news in the presidential contest, Democrats received good news on several fronts. First, the election returns indicated that they had avoided any further erosion of their share of the state's presidential votes. Second, Senator Jim Sasser's success in repeating Al Gore, Jr.'s, 1984 capture of a majority of the senatorial votes cast in traditionally Republican east Tennessee and Dudley Taylor's encouraging performance in the Second Congressional District provided evidence of the region's increasing receptivity to strong Democratic candidates. Finally, the Democrats' retention of their two to one majority in the Volunteer State's congressional delegation and their continued dominance in both houses of the State Legislature suggested a continuation of the party's newly regained (since 1986) ascendent position in Tennessee politics.

Although the overwhelming success of George Bush and Dan Quayle gave the Republican party cause to rejoice, the results in other contests proved somewhat disappointing. The continued inability of the party's candidates to recapture either a senatorial seat or the House seat in the Third Congressional District dampened any post-election euphoria. The GOP's failure to substantially reduce the Democratic majorities in the State Senate and the State House of Representatives also proved disheartening.

The 1988 election also offered additional evidence of a dealigned electorate, one characterized by widespread ticket splitting and by a willingness of self-identified partisans to cross party lines when casting their ballots. The substantial victories recorded by George Bush and Jim Sasser required massive ticket splitting, and the results of the NBC News Exit Poll indicate that Independents cast a large share of these split ballots. The exit poll findings also show that over one-fourth of the Republican identifiers voted for Sasser, while 13 percent of Democratic voters chose George Bush, evidence of the diminished importance of partisan identification in the decisions reached by voters in the Volunteer State.

Finally, the 1988 election represented the first recent presidential election contest in which voter turnout fell below that recorded four years earlier, a disturbing development that should give pause both to partisans and to political analysts. The decline in turnout, when taken in conjunction with evidence of continued ticket splitting and the ongoing erosion of the distinctive partisan character of Tennessee's three grand divisions, suggests a future of continued electoral volatility and competition. Indeed, the results of 1988 point to the importance of incumbency, strong candidates, and well-run, aggressive campaigns as critical elements in determining Tennessee's officeholders.

NOTES

1. Numan V. Bartley and Hugh D. Graham, *Southern Politics and the Second Reconstruction* (Baltimore: Johns Hopkins University Press, 1975), 80–81.

2. Jack Bass and Walter DeVries, *The Transformation of Southern Politics* (New York: Basic Books, 1976), 292.

3. Interview with Jim Hall, Executive Assistant to Governor Ned McWherter, January 19, 1988.

4. Robert H. Swansbrough and David M. Brodsky, "Tennessee: Weakening Party Loyalties and Growing Independence," in *The South's New Politics: Realignment and Dealignment*, ed. Robert H. Swansbrough and David M. Brodsky (Columbia: University of South Carolina Press, 1988), 81–93.

5. Anne H. Hopkins, William Lyons, and Steve Metcalf, "Tennessee," in *The 1984 Presidential Election in the South: Patterns of Southern Party Politics*, ed. Robert P. Steed, Laurence W. Moreland and Tod A. Baker (New York: Praeger, 1985), 225.

6. *Knoxville News-Sentinel*, November 6, 1988.

7. *Memphis Commercial Appeal*, October 25, 1988.

8. Ibid.

9. Interview with Thomas A. Hopper, Political Director, Tennessee Republican Party, December 20, 1988.

10. *Chattanooga Times*, August 20, 1988.

11. *Memphis Commercial Appeal*, October 26, 1988.

12. *Knoxville News-Sentinel*, November 6, 1988.

13. Interview with Jim Hall, Executive Assistant to Governor Ned McWherter, January 19, 1988.

14. Interview with Eugene Forrester, Executive Director, Tennessee Democratic Party, December 15, 1988.

15. Interview with Jim Hall, Executive Assistant to Governor Ned McWherter, January 19, 1988.

16. *Chattanooga Times*, February 2, 1988.

17. *Chattanooga Times*, August 30, 1988.

18. *Knoxville News-Sentinel*, November 6, 1988.

19. *Memphis Commercial Appeal*, October 26, 1988.

20. *Chattanooga Times*, June 17, 1988.

21. *Chattanooga Times*, August 22, 1988.

22. Ibid.

23. *Chattanooga Times*, November 1, 1988.

24. *Tennessean*, October 30, 1988.

25. *Memphis Commercial Appeal*, October 13, 1988.

26. *Knoxville News-Sentinel*, October 24, 1988.

27. *Tennessean*, October 30, 1988.

28. *Memphis Commercial Appeal*, October 21, 1988.

29. *Tennessean*, November 9, 1988.

30. *Memphis Commercial Appeal*, October 16, 1988.

31. *Knoxville News-Sentinel*, October 16, 1988.

32. *Tennessean*, October 16, 1988.

33. *Chattanooga Times*, October 28, 1988.

34. *Memphis Commercial Appeal*, October 2, 1988.

35. *Knoxville News-Sentinel*, November 10, 1988.

36. *Memphis Commercial Appeal*, October 6, 1988.

37. *Tennessean*, October 6, 1988.

38. *Memphis Commercial Appeal*, October 11, 1988.

39. *Memphis Commercial Appeal*, October 17, 1988.

40. Ibid.

41. *Chattanooga News-Free Press*, October 26, 1988.

42. *Memphis Commercial Appeal*, October 28, 1988.

43. *Chattanooga News-Free Press*, October 24, 1988.

44. *Knoxville News-Sentinel*, October 17, 1988.

45. *Knoxville News-Sentinel*, November 10, 1988.

46. *Memphis Commercial Appeal*, October 27, 1988.

47. *Tennessean*, November 6, 1988.

48. *Knoxville News-Sentinel*, October 20, 1988.

49. *Knoxville News-Sentinel*, October 11, 1988.

50. *Knoxville News-Sentinel*, October 27, 1988.

51. *Chattanooga Times*, October 27, 1988.

52. *Chattanooga Times*, November 9, 1988.

53. Certified General Election Results, November 8, 1988, Secretary of State, Tennessee.

54. NBC News Tennessee Exit Poll, November 8, 1988.

12

Texas: Toward an Ideological Politics

DENNIS S. IPPOLITO

INTRODUCTION

During the 1950s, the Democratic party's grip on the "solid South" began to weaken, with one of the most prominent defecting states being Texas. The Republican national ticket carried Texas in 1952 and again in 1956. In 1960, Democratic presidential nominee Senator John F. Kennedy attempted to revive his party's electoral prospects in Texas by selecting Senator Lyndon B. Johnson as his vice presidential running mate. Under a unique Texas law that he had persuaded the Texas legislature to pass, Johnson was able to run a dual campaign for re-election to the Senate and election as Vice President.

Kennedy's strategy was successful, if barely so. The Kennedy-Johnson ticket carried Texas by slightly more than 45,000 votes out of the 2.3 million cast. Johnson's Senate campaign was, as expected, victorious as well, although Johnson was held to less than 60 percent of the vote by a young and relatively unknown Republican challenger, John G. Tower. (In an unexpected postscript, Tower managed to win a special election for Johnson's vacated seat the following year. Republicans have kept it ever since.)

In 1988, Michael S. Dukakis replayed the Kennedy strategy, choosing Texas Senator Lloyd Bentsen as his vice presidential candidate. The Democratic party, as in 1960, was coming off two successive losses in Texas to a popular Republican president. The Republican presidential candidate in 1988, as in 1960, was the

222

The Rim South

Table 12.1
Republican Party Victories in Congressional, State, and Local Races

Year	State Senate	State House	Local/Judicial	U.S. House
1964	0	1	1	0
1966	1	7	0	2
1968	2	9	0	3
1970	2	10	0	3
1972	3	17	0	4
1974	3	16	0	3
1976	4	19	67	2
1978	5	22	0	4
1980	8	35	166	5
1982	5	36	270	5
1984	6	52	377	10
1986	6	56	504	10

Source: <u>Dallas Morning News</u> (30 October 1988), 26A.

incumbent Vice President. In 1988, unlike 1960, however, the Republican national ticket carried the state, and it did so by a wide margin.

Presidential Republicanism

The parallels between 1960 and 1988 were deliberately and explicitly drawn by Michael Dukakis.[1] That they proved to be quite inexact reflects the degree to which the Texas political landscape has shifted in the intervening years. Three decades ago, the electoral problems of Texas Democrats were real but narrowly confined. What V. O. Key, Jr., had termed the "Presidential Republican" voter had complicated political life in Texas, and other southern states, by supporting Republican presidential nominees.[2] In state and local elections, however, this "strange political schizophrenic" remained a Democrat.[3]

Rapid population growth in Texas during the 1960s and 1970s, however, added new elements to the Republican electorate. As a result, Texas has shifted much more strongly into the Republican presidential base. In 1972, 1980, and 1984, the Republican national ticket averaged nearly 62 percent of the total vote in Texas, approximately 5 percentage points higher than the party's share nationwide. With these victories, there came a steady improvement in the Republican party's performance in state and local races.

In 1978, for example, the Republicans finally captured the Governor's office. Republican William Clements lost his bid for re-election in 1982 but swept to an impressive victory four years later, and, throughout this period, Republican representation in the U.S. Congress and in state and local offices had climbed upward, accelerated greatly by the Reagan victories in 1980 and 1984 (see Table 12.1).

Texas and the South

Against this backdrop, the 1988 presidential election posed a twofold concern for Texas Democrats. The first was having a Democratic ticket that would be seriously competitive in the state. The second was preventing further erosion in the party's electoral strength at other levels.

The choice of Lloyd Bentsen was a signal that the Dukakis campaign recognized the severe problems it faced in Texas and the rest of the South. Southern Democratic leaders were quick to seize on this newfound sense of political realism on the part of the national party as a basis for uniting the state parties across the South. Immediately after Dukakis announced Bentsen's selection, Oklahoma Senator David L. Boren enthusiastically declared that the Dukakis-Bentsen ticket "has philosophical balance, and it has regional balance."[4] Louisiana Senator John B. Breaux predicted that enthusiastic support from local Democratic officials would "give [his] state to Dukakis and Bentsen."[5] Georgia Senator Sam Nunn emphasized that "this time around . . . we're not going to run away from the ticket."[6]

The acid test of the Democratic party's Southern Strategy, however, was obviously going to be Texas. With its twenty-nine electoral votes, Texas was not only the biggest electoral prize in the South, but also the arena in which virtually all the supposed elements of a Democratic revival were solidly in place. It was represented on the ticket by a conservative and influential Democrat who had repeatedly demonstrated his appeal among all factions of an ideological disparate party. Bentsen's dual campaign, moreover, put not only his superb organization but his very generous Senate campaign funding at the service of the Dukakis-Bentsen ticket. At the beginning of the campaign, it was anticipated that Bentsen's Senate race would add over $10 million to the $7–10 million already targeted for Texas by the Dukakis campaign managers.[7] Finally, the state's economy was in the midst of a prolonged and severe recession. Senator Phil Gramm, who nominated George Bush at the Republican convention, declared in August that "Texas is clearly the battleground of the campaign."[8]

In the end, however, the long-term realignment in Texas presidential politics overwhelmed all these short-term factors, as George Bush carried the state by 56 to 44 percent. For the fourth time in five elections, the Republican national ticket ran more strongly in Texas than nationally.[9] For the first time, Republicans captured less visible statewide offices that represented the last bastion of exclusive Democratic control.

Bentsen was, as hoped by Texas Democrats, a "stopper," easily retaining his own seat and triggering more than 700,000 split tickets that bolstered Democrats in down-the-ballot races.[10] Nevertheless, the Dukakis-Bentsen ticket proved to be only moderately more competitive than Mondale-Ferraro had been in Texas and across the South. For many Democrats, the immediate focus of post-election explanations was the campaign "mismanagement" by Dukakis and his staff. For others, the more serious question was whether the party could compete for the presidency under "normal" circumstances.

THE CAMPAIGN

A statewide survey conducted in late August found the presidential race in Texas to be a toss-up.[11] Among likely voters, Bush was perceived more favorably than Dukakis. His advantage was modest, however, compared to the gap between the vice presidential candidates. The net effect was precisely what the Democrats had hoped for when the Dukakis-Bentsen team was put together.

In mid-October, re-interviews with many of these same respondents showed Bush holding a 10 percentage point lead, and estimated that without Bentsen the margin would have been an overwhelming 56 to 40 percent.[12] By the end of October, Texas Democratic officials were reported to be "shifting their sights ... to races below the presidential and senatorial contests."[13] As one "down-ballot" Democratic candidate explained, "Bentsen is indispensable to us. You saw what happened in 1984 when we didn't have a stopper."[14] A Democratic state legislator agreed, "We'd probably lose a net of 10 seats in the Texas House if Bentsen weren't on the ticket."[15]

The decline of Democratic hopes in Texas paralleled what was occurring elsewhere. The *Washington Post* reported in mid-October that Dukakis had in fact scaled back his nationwide effort.[16] Conspicuously absent from the new Dukakis strategy was Texas, and indeed the rest of the South.

The Democratic Effort

The Democratic presidential campaign in Texas had some clearly identifiable targets. One was heavily Hispanic south Texas, where Mondale had run comparatively well in 1984. Among Hispanic voters, it was expected that Dukakis-Bentsen would also run strongly, but just how strongly and with what turnout level were unclear. While Hispanic registration had climbed over 80 percent between 1976 and 1984, Hispanic turnout rates had not kept pace. For 1984, it was estimated that turnout among registered Hispanic voters was less than 50 percent, compared to nearly 70 percent for all registered voters in Texas.[17] As a consequence, Hispanics accounted for just over 9 percent of the total vote in 1984, only a slight increase over their 8 percent in 1976.[18]

A second Democratic focus was east Texas, where Reagan had accelerated a long-term erosion in Democratic support among rural whites. This had once been a staunchly Democratic area, with a demographic mix and economic composition akin to much of the Deep South. George Wallace's presidential race had attracted strong support in 1968 among east Texas whites, and Democratic presidential candidates had faced problems here ever since. For Texas Democrats, east Texas was viewed as a key battleground since it offered the opportunity to bring rural whites back into the party.

The political strength of Lloyd Bentsen in Texas had been built on his ability to weld together these disparate groups and to add to them conservative and moderate whites in more urban areas of the state. The third dimension of the

Democrats' Texas strategy, therefore, was to minimize losses among the former and to compete seriously for the latter.

The bulk of the Democrats' personal campaigning in Texas was, of course, handled by Lloyd Bentsen, but there were numerous joint appearances by Dukakis and Bentsen, along with some individual forays by Dukakis. On October 6, the day after Bentsen had clearly outshone Dan Quayle in the campaign's only vice presidential debate, Dukakis joined Bentsen in Lone Star to celebrate his victory and to launch a major effort to focus public attention on Bentsen-Quayle comparisons.[19] The choice of a running mate, declared Dukakis, was the first "presidential" decision he and Bush had made, and he urged voters to "judge us by how we made it and who we chose."[20]

Selling Bentsen to Texans, however, was hardly necessary. More necessary, and typical of the campaign, was Bentsen's trying to sell Dukakis. As the campaign wore on, Bentsen took on the major responsibility for defending Dukakis, and his record, against Republican attacks. On Saturday, October 22, Bentsen brought Dukakis to economically troubled southeast Texas and complained about the "vicious things and lies about Mike Dukakis" being spread by the Bush campaign.[21] Declared Bentsen, "The Republican campaign of distortion just has to stop."[22]

Democrats were also counting on Bentsen to help them with turnout. In 1982, Bentsen's contested Senate race had been credited with boosting Democratic voter turnout to such high levels that the party was able to regain the Governor's Office.[23] Bentsen's organizational and financial resources, along with his presence on the ticket, were expected to yield similar, if less spectacular, benefits in 1988. Bentsen's financial backing of the Southwest Voter Registration Education Project, for example, was expected to raise Hispanic voter registration and turnout.[24] Moreover, a new Texas law allowing no-excuse absentee voting over a two-week period prior to the election was widely perceived as benefiting Democratic efforts to maximize minority voter turnout.[25]

The tangible elements of an effective Democratic campaign were certainly in place in 1988. The campaign had at its disposal a proven, statewide organization. There was a financial gap between the parties, but this time the Democratic national ticket had the advantage. Further, the Dukakis campaign had raised and distributed to state parties more "soft money"—campaign contributions not covered by federal laws and regulations—than any previous Democratic candidate.[26] The electoral targets on the Democratic side had been clearly identified, and Bentsen had already demonstrated his appeal among them. Finally, Dukakis had shown considerable strength among Hispanics and other core Democratic constituencies in winning the Super Tuesday primary in Texas.

The Republican Strategy

For George Bush and his campaign advisors, the Texas campaign was aimed exclusively against Dukakis from the beginning. Its objectives were to portray Dukakis as unacceptably liberal for Texas and to separate Dukakis from Bentsen.

Bentsen's Senate opponent, a two-term U.S. House member from west Texas named Beau Boulter, was essentially ignored by the Bush campaign. Prior to Bentsen's selection by Dukakis, Boulter's candidacy had been shunned by Texas Republican leaders, who preferred to minimize Bentsen's electoral efforts. After Bentsen's dual candidacy was announced, Boulter received support from the Republican Senatorial Campaign Committee in challenging Bentsen's use of his Senate campaign funds. The Federal Election Commission dismissed their complaint in late July, and an effort to have the federal courts intervene was also unsuccessful.

This brief confluence of interests, however, quickly evaporated, and official Republican efforts to assist the Boulter candidacy never materialized. Instead, the Republican presidential campaign in Texas gave its not-so-subtle endorsement to what became known as the "Texas Ticket"—George Bush for president and Lloyd Bentsen for the U.S. Senate. Bentsen, who usually avoided discussions about his dual candidacy, actually wound up complaining about the Republican efforts to boost his Senate campaign. On October 22, he declared, "The Republicans are trying to peddle the notion that you can vote twice for Texas by voting for George Bush and Lloyd Bentsen."[27] Bentsen's counter, however, was aimed not at Bush but at Quayle: "Let me make this one clear—a vote for George Bush is a vote for Dan Quayle. And a vote for Dan Quayle sure isn't a vote for Lloyd Bentsen."[28]

The Bush campaign's concern over Bentsen was well-founded. In mid-July, after the Bentsen choice was announced, a statewide poll in Texas found Bush with a minuscule 45 to 44 percent edge over the Democratic ticket.[29] Two nationwide Gallup polls conducted during late July showed the Democrats with a 17 percentage point lead.[30] By late August, while new Gallup surveys reported that Bush had overcome this gap and moved ahead nationally, the Texas race still appeared to be stuck on dead center.[31]

Moreover, the closeness of the contest in Texas contrasted with Bush's clear advantage over Dukakis on various dimensions of voter evaluation. As shown in Table 12.2, potential voters' assessments of the candidates' leadership qualities and their abilities to handle domestic and foreign policy issues consistently favored Bush even before the fall campaign had officially begun. Nevertheless, the Bush-Quayle ticket led Dukakis-Bentsen by only 47 to 44 percent.[32]

A statewide Texas Poll conducted prior to Labor Day, however, indicated that even a narrow Bush lead had a firm foundation.[33] Among registered voters who were surveyed, economic issues were the most prominent concerns, and the Republicans were perceived as better able to deal with economic matters by an almost two to one margin. Moreover, while comparable percentages of Democratic identifiers (81 percent) and Republican identifiers (92 percent) reported that they were likely to support their respective presidential tickets, Bush's lead among Independents was 50 percent to 30 percent.

Dukakis, unlike Bush, was also entering the formal phase of the fall campaign with a very narrow gap between his positive and negative ratings.[34] Dukakis's

Table 12.2

Texas Statewide Survey Results, Voter Assessments of Bush and Dukakis, August 26–September 2, 1988 (in percent)*

Voter Assessment of Candidate's Ability to—	Percentage of Likely Voters Choosing	
	Bush	Dukakis
Provide strong leadership	50	41
Deal with economy	50	41
Deal with Soviet relations	58	28
Deal with strong defense	60	29
Deal with helping Texas	47	38
Deal with fighting drugs	41	35

*Reported sample size of 1,001 respondents; reported margin of error plus or minus 3 percentage points.

Source: Dallas Morning News Poll (5 September 1988), 1A, 18A.

liberalism, moreover, had been firmly established for many voters, 50 percent of whom thought that he was more liberal than most Texans. As the director of the Texas Poll presciently concluded, "At this point in the campaign, the Bush lead is supported by perceptions and opinions that suggest it may be hard to erase. . . . If there is an issue that could provide a wedge for Dukakis in Texas, it is not obvious what it is."[35]

The aggressive advertising campaign against Dukakis that unfolded after Labor Day, therefore, served primarily to cement Bush's initial advantages in direct comparisons to Dukakis. The Bush organization invested substantial funds in television advertisements attacking Dukakis's record on crime, his opposition to the death penalty, and his prison furlough program.[36] The Pledge of Allegiance issue was also played prominently, and an unusual emphasis was placed on defense and gun control. The former was simply a continuation of an attack line against Democratic presidential candidates that Republicans had used effectively since 1972. The latter was a relatively new addition to presidential campaigning, designed to strike a responsive chord in a heavy gun-ownership state such as Texas and to be an integral part of the effort to portray Dukakis as a liberal extremist. George Christian, an Austin political consultant and former press secretary to Lyndon Johnson, noted the anxiety among Democrats that gun control could be enormously effective if "combined with other things: the [Massachusetts] prison furlough [program] and his [Dukakis's] alleged softness on crime."[37]

The effectiveness of the Bush campaign in exploiting the social issue "combinations" was reflected in Dukakis's declining voter ratings. By the third week in October, Dukakis was receiving negative ratings from nearly half (49 percent) of the respondents in a statewide survey, a level that compared unfavorably not only to Bush and Bentsen but also to Quayle.[38] In addition, Bush was widely perceived as having won the second presidential debate, and Lloyd Bentsen's performance in his vice presidential debate was not having the decisive impact for which Democrats had hoped.[39]

The Republican campaign had, at this point, propelled Bush into a strong lead in every region of the state except south Texas.[40] His overall lead of 52 to 42 percent was not overwhelming, but it was solidly based, especially given the continuing Bentsen effect.[41] Among whites, Bush's lead was 65 to 30 percent, while Independents favored Bush by 70 to 21 percent. Without blacks and Hispanics, in sum, the Democratic national ticket would have been facing another landslide.

The Republican presidential campaign in Texas was not just commercials and attacks. It was backed up by a formidable vote-targeting organization that drew on the expertise developed during the Reagan campaigns.[42] The negative campaigning that was deplored so widely elsewhere, moreover, was not especially troublesome in Texas. As one *Wall Street Journal* reporter pointed out in September: "Presidential politics here is a bit like an East Texas deer hunt. No one minds pumping Bambi full of lead; the issue is whether to bring along the dogs as well as the Winchester."[43]

The Bush campaign had no qualms about bringing along the dogs, and the Dukakis campaign never developed an effective rejoinder. Even if Dukakis had been able to shift the campaign debate to economic issues, he would have had to overcome a perhaps surprising advantage that Bush enjoyed on these issues throughout the campaign in Texas. On energy issues, where Texas's economic decline offered an opening, Dukakis's positions (opposition to oil import fees and support for a windfall profits tax) did not provide much leverage.[44] (Instead, Dukakis pledged to Texas energy representatives in Houston that he would make Bentsen chairman of a bipartisan summit on energy policy.)[45] On defense, Dukakis struggled to make himself credible to voters throughout the campaign, and not just in Texas.

Ronald Reagan, who had come to Texas earlier in the campaign, returned on the Saturday before election day to declare the contest "a referendum on liberalism" and to pronounce that a Bush administration would be a continuation of his own.[46] At this point, the Bush lead had ballooned to 17 percentage points.[47]

RESULTS AND ANALYSIS

For the Republican party, the Bush-Quayle victory in Texas was solid, if not nearly as spectacular as the Reagan triumph four years earlier. The total numbers of votes cast in 1984 and 1988 were similar, but the Republican presidential vote dropped (and Democratic presidential vote increased) by approximately 400,000 (see Table 12.3). A portion of this difference, and perhaps the bulk of it, reflected Bentsen's presence on the ticket, since the shift in votes for the Senate between 1984 and 1988 was dramatic.

For Michael Dukakis, however, the Bentsen gambit did not work. Despite

Table 12.3

Presidential and U.S. Senate Election Results in Texas, 1984 and 1988

Election	1984				1988			
	Republican		Democratic		Republican		Democratic	
	Vote*	Percent	Vote*	Percent	Vote*	Percent	Vote*	Percent
Presidential Vote	3.4	64	1.9	36	3.0	56	2.3	44
U. S. Senate Vote	3.1	59	2.2	41	2.1	40	3.1	60

*In millions.

Source: The 1984 data are from Richard M. Scammon and Alice V. McGilli-vray, America Votes 16 (Washington, D.C.: Congressional Quarterly, 1985), 396-407; the 1988 data are based on complete but unofficial election tabulations by the Secretary of State, State of Texas.

his impressive performance as a campaigner and the most positive voter eval-uations of any of the four national candidates in Texas, Bentsen could not deliver the state. For the Texas Democratic party, the Bentsen candidacy produced some tangible benefits in down-ballot races. For the national Democratic party, Bent-sen's candidacy failed to resolve, and perhaps even exacerbated, questions about the party's competitiveness in presidential elections.

The Presidential Vote

The Republican "drop-off" between 1984 and 1988 was reasonably uniform across the state. In the five largest counties, accounting for approximately 45 percent of the state's total population, the decline in Republican strength between 1984 and 1988 averaged about 8 percentage points (see Table 12.4). Neverthe-less, the largest of these counties (Harris and Dallas) remained comfortably Republican. Even Bexar County, with a Hispanic population of nearly 50 percent, was carried by the Bush-Quayle ticket, while only Travis County, the smallest of the major counties, switched to the Democrats.

In the Dallas and Houston metropolitan suburbs, a similar pattern emerged in 1988. The Republican percentage of the two-party vote decreased by an average of about 8 percentage points, but the decrease materially affected the result in only one county (Galveston). In heavily Hispanic counties, Bush did not run as well as Reagan had in 1984, but the Republican decline was not significantly greater than in the larger urban and suburban counties.

Congressional Voting

In addition to Bentsen's easy retention of his Senate seat, Texas Democrats also extended their advantage in the U.S. House. In 1984, the Republican party

Table 12.4
Republican Presidential Voting, 1984 and 1988, by Selected Counties (in percent)

Selected Counties	Percentage of Two-Party Vote		Change
	1984	1988	
Five Largest Counties			
Harris	62	57	-5
Dallas	67	59	-8
Bexar (San Antonio)	60	53	-7
Tarrant (Fort Worth)	67	61	-6
Travis (Austin)	57	45	-12
Dallas and Houston Metro-			
politan Counties			
Collin (Dallas)	82	75	-7
Denton (Dallas)	76	69	-7
Brazoria (Houston)	68	59	-9
Fort Bend (Houston)	69	63	-6
Galveston (Houston)	53	47	-6
Montgomery (Houston)	76	69	-7
Larger Hispanic-Majority			
Counties			
El Paso	56	47	-9
Hidalgo (McAllen)	44	35	-9
Cameron (Brownsville)	53	44	-9
Webb (Laredo)	41	32	-9

Source: The 1984 data are from Richard M. Scammon and Alice V. McGillivray, America Votes 16 (Washington, D.C.: Congressional Quarterly, 1985),
396-407; the 1988 data are based on complete but unofficial election
tabulations by the Secretary of State, State of Texas.

had doubled (to ten seats) its share of the twenty-seven-member Texas U.S. House delegation. The party managed to retain all its seats in 1986, but in 1988 two were lost. One of these was held by a two-term incumbent. The other was an open seat created when Beau Boulter decided to run for the Senate.

Of the eight remaining Republican-held seats, all but one were contested by Democratic challengers. In none of these, however, did the Republican share of the two-party vote drop below 68 percent. Among Democratic incumbents, only six of whom had Republican opponents, re-election percentages were similarly one-sided. None of these challenged Democrats received less than 60 percent of the vote.

State and Local Races

For the Republican party, a conspicuous bright spot in 1988 was its showing in several statewide races. The party managed to retain, by a 55 to 45 percent margin, a Railroad Commission seat to which its candidate had previously been appointed. Republicans also won three of six Supreme Court seats being contested. For both the Railroad Commission and the Supreme Court, these were modern-day firsts. Whether they were significant breakthroughs may be problematical, since there were unusual aspects to the Republican victories. The Republican candidate for the Railroad Commission, for example, was Kent Hance, a former Democrat. The Supreme Court elections featured not only a scandal-plagued court but also two Republican incumbents who had recently been appointed to fill seats vacated by resigning Democrats.

In state legislative elections, the balance between the parties remained largely unchanged. Republicans won five of fifteen state Senate races, including all three held by Republican incumbents. Republicans also picked up one open seat and defeated a Democratic incumbent. In the Texas House, Republicans managed to increase their representation from 52 seats to 57 (of 150). Local election results showed little significant change, with Republicans holding on to most of the gains made in 1984 and 1986, but with no major extensions into Democratic-controlled areas.

CONCLUSION

At the presidential level, the Republican party is dominant in Texas, because party labels are, for many Texans, reliable guides to "presidential issues"—leadership, economics, and foreign affairs. The Bush campaign's preoccupation with crime and social issues notwithstanding, Texas voters consistently, and by a wide margin, favored Bush over Dukakis on presidential issues. What the Bush campaign accomplished, moreover, was to divert Dukakis from seriously engaging Bush on these issues.

Below the presidential level, party labels are less reliable and less determinative. In 1984, with a liberal national ticket and a liberal U.S. Senate candidate in Texas, the Republican party gained landslide victories in both contests and scored well in down-the-ballot races. In 1988, Lloyd Bentsen's Senate race severed the choices at the top of the ticket and greatly limited the impact of the presidential election on other offices.

The salient division in Texas politics is a liberal–conservative one. Where this is reflected in a visible, statewide race, the Republican party has a decided advantage. In state and local races where the division is blurred or ideology is less salient, that advantage disappears.

The problem for Democrats is that ideology is hard to avoid in presidential elections. Since 1972, Democratic presidential candidates have averaged just over 40 percent of the vote in Texas. More effective campaigns are not going to erase this kind of deficit. The realignment of presidential party strength in Texas has already occurred, and the Democratic party must find some way to break up the Republican majority. Michael Dukakis was undoubtedly sincere about contesting for Texas, but he never developed his challenge beyond selecting Lloyd Bentsen. In fairness, however, it is difficult to see what issues he could have used against Bush in Texas. The insistence of Texas Democratic party leaders that the Dukakis campaign was mismanaged may have some basis, but is beside the point. Texas is simply unlikely to support any Democrat capable of being nominated by the national party because that candidate will inevitably be vulnerable to ideological attack. Despite Dukakis's protestations, Texas voters were never persuaded that ideology was irrelevant because of Bentsen, nor could they be convinced that Dukakis was ideologically indistinguishable from Bush.

The pace of party realignment in Texas below the presidential level, however, was not greatly affected by the 1988 election. The Democratic party has lost most of its advantage in party identification, but it still retains significant electoral strength, and there remains considerable insulation between presidential and state politics. In the absence of a truly disastrous Democratic national ticket, therefore, future Republican gains are likely to come slowly. At the same time, demographic and economic factors mitigate against any serious retrenchment in Republican strength. There was no Democratic resurgence in 1986, when Democrats hoped for a replay of 1982. There was none in 1988, with Reagan absent from the ticket.

It is important to remember that the Democratic party has not deliberately written off the South or Texas. Even in 1984, Walter Mondale flirted with the notion of running with Lloyd Bentsen and insisted that the South was crucial to his hopes. In 1988, Dukakis went beyond flirting. He entered the election campaign with a united party and a geographically balanced ticket. His loss leaves the Democrats with no ready answers for resolving their problems in Texas and the South. Thus, the real significance of 1988 may lie in the explanations that the Democrats draw from yet another defeat and in the solutions around which they unite.

NOTES

1. As reported after Dukakis's July 12 selection of Bentsen, "Dukakis . . . immediately cited the successful pairing of Johnson with John F. Kennedy in 1960." In addition:

It was Dukakis who ultimately decided against a defensive vice presidential choice. By choosing not to reinforce states where he ought to win, he avoided trapping himself in a fortress that might be impossible to defend . . . [and] opted for offense—using the running mate to attack Bush where he lives, both electorally and psychologically. (*Congressional Quarterly Weekly Report* 46 [July 16, 1988]: 1954, 1955)

2. V. O. Key, Jr., *Southern Politics* (New York: Vintage Books, 1949), 278–280.
3. Ibid., 278.
4. *National Journal* 20 (July 23, 1988): 1948.
5. Ibid.
6. Ibid.
7. *National Journal* 20 (August 20, 1988): 2157.
8. Ibid.
9. The only recent exception was 1976, when Jimmy Carter carried Texas. In the Carter–Gerald Ford race, the Republicans received 48.0 percent of the total vote in Texas, compared to 48.4 percent nationwide.
10. There were 5.4 million votes cast for President in Texas in 1988, and 5.3 million

for the U.S. Senate seat. The Bush-Quayle ticket received approximately 3.0 million votes, compared to 2.3 million for Dukakis-Bentsen. For the Senate, however, Bentsen received 3.1 million votes.

11. *Dallas Morning News*, September 5, 1988, 1, 18A. The results reported here are from a statewide poll conducted for the *Dallas Morning News* and *Houston Chronicle* from August 26 through September 2. The survey was conducted among 1,001 "likely Texas voters," with a reported margin of error of plus or minus 3 percentage points.

12. *Dallas Morning News*, October 23, 1988, 1, 26A. These results are based on interviews with 776 of the 1,001 "likely Texas voters" originally surveyed August 26 through September 2. The survey was conducted for the *Dallas Morning News* and *Houston Chronicle*. The report margin of error was plus or minus 4 percentage points.

13. *Dallas Morning News*, October 30, 1988, 1, 26A.

14. Ibid., 1.

15. Ibid., 26A.

16. See *Congressional Quarterly Weekly Report* 46 (29 October 1988): 3108.

17. *Dallas Morning News*, October 17, 1988, 9A.

18. Ibid.

19. *Dallas Times Herald*, October 7, 1988, 1.

20. *Wall Street Journal*, October 7, 1988, A14.

21. *Dallas Morning News*, October 23, 1988, 26A.

22. Ibid.

23. In 1982, Bentsen received nearly 60 percent of the vote in his Senate race. The total vote in 1982 was more than 800,000 votes higher than in 1978, when Republican William Clements won the governor's race. In 1982, Clements improved his 1978 showing by about 300,000 votes, but the higher turnout swamped his increase, and he lost by a 54 to 46 margin. Clements and Republican officials had argued against challenging Bentsen, fearing that Bentsen's organization would produce an unusually high off-year turnout.

24. *Wall Street Journal*, September 20, 1988, 28.

25. Ibid.

26. *National Journal* 20 (October 8, 1988): 2516.

27. *Dallas Morning News*, October 23, 1988, 26A.

28. Ibid.

29. *Dallas Morning News*, September 5, 1988, 18A.

30. *Congressional Quarterly Weekly Report* 46 (September 17, 1988): 2561.

31. Gallup poll results are from *Congressional Quarterly Weekly Report* 46 (September 17, 1988): 2561. The Texas poll results were reported in the *Dallas Morning News*, September 5, 1988, 1.

32. Ibid., 1, 18A.

33. *The Polling Report* 4 (October 3, 1988): 1, 4.

34. Ibid., 4.

35. Ibid.

36. *Wall Street Journal*, September 20, 1988, 28.

37. *Dallas Morning News*, September 11, 1988, 26A.

38. *Dallas Morning News*, October 23, 1988, 26A.

39. Ibid. According to the survey results reported here, 75 percent of the respondents stated that the presidential debates would not influence their votes, while 72 percent stated that the vice presidential debate would have no impact.

40. *Dallas Morning News*, October 23, 1988, 26A.
41. Ibid.
42. *National Journal* 20 (July 23, 1988): 1921.
43. *Wall Street Journal*, September 20, 1988, 1.
44. *National Journal* 20 (August 20, 1988): 2157.
45. *Wall Street Journal*, September 20, 1988, 28.
46. *Dallas Morning News*, November 6, 1988, 1.
47. Ibid.

13

Virginia: A Republican Encore in the Old Dominion

LARRY SABATO

At times in the autumn of 1988 it was difficult to determine whether Virginia was included in the national elections. Virtually ignored by the presidential contenders, with its airwaves nearly bereft of national advertising (save for network spots), Virginia once again did the predictable and voted solidly Republican on November 8, thereby justifying the decisions of both parties not to lavish attention on the Old Dominion. Adding to the electoral languor were easy re-elections for all ten incumbent U.S. House members and, as expected, a landslide victory for former Governor Charles S. Robb in the Senate contest. Virginians also made it two in a row for gambling, adding support for pari-mutuel horse-race betting to the previous year's referendum approval of the lottery.

VIRGINIA'S RECENT POLITICAL HISTORY

Virginia has a nearly consistent record of support for Republican presidential candidates in the post–World War II era, but a more complex picture of the state's political leanings emerges when contests for state offices are considered. Only Harry Truman in 1948 and Lyndon B. Johnson in 1964 among recent Democratic presidential nominees have proven able to carry the Old Dominion (see Table 13.1). Even the South's 1976 favorite son, Jimmy Carter, narrowly

Table 13.1
Presidential General Election Results in Virginia, 1948–1984

Year	Democratic Candidate	Percent of Vote	Republican Candidate	Percent of Vote
1948	Harry S. Truman*	47.9	Thomas E. Dewey	41.0
1952	Adlai E. Stevenson	43.4	Dwight D. Eisenhower*	56.3
1956	Adlai Stevenson	38.4	Dwight D. Eisenhower*	55.4
1960	John F. Kennedy	47.0	Richard M. Nixon*	52.4
1964	Lyndon B. Johnson*	53.5	Barry M. Goldwater	46.2
1968	Hubert H. Humphrey	32.5	Richard M. Nixon*	43.4
1972	George McGovern	30.1	Richard M. Nixon*	67.8
1976	Jimmy Carter	48.0	Gerald R. Ford*	49.3
1980	Jimmy Carter	40.3	Ronald Reagan*	53.0
1984	Walter Mondale	37.1	Ronald Reagan*	62.3

*Denotes the winner in Virginia. The percentages of votes for the Demo-
cratic and Republican candidates do not add to 100 percent because of
votes received by independents and third-party nominees.

Source: Compiled by author from returns provided by the Virginia State
Board of Elections.

lost Virginia—the only southern state he failed to add to his electoral column.
Ronald Reagan defeated Carter far more handily in 1980 than Gerald Ford had
done four years earlier, securing 53.0 percent of the vote to Carter's 40.3 percent.

Prior to 1952, Virginia had defected from the Democratic party in presidential
contests only once in post-Reconstruction times, when the 1928 Democratic
nominee Al Smith—an anti-Prohibition Catholic—proved too much for publicly
dry, Protestant Virginia to bear. Franklin Roosevelt returned Virginia to the
Democratic column in 1932, where she stayed for two decades.

As the national Democratic party moved leftward, however, friction with the
conservative Democratic machine in Virginia became inevitable. The machine's
leader, Virginia Governor (1926–1930) and U.S. Senator (1933–1965) Harry F.
Byrd, Sr., developed an antipathy for Roosevelt and, eventually, Truman, whose
pro–civil rights tilt was especially offensive to Byrd. By 1952 Byrd had officially
adopted a policy of "golden silence" in presidential years—a signal to his
machine's troops to regularly split their tickets, backing the GOP presidential
standard-bearer while voting solidly Democratic for state and local offices.

The Byrd machine declined after the abolition of the poll tax and the passing
of the Voting Rights Act of 1965 destroyed the limited electorate that had
sustained it, but the habit of ticket splitting remained strong. A heavily Dem-

ocratic state legislature was regularly returned to office, while from 1968 to 1980 the Republicans won every gubernatorial and presidential election, and in 1972 captured a majority of the House of Representatives delegation as well as a Senate seat.

In recent years, Virginia's strong two-party competitiveness has been even more evident. In 1981, Democrat Charles S. Robb, President Lyndon Johnson's son-in-law, captured the governorship and led a Democratic sweep of statewide offices. Just a year later, though, the Republicans added the Senate seat of retiring independent U.S. Senator Harry F. Byrd, Jr., to their column, with Paul S. Trible joining incumbent Senator John Warner (R) in Washington. At the same time, Democrats recaptured three U.S. House seats from the Republicans, reducing the GOP edge in the state's delegation from 9-to-1 to 6-to-4. As almost everywhere, 1984 was a good Republican year in Virginia, with Ronald Reagan and John Warner cruising to easy re-elections (with 62 and 70 percent of the vote, respectively). However, in 1985 the Democrats repeated their 1981 triumph, retaining all three statewide posts. The new Democratic governor, Gerald Baliles, was joined in the winner's circle by Virginia's first black and woman statewide officeholders, Lieutenant Governor L. Douglas Wilder and Attorney General Mary Sue Terry. The Democrats extended their winning streak in 1986, capturing yet another formerly Republican congressional seat to split the state's House delegation 5 to 5 with the GOP. This was the Democrats' largest House contingent since 1974–1976.

U.S. SENATE PRELIMINARIES

The unexpected retirement of one-term Republican U.S. Senator Paul S. Trible, Jr., dramatically changed the shape of the 1980 Senate race. Trible, citing a desire to spend more time with his family as well as frustration with the legislative process, renounced a re-election bid in September 1987. Trible also may have feared defeat at the hands of the likely Democratic senatorial nominee, former Governor Charles S. Robb.

Robb did indeed become the Democratic Senate nominee at the party's June 3–4 convention in Virginia Beach. Robb was unopposed, though several dozen Jesse Jackson delegates noisily protested his coronation, objecting primarily to Robb's opposition to their presidential favorite. (Robb's convention acceptance speech was temporarily interrupted by Jackson chants, but Robb's equally ardent and far more numerous supporters quickly drowned out the dissidents.)

The Republican state convention a week later in Roanoke was, if anything, even more exciting. The Republicans made history by nominating Virginia's first black major-party U.S. Senate candidate, Maurice Dawkins. The sixty-seven-year-old Baptist minister easily won a first-ballot victory over the pre-convention favorite, Andrew Wahlquist, former administrative assistant to U.S. Senator John W. Warner, as well as lawyer W. Gilbert Faulk, Jr. Dawkins triumphed after he electrified the convention with a stem-winding speech extolling the virtues of conservative philosophy. The overwhelmingly white delegates may also have recognized an opportunity to confound some voters' stereotype of the GOP as an undiversified, exclusive party. Also, many Republican leaders were looking ahead to the 1989 Governor's race and the Democrats' expected gubernatorial nomination of black Lieutenant Governor L. Douglas Wilder. By selecting Dawkins, Republicans tried to "make history" ahead of their rivals, thereby—they hoped—taking some of the precedent-shattering luster off Wilder's bid and inoculating themselves against possible charges of racial prejudices during the 1989 campaign. Finally, of course, the GOP believed that Dawkins could attract a larger-than-usual share of the black vote, though there were few illusions of a major breakthrough. At the same time, the novelty of a black Republican conservative, it was thought, might help to secure free media attention and financial support for the candidate.

Of course, Democrats were quick to note that Republicans had chosen a black only for a "token" nomination that was widely viewed as nearly worthless given Robb's electoral strength. The absence of any present or former officeholders in the GOP's candidate field certainly supports that contention. Nonetheless, Dawkins's victory was significant. After all, such an event would have been scarcely imaginable even a decade ago, and, as such, the nomination can be reasonably viewed as evidence of further progress in race relations in the Old Dominion. Unfortunately for the Republicans, though, they would receive little credit for this milestone, nor accomplish (for the most part) the other objectives mentioned earlier because of the numbing ineptness of Dawkins's autumn campaign as well as the lack of financial and organizational support extended to Dawkins by many state and local GOP activists, committees, and financiers.

THE GENERAL ELECTION CAMPAIGNS

The presidential race all but bypassed Virginia. Michael Dukakis made a quick foray into the state for a rally at the Governor's Mansion in late summer; he was not seen in the state again. Bush made not a single visit. The vice presidential candidates did make several brief appearances in the Old Dominion, however. The most time was spent by the GOP's Dan Quayle, who was mainly sent into safe, friendly territory when he could presumably cause little trouble for his ticket. Virginians were also spared the television advertising war, for the most part; state television stations reported small or nonexistent "buys" by the two campaigns. (Nationally aired spots could still be seen on the networks, of course.)

Incredibly, the state's own Senate contest was only slightly more visible. Dawkins ran a shoestring campaign, raising and spending less than $300,000. (Dawkins's war chest was smaller than that of every House incumbent in a contested Virginia race; a House district, of course, contains just one-tenth the state's population.) Moreover, Dawkins's effort was understaffed, disorganized, and prone to error. The inexperienced candidate was simply never taken seriously and provided people with little reason to do so. By contrast, the Robb campaign was flush with tested managers and ten times as much money ($3.2 million raised and $2.8 million spent). Robb's main opponent was his own social life. Newspapers (especially the *Virginian Pilot*, the *Richmond Times-Dispatch*, the *Washington Times*, and the *Washington Post*) revealed assorted and sordid details of Robb's extensive socializing with an unsavory, drug-oriented jet-set crowd at the resort city of Virginia Beach before, during, and after his governorship, despite warnings from political associates of the dangers involved. While illegal drugs were certainly present at these parties, no proof was ever offered that Robb had used drugs or knew that drugs were there, and Robb denied any improprieties. Dawkins attempted to capitalize on the scandal, but lacked the resources and standing to bring it off.

THE GENERAL ELECTION

On Election Day, voters followed the script written in advance by conventional wisdom, and George Bush and Chuck Robb both scored landslides. Bush received 59.7 percent of the presidential vote, about his average proportion in the South as a whole and not too far off Ronald Reagan's 1984 Virginia pace of 62.3 percent. Dukakis secured 39.2 percent, with minor-party candidates Lenora Fulani and Ron Paul barely noticeable at 0.7 percent and 0.4 percent, respectively. Robb garnered 71.2 percent to Dawkins's 28.7 percent in the U.S. Senate contest, a margin slightly greater than that achieved by Republican U.S. Senator John W. Warner in his 1984 re-election race.[1]

Both Bush and Robb carried all ten congressional districts (see Table 13.2). Bush's largest pluralities came in the heavily Republican Piedmont Seventh and Richmond Third districts, and his narrowest edge in the southwest Ninth. Dukakis won more than 40 percent of the vote in only two districts (the Tidewater Fourth and the Ninth). Robb did best in the eastern Second and Fourth districts, but his "worst" performance (in the Third, at 67.2 percent) was merely testimony to his strength everywhere, and to the relative uniformity of the vote by districts. Dawkins won more than 30 percent in only three districts (the Third, Fifth, and Seventh). Bush carried twenty-eight cities and eighty-two counties, while Dukakis won just thirteen cities and thirteen counties, scarcely better than Walter Mondale in 1984. Dukakis ran relatively well only in the economically troubled "coal counties" in the southwest, liberal white enclaves such as Arlington and Charlottesville, and localities with large black populations. By contrast, Robb carried every locality in the state. The only mild surprise may have been that Dawkins managed to secure nearly 30 percent of the total vote after pre-election polls had shown him barely above the mid-teens. Undoubtedly, Bush provided some coattails that expanded Dawkins's vote proportion to a slightly less embarrassing level.

The most disturbing aspect of the election unquestionably was the turnout. In the country as a whole, only about half the potential voting population (those aged eighteen and over) bothered to cast a ballot, the lowest proportion since

Table 13.2
Virginia General Election for President and U.S. Senator in 1988: Results by Congressional District (in percent)

District	Dukakis	Bush	Others	Robb	Dawkins
1	38.3	60.4	1.3	73.1	26.9
2	39.8	59.5	0.7	74.1	25.9
3	36.1	63.0	0.9	67.2	32.6
4	44.3	54.8	0.9	74.3	25.6
5	36.7	61.7	1.5	68.7	31.3
6	37.7	61.2	1.1	71.2	28.8
7	33.4	65.6	1.1	67.3	32.7
8	39.2	60.1	0.7	71.9	28.0
9	45.0	53.6	1.5	72.8	27.2
10	39.2	59.7	1.1	72.5	27.4
Statewide	39.2	59.7	1.1	71.2	28.7

Source: Official election results provided by the State Board of Elections.

1924. Because of Virginia's restricted franchise until the 1960s, the state's 1988 voter participation rate does not compare so badly with the recent past; Virginia's rate of 50.0 percent in 1988 was slightly better than 1986 and 1980, and a great improvement over all elections prior to 1964. However, as a percentage of the potential voting population, Virginia's 1988 turnout fell almost 2 percent from 1984, was still about a percentage point behind the national average, and showed the smallest gain in absolute number of voters in recent history (just 2.4 percent).[2] As across America, the 1988 campaigns failed to engage the interest of half the Virginians of voting age.

The Urban Vote

George Bush swept the Urban Corridor, Virginia's Standard Metropolitan Statistical Areas, and the state's rural regions with about equal strength (at or near 60 percent; see Table 13.3). The Bush/Dukakis contest was demographically a virtual carbon copy of the 1984 Reagan/Mondale matchup; the only notable change was that Dukakis increased Mondale's vote slightly (by 2 to 3 percent in each urban vote category). Dukakis captured the central cities with 53.6 percent—well below the usual victory margin for a Democrat in the territory

Table 13.3
Urban Vote, 1988 Virginia General Election for President and U.S. Senator (in percent)

Urban Measure	Percent of Total Vote	Dukakis	Bush	Others	Robb	Dawkins
Urban Corridor*	61.7	39.2	60.0	0.8	71.5	28.5
Metropolitan Statistical Areas**	67.6	39.7	59.4	0.9	71.6	28.4
(Central Cities)	(15.0)	(53.6)	(45.2)	(1.2)	(76.1)	(23.9)
(Suburbs)	(52.6)	(35.8)	(63.4)	(0.8)	(70.3)	(29.7)
Rural Areas***	28.2	38.6	60.0	1.4	70.6	29.4

*Includes cities of Alexandria, Chesapeake, Colonial Heights, Fairfax, Falls Church, Fredericksburg, Hampton, Hopewell, Manassas, Manassas Park, Newport News, Norfolk, Petersburg, Poquoson, Portsmouth, Richmond, Virginia Beach, and Williamsburg; and the counties of Arlington, Caroline, Charles City, Chesterfield, Clarke, Dinwiddie, Fairfax, Fauquier, Hanover, Henrico, James City, Loudoun, New Kent, Prince George, Prince William, Spotsylvania, Stafford, and York.

**The nine Standard Metropolitan Statistical Areas (SMSAs) for Virginia, as established by the U.S. Census Bureau, are Charlottesville, Danville, Lynchburg, Washington, D.C., Newport News-Hampton, Norfolk-Portsmouth, Petersburg-Colonial Heights, Richmond, and Roanoke. "Central cities" and "suburbs" are included in the SMSA figures. The Charlottesville and Danville SMSAs were first designated after the 1980 Census.

***All Virginia localities not included in either an SMSA or the Urban Corridor.

Source: Compiled by author from official election results provided by the Virginia State Board of Elections.

most favorable to that party's candidates (see Table 13.4). Bush's 63.4 percent landslide in the GOP-leaning suburbs was healthy even for a Republican, and compares favorably to most other GOP standard-bearers in recent elections. Once again, a Republican candidate was assisted by the relentlessly growing clout of the suburbs. These localities collectively hit another all-time high as a proportion of the total statewide general election vote (52.6 percent). At the same time, the Democratic-leaning central cities sank to an all-time general election low: Just 15.0 percent of the statewide vote originated there. Robb, of course, captured every segment of the urban and rural vote by massive margins. Robb's lead was greatest in the central cities (76.1 percent) and "least" in the suburbs (70.3 percent), but even in the latter, most Republican urban category, Dawkins failed to cross the 30 percent mark.

The Black Vote

Black turnout was relatively poor in 1988, with just 64.4 percent of black registered voters in a standard set of forty-four selected predominantly black

Table 13.4

**Major Statewide Elections in Virginia by Demographic and Black Voting
Patterns, 1969–1988 (in percent)**

Election and Winning Candidate	Central Cities*	Suburbs*	Black Vote**
General Elections			
1969 Governor, Linwood Holton	50.9	56.5	37.2
1970 U.S. Senator, Harry Byrd, Jr. (I)	52.2	55.9	3.0
1971 Lieutenant Governor, Henry Howell (I)	50.6	39.8	91.7
1972 President, Richard Nixon (R)	60.3	70.1	8.8
1972 U.S. Senator, William Scott (R)	42.5	52.7	6.7
1973 Governor, Mills Godwin (R)	43.2	54.6	5.7
1976 President, Gerald Ford (R)	43.6	53.9	5.0
1976 U.S. Senator, Harry Byrd, Jr. (I)	51.4	55.9·	4.4
1977 Governor, John Dalton (R)	47.9	59.9	5.0
1977 Lieutenant Governor, Charles Robb (D)	61.2	51.1	94.9
1977 Attorney General, Marshall Coleman (R)	47.7	56.6	32.7
1978 U.S. Senator, John Warner (R)	45.4	53.7	7.1
1980 President, Ronald Reagan (R)	41.3	58.4	3.4
1981 Governor, Charles Robb (D)	64.5	49.5	96.4
1981 Lieutenant Governor, Dick Davis (D)	67.2	52.3	95.5
1981 Attorney General, Gerald Baliles (D)	62.7	45.4	95.9
1982 U.S. Senator, Paul Trible (R)	39.6	55.1	5.7
1984 President, Ronald Reagan (R)	47.9	66.8	8.2
1984 U.S. Senator, John Warner (R)	57.6	72.9	21.2
1985 Governor, Gerald Baliles (D)	66.2	51.5	94.1
1985 Lieutenant Governor, Douglas Wilder (D)	64.4	48.8	96.6
1985 Attorney General, Mary Sue Terry (D)	71.3	58.6	95.6
1988 President, George Bush (R)	45.2	63.4	8.6
1988 U.S. Senator, Charles Robb (D)	76.1	70.3	83.7
Democratic Primary Elections*			
1969 Governor, William Battle (first primary)	31.8	40.6	11.8
1969 Governor, William Battle (runoff)	40.7	51.2	4.8
1977 Governor, Henry Howell	59.6	50.6	86.1
1977 Lieutenant Governor, Charles Robb	35.0	39.1	26.6
1977 Attorney General, Edward E. Lane	37.8	32.0	15.8
1988 President, Jesse Jackson	64.1	38.2	93.8
Republican Primary Election			
1988 President, George Bush	54.5	52.5	37.7

*Central cities and suburbs used in this table are designated components
of Virginia's Standard Metropolitan Statistical Areas (SMSAs), as established by the U.S. Bureau of the Census: Lynchburg, Washington, D.C.,
Newport News-Hampton, Norfolk-Portsmouth, Petersburg-Colonial Heights,
Richmond, and Roanoke. After 1980 the newly designated Charlottesville
and Danville MSAs are also included.

**Estimates of the black vote are based on results in the selected predom-
inantly black precincts used in various previous editions of Virginia
Votes.

***Figures for the 1970 Democratic primary for U.S. senator are not
included in this table; voter turnout in that election was miniscule.

Source: Calculated by the author from data supplied by the Virginia State
Board of Elections.

Table 13.5
**Turnout in Selected Black Precincts versus Statewide Turnout in Virginia,
1976–1988 (in percent)**

Year	Election	Overall Turnout*	Selected Black Precincts**
1976	President	80.8	76.4
1977	Governor	61.9	62.8
1978	U.S. Senator	60.3	56.4
1980	President	81.3	75.4
1981	Governor	64.9	67.5
1982	Lottery Referendum/ General Assembly	59.1	49.6
1988	President	77.6	64.4

*Percent of registered voters. Overall turnout includes black turnout; therefore, the differential between black and white turnout in each year is obviously greater than the figures in this column can indicate. Overall turnout includes black turnout; therefore, the differential between black and white turnout in each year is obviously greater than the figures in this column can indicate.
**Black turnout is measured by use of forty-four predominantly black precincts selected by the author.

Source: Compiled by author from Virginia Votes for the years indicated.

precincts in Virginia cities casting a ballot. This was more than 13 percent below the overall turnout of registered voters—by far the worst comparative differential in the ten most recent statewide elections reviewed in Table 13.5. In off-year elections, black turnout frequently exceeds overall turnout. In presidential elections, blacks usually participate at a lesser rate than whites, but not nearly as low as in 1988. Lack of black enthusiasm for Dukakis and Robb may have been a major factor at work here. Whatever the specific cause, it is clear that blacks were not excited enough to vote in large numbers in 1988.

Blacks who did vote cast their usual Democratic ballots, for the most part (see Table 13.6). Dukakis won 90.1 percent of the votes in the sample black precincts, about 1 percent less than Mondale did in 1984. Bush's proportion of 8.6 percent was hardly impressive, though it improved slightly over Reagan's 8.2 percent showing in 1984 (and was more than double Reagan's especially poor share of 3.4 percent in 1980). Robb won 83.7 percent, considerably off his 1981 gubernatorial pace of 96.4 percent, but still good considering that his opponent was black. Dawkins's 16.3 percent was reasonably impressive for a nonincumbent Republican, yet given the GOP's high hopes for a breakthrough in the black community, it can also be counted as a disappointment for Republicans. After all, three white Republicans have achieved higher proportions of

Table 13.6
Voting in Selected Predominantly Black Precincts in Virginia Cities, 1988 General Election for President and U.S. Senator

City	Number of Precincts	Dukakis	Bush	Others	Robb	Dawkins
Charlottesville	1	82.2	17.2	0.6	77.4	22.4
Virginia Beach	1	57.0	42.2	0.8	77.9	22.2
Hampton	2	77.7	20.7	1.6	82.3	17.7
Newport News	8	92.4	6.3	1.3	84.3	15.7
Norfolk	10	94.0	5.2	0.8	88.5	11.5
Portsmouth	2	94.2	5.1	0.7	78.9	21.1
Richmond	15	90.9	7.4	1.7	81.2	18.8
Emporia	1	92.6	6.2	1.2	87.5	12.5
Petersburg	4	92.2	6.1	1.7	82.7	17.3
Totals	44	90.1	8.6	1.3	83.7	16.3

Source: Official election results provided by the Virginia State Board of Elections.

the black vote than Dawkins in recent years: Linwood Holton for Governor in 1969 (37.2 percent), J. Marshall Coleman for Attorney General in 1977 (32.7 percent), and John W. Warner for U.S. Senator in 1984 (21.2 percent). In 1988, blacks simply chose party and ideology over race, not only in the U.S. Senate contest but also for a U.S. House seat (discussed in a later section).

Given the low turnout, blacks may have comprised little more than 10 percent of the statewide electorate in 1988.[3] Nonetheless, blacks probably comprised nearly a quarter of Dukakis's votes. By contrast, Bush's vote was about 98 percent white. Overall, Bush received approximately 65 percent of the white vote to Dukakis's 35 percent.

The Senate race had a very different complexion, of course. Robb attracted nearly 70 percent of the white vote—not far off his statewide pace—while blacks comprised just 12 percent of his total voters. The composition of Dawkins's vote was actually whiter than Robb's: Ninety-four percent of the Republicans' vote total came from whites, and only 6 percent from blacks. Meanwhile, Robb joined a very exclusive club of Democrats who have won a clear majority of Virginia's white vote since 1969. Andrew Miller and Mary Sue Terry in their 1973 and 1985 bids for Attorney General are the only other members.

U.S. HOUSE OF REPRESENTATIVES: NOMINATIONS

Only seven of Virginia's ten U.S. House districts hosted any competition in 1988. As usual, all the incumbents were unopposed for renomination: Democrats Owen Pickett of the Norfolk–Virginia Beach Second district, Norman Sisisky of the Tidewater Fourth, Jim Olin of the Roanoke Sixth, and Rick Boucher of the Southwest Ninth; and Republicans Herbert Bateman of the Hampton First,

Thomas Bliley of the Richmond Third, French Slaughter of the Piedmont Seventh, and Stan Parris and Frank Wolf in northern Virginia's Eighth and Tenth districts. (Sisisky, Bliley, and Slaughter were unopposed in the general election as well.) Challengers unopposed for their party nominations included Democratic lawyer James Ellenson in the First, Democratic Delegate David Brickley in the Eighth, Republican Charles Judd in the Sixth, and Republican Delegate John Brown in the Ninth. The Tenth district featured the only U.S. House primary, where in a very low turnout (2.7 percent of the registered voters), Robert L. Weinberg easily defeated fellow party member MacKenzie Canter III by 6,880 votes (76.8 percent) on June 14. The Second District was the site of a GOP convention contest between Jerry R. Curry and Stephen C. Shao. Curry, a black retired army major general, won over Shao, a 1986 Independent candidate for the House seat, by nearly a two to one margin in a May 14 party conclave.

Only in the Southside Fifth District were voters treated to a rousing political spring. The January 1988 death of nineteen-year veteran congressman W. C. "Dan" Daniel, a conservative Democrat, triggered a special election for the unexpired term on June 14. Both parties chose to nominate by convention. On March 26, Democrat L. F. Payne, a wealthy forty-two-year-old developer and chairman of the Wintergreen Resort in Nelson County, easily prevailed in his party's convention.[4] A political neophyte, Payne was nonetheless the choice of party leaders including Governor Gerald Baliles, and the Democrats quickly unified around Payne.

There was much more discord in Republican ranks. Former Reagan White House aide Linda Arey, forty-three, won a narrow convention victory over state Senator Onico Barker of Danville, 227 votes for Arey to 163 for Barker. Bitterness was apparent among many Barker supporters, who viewed Arey as an interloper who had lived out of the district for many years. Barker himself sat out the election, refusing to back his party rival.

Not incidentally, supporters of the controversial Reverend Jerry Falwell of Lynchburg were also instrumental in Arey's nomination; Falwell had resented Barker's vote against a tax break for Falwell's Liberty University during the 1987 General Assembly session.[5] Arey's Falwell connection made her additionally suspect in the minds of some Republican regulars who fear the influence of the "religious right" in the GOP.

Arey would have been Virginia's first-ever woman U.S. House member, but it was not to be. Payne's lack of a voting record, which left him free to position himself in the district's moderate-conservative mainstream; coupled with Arey's problems and Payne's outspending of Arey, by $563,000 to $348,000, produced a Payne victory.[6] Despite a Danville visit by Vice President George Bush on Arey's behalf two days prior to the election, Payne won a sizeable majority of 55,469 votes to 38,063 votes for Arey (59.3 percent to 40.7 percent).[7] The turnout was 38.2 percent of the registered voters, a moderately good participation rate for a special election.

Arey withdrew as the general election candidate, and the Republican party substituted Delegate Charles Hawkins of Pittsylvania County, a seven-year veteran of the State House.

U.S. HOUSE OF REPRESENTATIVES: GENERAL ELECTIONS

Virginia's general election House contests were all routs, and the ten-member delegation remained split evenly between the two parties. Just one incumbent, the Fifth's L. F. Payne, failed to top the 60 percent mark, but his 54.2 percent victory was still reasonably comfortable for an incumbent with only five months prior tenure. (His Republican opponent, Charles Hawkins, finished with 43.7 percent, with 2.1 percent for an Independent candidate.) The First's Herbert Bateman was lifted above 60 percent for the first time in his four successful contests (up to 73.3 percent), as was the Second's Owen Pickett (60.5 percent) to gain his sophomore term. The other members of Virginia's House delegation breezed to victory as well. Democrats had touted Delegate David Brickley's chances for an upset in the Eighth, but instead, Stan Parris proved anew that he has firmed up his hold on a marginal district, and secured 62.3 percent. The same electoral signal was sent by Frank Wolf in the Tenth (68.0 percent), Rick Boucher in the Ninth (63.4 percent), and Jim Olin in the Sixth (63.9 percent, see Table 13.7). Virginia's 100 percent rate of incumbency re-election fit nicely into the national picture where, for the second consecutive election, 98 percent of all House members who sought another term won again. Moreover, nationally, 95 percent of the triumphant incumbents won by at least 10 percentage points, as did all the Old Dominion's solons.

The GOP amassed a greater portion of total congressional votes across Virginia (56.9 percent) than in any modern election except for 1980 (when the party won nine of ten House seats in the Reagan landslide). When only the seven contested districts are considered, however, the Democrats had fewer worries. The proportion of the vote won by Democratic House candidates (46.6 percent) increased slightly over 1982, 1984, and 1986. This was partly due to the fact that two of the most popular GOP incumbents (Bliley and Slaughter) were unopposed, compared to just one of the Democrats' champion vote-getters (Sisisky).

Black voters, as we have already seen, gave little support to the black Republican U.S. Senate contender, Maurice Dawkins. Blacks gave even less backing to the black GOP U.S. House candidate in the Norfolk–Virginia Beach Second district. Jerry Curry won only about 8.5 percent of Norfolk's black voters, compared to Democrat Owen Pickett's 85.5 percent (and 6.0 percent for Independents). On the other hand, Republican Herb Bateman in the Peninsula First District did relatively well with blacks, given his party label, securing 18.9 percent in Newport News's sample black precincts and 36.8 percent of Hampton's. Bateman was certainly aided by the token nature of his opponent's campaign—yet the white Congressman fared better than either of the GOP's black candidates in 1988. Incidentally, another white Republican House incumbent,

Table 13.7

Election Results and Campaign Expenditures, 1988 Virginia General Election for U.S. Representatives

District	Candidates*	Total Campaign Expenditures	Percent of Votes
1	+Herbert H. "Herb" Bateman (R)*	$377,559	73.3
	James S. Ellenson (D)	30,303	26.7
	Totals	$407,862	100.0
2	Jery R. Curry	$175,000	35.5
	+Owen B. Pickett (D)*	412,762	60.5
	Stephen P. Shao (I)	7,263	2.4
	Robert A. Smith (I)	7,299	1.5
	Totals	$602,304	100.0
3	+Thomas J. Bliley, Jr. (R)*	$341,870	99.7
	Write-ins		0.3
	Totals	$341,870	100.0
4	+Norman Sisisky (D)*	$ 92,136	99.9
	Write-ins		0.1
	Totals	$ 92,136	100.0
5	+L.F. Payne, Jr. (D)*	$271,036	54.2
	Charles Hawkins (R)	102,792	43.7
	J. F. "Frank" Cole (I)	NA	2.1
	Totals	$373,828	100.0
6	Charles E. Judd (R)	$105,305	36.1
	+James R. "Jim" Olin (D)	318,129	63.9
	Totals	$423,434	100.0
7	+D. French Slaughter, Jr. (R)*	$ 85,412	99.6
	Write-ins		0.4
	Totals	$ 85,412	100.0
8	+Stanford E. "Stan" Parris (R)*	$640,397	62.3
	David G. Brickley	268,456	37.7
	Totals	$908,853	100.0
9	+Frederick C. "Rick" Boucher (D)*	$593,156	63.4
	John C. Brown (R)	137,099	36.6
	Totals	$730,255	100.0
10	+Frank R. Wolf (R)*	$656,957	68.0
	Robert L. Weinberg (D)	224,072	32.0
	Totals	$881,029	100.0
	Total	$4,847,003	

Key: NA indicates no data available; + denotes winner; * denotes incumbent; D denotes Democrat; I denotes independent; and R denotes Republican. Total campaign expenditures are those from 1 January 1987 to 8 December 1988, as reported to the Federal Election Commission, Washington, D.C. The FEC requires the filing of campaign finance data only by candidates who spend more than $5,000. The presumption is that the candidates for whom no report was filed spent less than the threshold sum.

Source: Compiled by author from official election results provided by the Virginia State Board of Elections.

Thomas J. Bliley of the Richmond Third District, managed to win a 34.5 percent share of the black vote under conditions somewhat similar to Bateman's in 1986.

To no one's surprise, all the incumbents handily outspent their losing rivals. The incumbents' financial edge ranged from a ratio of about two and a half to one in the Second, Fifth, and Eighth districts, up to a massive twelve and a half to one in the First District. However, there was one welcome development in campaign finance: The total 1988 statewide spending of $4.85 million represented a drop of 26 percent compared to 1986. This occurred despite the fact that seven House districts were party-contested in 1988, one more than two years earlier. The spending decline followed an increase of 12 percent in 1986 (over 1984) and a surge of 45 percent in 1984 (over 1982). No candidate in 1988 came close to spending over $1 million, which the Tenth's Frank Wolf did in 1986, and while three districts in 1986 featured total expenditures of at least a million dollars, none did so in 1988. The spending decrease may have been due in part to the intense fund-raising competition provided by the presidential, senatorial, and already-organizing 1989 gubernatorial campaigns. One financial footnote: Unopposed Third District incumbent Bliley reported disbursing more money ($342,000) than nine other party nominees in contested districts.

PARI-MUTUEL BETTING

Virginia's urge to gamble was on display again in 1988, as the state's voters followed up their approval of a state lottery a year earlier with an authorization for pari-mutuel betting on horse races. In fact, the two separate votes were amazingly similar. The east–west split was virtually identical; the overall vote proportions tracked closely (56.6 percent for the lottery and 55.9 percent for pari-mutuels); and the Urban Corridor stretching from northern Virginia through Richmond into Tidewater again proved decisive. Out of 136 localities, just 10 switched sides on the gambling questions from 1987 to 1988—a remarkable degree of constancy.[8] The same three congressional districts (the Fifth, Sixth, and Ninth) that had opposed the lottery tried to stop pari-mutuels, but they were once again overridden by the other seven districts. All ten districts voted "yes" and "no" in about the same proportions in both 1987 and 1988.

There was a much greater sea change from the pari-mutuel betting vote a decade earlier. While not a single locality that had backed pari-mutuels in 1978 went into opposition in 1988, twelve cities and twenty-two counties that had voted "no" in 1978 said "yes" in 1988.[9] Overall, thirty-nine counties, every one of them in the more rural, western half of the state, were in opposition to horse-race betting, and all fifty-six easterly counties were solidly in favor. The pattern was not quite as geographically tidy among cities; all fifteen cities that opposed pari-mutuels were in the western half of the state, as expected, but three of the twenty-six cities that gave electoral assent to the referendum were deep in western territory (Clifton Forge, Norton, and Roanoke). Still, this was the sort of sharp regional voting pattern that has been rare in modern Virginia history.

The pari-mutuel vote, like the lottery vote that preceded it, seemed to represent the existing social and cultural divide in the state rather than one based on purely political interests. In this respect, the two votes taken together may tell a fascinating tale of some fundamental differences in values and ways of life between the two broad regions of Virginia.

As the results of both referenda indicated, there is no doubt which set of values predominates in a state increasingly dominated politically by its Urban Corridor. The east–west split was accented with the flavor of an urban/suburban versus rural clash. The Urban Corridor and the Standard Metropolitan Statistical Areas (SMSAs) strongly favored horse racing, by 59.8 percent and 58.3 percent, respectively. The only demographic category found in opposition was rural Virginia, though the vote was close (48.9 percent in favor and 51.1 percent opposed). The central cities were especially inclined toward pari-mutuels (62.5 percent in favor), and the suburbs slightly less so (57.2 percent in favor).

What changed from 1978 to 1988? The following comparisons sketch the shape of the voting shift:

	"Yes Vote (rounded percent)		
	Pari-mutuels	Lottery	Pari-mutuels
	(1978)	(1987)	(1988)
Urban Corridor	55	62	60
SMSAs	53	60	58
Central Cities	53	63	62
Suburbs	53	59	57
Rural Areas	40	49	49

Clearly, urban areas—especially central cities but also suburbs—became much more willing to back gambling, but so did rural Virginia. While a narrow 51 percent majority still fought the change in 1987 and 1988, support for betting had grown by 9 full percentage points in a decade. Viewed in this light, the urban/rural divide seems more of a modest gap and less of a fearsome chasm.

One population group solidly in the pro–pari-mutuels camp was blacks. Black voters in the selected precincts shown in Table 13.6 gave 71.0 percent support to horse-race betting—much higher than the overall approval rating of 55.9 percent. White voters, by contrast, favored the referendum much more narrowly, by approximately a 54 to 46 percent margin.[10] The same black/white differential was apparent in the 1987 lottery vote, but in the lottery balloting, blacks were even more enthusiastic relative to whites in support of it (77.0 percent in favor). In one other way it was clear that black voters were less excited by horse-race betting than by the prospects of a lottery. Black participation in the pari-mutuel referendum was low (44.8 percent in the sample precincts) compared to the lottery (49.6 percent). Moreover, while ballot fall-off for blacks and whites was virtually the same in 1987, the 1988 rate for blacks voting on pari-mutuels was about double that of whites. Fall-off for whites was approximately 10 percent, but for blacks it was almost 20 percent.

The overall voter participation on the pari-mutuel question (black and white electorates combined) was 87.2 percent, a slightly lower level of participation than for the 1987 lottery (89.1 percent) and the 1978 horse-racing vote (90.7 percent). However, both the earlier contests were off-year elections that had featured shorter ballots, so a smaller fall-off in those referenda was to be expected. The 1988 fall-off for offices higher on the ballot was also at normal levels, and it followed the pattern set in the last presidential contest almost precisely. The ballot fall-off rates were just one more reminder that 1988 was an election year with few surprises.

The campaigns for and against pari-mutuel betting were not equally potent. The pro side counted in its corner almost every major current and former statewide official save Attorney General Mary Sue Terry (who was concerned about organized crime's potential influence in a betting operation). Governor Baliles, who had opposed the lottery, announced his support. The horse breeders were active in the pro efforts, of course, and contributed the money necessary to run it.

The opposition was far more ragtag, dominated by many of the same religious groups and preachers who had caused something of a backlash in their anti-lottery crusade in 1987. Marching into battle again was the Reverend Jerry Falwell, who personally bought television advertising time to denounce pari-mutuels on the weekend prior to Election Day. Private polls have consistently shown Falwell to be one of the most unpopular public figures in the state, and his endorsement—whenever active, highly visible, and timed for maximum notice at the end of a campaign—has long been thought to lose far more votes than it wins.[11] Just such a backlash may have been unwittingly created again by Falwell in 1988, since his advertisements were the last new piece of information many voters received on the pari-mutuel issue.

Pari-mutuel betting ultimately passed handily, suggesting again the political and demographic changes that have occurred in the state over the past decade. In 1978 when pari-mutuels went down to defeat, Virginia was considered solidly conservative, with a more pronounced rural influence and character. Ten years later, the state has clearly moderated politically. While certainly not liberal in attitudes or voting habits, Virginians feature a conservatism that seems increasingly tempered by moderation and, on occasion, a kind of progressive centrism. Most of all, the Urban Corridor rules—and all statewide candidates, not to mention the state's less favored regions, must inevitably adjust to and accommodate that reality.

NOTES

1. Robb's vote proportion was the best for a U.S. Senate election since Democratic incumbent A. Willis Robertson was re-elected to his Senate seat with 81.3 percent over two Independents in 1960. If the comparison is restricted to two-party contests, one has

to return to 1934, when Harry Byrd, Sr., won 76.0 percent of the vote over a token GOP challenger. In recent years the only Republican to run more poorly statewide than Dawkins was Senate nominee Ray Garland, who received 15.3 percent in a three-way race won by incumbent Harry Byrd, Jr., in 1970.

2. As one might expect, there was also a drop in the participation rate among those actually registered to vote. In 1988, 77.6 percent of the registered population cast a ballot, down from 81.5 percent in 1984 and a nearly identical 81.4 percent in 1980.

3. Thus, perhaps 225,000 blacks voted out of a total turnout of approximately 2,232,000.

4. The three other candidates were Claude Whitehead of Halifax County, Ron Milner of Bedford County, and Frank Cole of Halifax County. Payne reached an absolute majority before the end of the first ballot, and the tally had not been completed before the nomination was made unanimous.

5. See, for example, Tyler Whitley, "GOP Nominee Embarks on 5th District Tour," *Richmond News Leader*, April 11, 1988, p. 6.

6. Almost half Payne's war chest was supplied by the candidate himself.

7. There were also eighty write-ins, for a total turnout of 93,612.

8. Six localities switched from being pro lottery to anti pari-mutuels: Bedford City and the counties of Buckingham, Charlotte, Craig, Lee, and Prince Edward. Four localities made the opposite switch: Mecklenburg County and the cities of Charlottesville, Clifton Forge, and Roanoke.

9. One county (Cumberland) that had registered a tie vote in 1978 also voted affirmatively for pari-mutuels in 1988.

10. This estimate takes into account ballot fall-off after assuming that blacks were about 10 percent of the total election day turnout. Fall-off is the degree of voting for top-of-the-ballot items compared to voting on issues lower on the ballot. There is always some fall-off or drop-off from top to bottom, but it varies considerably from year to year and issue to issue.

11. See the 1981 Robb-Coleman example in *Virginia Votes 1979–1982* (Charlottesville: Institute of Government, University of Virginia, 1983), 84. Other Democratic candidates (Dick Davis in his 1982 U.S. Senate bid and Gerald Baliles in his 1985 gubernatorial battle, for instance) have found Falwell a tempting target because of his high negative ratings. Candidates with close ties to Falwell, such as the 1988 GOP House nominee in the Roanoke Sixth District, Charles Judd, and a 1983 Republican candidate for the state Senate in Falwell's own home area, Harry Covert, have lost badly (see *Virginia Votes, 1983–1986*, [Charlottesville: Institute of Government, University of Virginia, 1987], 12).

PART IV

CONCLUSION

14

The 1988 Presidential Election and the Future of Southern Politics

EARL BLACK AND MERLE BLACK

In the 1988 presidential election the Republican party once again convincingly swept the South. George Bush defeated Michael Dukakis by a ratio of almost three to two, a margin of victory unapproached in any other region of the nation. In most southern states, the campaign was essentially over by the second presidential debate. The Democratic party, having nominated a candidate who could be lambasted regionally as the most preposterous and parochial sort of northeastern liberal, lacked both a convincing message and a credible messenger. Vice President Bush, whose image metamorphosed during the campaign from Ronald Reagan's trusty, self-effacing, Yale-educated butler to a "kinder, gentler" George the Ripper, easily attracted the overwhelming white majorities that continue to be the hallmark of Republican victories in the South.

There was more to the election, of course, than the candidates' contrasting images. Bush benefited enormously from the resurgence of President Ronald Reagan's popularity after he signed an arms reduction treaty with the Soviet Union in the summer of 1988. Bush's background in foreign affairs became a significant asset in comparison with Dukakis's inexperience in this vital dimension of presidential responsibility. Moreover, the election took place in a relatively favorable economic climate for many southerners. A majority of the region's adults believed that their personal economic situation was better in 1988 than it had been in 1980, when a Democrat had been president.[1]

THE REPUBLICAN PRESIDENTIAL ADVANTAGE
IN THE SOUTH

Over the past half century, the South has shifted from a region overwhelmingly Democratic in presidential elections (through 1944) to one characterized by balanced competition between the two parties (1952–1964), and subsequently by a distinct Republican advantage.[2] The 1988 contest in the South provides a compelling demonstration of the Republican party's superior position in post–Great Society presidential elections. Lyndon Johnson's administration (1963–1969) combined racial, economic, and cultural liberalism in domestic affairs with ineffective intervention in foreign policy. These unpopular policies divided the southern Democratic party into antagonistic and sometimes irreconcilable factions. Once the third-party efforts of George Wallace had been exhausted, Republican presidential candidates had many salient issues that could be used to fashion southern victories.[3]

Republican presidential candidates have now carried all or most of the region's electoral vote in five of the last six elections. Far better than the Democrats, the Republicans have understood the dynamics of partisan dealignment in the South. Southern voters are now splintered into Democrats, Republicans, and Independents, with neither of the two parties able to attract a majority.

In this broken field of partisans and Independents, the formula for general election success is straightforward for both minority parties. Each party needs to unite the various factions that constitute its base. However, even a completely unified Democratic party is no longer big enough to win by itself, and even the most united Republican party still falls far short of constituting a majority of the entire electorate. Both southern parties have to go beyond their identifiers to win. Since the end of the Great Society, Republican presidential candidates have usually beaten their Democratic rivals at both tasks. Southern Republicans have rallied more cohesively than southern Democrats around their presidential nominees. Even more important, Republican presidential candidates have run well among white Independents and conservative Democrats. By contrast, all the recent Democratic presidential candidates, with the sole exception of Jimmy Carter in 1976, have fared poorly among Independents. None of the Democratic nominees has generated appreciable support from Republicans.

Several underlying factors have helped the Republicans secure enormous votes from southern whites in the post–Great Society era. The list begins—but hardly ends—with the parties' contrasting positions on civil rights and race relations. Traditional southern one-party politics was premised in part on the notion that the Democratic party was the white South's instrument in national politics for maintaining racial segregation. When the Democratic party shifted to a pro–civil rights position in response to the civil rights movement of the early 1960s, southern Democratic politicians correctly expected the party to lose support among white conservatives. Shortly after the Civil Rights Act of 1964 was passed,

President Johnson told an aide, "It think we just delivered the South to the Republican party for a long time to come."[4]

As Johnson took the Democrats to the left on civil rights, Arizona Senator Barry Goldwater led the Republicans to the right.[5] Many white southerners now support important, permanent changes in race relations (such as ensuring the right to vote and providing equal access to places of public accommodations). However, numerous whites remain unsympathetic to governmentally sponsored efforts to desegregate schools (particularly in metropolitan areas that would require extensive busing) and to monitor racial discrimination in employment. Affirmative action programs are especially unpopular, and most whites prefer to live in all-white neighborhoods. Enormous social distance persists between most blacks and most whites. In the South, as in the rest of the nation, very few whites feel "close" to blacks, nor do most blacks feel "close" to whites.[6]

Compared to their domestic rivals, Republican presidential candidates have usually been far more understanding of and sympathetic toward the views of the white majority in the South. Among many southern whites who think about these matters, the Republicans are generally seen as closing the door against governmentally initiated racial change, while the Democrats are commonly perceived as opening the door.

Presidential politics offers many ways to use race to win votes. "Direct appeals to racial prejudice may no longer be acceptable in American politics," Thomas B. Edsall has observed, "but race, in an indirect and sometimes subliminal way, remains a driving force in the battle today between Republicans and Democrats."[7] The potential still exists for exploiting prejudicial feelings and conflicts of interest between whites and blacks, especially when the appeal can be packaged in symbols or issues that have no necessary connection with race.

While the Republicans' advantage in presidential politics stems in part from racial matters, their appeal among southern whites goes far beyond these concerns. The perennial issue of fostering prosperity has worked in favor of the GOP, especially over the past decade. Jimmy Carter, the sole Democratic president in the post–Great Society era, presided over a period of high interest rates and serious inflation, thereby associating the Democratic party in the experience of many white southerners with adverse economic conditions. In contrast, economic recovery after the recession of 1982–1983 has prompted millions of southerners to view the Republican party as an instrument of economic opportunity and upward mobility. The Reagan tax cuts have allowed Republican strategists to claim that the GOP is anxious to let Americans keep more of what they make rather than having their earnings taxed away by the federal government.

Republican presidential candidates have also benefited from the perception that they will better defend the nation's international interests than their Democratic opponents. Again, the comparison between the Carter and the Reagan years is instructive. Whether rightly or wrongly, President Carter came to be viewed as too irresolute in national security affairs to stand up to the Iranians, much less to the Soviets. Although the Reagan record on national security was not a string of unbroken victories, the president did revive national pride. President Reagan sharply increased military expenditures and concluded an arms reduction treaty with the Soviet Union only months before the election, allowing Vice President Bush to claim that the Reagan approach of bargaining through strength had actually worked.

Beyond providing peace and prosperity, the Republicans have emphasized the importance of symbolic conservative values (maintaining traditional family values, the importance of religion, support for capital punishment, and opposition to gun control, among others). The rhetoric of the Reagan administration was warmly received by many conservative and moderate southern whites who agreed with many positions embracing cultural conservatism.

Thus, recent Republican presidents have been viewed by many white southerners as more committed than their Democratic rivals to protecting their values and advancing their interests over a wide range of questions: pocketbook economic issues, defending the nation in a hostile world, throttling the pace of governmentally sponsored racial change, and preserving traditional cultural values. Many factors, not a single grand factor, account for the Republicans' southern advantage in presidential politics.[8]

THE NATIONAL CONTEXT OF THE 1988 ELECTION

Just as the Democrats enjoyed a decisive advantage in New Deal presidential elections, since 1968 Republicans have been much better situated than Democrats to win the presidency. The GOP's advantage going into the 1988 campaign can be identified by analyzing state voting histories in post–Great Society presidential elections.[9] A partisan state, whether Democratic or Republican, is defined as one in which the same party has carried the state in at least three-fourths of the elections. Any state not qualifying as partisan is considered mixed.

In the aftermath of the Great Society, the Republican party has developed its broadest national base ever in presidential politics. It is a political fact of the utmost significance that forty-one states, controlling 77 percent of the nation's electoral vote, have been reliably Republican in recent presidential elections. Provided the Republicans could simply recapture most of their base, victory would be assured in 1988.

The South has become a cornerstone of the Republican base. Apart from Georgia, which twice remained loyal to its native son and was therefore mixed in its voting behavior, all the southern states qualified as reliably Republican in post–Great Society elections.

The unprecedented breadth of the Republican presidential base contrasted sharply with the Democrats' situation. With a national base consisting only of Minnesota and the District of Columbia (2 percent of the electoral vote), the Democratic party after 1964 has been relegated to its weakest position in presidential elections since the disastrous period in the Civil War and Reconstruction.

Under these circumstances, a Democratic presidential victory in 1988 necessitated carrying the party's meager base, sweeping the mixed states, and winning many other states that have ordinarily gone Republican in recent times. Although a Democratic victory in 1988 was certainly not impossible, neither was it probable unless many short-term factors—candidates, issues, conditions, and events—interacted in state after state to discredit the Republican candidate and legitimize the Democratic nominee.

IMAGINATIVE SLEDGEHAMMERING: THE SUCCESSFUL REPUBLICAN PRESIDENTIAL CAMPAIGN

The initial Republican advantage in the 1988 campaign appeared in Bush's Super Tuesday victories. Lee Atwater, Bush's campaign manager, had long predicted that Super Tuesday would benefit Bush far more than any Democratic politician. As usual, Atwater was right. Bush's decisive victory in South Carolina on the Saturday preceding March 8 set up a rout of his Republican opponents in the rest of the South on Super Tuesday.[10]

The Vice President's unambiguous success made his nomination a dead certainty and enabled the Bush campaign to begin unifying the Republican party. Bush strategists were not always immediately successful in assimilating the activists from the losing campaigns, but party unification accelerated after Bush appeased conservatives by selecting Indiana Senator Dan Quayle for Vice President. If a minority party's success in the general election requires uniting the various party factions behind the nominee, the Republicans had a head start over the Democrats in this task and a better understanding of how to achieve it.

However, in the spring and summer of 1988, not all the factors that had previously helped the Republicans win the presidency seemed to be in place. Bush faded from public attention after he cinched the nomination, while Dukakis rose in the polls as he defeated Jesse Jackson. Gallup polls in March and April showed Bush holding leads of only 4 and 3 points over Dukakis in the South. An early June poll, in the wake of Dukakis's victory over Jackson in the California primary, even showed the Massachusetts governor with an 11 point lead over Bush. Two weeks later, Bush again had gone ahead of Dukakis by 7 points in the South, but the Vice President continued to trail elsewhere.[11]

In addition to Bush's apparent weakness, two other important indicators were moving in the wrong direction for the GOP. The Vice President's intimate association with President Reagan was obviously one of his most significant political assets, but the President's job approval rating among southerners dropped from 57 percent in May to 54 percent in the first week of July. The midsummer rating was far below Reagan's approval rating around the time of the 1984 election, when 65 percent of southerners had approved of the president's job performance.[12]

Furthermore, southerners had become more dissatisfied with the president's handling of the economy between May and July. In the spring, 49 percent of

southerners—the highest of any region—approved of President Reagan's economic policies, while 45 percent disapproved. By July, though, only 43 percent
of southerners still approved of the president's handling of the economy, and
49 percent disapproved. In midsummer it was not at all clear that pocketbook
issues would work so favorably for the GOP as in the past.[13]

In this setting of uncertainty and concern about Bush's success in the fall
election, Republican campaign strategists began in midsummer to execute a
strategy designed to elevate Bush by discrediting Dukakis as a viable presidential
candidate. The sledgehammer campaign Bush waged against Dukakis was thor-
oughly familiar to observers of partisan politics in the South. As Thomas B.
Edsall observed, the 1988 Bush campaign amounted to a "classic southern
Republican challenge to a 'national' Democrat," a type of campaign that Republicans have often conducted in the region.[14] It involved the Vice President
aggressively nailing Dukakis to the wrong side of a host of conservative valence
issues and sacred symbols as well as directly assailing his character, judgment,
and values.

Atwater summarized the Bush campaign's general election strategy in a post-
election interview. "The strategic concept was developed way before we knew
who the Democratic nominee was," Atwater said. "Whoever it was, we had to
paint him as a frostbelt liberal who is out of the mainstream, and is not in tune
with the values of the mainstream voters. What we did was find the actual issues
that allowed us to paint the picture."[15]

Careful examination of Dukakis's past by Republican researchers generated
a bumper harvest of words and deeds that could be exploited with devastating
effect against the Massachusetts governor among white southerners.[16] "With
Dukakis," Bush's Virginia coordinator explained, "picking issues is like looking
at a cart with 100 of the best-looking chocolate desserts. It's really tough to
choose."[17] "There are only four words we need to mention," claimed the director
of Bush's Tennessee campaign. "ACLU. Gun Control. Furloughs. Taxes. Down
here, one of those four is bound to hit home."[18] Bush's Texas campaign manager
discerned an abundance of "hot button" issues to exploit. "It's almost like going
down the list, shutting your eyes, and saying, 'Where should we hit him this
week?'"[19] Simply on the issue of being "soft on crime," which many Republicans
considered Dukakis's most vulnerable area, numerous stones could be hurled.
"Whether it is the furlough program, Dukakis' opposition to the death penalty,
vetoing mandatory sentencing for drug dealers or gun control—the mix of these
four issues is overwhelming," said Lanny Griffin, the Bush campaign's chief
southern strategist.[20]

Once the voters were adequately alerted to Dukakis's past positions, Republicans were confident that the governor's efforts to present himself as a nonideological, pragmatic moderate would collapse, and that he would be isolated
as a liberal. If Bush could convincingly flog Dukakis as an unadulterated liberal—
a Teddy Dukakis—then all the advantages conservatives hold over liberals in
the South would come into play.

Very few southerners identify themselves as liberals (only 14 percent of the 1988 southern voters), and they are easily outnumbered by conservatives (38 percent, the highest in the nation; see Table 14.3). Moreover, many "moderates" take conservative positions on a variety of social, racial, defense, and some economic question. Aware of the conservative ideological tilt among the region's white voters, the Republicans sought to make the election a referendum on Massachusetts-style liberalism.

Throughout his southern campaign, Bush fiercely denounced Dukakis's judgment and values. Two examples illustrate the tone of the Bush assault. On August 27, in the east Texas town of Longview, Bush assumed the role of a "bare-knuckled, street-brawler" as he "launched one of his harshest, most sharply worded attacks on . . . Dukakis, portraying his opponent as a 'liberal Massachusetts governor' who opposes gun ownership, the Pledge of Allegiance, prayer in public schools, and is weak on crime." According to the *Washington Post*, "The crowd loved the rhetoric, cheering each new attack." As one retired white person put it, "Texans are basically conservative. They believe in God and the right of the individual," he said, "They still pray a lot in public schools down here. I guess it's against the law, but they're still doing it. Bush is really talking about where we live."[21]

A few days later, Bush spoke in Rocky Mount, North Carolina, a city in the eastern part of the state that had once been a Democratic stronghold but that now tended to go Republican in presidential elections. "I can't understand the type of thinking," Bush complained, "that lets first degree murderers who haven't even served enough time to be eligible for parole out on parole so they can rape and plunder again and then isn't willing to let the teachers lead the kids in the pledge of allegiance."[22]

The furlough issue—made concrete by the episode in which Willie Horton, a black man sentenced to life imprisonment for first-degree murder who raped a white woman after escaping while on a weekend furlough from a Massachusetts prison—was political dynamite against Dukakis in the South. Using a black convict to depict Dukakis as soft on criminals illustrated the persisting importance of racial appeals. In particular, the Horton case focused "on one of the traditionally most divisive and frightening examples of race relations: the black rapist and the white woman, an image exploited in the past by southern segregationists."[23]

On other matters of concern to southerners, the Republican campaign accentuated the positive. "President Reagan has given his vice president the greatest campaign gift of all: a warm feeling of peace and prosperity among the voters who count the most," concluded Kenneth R. Weiss of the *New York Times* Regional News Service.[24] The Republican campaign stressed huge differences between Bush's experience and Dukakis's inexperience in international affairs and national security policy; claimed that the arms reduction treaty signed by President Reagan with the Soviet Union proved the wisdom of strengthening the military before bargaining with the Russians; accused the Massachusetts governor

Table 14.1
Party Identification, Region, and the 1988 Bush Vote (in percent)*

| Area | Party Identification of Voters in 1988 | | | Area Bush |
	Democrat	Independent	Republican	Vote
South	21 (37)	63 (24)	94 (35)	58
West	14 (37)	50 (22)	90 (38)	52
Midwest	14 (36)	55 (28)	92 (34)	52
Northeast	18 (38)	51 (28)	87 (32)	50
United States	17 (37)	55 (26)	91 (35)	53

*Each entry is the percentage of a region's popular vote won by George Bush. Regions are ranked (highest to lowest) according to the total popular vote for Bush. Figures in parentheses report the percentage of voters for a given category of partisanship.

Source: New York Times/CBS News Exit Poll, New York Times (10 November 1988).

of wanting to raise taxes in contrast to Bush's pledge (''read my lips'') of no new taxes; and favorably contrasted economic recovery under the Reagan-Bush administration to high rates of inflation and interest under the last Democratic administration.

Bush's aggressive mixture of negative and positive campaigning gave southern whites several reasons to stick with the Republican candidate. As the fall campaign proceeded, Republican ranks closed around Bush, and the Vice President developed growing support among white Independents and Reagan Democrats. Bush's slashing attacks on Dukakis resolved whatever doubts Dole, Kemp, and Robertson supporters in the southern Republican party might have held about his ability to take the fight to the Democrats. For example, North Carolina Senator Jesse Helms, who had not endorsed any candidate in the primaries, was fully on board for the fall campaign. ''My supporters back the Bush-Quayle ticket 102 percent,'' he announced. ''Dukakis is the best thing Bush has going for him,'' Helms emphasized. ''People look at Dukakis and they get frightened. They're scared to death.''[25]

The Bush organization and the state Republican parties used a combination of paid and free media, direct mail, and phone banks to identify, inform, and bring to the polls registered Republicans for the fall election. In the end, the Republican campaign paid off in an extraordinarily cohesive party vote for Bush (see Table 14.1). The Vice President received 94 percent of the vote cast by self-identified Republicans, approximately the same level of support that Reagan had received four years earlier.

Bush also secured the landslide he needed from the ''swing'' voters—Independents and ''Reagan Democrats.'' After all, the sledgehammer strategy had been originally designed to appeal specifically to the values, beliefs, interests, and fears of these whites. Most of these voters, Bush strategists believed, would reject a candidate associated with the positions Republicans attributed to Dukakis. ''After they have had a chance to be better acquainted with the two candidates,'' Bush-strategist Lanny Griffin said, ''they are siding overwhelmingly with us. Among ticket splitters and Reagan Democrats, we are getting enough to win.''[26]

The net impact of the multiple attacks on Dukakis was to make the Massachusetts governor unacceptable to millions of southern white swing voters, while Bush appeared tough enough to keep the peace and preserve prosperity. According to the *New York Times*/CBS News Exit Poll, Bush won 63 percent of the self-classified Independents and 21 percent of Democrats in the South. These percentages, though slightly lower than Reagan's figures in 1984, were still high enough to defeat Dukakis convincingly among the Independents and to deny Dukakis the cohesive Democratic vote he had sought. By combining Bush's strength among Independents and Reagan Democrats with his powerful mobilization of the Republican base vote, the Vice President was able to poll 67 percent of the region's white voters, who themselves comprised 85 percent of the southern voters. The Bush campaign was a resounding success.

ANOTHER LOST CAUSE: THE DUKAKIS CAMPAIGN IN THE SOUTH

Southern Democrats approached the 1988 campaign as regional underdogs but with considerably more optimism than in 1984. President Reagan's retirement meant that the Democrats would compete against a weaker opponent. Nonetheless, the Democrats faced real problems in carrying the region. For one thing, there were far fewer southern Democrats in 1988 than in 1980. In addition, liberals continued to be a beleaguered and unpopular minority within the region, vastly outnumbered by conservatives and moderates. Geographically, the Democrats' traditional base of support had collapsed over the past two decades, while the Republicans' consistent support had rapidly expanded in many cities and suburbs.[27] At the minimum, a Democratic victory in the South depended on the right candidate and the right campaign. Southern Democrats got neither from Dukakis, and again they suffered a lopsided defeat.

SUPER TUESDAY BACKFIRES

Super Tuesday produced a ''Democratic muddle.''[28] Three Democrats claimed victory in the South. Dukakis secured pluralities of the vote in Texas and Florida, the region's largest states. Jesse Jackson won pluralities in Alabama, Georgia, Louisiana, Mississippi, and Virginia, and a majority of the South Carolina caucus vote on March 12. Al Gore, Jr., rallied in the closing days to carry Arkansas, North Carolina, and Tennessee. More than two months of tough, abrasive campaigning were necessary before the Massachusetts governor eliminated his rivals.

In the South, Dukakis's nomination again gave the Democrats a potentially weak candidate. His success in the March primaries had been limited to states that were typically Republican strongholds in presidential elections. It was exceedingly unlikely that Dukakis could beat Bush in Texas, where the Vice President had first won elective office, or in Florida, which had gone Republican in all but two presidential elections since 1952.

Dukakis finished a distant second in Arkansas, and he ran third in the remaining southern states. This is very important. In effect, the Democrats nominated for the presidency a politician who had run so poorly in the initial southern primaries that he would not even have qualified for the runoff in most southern states. Dukakis's weak showing in most states and plurality "victories" in states likely to go for Bush in the fall were early signals of another successful Republican march through the South in the general election.[29]

THE DUKAKIS SOUTHERN STRATEGY

Initially, the Dukakis organization refused to write off the South. "If anyone tells you that we can't win in the South, or that we can't win in the West, or that we can't win in the great state of Texas," Dukakis told the Texas State Democratic Convention, "don't you believe it."[30] Interviews with chairmen and executive directors of state parties led David S. Broder to conclude that "after hiding from their national ticket four years ago, southern Democratic officials are telling aides of the Massachusetts governor that Vice President Bush does not have their region's electoral votes locked up—unless Dukakis decides to default."[31]

Dukakis's apparent Southern Strategy had three parts. First, he sought to position himself as a moderate, pragmatic Democrat skilled in the art of governing rather than as a liberal Democrat. Second, Dukakis tried to capitalize on the feeling of many southern Democrats—which was widespread in the spring and summer of 1988—that Bush was weak and beatable. Finally, he attempted to regain the support of conservative Democrats and Independents by selecting Texas Senator Lloyd Bentsen as his running mate. None of these tactics worked.

THE ATTEMPT TO PUT IDEOLOGY OFF LIMITS

In his acceptance speech to the Democratic National Convention, Dukakis asserted that "this election isn't about ideology. It's about competence." The governor added that "It's not about meaningless labels. It's about American values. Old-fashioned values like accountability and responsibility and respect for the truth."[32] Dukakis mixed progressive and conservative themes in his effort to appeal to southerners.

As part of his progressive appeal, he urged "good jobs at good wages for every citizen in the land, no matter who they are or where they come from or what the color of their skin." In August, campaigning in Birmingham, Dukakis eulogized the four black girls killed by a bomb in a church twenty-five years ago, and pledged that "we will not rest until every form of bigotry and racism and religious intolerance will be banished from this land.''[33]

However, the Massachusetts governor also stressed conservative themes when campaigning in the South. Robin Toner captured the spirit of a June campaign swing:

In three days of traveling the South, the New Englander had tried hard to immerse himself in this region's political culture, and to dispel the notion that another liberal northern Democrat had captured the nomination and was about to lead the ticket on another doomed crusade across the South. [The Democratic nominee] was doing his best to avoid the labels that can mean political catastrophe in the deep South—such as "ultraliberal." He was talking about fighting crime and illicit drugs. He was talking about strengthening families.[34]

According to T. R. Reid, the purpose of Dukakis's southern trip was "to create a positive image for this largely unknown Democratic Yankee" by showing "a picture of a tough crime-fighter, a worthy commander in chief for the war on drugs."[35]

While Dukakis's attempt to present himself as a moderate who had something to offer both progressive and conservative southerners made political sense, the real question was whether his self-definition would prevail against the expected Republican efforts to define him as a Teddy Kennedy liberal. Susan Estrich, his campaign manager, foresaw the attacks but professed little concern. "I expect the Republicans will be very negative about Dukakis. They've run out of positive things to say about Bush. We're ready for it."[36]

Some of the southern Democrats, though, who were much more experienced in the type of campaigning Republicans had practiced against moderate to liberal Democrats, were worried about the coming onslaught. "In one way or another," reported columnist David Broder, "most of the southerners express fears that Republicans will move to label Dukakis a typical northeastern liberal, whose values are alien to the 'God, flag, and country' psychology of the South." One veteran southern campaign manager argued correctly that " 'symbolism is important in the South. People will tolerate a good deal of difference on policy, but if they don't think you share their values, they write you off.' ''[37]

As the campaign proceeded, of course, Dukakis's self-definition collapsed. "Initial reaction to the governor here in the South was positive," commented John Dillin. "But in August and September, the governor's political standing was devastated among white Southerners on gun control, the death penalty, the Pledge of Allegiance and prison furloughs—visceral issues that grabbed the public's attention."[38] For weeks, Dukakis mounted no effective counterattack against the Republican charges, much to the disgust of southern Democratic leaders who urged immediate replies to the Republican "lies." Al LaPierre of the Alabama Democratic party complained that " 'We know how to run and do what the Republicans are doing—a down and dirty campaign. We're used to it.' ''[39]

The net impact of the Republicans' multiple attacks on Dukakis's beliefs, values, and past behavior was to make him unacceptable to many southern white swing voters. Analyzing interviews with Reagan Democrats and Independents, Kenneth R. Weiss concluded that "all but a handful of these Southern swing voters consider themselves either conservative or moderate in their political beliefs. From this political orientation, two out of three of these voters believe Dukakis is 'too liberal.' "[40] "President Dukakis just doesn't sound like an American president," said one Tennessee voter. "It sounds like somebody in Indonesia or Greece or someplace overseas."[41]

Conservative Republican Senator Phil Gramm of Texas, a former Democrat who switched to the Republican party, compared the voters' options this way late in the campaign:

I think there's growing evidence all over the state that people are closing the book on Mike Dukakis. There's no one silver bullet, but you combine three or four of those issues and it induces Joe to say to Sarah across the kitchen table, "Honey, this Dukakis guy is not our kind of person."[42]

THE SOUTHERN DEMOCRATS UNDERESTIMATE BUSH

The second initial basis for Democratic optimism involved a gross underestimation of Bush's strength as a campaigner. David Broder's interviews with southern Democratic leaders underscored the point that "much of the increased optimism about Democratic inroads in the South rests less on an estimate of Dukakis' strengths than on Bush's perceived weaknesses." A few weeks later, Robin Toner reported that "many of these Southern Democrats smell the possibility of victory" and that "some party leaders seemed delighted at the prospect of a race against Vice President Bush."[43]

" 'We're not just going to drive little Georgie Bush out of office. We're going to drive him plumb crazy,' " boasted Jim Hightower, the populist Texas Commissioner of Agriculture. Frank Holleman, the South Carolina state chairman, believed "Bush is a fundamentally weak personality and a weak candidate. That's why we have a chance."[44] Disrespect for Bush peaked at the Democratic National Convention, where the Vice President was ridiculed mercilessly by numerous speakers.

There was, in truth, some justification for the Democrats' eagerness to take on Bush, since the Vice President's performance in the Republican primaries was often inconsistent. At times he looked like an authentic leader; at other times he seemed a parody of leadership. Bush operated in Reagan's shadow and did not emerge as an independent figure until the Republican National Convention.

However, the Democrats' contempt for Bush blinded them both to Bush's potential strengths in the general election and to the likelihood that the Vice President's managers, all experienced in the demands of national campaigns, would know how to make the most of the material at hand. In the end, southern

Democrats underestimated Bush and overestimated Dukakis.

During the Super Tuesday campaign, Dukakis had already revealed a tin ear for the subtleties of southern political culture. The Massachusetts governor essentially advised southerners that they were the same as Americans everywhere, which may or may not be true, but which contradicted the belief of many white southerners that they possessed a special culture in which they took enormous pride.[45] It was not surprising that Dukakis (and his Massachusetts advisors) would fail to take seriously the potential political damage arising from Bush's shrewd attacks on the governor's beliefs and values.

GOING FOR TEXAS: THE BENTSEN STRATEGY

When Dukakis campaigned in the South before the convention, he was everywhere advised to balance his ticket with a southerner. Apparently unconvinced that he could make inroads into the region based solely on his own strength and Bush's weaknesses, Dukakis chose the most popular Democrat in Texas to broaden the ticket's appeal to white southerners. Senator Lloyd Bentsen had repeatedly demonstrated his ability to unite all wings of the fractious Texas Democratic party. His selection as the Democratic vice presidential nominee immediately brought support from many moderate and conservative Democratic elected officials and state party chairpersons in the region.

Apart from activating officeholders and politicians who had a personal stake in a Democratic presidential victory, the real question was whether rank and file southern Democrats and many Independents would support the Dukakis-Bentsen ticket. In "his role as a Southerner working the Southern territory for a Yankee," Bentsen pleaded with Democrats to return to the party:

"This year Michael Dukakis reached out to the South," he said. "He chose one of you. He took the extra step to bring us home again. He came here and listened to us. He campaigned among us. He asked a Southerner to join him on the ticket, and one reason I accepted was because I want to help bring Texas and Tennessee and Arkansas and Mississippi back into the Democratic party."[46]

The strategy was only partially successful. It did not win back all the rank and file conservative Democrats, nor did a majority of white Independents vote Democratic. Party leaders acknowledged that "having Mr. Bentsen on the ticket means little to the average voter. 'You don't have guys out there driving Trans Ams with Bentsen stickers,' said one Democratic activist. 'It's at a higher level.' "[47] The nub of the problem was that Democratic politicians were no longer opinion leaders for many voters. "Most voters today," observed Hastings Wyman, Jr., "make up their minds independent of state and local leadership."[48]

By September the Dukakis campaign was in trouble, and its prospects worsened after the first presidential debate. "Nowhere in the South are the Democrats running any better than even," reported Douglas Jehl on October 2. " 'We're really sucking wind down here,' said one state director who spoke on condition he not be identified."[49] On Saturday, October 1, a secret meeting of Dukakis campaign officials from the so-called "Big Five" states (North Carolina, Tennessee, Arkansas, and Georgia, plus the border state of Kentucky) occurred in Atlanta to "fashion a fallback strategy that will focus on the five southern states where a Democratic victory still seems possible." Dukakis officials from other southern states were not invited to attend, a sign that the Dukakis campaign was writing off most of the region a month before the election.[50] After the second debate, polls showed Dukakis virtually out of the race in all the region's states, and the governor's organization virtually abandoned the South to concentrate on eighteen states outside the region.[51]

THE 1988 RESULTS

The 1988 presidential election added a fresh verse to the new song of a Republican Solid South. Just as Nixon had done in 1972 and Reagan in 1980 and 1984, the Bush campaign unified its base, won most of the Independents, and took a respectable share of the region's Democrats. Even though Dukakis ran a stronger race than Walter Mondale among southern Democrats, the Massachusetts governor secured little support from the large majority of southern voters who are not Democrats.

Republican strategists were light-years ahead of their Democratic counterparts in assessing the vulnerabilities of the opposition and in selecting the specific "hot button" issues and symbols that could motivate anti-Dukakis feelings. In a slashing rhetorical style that owed something to the political warfare that George Wallace had conducted against his enemies, Bush personally savaged Dukakis's record. Nonetheless, the Bush victory was not based entirely on the exploitation of negative feelings toward Dukakis. The Vice President stressed his close ties with President Reagan (whose popularity was again rising), his superior experience in national decision making, and the Republicans' accomplishments in maintaining peace and promoting prosperity.

An *Atlanta Journal-Constitution* poll conducted in the first week of October, for example, showed that the ingredients of Republican success were now settling into place. According to Tom Baxter, "Mr. Bush's eight years as vice president have made him better known than Mr. Dukakis among Southern voters and given them greater confidence in his experience and abilities." A month before the election, the Vice President had managed "to shape the focus of the campaign around the same issues the Republicans have used to win the region in four of the past five presidential elections: defense, crime, and patriotism." Moreover, the issue of relative economic prosperity had begun to work in Bush's favor. Baxter noted that

most people think they are financially better off than they were when Mr. Reagan first was elected. Therefore they seem more likely to listen to Mr. Bush when he discusses the progress made since the "bad old days" of high inflation and double-digit interest rates under President Jimmy Carter and less likely to agree with Mr. Dukakis's claim that in real terms most middle-class voters have lost ground.[52]

As William Graham, Bush's North Carolina coordinator, put it, "If we can't sell peace and prosperity, we don't deserve to win."[53]

In 1988, for the fourth time in six elections, the South was the least Democratic region in the country (see Table 14.2). The Democratic vote in the South (41 percent) trailed the other regions by 6 to 8 points and was far too low to generate any electoral college votes. Although the Massachusetts governor was much more closely competitive with Bush in the popular vote outside the South, Dukakis won only 28 percent of the North's electoral vote.

In pondering Bush's success in the South, it is important to bear in mind the tremendous impact of the Reagan presidency in changing the underlying patterns of partisanship. The Reagan years—especially after the recovery from the recession of 1982–1983—stimulated identification with the Republican party and undermined Democratic partisanship. According to the *New York Times*/CBS News Exit polls, in the 1980 presidential election there were nearly twice as many self-identified Democrats (52 percent) as Republicans (26 percent) in the South. Four years later, the Democratic majority among southern voters had vanished. The share of Republicans among the region's voters rose to 35 percent, while Democrats dropped to 39 percent. No longer did the South stand out in party identification as the most Democratic and least Republican region of the country.[54] By 1988 the Republicans (still 35 percent) had achieved approximate parity with the Democrats (37 percent) in the southern presidential electorate (see Table 14.1). Moreover, Bush ran stronger in the South among all three groups—Republicans, Independents, and Democrats—than he did in any other region.

Part of the reason for Bush's greater strength in the South lies in the fact that the southern electorate contains comparatively more conservatives and relatively fewer liberals than elsewhere in the nation (see Table 14.3). Self-described moderates made up 43 percent of the region's voters in 1988, and they went narrowly for Bush. Had the southern electorate been comprised solely of moderates, the election would have been very close. Among the voters who labeled themselves liberals or conservatives, however, there were acute differences in partisan support. Bush carried four-fifths of the conservatives but only about a fifth of the southern liberals. Moreover, conservatives had a considerable practical advantage because they outnumbered liberals by almost three to one. The Vice President's votes among the larger group of conservatives swamped Dukakis's yield among the much smaller group of liberals.

Once again, the southern electorate, like the rest of the nation, was sharply polarized between whites and blacks. Bush won two-thirds of the southern white vote, but merely one-eighth of the black vote (see Table 14.4). In the past three presidential elections, the Republicans have consistently won their largest white

Table 14.2
Democratic Performance in Post–Great Society Presidential Elections:
Comparison of Democratic Percentage of Popular Vote and Electoral Vote by
Region, 1968–1988*

Item	Popular Vote							Electoral Vote						
	68	72	76	80	84	88	NDX	68	72	76	80	84	88	NDX
South	31	29	54	45	37	41	35	20	0	91	9	0	0	5
Border	43	36	53	45	42	48	42	38	6	84	37	6	18	17
West	44	39	46	34	39	47	42	14	0	4	4	0	19	8
Midwest	44	40	48	41	41	47	43	23	0	35	8	8	23	13
Northeast	50	41	51	42	44	49	46	81	11	70	3	0	47	35
Nation	43	38	50	41	41	46	42	35	3	55	9	2	21	15
North	46	40	49	40	42	48	44	40	4	44	9	3	28	19
Northern Democratic Target	55	55	49	52	54	53	54	60	66	37	63	67	67	65
Northern Democratic Gap	-9	-15	0	-12	-12	-5	-10	-20	-62	+7	-54	-64	-39	-46

*Regions are ranked (lowest to highest) according to the mean Democratic vote for the four elections (1968, 1972, 1984, and 1988) in which the Democratic nominee was not a southerner.

Key: NDX = mean Democratic votes for the four elections (1968-72, 1984-88) in which the Democratic presidential nominee was a northerner.
      South = Alabama, Arkansas, Florida, Georgia, Louisiana, Mississippi, North Carolina, South Carolina, Tennessee, Texas, and Virginia.
      Border = Delaware, District of Columbia, Kentucky, Maryland, Missouri, Oklahoma, and West Virginia.
      Northeast = Connecticut, Maine, Massachusetts, New Hampshire, New Jersey, New York, Pennsylvania, Rhode Island, and Vermont.
      Midwest = Illinois, Indiana, Iowa, Kansas, Michigan, Minnesota, Nebraska, North Dakota, Ohio, South Dakota, and Wisconsin.
      West = Alaska, Arizona, California, Colorado, Hawaii, Idaho, Montana, Nevada, New Mexico, Oregon, Utah, Washington, and Wyoming.
      North = United States minus the South.
      Northern Democratic Target = the minimum percentage of the non-southern popular vote and electoral vote needed by the Democrats to win 50.1 percent of the national popular vote and 50.1 percent of the national electoral vote, given the Democrats' performance in the South.
      Northern Democratic Gap = net difference between the northern Democratic target and the northern vote actually received.

Source: Calculated by authors.

majorities in the South. While black southerners mostly stayed with Dukakis, they accounted for only 15 percent of the region's voters.

Within the South, Dukakis was slightly more successful than any other northern Democratic presidential candidate since 1968. However, the 1988 vote continued to reveal the Democrats' inability to wage competitive races except when popular southern Democrats have headed the presidential ticket (see Table 14.5). Of the

Table 14.3
Political Ideology, Region, and the 1988 Bush Vote*

| Area | Political Ideology of Voters in 1988 | | | C/L |
	Liberal	Moderate	Conservative	
South	22 (14)	52 (43)	81 (38)	2.7
West	15 (18)	47 (44)	78 (35)	1.9
Midwest	19 (17)	48 (49)	78 (31)	1.8
Northeast	15 (23)	47 (45)	81 (30)	1.3
United States	18 (18)	49 (45)	80 (33)	1.8

*Each entry is the percentage of a region's popular vote won by George
Bush. Regions are ranked (highest to lowest) according to the ratio of
conservative voters to liberal voters. Figures in parentheses report the
percentage of voters for a given category. C/L reports the conservative
to liberal ratio.

Source: New York Times/CBS News Exit Poll, New York Times (10 November
1988).

Table 14.4
The Republican Presidential Vote, 1980–1988, by Race and Region*

| Area | White Voters | | | Black Voters | | |
	1980	1984	1988	1980	1984	1988
South	61	71	67	9	10	12
West	55	66	58	--	--	13
Midwest	55	64	57	11	6	8
Northeast	51	57	54	12	7	12
United States	55	64	59	11	9	12

*Each entry is the percentage of a region's vote won by the Republican
presidential candidate. Regions are ranked (highest to lowest) according
to the mean white Republican vote.

Source: New York Times/CBS News Exit Poll, New York Times (10 November
1988).

forty-four state campaigns between 1968 and 1988 involving Democratic nominees who were northern liberals, only one (Louisiana in 1988, with the nation's
highest rate of unemployment) produced a Democratic presidential vote that
reached 45 percent.

Although Dukakis's percentages of the total vote did not vary greatly among
the southern states (ranging from 38 percent in South Carolina to 45 percent in
Louisiana), much greater diversity appeared among white southerners (see Table
14.6). In every southern state Dukakis lost the vast majority of the white vote.
Generally, the size of Dukakis's white vote was inversely related to the size of

Table 14.5
Democratic Share of the Presidential Vote in the Southern States, 1968–1988*

Political Unit	Presidential Election						Mean Vote		
	68	72	76	80	84	88	68–88	68–72 84–88	76–80
Mississippi	23	20	50	48	37	40	36	30	49
Alabama	19	26	56	47	38	40	38	31	52
South Carolina	30	28	56	48	36	38	39	33	52
Georgia	27	25	67	56	40	40	42	33	61
Florida	31	28	52	39	35	39	37	33	45
North Carolina	29	29	55	47	38	42	40	34	51
Virginia	33	30	48	40	37	40	38	35	44
Louisiana	28	28	52	46	38	45	40	35	49
Tennessee	28	30	56	48	42	42	41	35	52
Arkansas	30	31	65	48	38	43	42	36	56
Texas	41	33	51	41	36	44	41	39	46
Deep South	25	25	57	49	38	41	39	32	53
Peripheral South	34	30	53	42	37	42	40	36	48
All South	31	29	54	45	37	41	40	35	49

*States are ranked (lowest to highest) according to the mean Democratic vote for the four elections (1968, 1972, 1984, and 1988) in which the Democratic nominee was not a southerner.

Source: Calculated by the authors from appropriate volumes of Richard M. Scammon and Alice v. McGillivray, eds., America Votes, and from the New York Times (10 November 1988).

the black population. Deep South whites, particularly those residing in South Carolina and Mississippi, were even less attracted to the Democratic ticket than were peripheral South whites, who lived in states with smaller black populations. In neither subregion did the Democrats come close to winning the minority of the white vote they needed for victory.[55]

THE FUTURE

Post–Great Society presidential elections have been distinguished by the Republicans' ability to win repeated victories in every region. When the fifty states are reclassified on the basis of their votes in the 1968–1988 elections (1972–1988 for the southern states lest George Wallace's victories in 1968 obscure the Republicans' subsequent success in the region), the South emerges as the most pro-Republican region in the nation, followed closely by the West and Midwest (see Table 14.7).

The disappearance of the Democratic Solid South and its replacement in many elections by a Republican Solid South have profound strategic implications for partisan control of the presidency. Table 14.2 compares the Democratic popular and electoral college votes for post–Great Society presidential elections for the South and four other regions (Border, Northeast, Midwest, and West). With the

Table 14.6

Too Few Southern Whites for Dukakis: Comparison of Estimated White Vote Won by Michael Dukakis with Estimated Minimum White Vote Needed for a Democratic Victory in the 1988 Presidential Election (in percent)

Political Unit	White Vote Won	White Vote Target	White Vote Won as a Percentage of White Vote Target
South Carolina	21	38	57
Mississippi	24	38	64
Georgia	28	41	69
Alabama	29	41	70
Virginia	31	43	72
Louisiana	32	39	82
North Carolina	33	43	77
Florida	34	46	74
Tennessee	36	45	79
Arkansas	37	45	81
Texas	39	46	85
Deep South	28	40	70
Peripheral South	36	45	79
All South	33	44	77

Source: Calculated by the authors from voter registration data reported in the 1988 Statistical Abstract of the United States (Washington, D.C.: U.S. Government Printing Office), 320; and from the estimated Democratic share of the southern black vote reported in the 1988 New York Times/CBS News Exit Poll, New York Times (10 November 1988). In preparing the estimates it was assumed that the proportion of black voters equalled .9 of the proportion black of all registered voters in 1986. Figures for Texas overestimate the Anglo Democratic vote because Hispanics have not been distinguished from Anglos. For procedures, see Earl Black and Merle Black, Politics and Society in the South (Cambridge: Harvard University Press, 1987), 140-142.

exception of the two elections in which Jimmy Carter headed the ticket, the region that once routinely provided landslide Democratic presidential votes has been the least Democratic of the five regions in recent presidential politics.

As the southern electoral vote has shifted to the Republicans, Democratic presidential victories have consequently come to depend on winning extraordinary majorities of the electoral vote outside the South. Because the South contains more electoral votes than any other region (slightly more than a fourth in 1988) and because it has often been exceptionally cohesive (awarding nine-tenths or more of its electoral vote to one candidate in every election since 1972), the South occupies an especially important strategic position in presidential politics.

Two rules of thumb for winning the presidency follow from the South's size and cohesion. First of all, a party that wins no electoral votes in the South needs a minimum of two-thirds of the electoral vote in the rest of the nation in order to win a bare majority of the total electoral vote. Indeed, since the South will have more electoral votes after the 1990 reapportionment than it had in 1988, the northern target for a party completely defeated in the region will be slightly

Table 14.7

The 1992 Presidential Election in Context: Percentage of Electoral Vote Controlled by Democratic, Mixed, and Republican States in 1968–1988 Presidential Elections, by Region and Nation*

Region	Democratic	Mixed	Republican	EVS**
South	0	9	91	(26)
West	0	13	87	(21)
Midwest	8	9	83	(23)
Border	6	32	62	(9)
Northeast	0	69	31	(21)
United States	2	24	73	(100)
North	3	30	67	(74)

*Each entry is the percentage of a region's electoral vote cast by each type of state (Democratic, Mixed, or Republican). Partisan states are those in which the same political party carried the state in at least 75.0 percent of the 1968-1988 elections. Southern states are classified on the basis of the 1972-1988 elections. States not classified as Democratic or Republican are defined as Mixed. Regions have been ranked (highest to lowest) according to the percentage of the region's electoral vote cast by Republican states.

**EVS = electoral vote share (region's share of the nation's electoral vote for the 1988 presidential election).

Source: Calculated by the authors.

higher in the 1992 presidential election. Second, a party that wins the entire electoral vote of the South can secure a majority in the electoral college by capturing one-third of the northern electoral vote. Again, that northern target will be marginally lower in 1992 because of reapportionment.

A large and united South can have a substantial impact on presidential campaigns, enabling the party with a comprehensive southern base to concentrate its resources on a small number of carefully selected northern states while forcing the party without southern support to campaign successfully in a great many northern states. As a matter of practical politics, the South's size and cohesion give the Republicans a significant advantage, since they can afford to lose much more of the electoral vote in the rest of the country than can the Democrats.

Given their recent success in the South, Republican strategists will again try to use the region as the cornerstone of their electoral college base in presidential politics. However, by running nationally the type of campaign that has often enabled southern Republicans to defeat southern Democrats, the GOP may have hurt itself outside the region. Kevin P. Phillips has argued that "the GOP presidential coalition is now so overconcentrated in the South that a Democrat could win the electoral college with narrow margins in the big states."[56] Outside the South, the 1988 election was too close for comfort for the GOP. Modest voting shifts would have produced Democratic victories in many important states.

Although the current Republican advantage in the South is manifest, it is worth emphasizing that the new Republican Solid South differs from the Democratic Solid South in a crucial respect. The Republicans cannot take the South for granted as the Democrats once did. From 1920 to 1944, Democratic presidential candidates averaged 70 percent of the South's popular vote. During the New Deal era, average support for Roosevelt even grew to 78 percent of the southern vote.

By these standards, the modern Republican Solid South is based on a much smaller share of the popular vote. GOP presidential candidates have averaged slightly over 57 percent of the popular vote in the last five contests, enough to make the Democratic candidate an underdog, but not large enough to put an occasional Democratic victory beyond reach.[57]

Republican presidential candidates have done well because, more often than not, substantial majorities of southern whites have liked the general conditions under Republican rule and disliked the conditions under the Democrats.

"I don't particularly like Bush. Who does?" acknowledged a Tennessee real estate salesman. "But I like what's happened the last eight years. We got inflation under control. We got some respect in the country on national defense. We got Russia afraid of us. If something's not broken, you don't fix it."[58]

Continued support for Republican presidents in the South is not inevitable. Major economic setbacks, problems in foreign affairs, the revival of racial unrest, or a multitude of other controversies might prompt voters to reevaluate their support of the GOP. Much will rest on perceptions of President Bush's ability to lead the nation.

The Democrats again face an uphill battle to regain presidential standing in the region. The national Democratic party has lost so much stature among many white southerners that significant changes in white perceptions of the consequences of Republican rule will probably be required before they begin to pay serious attention to Democratic presidential candidates.

Because the Republicans' rhetoric resonates so powerfully with the beliefs and values of many middle-class and working-class whites, Democratic presidential candidates have been forced to state their case in terms of the probability of adverse future outcomes. Democratic arguments about what might possibly go wrong in the future have not been as persuasive as GOP appeals to current perceptions of "peace and prosperity." However, if and when the nation's future does turn out to be as perilous as some Democrats warn, their presidential candidates will be back in business in the South.

What the Democrats can realistically attempt in 1992 will turn on many factors that are now unknowable. The condition of the economy in various states, evaluations of the President's performance in domestic and foreign affairs, the quality of the Democratic nominee, and other similar factors will enter into assessments of what would constitute a reasonable Democratic presidential strategy for the region in comparison to other parts of the nation.

Democrats have three broad options about the role of the South in presidential politics. They can completely write off the South, go all out in every southern state, or campaign selectively in the region.

Based on the historical record, conceding the entire region to the Republicans makes little sense as a winning strategy. It gives up (by 1992) almost 150 electoral votes, more than half the total needed for victory, and no Democratic presidential candidate has ever been elected by this route. However, given the Democratic party's decimation in the South since the Great Society, it might be necessary for the Democrats to pioneer a new way of electing a president. The outlines of such a winning strategy can be discerned in Dukakis's performance outside the South. If a future Democratic nominee could carry the states won by Dukakis plus the states in which Dukakis polled at least 45 percent of the popular vote, it would be possible in principle for a Democrat to win the presidency without a single electoral vote from the South. Such a Democratic campaign would concentrate on a carefully selected group of states located in the Northeast, Border, Midwest, and coastal West. The riskiness of this strategy is obvious. The Democratic nominee would have virtually no margin for defeat in any of the northern target states. A Democratic northern strategy would allow the Republicans to assemble more than half their electoral college majority without a contest, and to concentrate their resources on the right combination of northern states to checkmate the Democrats.

On the other hand, a strategy that assumed the entire South could go Democratic in the 1992 presidential election would make little sense unless the Bush administration experienced major setbacks or the Democrats nominated a candidate who could elicit genuine enthusiasm in the South. Even a southerner at the top of the Democratic ticket would not guarantee winning the entire region.

Absent a total Republican collapse, the most reasonable strategy for the Democrats would be to concentrate on states outside the region, but to allocate some of their campaign resources to a small number of southern states—Arkansas and Tennessee, for example, plus any others that might be experiencing severe economic difficulties in the election year—where majority biracial coalitions might be constructed. Denying the Republicans a complete sweep of the South is probably the most realistic outcome for which the Democrats can hope in the near future.

In any event, the 1988 presidential election in the South confirms the distinct advantage that Republicans have created in the wake of the Great Society. Southern outcomes are mainly shaped by the majority of the "white South," just as they have been since the end of Reconstruction. Though most whites have shifted from the Democratic to the Republican party in terms of presidential preference, the abiding continuity is that the region's outcomes are fundamentally set by the perceived interests, aspirations, and emotions of white southerners. It is an environment in which the Republicans will endeavor to construct a Solid

South, while the Democrats will strive to win bits and pieces of their former base.

NOTES

1. *Atlanta Journal/Atlanta Constitution*, October 9, 1988.

2. Earl Black and Merle Black, *Politics and Society in the South* (Cambridge, Mass.: Harvard University Press, 1987), 259–264.

3. See, for example, Kevin P. Phillips, *The Emerging Republican Majority* (Garden City, N.Y.: Anchor Books, 1970), 187–289; Numan V. Bartley and Hugh D. Graham, *Southern Politics and the Second Reconstruction* (Baltimore: Johns Hopkins University Press, 1975), 81–135; James L. Sundquist, *Dynamics of the Party System*, rev. ed. (Washington, D.C.: Brookings Institution, 1983), 269–297, 352–375; and Dewey W. Grantham, *The Life and Death of the Solid South* (Lexington: University Press of Kentucky, 1988), 149–203.

4. Joseph A. Califiano, "Tough Talk for Democrats," *New York Times Magazine*, January 8, 1989, 28.

5. Goldwater voted against the Civil Rights Act of 1964 and thereby became a hero to many southern white conservatives, especially in the Deep South. Barry M. Goldwater with Jack Casserly, *Goldwater* (New York: Doubleday, 1988). Goldwater's recollections about the Civil Rights Act are on pages 3, 171–173, 193–194.

6. Black and Black, *Politics and Society*, 98–171, 195–212.

7. *Washington Post National Weekly Edition*, August 8–14, 1988.

8. Harold W. Stanley has emphasized multiple reasons for Republican success in the South, although he places considerably less emphasis on race-related factors than do these authors. See Harold W. Stanley, "The 1984 Presidential Election in the South: Race and Realignment," in Robert P. Steed, Laurence W. Moreland, and Tod A. Baker, eds., *The 1984 Presidential Election in the South* (New York: Praeger, 1985), 315–322.

9. For detailed assessments, see Earl Black and Merle Black, "The Regional Basis of the Republican Advantage in Presidential Politics" (Paper delivered at the 1988 Citadel Symposium on Southern Politics, Charleston, S.C., March 3–4, 1988); and Earl Black and Merle Black, "The Rise and Decline of the Solid South in National Politics" (Paper delivered at the 1988 annual meeting of the American Political Science Association, Washington, D.C., September 1–4, 1988).

10. Charles D. Hadley and Harold W. Stanley, "An Analysis of Super Tuesday: Intentions, Results, and Implications" (Revision of a paper presented at the annual meeting of the Midwest Political Science Association, April 14–16, 1988), 5. See chapter 1 in this volume by Charles S. Bullock III.

11. *Gallup Report*, April 1988, 4; May 1988, 3; July 1988, 3.

12. *Gallup Report*, June 1988, 20; July 1988, 19; December 1984, 9.

13. *Gallup Report*, June 1988, 24; July 1988, 24.

14. *Washington Post*, January 20, 1989.

15. *Washington Post*, January 20, 1989.

16. *Washington Post National Weekly Edition*, November 7–13, 1988.

17. *Richmond Times Dispatch*, November 6, 1988.

18. *Raleigh News and Observer*, October 2, 1988.

19. *Washington Post*, September 25, 1988.

20. *Tuscaloosa News*, October 25, 1988.

21. *Washington Post*, August 27, 1988.

22. *Wall Street Journal*, September 6, 1988.

23. *Washington Post National Weekly Edition*, August 8–14, 1988.

24. *Wilmington Sunday-Star News*, October 23, 1988.

25. *Durham Sun*, August 30, 1988.

26. *Wilmington Sunday-Star News*, October 23, 1988.

27. Black and Black, *Politics and Society*, 213–219, 232–275.

28. Charles D. Hadley and Harold W. Stanley, " 'Super Tuesday'—Did the South Gain?'' *Baton Rouge Sunday Advocate*, April 10, 1988.

29. Merle Black and Earl Black, "Don't Underestimate Bush," *New York Times*, March 13, 1988.

30. *New York Times*, June 18, 1988.

31. *Washington Post National Weekly Edition*, May 30–June 5, 1988.

32. *New York Times*, July 22, 1988.

33. *New York Times*, July 22, 1988; August 19, 1988.

34. *New York Times*, June 20, 1988.

35. *Washington Post*, June 19, 1988.

36. *Wall Street Journal*, July 22, 1988.

37. *Washington Post National Weekly Edition*, May 30–June 5, 1988.

38. *Christian Science Monitor*, October 25, 1988.

39. *New York Times*, October 28, 1988.

40. *Wilmington Sunday-Star News*, October 23, 1988.

41. *Raleigh News and Observer*, October 16, 1988.

42. Peter Applebome, "The Battle for Texas," *New York Times Magazine*, October 30, 1988, 66.

43. *Washington Post National Weekly Edition*, May 30–June 5, 1988; *New York Times*, June 20, 1988.

44. *New York Times*, June 20, 1988; *Washington Post National Weekly Edition*, May 30–June 5, 1988.

45. See, for example, John Shelton Reed, *The Enduring South* (Chapel Hill: University of North Carolina Press, 1986).

46. *New York Times*, September 18, 1988.

47. *Atlanta Constitution*, August 18, 1988.

48. *Southern Political Report*, September 13, 1988.

49. *Raleigh News and Observer*, October 2, 1988.

50. Ibid.

51. *Washington Post National Weekly Edition*, October 24–30, 1988.

52. *Atlanta Journal/Atlanta Constitution*, October 9, 1988.

53. *Raleigh News and Observer*, September 21, 1988.

54. *New York Times*, November 10, 1988. For analyses of changing partisanship in the South, see Black and Black, *Politics and Society*, 232–256; John R. Petrocik, "Realignment: New Party Coalitions and the Nationalization of the South," *Journal of Politics* 49 (May 1987): 347–375; and Harold W. Stanley, "Southern Partisan Changes: Dealignment, Realignment or Both?" *Journal of Politics* 50 (February 1988): 64–88.

55. The 1988 results were by no means new. See Earl Black, "Competing Responses to the 'New Southern Politics': Republican and Democratic Southern Strategies, 1964–

76,'' in Merle Black and John Shelton Reed, eds., *Perspectives on the American South*, vol. 1 (New York: Gordon and Breach, 1981), 151–164.

56. "The Inept Campaign," *New York Review of Books*, December 22, 1988, 18.

57. According to Stanley, the "expected Republican majority [of the southern presidential vote was] a thin one, ranging from 51% to 53% of the vote" ("Southern Partisan Changes," 79). This estimated range of popular support is actually 4 to 6 percentage points below what Republican presidential candidates have averaged over the five elections from 1972 to 1988.

58. *Raleigh News and Observer*, October 16, 1988.

Index

About the Editors and Contributors

LAURENCE W. MORELAND (M.A., Duke University) is professor of political science at The Citadel. He is a codirector of The Citadel Symposium on Southern Politics and has conducted research on political party activists, southern politics, and elections. In addition to authoring a number of publications and professional papers, he has coedited seven books, including *Contemporary Southern Political Attitudes and Behavior*. He is currently engaged in analyzing data on state party activists and political party precinct officials.

ROBERT P. STEED (Ph.D., University of Virginia) is professor of political science at The Citadel. He is a codirector of The Citadel Symposium on Southern Politics, has codirected a survey of 1984 state convention delegates in twelve states, and has coedited seven books dealing with southern politics, including *The Disappearing South? Studies in Regional Change and Continuity* and *The Transformation of Southern Party Coalitions*. He has done substantial research and publication on southern politics, party politics, the presidency, political socialization, and South Carolina politics, and is currently involved in research on local party activists in the South.

TOD A. BAKER (Ph.D., University of Tennessee) is professor of political science at The Citadel. He has codirected an extensive survey of delegates to the 1984 state party conventions in twelve states, and is presently codirector of The Citadel Symposium on Southern Politics. He has been involved in the development of a number of professional papers and publications in the areas of urban politics, southern politics, and party activists, and has coedited seven books on various aspects of southern politics. He is currently continuing his work on southern politics with special attention to the role of religion in the region.

ALAN I. ABRAMOWITZ (Ph.D., Stanford University) is professor of political science at Emory University. He has coauthored and coedited three books, and has published widely in a variety of professional journals. A regular contributor of papers at professional conferences, he is currently engaged in research, funded by a grant from the National Science Foundation, on those attending state party caucuses connected with the 1988 presidential nominating process.

EARL BLACK (Ph.D., Harvard University) is Olin D. Johnston Professor of Political Science at the University of South Carolina. In addition to having written numerous journal articles, book chapters, and professional papers, is is the author of *Southern Governors and Civil Rights: Racial Segregation as a Campaign Issue in the Second Reconstruction* (1976) and coauthor of *Politics and Society in the South* (1987).

MERLE BLACK (Ph.D., University of Chicago) is Asa B. Candler Professor of Politics and Government at Emory University. He has coedited a number of books, including *Perspectives on the American South* (1981); written extensively for professional journals and professional conferences; and coauthored *Politics and Society in the South* (1987).

DIANE D. BLAIR (M.A., University of Arkansas) is associate professor of political science at the University of Arkansas. She is the author of two books and twenty book chapters and journal articles. She has served in a number of appointive positions, has done extensive work for various governors of Arkansas, and is a recognized authority on contemporary Arkansas politics.

LEWIS BOWMAN (Ph.D., University of North Carolina) is professor of political science at the University of South Florida. His past research has produced a variety of journal articles, technical reports, and professional conference papers on party activists, urban services, public health care, vocational rehabilitation, and public opinion. He is currently directing a multistate survey of local party officials in the South.

DAVID M. BRODSKY (Ph.D., Emory University) is the University of Chattanooga Foundation Professor of Political Science at the University of Tennessee at Chattanooga. A coeditor of *The South's New Politics: Realignment and De-*

alignment, his research interests range from southern politics to budgeting and the policy process.

CHARLES S. BULLOCK III (Ph.D., Washington University, St. Louis) is Richard B. Russell Professor of Political Science at the University of Georgia. His extensive research has resulted in over seventy journal articles and book chapters, nine books, and almost fifty professional conference papers, plus two technical reports. He has received numerous research grants and has served in a variety of consulting positions.

PATRICK R. COTTER (Ph.D., Ohio State University) is associate professor of political science at the University of Alabama. His past affiliations with the Capstone Poll at the University of Alabama and the National Network of State Polls has focused much of his research and publication on public opinion and political behavior, especially in the South, but he has also done research on such topics as social services and the aging, and voting behavior in Central America.

WENDY DAVIS (B.A., Berry College) is a Ph.D. student at Emory University. She is doing research in electoral politics.

CHARLES D. HADLEY (Ph.D., University of Connecticut) is professor of political science at the University of New Orleans. He is coauthor of *Transformations of the American Party System* (1978), has published in a number of journals including *Public Opinion Quarterly* and the *Journal of Politics*, and is coeditor of *Political Parties in the Southern States* (1990). His current research interests include black politics in the South, interest groups, party activists, and recent developments in Louisiana politics.

WILLIAM E. HULBARY (Ph.D., University of Iowa) is associate professor of political science at the University of South Florida. His research interests include political socialization, judicial politics, and party activism. He is currently involved in a long-term study of local party officials in Florida and other selected southern states.

DENNIS S. IPPOLITO (Ph.D., University of Virginia) is the Eugene McElvaney Professor of Government and Chair of the Department of Political Science at Southern Methodist University. He is the author or coauthor of numerous books, book chapters, and professional journal articles, including the volumes *Political Parties, Interest Groups, and Public Policy* and *Hidden Spending: The Politics of Federal Credit Programs*. His research interests range from political parties to public opinion to public policy.

ANNE E. KELLEY (Ph.D., Florida State University) is associate professor of political science at the University of South Florida. She has done research in political socialization, party activism, and Florida politics. Her current research concentrates on party politics in Florida and involves analysis of data on local party officials; the project is being expanded to include other southern states as well.

CHARLES L. PRYSBY (Ph.D., Michigan State University) is professor of political science at the University of North Carolina at Greensboro. He has contributed to the development of one book, *Political Choices* (1980), a series of four computer-based instructional packages on voting behavior, and numerous journal articles, book chapters, and professional papers. Additionally, he has served since 1980 as the North Carolina State Manager for News Election Service.

LARRY SABATO (D.Phil., Oxford University) is an election analyst and associate professor of government and foreign affairs at the University of Virginia. A former Rhodes Scholar and Danforth Fellow, he is recognized as the leading academic authority on Virginia politics. He has written nine books and monographs; is the author of the *Virginia Votes* series, which analyzes Virginia elections; and has served as an election analyst for numerous newspapers and electronic media reports.

STEPHEN D. SHAFFER (Ph.D., Ohio State University) is associate professor of political science at Mississippi State University. He has been associated with the university's Social Science Research Center, and has been involved in numerous surveys of public opinion and political behavior in Mississippi. In addition to publishing over a dozen book chapters and journal articles, he has presented numerous research papers at a variety of professional conferences.

HAROLD W. STANLEY (Ph.D., Yale University) is associate professor of political science at the University of Rochester. A Rhodes Scholar, he has written two books, coedited a third, and contributed articles to a number of professional journals. He has done extensive research on southern politics, including an examination of the presidential nomination process, during a year as a visiting research professor at the University of Alabama.

ROBERT H. SWANSBROUGH (Ph.D., University of California at Santa Barbara) is professor of political science at the University of Tennessee at Chattanooga. A coeditor of *The South's New Politics: Realignment and Dealignment*, he has held a number of positions in Washington and has done extensive research on Tennessee politics.